The Hatherleigh Guides Master Index

Volumes 1–10

The Hatherleigh Guides series

The Hatherleigh Guides Master Index

Volumes 1–10

 Hatherleigh Press • New York

The Hatherleigh Guides Master Index, Volumes 1–10

Project Editor: Stacy M. Powell
Indexer: Angela Washington-Blair, PhD
Cover Designer: Gary Szczecina

© 1998 Hatherleigh Press
A Division of The Hatherleigh Company, Ltd.
1114 First Avenue, Suite 500, New York, NY 10021-8325

Compiled under the auspices of the editorial boards of *Directions in Mental Health Counseling, Directions in Clinical Psychology*, and *Directions in Rehabilitation Counseling*.

Library of Congress Cataloging-in-Publication Data
    ISBN 1-886330-52-2 (alk. paper)

The Hatherleigh guides master index, volumes 1–10 —1st ed.
    p.   cm.
    Includes index.
    ISBN 1-886330-52-2 (paperback: acid-free paper)
    1. Hatherleigh guides series--Indexes. 2. Psychotherapy--Indexes.
        I. Hatherleigh Press.
    RC456.H38 1998 Index
    016.61689--dc21   97-25688
                                                                CIP

August 1998

10 9 8 7 6 5 4 3 2 1
Printed in Canada

The *Hatherleigh Guides* series was compiled under the auspices of the editorial boards of *Directions in Mental Health Counseling, Directions in Clinical and Counseling Psychology,* and *Directions in Rehabilitation Counseling*

Gary Holmes, PhD, CRC
Emporia State University (Emporia, KS)

John Homlish, PhD
The Menninger Clinic (Topeka, KS)

Sharon E. Robinson Kurpius, PhD
Arizona State University (Tempe, AZ)

Marilyn J. Lahiff, RN, CRRN, CIRS, CCM
Private practice (Englewood, FL)

Chow S. Lam, PhD
Illinois Institute of Chicago (Chicago, IL)

Paul Leung, PhD, CRC
Deakin University (Burwood Vicotria, Australia)

Carl Malmquist, MD
University of Minnesota (Minneapolis, MN)

Robert J. McAllister, PhD
Taylor Manor Hospital (Ellicott City, MD)

Richard A. McCormick, PhD
Cleveland VA Medical Center-Brecksville Division (Cleveland, OH)

Thomas Miller, PhD, ABPP
University of Kentucky College of Medicine (Lexington, KY)

Jane E. Myers, PhD, CRC, NCC, NCGC, LPC
University of North Carolina–Greensboro (Greensboro, NC)

Don A. Olson, PhD
Rehabilitation Institute of Chicago (Chicago, IL)

William Pollack, PhD
McLean Hospital (Belmont, MA)

Keith M. Robinson, MD
University of Pennsylvania (Philadelphia, PA)

Susan R. Sabelli, CRC, LRC
Assumption College (Worcester, MA)

Gerald R. Schneck, PhD, CRC-SAC, NCC
Mankato State University (Mankato, MN)

George Silberschatz, PhD
University of California–San Fransisco (San Fransisco, CA)

David W. Smart, PhD
Brigham Young University (Provo, UT)

Julie F. Smart, PhD, CRC, NCC
Utah State University (Logan, UT)

Joseph Stano, PhD, CRC/LRC, NCC
Springfield College (Springfield, MA)

Anthony Storr, FRCP
Green College (Oxford, England)

Hans Strupp, PhD
Vanderbilt University (Nashville, TN)

Retta C. Trautman, CCMHC, LPCC
Private practice (Toledo, OH)

Patricia Vohs, RN, CRRN, CRC, CIRS, CCM
Private practice (Warminster, PA)

William J. Weikel, PhD, CCMHC, NCC
Morehead State University (Morehead, KY)

Nona Leigh Wilson, PhD
South Dakota State University (Brookings, SD)

Table of Contents

Description of The Hatherleigh Guides   ix

About the Contributors   xxxi

Name Index   1

Subject Index   55

The Hatherleigh Guides Series

The *Hatherleigh Guides* have been developed for practicing professionals, students, and laypersons who need a comprehensive yet concise presentation of new research and clinical developments in the mental health sciences. Chapters have been carefully selected and edited to be stimulating presentations of updated information as the mental health profession prepares for the new challenges of the 21st century.

THE HATHERLEIGH GUIDE TO

Psychiatric Disorders

FEATURING ARTICLES WRITTEN BY EXPERT RESEARCHERS AND CLINICIANS, INCLUDING:

Obsessive-Compulsive Disorder: New Findings

•

Posttraumatic Stress Disorder

•

Diagnosis and Treatment of Dissociative Identity Disorder

•

Therapeutic Approaches to Anxiety Disorders

•

Psychotherapeutic Strategies for Borderline Personality Disorder

Hatherleigh Press

Psychiatric Disorders

An Update on Posttraumatic Stress Disorder
Thomas W. Miller, PhD, ABPP

Obsessive-Compulsive Disorder: New Findings
Thomas R. Insel, MD

The Diagnosis and Treatment of Dissociative Identity Disorder
Richard Kluft, PhD, MD, FAPA

Therapeutic Approaches to Anxiety Disorders
Robert L. DuPont, MD

Psychotherapeutic Strategies for Borderline Personality Disorders
Glen O. Gabbard, MD

The Criminal Personality
Stanton E. Samenow, PhD

Pathological Gambling
Richard A. McCormick, PhD

Pervasive Developmental Disorders
Sam Goldstein, PhD

Parent Training for Children with Attention-Deficit/Hyperactivity Disorder
Robert F. Newby, PhD, ABPP

Teaching Self-Help Strategies to Manic Clients
Mary Ellen Copeland, MS, MA

Self-Management Approaches for Seriously Mentally Ill Persons
Alex Kopelowicz, MD, and Robert Paul Liberman, MD

The *Hatherleigh Guide to Psychiatric Disorders* surveys a fascinating array of emotional and behavioral disorders encountered in contemporary American culture. DSM-IV is used as a framework within which some of the most notable experts in their fields present up-to-date information about diagnostic issues, etiologic factors, and treatment approaches specific to each disorder. Important new perspectives on these conditions provide clinicians with invaluable strategies to enhance their therapeutic effectiveness.

Psychotherapy

FEATURING ARTICLES WRITTEN BY EXPERT RESEARCHERS AND CLINICIANS, INCLUDING:

Current Practice and Procedures of Group Psychotherapy

•

Resistance to and Fear of Change

•

Therapeutic Approaches to Erotic Transference

•

Dealing with Difficult Clients

•

Current Approaches to Therapy with Elderly Clients

•

Power Imbalances in Therapeutic Relationships

Hatherleigh Press

Psychotherapy

"Repair" Versus "Growth"
Approaches to Therapy
Paul L. Adams, MD

Listening Processes in
Psychotherapy and Counseling
Fraser N. Watts, PhD

Resistance to and Fear of Change
James F. T. Bugental, PhD, and
Elizabeth K. Bugental, PhD

Dealing with Difficult Clients
George A. Harris, PhD

Brief Therapy with Difficult
Clients
Lynn Loar, PhD, LCSW

Research Findings on Short-
Term Psychodynamic Therapy
Techniques
Jeffrey L. Binder, PhD, ABPP

Current Practice and Procedures of
Group Psychotherapy
Martin G. Allen, MD

Avoiding Conflict in Group
Therapy: Ethical and Legal
Issues
Jim Gumaer, EdD, and
Alan Forrest, EdD

Marriage and Family Therapy:
Theories and Applications
Stanley C. Feist, PhD

A Problem-Centered Approach to
Interviewing in Family Therapy
Donald R. Catherall, PhD

Current Approaches to Therapy
with Elderly Clients
Victor Molinari, PhD

Power Imbalances in
Therapeutic Relationships
Michael L. Perlin, JD

Therapeutic Approaches to
Erotic Transference
Glen O. Gabbard, MD

On the Efficacy of Psychotherapy
Henry M. Bachrach, PhD

The Hatherleigh Guide to Psychotherapy brings you the work of 16 expert psychotherapists from a wide variety of research, clinical, and theoretical backgrounds. By reviewing the various types of strategies currently being used in both individual and group treatment, each chapter demonstrates how to tailor these strategies to the specific needs of clients. Using up-to-date research and case examples, this volume will enrich your beliefs about the human potential for change and will enable you to integrate a broad scope of perspectives into a style uniquely your own.

Managing Depression

FEATURING ARTICLES WRITTEN BY EXPERT RESEARCHERS AND CLINICIANS, INCLUDING:

Cognitive Therapy for Depression

•

Depression and the Immune System

•

Anorexia Nervosa, Bulimia Nervosa, and Depression

•

Treatment of Depression and the Restoration of Work Capacity

•

Psychosocial Therapies for Dysthymia

•

Decision Making in the Use of Antidepressants: Treatment Considerations

Hatherleigh Press

Managing Depression

Adaptive Styles in the Etiology of Depression
Peter C. Whybrow, MD

Depression and the Immune System
Elinor M. Levy, PhD, Cheryl Chancellor-Freeland, PhD, and Richard Krueger, MD

Post-Stroke Depression
Rajesh M. Parikh, MD, and Robert G. Robinson, MD

Anorexia Nervosa, Bulimia Nervosa, and Depression:
Arnold E. Andersen, MD

Group Counseling for Depressed Older Adults
Wanda Y. Johnson, PhD, PC

The Risk of Misdiagnosing Physical Illness as Depression
Mark S. Gold, MD, FCP, FAPA

Principles in Psychotherapy
Louis Jolyon West, MD

Cognitive Therapy for Depression
Robin B. Jarrett, PhD, and A. John Rush, MD

Behavioral Counseling for Older Adults with Depression
Duane A. Lundervold, RhD

The Management and Resolution of Dependency in the Depressed Client
John A. Birtchnell, MD, FRC Psych., DPM, Dip. Psychother., AFBPsS

Treatment of Depression and the Restoration of Work Capacity
Jim Mintz, PhD, Lois I. Mintz, PhD, Mary Jane Robertson, MS, Robert P. Liberman, MD, and Shirley M. Glynn, PhD

Psychosocial Therapies for Dysthymia
Robert H. Howland, MD

Alleviating Symptoms of Depression
Mary Ellen Copeland, MS

Decision Making in the Use of Antidepressants
Pedro L. Delgado, MD, and Alan J. Gelenberg, MD

The *Hatherleigh Guide to Managing Depression* distills recent research into the nature and treatment of depression and offers hands-on methods for helping depressed clients and patients. Chapters examine the roots and causes of depression, different approaches to treatment, strategies for managing the various forms of depression, the ways in which depression affects certain populations, and treatment considerations for administering antidepressant medications.

THE HATHERLEIGH GUIDE TO

Issues in Modern Therapy

FEATURING ARTICLES WRITTEN
BY EXPERT RESEARCHERS AND
CLINICIANS, INCLUDING:

Stress in the Workplace

•

Co-Dependence

•

Ethical Considerations
in Working with Survivors
of Sexual Abuse

•

A Rational-Emotive Approach
to Anger Management

•

Working with Self-Esteem
in Psychotherapy

•

Forgiveness

Hatherleigh Press

Issues in Modern Therapy

Recent Research Findings on
Stress Management Techniques
Paul M. Lehrer, PhD

Stress in the Workplace
Gerald A. Kraines, MD

Psychological Factors in the
Treatment of Cancer and
Coronary Heart Disease
*Ronald Grossarth-Maticek, MD, ScD,
PhD, and H. J. Eysenck, PhD, DSc*

Co-Dependence
*Robert L. DuPont, MD, and
John P. McGovern, MD, ScD, LLD*

Resent Research Findings on
Children of Alcoholics
Emil Chiauzzi, PhD

Therapeutic Approaches Toward
Patients with a History of Incest
in Childhood
A. Reese Abright, MD

Ethical Considerations in
Working with Survivors of
Sexual Abuse
*Judith C. Daniluk, PhD, and
Beth E. Haverkamp, PhD*

A Rational-Emotive Approach
to Anger Management
*Windy Dryden, PhD, and
Jack Gordon, BA (Hons)*

The Assessment and Treatment
of Relationship Wounds
*Richard W. Halstead, PhD, NCC,
LMHC*

Divorce as a Developmental
Catalyst
Judith H. Gold, MD, FRCPC

Working with Self-Esteem in
Psychotherapy
Nathaniel Branden, PhD

Forgiveness
Robert J. McAllister, PhD, MD

The *Hatherleigh Guide to Issues in Modern Therapy* provides mental health professionals with the practical information they need to better understand and address the issues that frequently arise in today's clinical practice. Sixteen expert psychotherapists present hands-on strategies and provide up-to-date research and case examples for managing a wide range of contemporary issues, such as stress in the workplace, co-dependence, divorce, sexual abuse, self-esteem, anger, and forgiveness.

Child and
Adolescent Therapy

**FEATURING ARTICLES WRITTEN
BY EXPERT RESEARCHERS AND
CLINICIANS, INCLUDING:**

Treatment and Prevention
for Sexually Abused Children

•

Attention-Deficit/
Hyperactivity Disorder

•

Adoption Psychopathology and
the "Adopted Child Syndrome"

•

Cognitive-Behavioral
Play Therapy

•

Diagnosis and Management
of Depression in Adolescents

•

Adolescent Suicide

Hatherleigh Press

Child and Adolescent Therapy

Anxiety Disorders in Children
and Adolescents
Alayne Yates, MD

Structured Treatment and
Prevention Activities for
Sexually Abused Children
Ann Hazzard, PhD

Attention-Deficit/Hyperactivity
Disorder
Sam Goldstein, PhD

Homelessness and Depression in
Children
*Janet Wagner, PhD, RN,
Catheryne L. Schmitz, PhD, ACSW
and Edna Menke, PhD, RN*

Adoption Psychopathology and
the "Adopted Child Syndrome"
David Kirschner, PhD

Cognitive-Behavioral Play
Therapy
Susan M. Knell, PhD

Diagnosis and Management of
Depression in Adolescents
Barry Sarvet, MD

Group Therapy for Adolescents
*Seth Aronson, PsyD, and Saul
Scheidlinger, PhD*

Aggression Replacement
Training in Children and
Adolescents
Barry Glick, NCC

Evaluation and Treatment
of the Substance-Abusing
Adolescent
R. Jeremy A. Stowell, MD, FAPA

Adolescent Suicide
James C. Brown, PhD

Protecting the Confidentiality
of Children and Adolescents
Edward E. Bartlett, PhD

C hildhood sexual abuse, academic failure, attention-deficit/hyperactivity disorder, substance abuse, depression, and suicide are among the most pressing mental health problems facing children and adolescents today. In *The Hatherleigh Guide to Child and Adolescent Therapy*, fifteen highly esteemed authorities in the field provide clinicians with important therapeutic strategies, up-to-date findings, and detailed case examples from their own front-line experience with these populations. Chapters offer a wide range of traditional and contemporary approaches, and a variety of resources for managing the numerous problems facing young people.

THE HATHERLEIGH GUIDE TO

Marriage and Family Therapy

FEATURING ARTICLES WRITTEN BY EXPERT RESEARCHERS AND CLINICIANS, INCLUDING:

Working with Families Headed by Single Fathers

•

Counseling Children of Divorce

•

The Death of a Child: Implications for Marital and Family Therapy

•

Family Caregiving of the Elderly

•

Hypoactive Sexual Desire Disorders in Couples: A Cognitive-Behavioral Perspective

•

The Clinical Management of Jealousy

Hatherleigh Press

Marriage and Family Therapy

Family Diagnostic Testing
Dennis A. Bagarozzi, PhD

Counseling Children of Divorce
Paul J. Ciborowski, PhD

**Working with Families Headed
by Single Fathers**
Geoffrey L. Greif, DSW

**Understanding and Treating the
Remarriage Family**
Florence W. Kaslow, PhD

**The Role of Family-Treatment
Approaches in Adolescent
Substance Abuse**
William H. Quinn, PhD

**Family-Therapy Interventions
with Inner-City Families
Affected by AIDS**
Gillian Walker, MSW

The Death of a Child
*Paula P. Bernstein, PhD, and
Leslie A. Gavin, PhD*

Family Caregiving of the Elderly
*Juanita L. Garcia, EdD, and Jordan I.
Kosberg, PhD*

**Relational Sexuality: An
Understanding of Low
Sexual Desire**
*Lynda Dykes Talmadge, PhD, and
William C. Talmadge, PhD*

**Hypoactive Sexual Desire
Disorders in Couples:
A Cognitive-Behavioral
Perspective**
*Gilles Trudel, PhD, Marc Ravart, MA,
and Sylvie Aubin, MA*

**The Clinical Management of
Jealousy**
*Paul E. Mullen, MBBS, DSc, MPhil,
FRCPsych, FRANZCP*

Mutuality in Couples Therapy
Paula Schneider, PhD, MSW

E ffective treatment of clients requires an understanding of the con-
text in which their problems have arisen, as well as those within
which they currently exist. One of the most important contexts is obvi-
ously marriage and family. Marital and family issues must be managed
in individual treatment, and therapy applications that deal with the
family as a whole. In a time of high divorce rates and single-parent
households, this presents quite a challenge, which mental health professionals must meet by. *The Hatherleigh Guide to Marriage and Family Therapy*
presents invaluable information in practical, jargon-free language for
treating couples and families. Chapters by experts in the field address
such timely issues as how divorce affects children, single parenting by
fathers, the remarriage family, family caregiving for the elderly, the
impact of a child's death on the family and others.

THE HATHERLEIGH GUIDE TO

Treating Substance Abuse Part I

FEATURING ARTICLES WRITTEN BY EXPERT RESEARCHERS AND CLINICIANS, INCLUDING:

Motivational Enhancement in the Treatment of Addictions

•

Marital and Family Therapy in the Treatment of Alcoholism

•

Naltrexone: A New Option for the Treatment of Alcohol Dependence

•

Trends in Hallucinogenic Drug Use: LSD, "Ecstasy," and the Rave Phenomenon

•

Caffeine and Anxiety Disorder

•

Cognitive-Behavioral Group and Family Treatment of Cocaine Addiction

Hatherleigh Press

Treating Substance Abuse, Part I

An Integrative Approach for the Evaluation and Treatment of Alcohol and Drug Abuse
Ralph E. Tarter, PhD

Medications Used in Rehabilitation Settings
Susan Gallagher-Lepak, RN, MSN, Fong Chan, PhD, Donald Kates, MS, Laura Dunlap, MA, Kristine M. Eiring, MS, and Joseph Cunningham, MS

Improved Detoxification from Drugs and Alcohol Through Nutrition
Jeffrey S. Bland, PhD

Naltrexone Pharmacotherapy for the Treatment of Alcohol Dependence
Robert L. DuPont, MD, and Mark S. Gold, MD, FCP, FAPA

Inpatient Versus Outpatient Treatment of Alcoholism
Barbara W. Reeve, MD, MS

Marital and Family Therapy in the Treatment of Alcoholism
Timothy J. O'Farrell, PhD

Trends in Hallucinogenic Drug Use: LSD, "Ecstasy," and the Rave Phenomenon
Mark S. Gold, MD, FCP, FAPA

Caffeine and Anxiety Disorder
Malcolm Lader, MD, PhD, DSc, FRCPsych

Cognitive-Behavioral Group and Family Treatment of Cocaine Addiction
Paul Richard Smokowski, MSW, and John S. Wodarski, PhD

Motivational Enhancement in the Treatment of Addictions
Emil Chiauzzi, PhD

Reducing Risk of Relapse in Addiction
Emil Chiauzzi, PhD

Improving Outcomes With Interagency Collaboration
Michael D. McGee, MD

The *Hatherleigh Guide to Treating Substance Abuse, Part I* is the first of a two-volume set that offers mental health professionals the theoretical and practical information they need to meet the challenges of treating patients who use and abuse alcohol and other drugs. In *Part I*, nineteen experts in the field address some of the most pressing general topics in the diagnosis and treatment of substance use disorders, and *Part II* focuses on treating specific populations of individuals. This volume presents up-to-date findings on the treatment of alcoholism and addiction to cocaine, caffeine, hallucinogens, and marijuana. Techniques and case examples are offered from a variety of approaches, including motivational enhancement therapy, marital and family therapy, and cognitive-behavioral therapy.

THE HATHERLEIGH GUIDE TO

Treating
Substance Abuse Part II

FEATURING ARTICLES WRITTEN
BY EXPERT RESEARCHERS AND
CLINICIANS, INCLUDING:

Substance Abuse
in the Workplace
•
Ethical Issues in Counseling
Adolescents Who Abuse Alcohol
and Other Drugs
•
Geriatric Alcoholism:
Identification and Elder-Specific
Treatment Programs
•
Counseling Chemically
Dependent Patients
with HIV Infection
•
Substance Abuse in Pregnancy
•
Comorbid Major Depression
and Alcoholism

Hatherleigh Press

Treating Substance Abuse, Part II

Substance Abuse in the Workplace: The Role of Employee Assistance Programs
John C. Thomas, PhD, CEAP, CSAC, NCC, NCAC II

Substance Abuse and Disability
Elizabeth de Silva Cardoso, MEd, Fong Chan, PhD, Kenneth Thomas, EdD, Gwen Roldan, PhD, and Kirby Ingraham, MSW

Substance Abuse in Pregnancy
Mindy Thompson Fullilove, MD, and Isabelle Dieudonné, MD

Clinical Profile and Evaluation of Comorbid Major Depression and Alcoholism
Jack R. Cornelius, MD, MPH, Ishan M. Salloum, MD, MP, Dennis C. Daley, MSW, and Michael E. Thase, MD

Overcoming Adolescent Addiction: Working with Families and the Role of 12-Step Programs
Robert L. DuPont, MD

Physical Fitness Programming for Prevention and Treatment of Adolescent Substance Abuse
Thomas R. Collingwood, PhD, FACSM

Ethical Issues in Counseling Adolescents Who Abuse Alcohol and Other Drugs
Tomás José Silber, MD, MASS, and Daniel Silber, PhD

Geriatric Alcoholism: Identification and Elder-Specific Treatment Programs
Jayne Reinhardt, MPH, and George Fulop, MD, MSCM

Counseling Chemically Dependent Patients with HIV Infection
Michael Shernoff, MSW, ACSW

Issues in the Diagnosis and Treatment of Comorbid Addictive and Other Psychiatric Disorders
Norman S. Miller, MD

Motivation-Based Assessment and Treatment of Substance Abuse in Patients with Schizophrenia
Douglas Ziedonis, MD, MPH, and William Fisher, EdD

T he *Hatherleigh Guide to Treating Substance Abuse, Part II* is the second of a two-volume set that offers mental health professionals the theoretical and practical information they need to meet the challenges of treating patients who use and abuse alcohol and other drugs. *Part I* focuses on some of the most pressing general topics in the diagnosis and treatment of substance use disorders; this volume, *Part II*, addresses important issues affecting special populations of individuals. Twenty-two experts in the field discuss strategies for treating sub-stance-abusing patients, including those with disabilities, psychiatric disorders, schizophrenia, and major depression; adolescents; older adults; and pregnant women.

THE HATHERLEIGH GUIDE TO

Vocational and Career Counseling

FEATURING ARTICLES WRITTEN
BY EXPERT RESEARCHERS AND
CLINICIANS, INCLUDING:

Cultural Diversity and Its Impact
on Career Counseling

•

Placement Practices and
Labor Markets for Clients
with Disabilities

•

Vocational Assessment
and the Americans
with Disabilities Act

•

Supported Employment:
An Overview

•

Vocational Evaluation of Clients
with Traumatic Brain Injury

•

Client Resistance
to Career Counseling

Hatherleigh Press

Vocational and Career Counseling

A Constructive Developmental
Perspective on Career
Counseling
Garrett McAuliffe, PhD

Client Resistance to Career
Counseling
Lewis E. Patterson, EdD

Vocational Assessment and the
ADA: Issues and Approaches for
the Rehabilitation Professional
Stephen W. Thomas, EdD, CVE, CRC

Personal Assistance: A Key to
Employability
*Margaret A. Nosek, PhD, and
Catherine Clubb Foley, PhD*

Placement Practices and Labor
Markets for Clients with
Disabilities
David Vandergoot, PhD, CRC

Supported Employment: An
Overview
*James Schaller, PhD, E
dna Mora Szymanski, PhD, and
Cheryl Hanley-Maxwell, PhD*

Work Hardening: A Dynamic
Process
*Rock Weldon, MA, CVE, and
Gary L. Sigmon, EdD*

Vocational Evaluation of Clients
with Traumatic Brain Injury
Robert T. Fraser, PhD, CRC

Vocational Rehabilitation for
Patients with Schizophrenia
*H. Richard Lamb, MD, and
Cecile Mackota*

Cultural Diversity and Its Impact
on Career Counseling
Jay W. Rojewski, PhD

Vocational Evaluation of
Hispanic Clients with
Disabilities
*Julie F. Smart, PhD, RC, NCC, LPC,
ABDA and David Smart, PhD*

The Effective Use of Vocational
Evaluation Services
Stephen W. Thomas, EdD, CVE, CRC

As we approach the end of the millennium, the fields of vocational and career counseling are undergoing rapid changes. Medical advances that allow more individuals with disabilities to work, changes in legislation (such as the Americans with Disabilities Act [ADA]), labor market conditions, assistive technology in the workplace, and changes in the demographic make-up of the United States—are just some of the changes that are influencing the services that professionals provide. *The Hatherleigh Guide to Vocational and Career Counseling* equips vocational rehabilitation professionals and career counselors with the information they need. Seventeen experts in the field synthesize leading theories and applications and present information on topics such as client resistance to career counseling, placement practices and labor markets for clients with disabilities, and vocational assessment and the ADA.

Ethics in Therapy

**FEATURING ARTICLES WRITTEN
BY EXPERT RESEARCHERS AND
CLINICIANS, INCLUDING:**

Sexual Boundary Violations

•

Dual/Multiple Relationships:
Toward a Consensus of Thinking

•

Ethics in Supervision: Managing
Supervisee Rights and
Supervisor Responsibilities

•

Lawsuit Prevention Techniques

•

Ethics and Multiculturalism:
The Challenge of Diversity

Ethics in Therapy

Current Ethical Issues in the
Practice of Psychology
Sharon E. Robinson Kurpius, PhD

Ethical Considerations in the
Development of Counseling Goals
Kerry Brace, PsyD

Codes of Ethics as Catalysts for
Improving Practice
*Barbara Herlihy, PhD, NCC, LPC, and
Gerald Corey, EdD, ABPP, NCC*

Preparing Rehabilitation
Counselors to Deal with Ethical
Dilemmas
Carolyn Rollins, PhD

Ethics in Supervision: Managing
Supervisee Rights and Supervisor
Responsibilities
*J. Michael Tyler, PhD, and
Catherine L. Tyler, MBA*

Expert Witness Testimony: Ethical,
Practical, and Legal Issues
Robert L. Sadoff, MD

Lawsuit Prevention Techniques
Barbara E. Calfee, JD, LSW

The "Duty to Protect" Others from
Violence
Michael L. Perlin, Esq

Ethics, Insanity Pleas, and Forensic
Psychology
Michael W. Millard, PhD, BCFE

The Multifaceted Ethical
Dimension of Treating the
Mentally Ill
Mary Ann Carroll, PhD

Dual/Multiple Relationships:
Toward a Consensus of Thinking
*Gerald Corey, EdD, ABPP, NCC, and
Barbara Herlihy, PhD, NCC, LPC*

Sexual Boundary Violations
Silvia W. Olarte, MD

Ethical Standards in Counseling
Sexually Active Clients with HIV
Elliot D. Cohen, PhD

Ethics and Multiculturalism:
The Challenge of Diversity
*Courtland C. Lee, PhD, and
Virginia Kurilla, MEd*

In today's complex and changing world of mental health practice, therapists are confronted with a range of ethical issues for which there are no easy answers. New ethical issues, some of which were not even anticipated at the time when many seasoned practitioners were originally trained, now present themselves. These include: a possible duty to warn partners of sexually active clients who are HIV positive; client rights and informed consent in a managed care environment; ethical implications of new technologies used to support psychotherapy services; and issues of therapist competence to counsel with an ethnically, racially, and culturally diverse client population. *The Hatherleigh Guide to Ethics in Therapy* presents contemporary thought on these and other issues by leading experts in the field, who draw on basic ethical principles such as respect for autonomy, beneficence, nonmalificence, justice, and fidelity.

About the Contributors

A. Reese Abright, MD
Chief of Child and Adolescent Psychiatry, St. Vincent's Hospital and Medical Center of New York; and Clinical Associate Professor of Psychiatry, New York Medical College, New York, NY.

Paul L. Adams, MD
Emeritus Professor of Child Psychiatry, University of Texas Medical Branch, Galveston, TX, and Visiting Professor of Child Psychiatry, University of Tennessee Center for Health Sciences, Memphis, TN. He maintains a private practice in Louisville, KY.

Martin G. Allen, MD
Clinical Professor of Psychiatry, Department of Psychiatry, Georgetown University School of Medicine; in private practice, Washington, D.C.

Arnold E. Andersen, MD
Professor of Psychiatry, The University of Iowa College of Medicine, Iowa City, IA.

Seth Aronson, PsyD
Assistant Director, Child/Adolescent Psychiatry, Bronx Municipal Hospital Center/Albert Einstein College of Medicine, Bronx, NY.

Sylvie Aubin, MA
Clinical Psychologist at a marital and family consultation clinic in Montreal, and a PhD candidate in Psychology at the University of Quebec.

Henry M. Bachrach, PhD
Clinical Professor of Psychiatry, New York Medical College at St. Vincent's Hospital and Medical Center of New York.

Dennis A. Bagarozzi, PhD
Director, Human Resource Consultants; Licensed Psychologist and Marriage and Family Therapist who holds a private practice in Atlanta, GA and Athens, GA.

Edward E. Bartlett, PhD
Associate Adjunct Professor, George Washington University School of Medicine, Washington, DC.

Paula P. Bernstein, PhD
Associate Clinical Professor, The University of Colorado Health Sciences Center; and Adjunct Associate Professor, The University of Denver, Denver, CO.

Jeffrey L. Binder, PhD, ABPP
Member of the Core Faculty of the Georgia School of Professional Psychology, Atlanta, GA.

John A. Birtchnell, MD, FRCPsych, DPM, Dip Psychother, AFBPsS
Honorary Senior Lecturer, the Institute of Psychiatry; Honorary Consultant Psychiatrist, the Maudsley Hospital, London, England.

Kerry Brace, PsyD
Psychotherapist, Allegheny East MHMR Center, Pittsburgh, PA.

Nathaniel Branden, PhD
Executive Director of the Branden Institute for Self-Esteem, Los Angeles, CA.

James C. Brown, PhD
Chairman, The Academy of Clinical Mental Health Counselors; and Associate Dean for Student Programs, School of Dentistry, University of Mississippi Medical Center, Jackson, MS.

Elizabeth K. Bugental, PhD
Formerly Assistant Director of Inter/Logue and now serves as a board member and consultant to several community agencies.

James F. T. Bugental, PhD
Rockefeller (Teaching) Scholar at the California Institute of Integral Studies, Emeritus Professor of the Saybrook Institute, and Emeritus Clinical Faculty of the Stanford University Medical School.

Barbara E. Calfee, JD, LSW
President, Barbara Calfee & Associates, Beachwood, OH.

Elizabeth Cardoso, MEd
Doctoral student, University of Wisconsin–Madison.

Mary Ann Carroll, PhD
Professor of Philosophy, Department of Philosophy and Religion, Appalachian State University, Boone, NC.

Donald R. Catherall, PhD
Executive Director, The Phoenix Institute, Chicago, IL.

Fong Chan, PhD
Professor and Co-Director of the Rehabilitation Research and Training Center on Career Development, Department of Rehabilitation Psychology and Special Education, University of Wisconsin–Madison.

Cheryl Chancellor-Freeland, PhD
Immunology Fellow, Department of Microbiology, Boston University School of Medicine, Boston, MA.

Emil Chiauzzi, PhD
Clinical Director of the Addictions Treatment Program, Waltham-Weston Hospital, Waltham, MA.

Paul J. Ciborowski, PhD
Associate Professor of Counseling, Long Island University, C. W. Post Campus, Brookville, NY, and Chair of the Brookhaven [NY] Youth Board.

Elliot D. Cohen, PhD
Professor, Department of Social Sciences, Indian River Community College, Fort Pierce, FL, and Editor-in-Chief of the *International Journal of Applied Philosophy.*

Thomas R. Collingwood, PhD, FACSM
Director, Fitness Intervention Technologies, Richardson, TX.

Mary Ellen Copeland, MS, MA
Counselor, Consultant, and Educator who specializes in the management of affective disorders and maintains a private practice in Brattleboro, VT.

Gerald Corey, EdD, ABPP, NCC
Professor of Human Services and Counseling, California State University at Fullerton, Fullerton, CA.

Joseph Cunningham, MS
Doctoral student in the Clinical Psychology Program, Department of Psychology at the Illinois Institute of Technology, Chicago, IL.

Judith C. Daniluk, PhD
Associate Professor of Counseling Psychology, the University of British Columbia, Canada.

Pedro L. Delgado, MD
Associate Professor of Psychiatry and Director of Psychopharmacology Research, University of Arizona College of Medicine, Tucson, AZ.

Isabelle Dieudonné, MD
Assistant Professor of Pediatrics and a neonatologist, The New York Hospital-Cornell Medical Center, New York, NY.

Windy Dryden, PhD
Professor of Counseling at Goldsmith's College, University of London, London, England; Fellow of the Institute for Rational-Emotive Therapy, New York, NY; and an accredited supervisor for training in Rational-Emotive Therapy.

Laura Dunlap, MA
Doctoral student in the Department of Rehabilitation Psychology and Special Education, University of Wisconsin–Madison.

Robert L. DuPont, MD
President, Institute for Behavior and Health, Inc., Rockville, MD, and Clinical Professor of Psychiatry, Georgetown University School of Medicine, Washington, DC.

Kristine M. Eiring, MS
Doctoral student in the Department of Rehabilitation Psychology and Special Education, University of Wisconsin–Madison.

H. J. Eysenck, PhD, DSc
Professor Emeritus in the Department of Psychology, Institute of Psychiatry, University of London, London, England.

Stanley C. Feist, PhD
Emeritus Professor of Psychology, The State University of New York College of Technology, Farmingdale, NY.

William Fisher, EdD
Research Associate and Project Director of the Dual Diagnosis Treatment and Research Program, Connecticut Mental Health Center, Department of Psychiatry, Yale University School of Medicine, New Haven, CT.

Frederic Flach, MD
Adjunct Associate Professor of Psychiatry, Cornell University Medical College, New York; Attending Psychiatrist at Payne Whitney Clinic of The New York Hospital and St. Vincent's Hospital and Medical Center, New York.

Catherine Clubb Foley, PhD
Assistant Professor, Department of Physical Medicine, and Senior Researcher, the Center for Research on Women with Disabilities, Baylor College of Medicine, Houston, TX.

Alan Forrest, EdD
Professor of Counselor Education at Radford University, Radford, VA, and a licensed professional counselor in private practice.

Robert T. Fraser, PhD, CRC
Professor in the Department of Neurology, with joint appointments in Neurological Surgery and Rehabilitation Medicine, University of Washington; and Consultant, Associates in Rehabilitation and Neuropsychology, Seattle, WA.

Mindy Thompson Fullilove, MD
Associate Professor of Clinical Psychiatry and Public Health, Columbia University and New York State Psychiatric Institute, New York, NY.

George Fulop, MD, MSCM
Assistant Professor, Departments of Community Medicine, Geriatrics, and Psychiatry, The Mount Sinai School of Medicine, New York, NY.

Glen O. Gabbard, MD
Bessie Walker Callaway Distinguished Professor at the Menninger Clinic; Training and Supervising Analyst, Topeka Institute for Psychoanalysis; and Clinical Professor of Psychiatry, University of Kansas School of Medicine, Topeka, KS.

Susan Gallagher-Lepak, RN, MSN
Doctoral student in the Department of Rehabilitation Psychology and
Special Education, University of Wisconsin–Madison.

Juanita L. Garcia, EdD
Associate Professor, Department of Gerontology, College of Arts and
Sciences, University of South Florida, Tampa, FL.

Leslie A. Gavin, PhD
Assistant Professor, the University of Colorado Health Sciences Center
and the National Jewish Center for Immunology and Respiratory Medicine, Denver, CO.

Alan J. Gelenberg, MD
Professor and Head, Department of Psychiatry, University of Arizona
College of Medicine, Tucson, AZ.

Barry Glick, PhD, NCC
Consultant, G & G Associates, Scotia, NY.

Shirley M. Glynn, PhD
Assistant Research Psychologist, Department of Psychiatry and Biobe-
havioral Sciences, UCLA School of Medicine, and Clinical Research
Psychologist at the West Los Angeles Veterans Affairs Medical Center,
Los Angeles, CA.

Judith H. Gold, MD, FRCPC
President, American College of Psychiatrists, 1992–1993; Editor, Clinical Practice Series, American Psychiatric Press, Washington, DC.

Mark S. Gold, MD
Potash Professor, University of Florida Brain Institute, Gainesville, FL.

Sam Goldstein, PhD
Clinical Director, Neurology Learning and Behavior Center, Salt Lake
City, UT; Clinical Instructor, Department of Psychiatry, and Adjunct
Professor, Department of Educational Psychology, University of Utah
School of Medicine, Salt Lake City, UT.

Jack Gordon, BA (Hons)
Graduate member of the British Psychological Society.

Geoffrey L. Greif, DSW
Professor, School of Social Work, University of Maryland at Baltimore.

Ronald Grossarth-Maticek, MD, ScD, PhD
Director, Institute for Preventative Medicine, European Center for Peace and Development, University of Peace (established by the United Nations), Heidelberg, Germany.

Jim Gumaer, EdD
Professor of Counselor Education at Radford University, Radford, VA, and a licensed professional counselor in private practice.

Richard W. Halstead, PhD, NCC, LMHC
Assistant Professor, the Counseling Institute, St. Joseph College, West Hartford, CT.

Cheryl Hanley-Maxwell, PhD
Associate Professor and Chair, University of Wisconsin–Madison, Madison, WI.

George A. Harris, PhD
Psychologist in private practice in Kansas City, MO; formerly a therapist in vocational rehabilitation and corrections.

Beth E. Haverkamp, PhD
Associate Professor of Counseling Psychology, the University of British Columbia, Canada.

Ann Hazzard, PhD
Associate Professor of Pediatrics and Assistant Professor of Psychiatry at Emory University School of Medicine, Atlanta, GA.

Barbara Herlihy, PhD, NCC, LPC
Associate Professor of Counselor Education, Loyola University of New Orleans, New Orleans, LA.

Robert H. Howland, MD
Assistant Professor of Psychiatry, Western Psychiatric Institute and Clinic, University of Pittsburgh School of Medicine, Pittsburgh, PA.

Kirby Ingraham, MSW
Senior Rehabilitation Counselor, Illinois Department of Rehabilitation Services, Elgin, IL.

Thomas R. Insel, MD
Director, Yerkes Primate Center, and Professor of Psychiatry, Emory University School of Medicine, Atlanta, GA.

Robin B. Jarrett, PhD
Associate Professor of Psychiatry, Department of Psychiatry, The University of Texas Southwestern Medical Center, Dallas, TX.

Wanda Y. Johnson, PhD, PC
Licensed Professional Counselor, Licensed Marriage and Family Therapist, Certified Hypnotherapist, and Certified Play Therapist in private practice in Arlington, TX.

Florence W. Kaslow, PhD
Director, Florida Couples and Family Institute, West Palm Beach, FL; Visiting Professor of Medical Psychology in Psychiatry, Duke University Medical Center, Durham, NC; and Visiting Professor of Psychology, Florida Institute of Technology, Melbourne, FL. She was the first president of the International Family Therapy Association.

Donald Kates, MS
Doctoral student in the Department of Rehabilitation Psychology and Special Education, University of Wisconsin–Madison.

David Kirschner, PhD
In private practice in Merrick, NY, and Woodbury, NY.

Richard P. Kluft, PhD, MD, FAPA
Clinical Professor of Psychiatry, Temple University School of Medicine, and Senior Attending Psychiatrist and Director of the Dissociative Disorders Program, The Institute of Pennsylvania Hospital, Philadelphia.

Susan M. Knell, PhD
Adjunct Assistant Professor, Cleveland State University; and Lecturer, Case Western Reserve University, Cleveland, OH.

Alex Kopelowicz, MD
NIMH Postdoctoral Research Fellow at UCLA School of Medicine, and Medical Director of the San Fernando Mental Health Center.

Jordan I. Kosberg, PhD
Professor, School of Social Work, Florida International University, North Miami, FL.

Gerald A. Kraines, MD
CEO, The Levinson Institute, Belmont, MA; Visiting Lecturer in Psychiatry, Harvard Medical School, Boston, MA; and in private practice.

Richard Krueger, MD
Assistant Clinical Professor of Psychiatry, Columbia College of Physicians and Surgeons, New York, NY; Attending Psychiatrist, Columbia Presbyterian Hospital and the New York State Psychiatric Institute, New York, NY.

Virginia Kurilla, MEd
Private counseling practitioner and a graduate student in the Counselor Education Program, University of Virginia.

Sharon E. Robinson Kurpius, PhD
Professor of Counseling Psychology, Division of Psychology in Education, Arizona State University, Tempe, AZ.

Malcolm Lader, MD, PhD, DSc, FRCPsych
Professor of Clinical Psychopharmacology, Institute of Psychiatry, London, UK.

H. Richard Lamb, MD
Professor of Psychiatry, University of Southern California School of Medicine, Los Angeles, CA.

Courtland C. Lee, PhD
Professor of Counselor Education, University of Virginia, Charlottesville, VA.

Paul M. Lehrer, PhD
Professor of Psychiatry, the University of Medicine and Dentistry of New Jersey, Robert Wood Johnson Medical School, Piscataway, NJ.

Elinor M. Levy, PhD
Associate Professor of Microbiology, Department of Microbiology, Boston University School of Medicine, Boston, MA.

Robert Paul Liberman, MD
Professor, Department of Psychiatry and Biobehavioral Sciences, UCLA School of Medicine; Director, Clinical Research Unit at Camarillo [CA] State Hospital; Director, Clinical Research Center for the Study of Schizophrenia; and Chief, Treatment Development and Assessment Unit, Community and Rehabilitative Psychiatry Section, Psychiatry Service, West Los Angeles Veterans Affairs Medical Center, Los Angeles, CA.

Lynn Loar, PhD, LCSW
Educational Coordinator of the San Francisco Child Abuse Council, San Francisco, CA.

Duane A. Lundervold, RhD
Family Therapist, Boone County Youth and Family Counseling, Boone County Hospital, Boone, IA.

Cecile Mackota
Former Director of Vocational Rehabilitation, San Mateo County Mental Health Services, San Mateo, CA.

Robert J. McAllister, PhD, MD
Senior Psychiatrist, Taylor Manor Hospital, Ellicott City, MD.

Garrett McAuliffe, PhD
Associate Professor of Counselor Education, Old Dominion University, Norfolk, VA.

Richard A. McCormick, PhD
Chief, Psychology S ervice at the Cleveland V.A. Medical Center, and Assistant Clinical Professor of Psychology, Case Western Reserve University, Cleveland, OH.

Michael D. McGee, MD
Dr. McGee is Medical Director of Massachusetts Biodyne Inc, and Psychiatrist in Chief at the Solomon Mental Health Center, Lowell, MA.

John P. McGovern, MD, ScD, LLD
Clinical Professor of Medicine, University of Texas Medical School at Houston; and Clinical Professor of Pediatrics and Microbiology, Baylor College of Medicine, Houston, TX.

Edna Menke, PhD, RN
Associate Professor, The Ohio State University College of Nursing, Department of Family and Community Medicine, Columbus, OH.

Michael W. Millard, PhD, BCFE
In private practice in Hopkins, MN. He specializes in forensic evaluations.

Norman S. Miller, MD
Associate Professor of Psychiatry, and Chief, Division of Addiction Psychiatry, the University of Illinois at Chicago.

Thomas W. Miller, PhD, ABPP
Chief of Psychology Services at the Department of Psychiatry, University of Kentucky Medical Center, Lexington, KY.

Jim Mintz, PhD
Professor, Department of Psychiatry and Biobehavioral Sciences, UCLA School of Medicine; Research Psychologist, West Los Angeles Veterans Affairs Medical Center; and Chief, Methodology and Statistical Services Unit, Clinical Research Center for the Study of Schizophrenia, Los Angeles, CA.

Lois I. Mintz, PhD
Assistant Research Psychologist, Department of Psychiatry and Biobehavioral Sciences, UCLA School of Medicine, Los Angeles, CA.

Victor Molinari, PhD
Director of Geropsychology at the Veterans Affairs Medical Center, Houston, TX, and Clinical Assistant Professor of Psychology in the Department of Psychiatry and Behavioral Sciences at Baylor College of Medicine, Houston, TX.

Paul E. Mullen, MBBS, DSc, MPhil, FRCPsych, FRANZCP
Director, Forensic Psychiatry Services, Rosanna, Australia; and Professor of Forensic Psychiatry, Monash University, Melbourne, Australia.

Robert F. Newby, PhD, ABPP
Child neuropsychologist and Associate Professor of Neurology, Medical College of Wisconsin, Milwaukee, WI.

Margaret A. Nosek, PhD
Associate Professor, Department of Physical Medicine and Director of the Center for Research on Women with Disabilities, Baylor College of Medicine, Houston, TX.

Timothy J. O'Farrell, PhD
Associate Professor of Psychology in the Department of Psychiatry at Harvard Medical School, Boston, MA, and Associate Chief of the Psychology Service at the Veterans Affairs Medical Center in Brockton and West Roxbury, MA, where he directs the Counseling for Alcoholics' Marriages (CALM) Project and the Alcohol and Family Studies Laboratory.

Silvia W. Olarte, MD
Clinical Professor of Psychiatry and faculty member of the Psychoana-
lytic Institute, Department of Psychiatry, New York Medical College,
Valhalla, NY.

Rajesh M. Parikh, MD
Associate Professor, Jaslok Hospital and Research Center, Bombay,
India.

Lewis E. Patterson, EdD
Professor Emeritus of Counseling, the College of Education at Cleveland State University, Cleveland, OH.

Michael L. Perlin, Esq
Professor of Law, New York Law School, New York, NY.

William H. Quinn, PhD
Associate Professor, Marriage and Family Program, Department of
Child and Family Development, University of Georgia, Athens, GA.

Marc Ravart, MA
Clinical Psychologist and Sexologist, the Human Sexuality Unit of
Montreal General Hospital, and PhD candidate in Psychology at the
University of Quebec.

Barbara W. Reeve, MD
Acting Chief of Psychiatry, Eastern Maine Medical Center, Bangor, ME,
and maintains a private practice in Ellsworth, ME.

Jayne Reinhardt, MPH
Public Health Educator, San Diego [CA] County Alcohol and Drug
Services.

Mary Jane Robertson, MS
Research Associate, Department of Psychiatry and Biobehavioral Sciences, UCLA School of Medicine, Los Angeles, CA.

Robert G. Robinson, MD
Professor and Head, Department of Psychiatry, University of Iowa
College of Medicine, Iowa City, IA.

Jay W. Rojewski, PhD
Associate Professor, Department of Occupational Studies, The University of Georgia, Athens, GA.

Gwen Roldan, PhD
Assistant Professor, Department of Psychology, Illinois Institute of Technology.

Carolyn Rollins, PhD
Assistant Professor, the Department of Rehabilitation, Social Work, and Addictions, Denton, TX.

A. John Rush, MD
Betty Jo Hay Professor of Psychiatry, Department of Psychiatry, The University of Texas Southwestern Medical Center, Dallas, TX.

Robert L. Sadoff, MD
Clinical Professor of Psychiatry and Director of the Center for Studies in Social-Legal Psychiatry, University of Pennsylvania, Philadelphia, PA.

Stanton E. Samenow, PhD
Clinical Psychologist and Consultant in Alexandria, VA.

Barry Sarvet, MD
Director of Training at the Division of Child and Adolescent Psychiatry, University of New Mexico School of Medicine, Albuquerque, NM.

James Schaller, PhD
Assistant Professor, The University of Texas at Austin.

Saul Scheidlinger, PhD
Professor Emeritus of Psychiatry (Child Psychology), Albert Einstein College of Medicine, Bronx, NY.

Cathryne L. Schmitz, PhD, ACSW
Assistant Professor, Saint Louis University School of Social Service, St. Louis, MO.

Paula Schneider, PhD, MSW
Associate Professor of Social Work, Regis College, Weston, MA, and practices couples therapy in Chestnut Hill, MA.

Michael Shernoff, MSW, ACSW
Founder and former Co-Director of Chelsea Psychotherapy Associates, New York, NY; currently in private practice and an Adjunct Faculty Member at the Hunter College Graduate School of Social Work, New York, NY.

Gary L. Sigmon, EdD
Vocational Consultant, Blue Ridge Vocational Services, Boone, NC.

Daniel Silber, PhD
Assistant Professor of Philosophy, Kent State University, Kent, OH.

Tomás José Silber, MD, MASS
Director of Education and Training, Department of Adolescent and Young Adult Medicine, Children's National Medical Center, and Professor of Pediatrics, The George Washington University School of Medicine and Health Sciences, Washington, DC.

David W. Smart, PhD
Professor, Counseling and Development Center, Brigham Young University, Provo, UT.

Julie F. Smart, PhD, CRC, NCC, LPC, ABDA
Assistant Professor, Department of Special Education and Rehabilitation, Utah State University, Logan, UT.

Paul Richard Smokowski, MSW
Student in the Doctoral Program in Social Welfare at the University of Wisconsin School of Social Work, Madison, WI.

R. Jeremy A. Stowell, MD, FAPA
Former Director of Adolescent Programs, Virginia Beach Psychiatric Center; currently Medical Director, the Division of Substance Abuse, Norfolk Community Services Board; and in private practice in Virginia Beach, VA.

Edna Mora Szymanski, PhD
Professor and Associate Dean, University of Wisconsin–Madison, Madison, WI.

Lynda Dykes Talmadge, PhD
Adjunct faculty member, Department of Psychology, Georgia State University, Atlanta, GA, and Clinical Psychologist in private practice.

William C. Talmadge, PhD
Adjunct faculty member, Department of Psychology, Georgia State University, Atlanta, GA, and in private practice.

Ralph E. Tarter, PhD
Professor of Psychiatry and Neurology, University of Pittsburgh [PA] Medical School; and Director, Center for Education and Drug Abuse Research (CEDAR), a consortium between St. Francis Medical Center and the University of Pittsburgh.

John C. Thomas, PhD, CEAP, CSAC, NCC, NCAC II
Employee Assistance Consultant with E. I. DuPont de Nemours & Company, Waynesboro and Front Royal, VA.

Kenneth R. Thomas, EdD
Professor, Rehabilitation Psychology Program, the University of Wisconsin–Madison.

Stephen W. Thomas, EdD, CVE, CRC
Professor and Director, Graduate Program in Vocational Evaluation, Department of Rehabilitation Studies, East Carolina University, Greenville, NC.

Gilles Trudel, PhD
Professor, Department of Psychology, The University of Quebec, Quebec, Canada; and Clinical Psychologist, The Behavioral Therapy Unit, Louis H. Lafontaine Hospital, Montreal, Canada.

Catherine L. Tyler, MBA
Former supervisor, State of Indiana, Division of Family and Children.

J. Michael Tyler, PhD
Assistant Professor, Department of Counseling, University of South Florida, Fort Myers, FL.

David Vandergoot, PhD, CRC
President, the Center for Essential Management Services, Oceanside, NY; and Faculty Member, Hunter College, New York, NY.

Janet Wagner, PhD, RN
Dean, Health and Human Services Division, Columbus State Community College, Columbus, OH.

Gillian Walker, MSW
Senior faculty member, The Ackerman Institute for Family Therapy, New York, NY.

Fraser N. Watts, PhD
Employed at the Medical Research Council's Applied Psychology Unit, Cambridge, England.

Rock Weldon, MA, CVE
Vocational Consultant, Weldon & Associates, Greenville, SC.

Louis Jolyon West, MD
Professor of Psychiatry, UCLA School of Medicine, Los Angeles, CA.

Peter C. Whybrow, MD
Professor and Chairman, Department of Psychiatry, University of Pennsylvania, Philadelphia, PA.

John S. Wodarski, PhD
The Janet B. Wattles Research Professor and Director of the Doctoral Program and Research Center, State University of New York at Buffalo, School of Social Work, Buffalo, NY.

Eileen Wolkstein, PhD
Adjunct Assistant Profession/Research Scientist, Rehabilitation Counseling Program, New York University, New York, NY; and Director of Training and Dissemination, NIDRR Funded Research and Training Center in conjunction with Drugs and Disabilities, Wright State University School of Medicine.

Alayne Yates, MD
Professor of Psychiatry, the University of Hawaii, Honolulu, HI.

Douglas Ziedonis, MD
Assistant Professor and Director of the Dual Diagnosis Treatment and Research Program, Connecticut Mental Health Center, Department of Psychiatry, Yale University School of Medicine, New Haven, CT.

Name Index

A

Aagesen, C. A., 3:219
Abbot, M. W., 7:225, 235
Abbott, J., 6:152, 164
Abboudi, Z.H., 7:149
Abelin, T., 8:163, 173
Abikoff, H., 1:192, 209
Ablow, K., 3:263
Abma, J.C., 8:97, 114
Abou-Saleh, M.T., 3:107, 109
Abramowitz, A.J., 5:59, 71
Abrams, D., 4:18, 29
Abrams, D.B., 7:228, 239
Abrego, P.J., 9:19, 32
Abright, A. R., 4:117, 128
Achenbach, T., 5:35, 36, 7:11, 22
Achenbach, T.M., 1:197, 209, 5:53, 71
Acierna, R., 7:181, 186
Ackerman, A.B., 2:123, 141
Ackerman, N.W., 2:8, 146, 161
Ackerman, P.T., 5:49, 71
Ackerman, R.J., 8:9, 44
Ackner, B., 1:64, 85
Adachi, J., 4:109
Adams, J.E., 9:47, 58
Adams, K., 1:223, 231
Adams, R.D., 3:34, 46
Addalli, K.A., 5:76
Ader, R., 3:32
Adey, M., 3:172
Adkins, B.J., 1:162, 167
Adlaf, E.M., 5:238, 246
Adler, A., 1:144, 151, 2:6, 11, 12, 101, 144
Adler, C.S., 4:19, 22
Adler, G., 1:120, 122, 130, 132
Adler, N., 1:155, 167
Adler, R., 5:12, 16
Adolph, M.R., 3:82, 90
Ager, R.D., 7:104, 127
Aghajanian, G.K., 7:137, 138, 140, 148
Agosti, V., 8:135
Agrell, B., 3:158, 171
Ahles, T.A., 4:23

Ahlgren, C., 9:125
Ahrons, C.R., 6:75, 83, 96
Akhtar, S., 1:35, 45
Akil, H., 3:266, 277
Akiskal, H., 1:31, 46, 3:13
Akiskal, H.S., 3:228, 231, 237, 241, 5:80, 98
Aldwin, C.M., 3:148, 171
Alessi, N.E., 5:15, 16
Alexander, B.K., 6:122, 144
Alexander, F., 2:66, 78
Alexander, F.M., 4:5, 22
Alexander, Franz, 2:6, 10
Alexander, M.J., 7:193, 212
Alexander, P.C., 4:145, 146, 148, 150
Alexander, R., 2:83, 93, 5:225
Allan, G., 6:170, 185
Allan, M., 5:270
Allan, M.J., 5:159, 169
Alldritt, L., 8:230, 242
Allen, D., 8:255, 264
Allen, F.E., 7:56, 61
Allen, F.H., 2:9
Allen, G.D., 5:238, 247
Allen, M.G., 2:100, 101, 103, 107, 118
Allison, R.B., 1:57, 78, 85
Allman, C., 5:270
Allman, C.J., 5:254, 269
Allodi, F., 1:2, 10, 13, 24
Allred, C.H., 1:76, 94
Allshouse, K.D., 7:194, 208, 210
Alman, P., 5:36
Almond, P.J., 1:183, 187
Alpert-Gillis, L.J., 6:47, 54
Alson, A., 2:109, 120
Alston, R.J., 9:192, 204
Altamura, A.C., 3:274, 277
Alterman, A.I., 7:68, 69, 74, 85, 99, 8:137
Altman, L., 6:133, 144
Aluwahlia, S., 5:38
Amado, K., 7:12, 24
Amaro, H., 8:114
Ambrosini, P., 5:38, 172

Ambrosini, P.J., 5:11, 14, 16, 165, 169
Amendola, C.A., 7:142, 150
Amerikaner, M., 4:16, 22
Ames, G., 8:15, 46
Amick, A., 1:26
Amoateng, A.Y., 5:238, 246
Amodei, N., 4:8, 22
Amos, O.C., 9:181, 206
Anastasi, A., 9:42, 58, 221, 222, 223, 225
Anch, A.M., 7:169
Andersen, A., 4:42, 47, 50
Andersen, A.E., 3:52, 60, 63
Andersen, G., 3:42, 46
Anderson, C., 2:48, 61, 4:102, 107, 6:192, 214
Anderson, C.M., 2:177, 190
Anderson, D., 5:226, 9:179, 204
Anderson, G., 1:51, 95
Anderson, J.C., 5:4, 174
Anderson, K.E., 7:51, 53, 61
Anderson, S., 10:76, 95
Andolfi, M., 2:146, 161
Andrasik, F., 4:11, 22, 23
Andrews, J., 5:166, 171
Andrezejewski, P., 3:43, 47
Andrulonis, P.A., 1:125, 132
Angermeier, L., 9:196, 207
Anglin, D., 8:287
Angold, A., 5:156, 158, 169
Angst, J., 3:269, 275, 277
Anker, A.L., 7:178, 186
Anmis, H.M., 6:112, 114
Annis, H.M., 7:89, 98
Annis, L.V., 10:149, 158
Annon, J., 6:193, 213
Ansbacher, H.L., 2:48, 61
Anthenelli, R.M., 8:125, 132
Anthony, J.C., 8:246, 247, 262
Anthony, W.A., 3:202, 203, 218
Antico, L., 3:174
Apfel, R., 10:196, 207
Aponte, J.F., 5:104, 122
Appelbaum, K.A., 4:23
Appelbaum, P.S., 10:150, 158, 196, 207
Appell, J., 5:205, 224
Applebaum, D.R., 6:150, 162
Apter, A., 5:254, 269
Arana, G.W., 7:35, 38, 45
Arato, M., 8:131, 133
Arbona, C., 9:194, 204, 211, 225
Arbuthnot, J., 5:219, 223
Ard, B.N., 6:258, 263

Arena, J.G., 4:22, 23
Aries, E., 3:78, 90
Arieti, S., 3:186, 190, 196
Aristotle, 2:100
Arkes, H.R., 10:26, 33
Armistead, L., 6:36, 54
Armitage, S., 7:18, 22
Armor, D.J., 7:216, 225, 236, 240
Armstrong, M.A., 8:126, 134
Arnalde, M.A., 9:230
Arnaud, M.J., 7:53, 62
Arnold, B., 9:210, 228
Arnold, B.R., 9:210, 225
Aronson, S., 5:177, 189
Arredondo, P., 9:178, 208, 218
Arredondo, P.M., 10:236, 237, 245, 247, 248
Arrendondo, P.M., 9:227
Arria, A., 5:228, 247
Arrick, J.R., 1:183, 187
Arrowood, A.A., 8:191, 194
Arruda, M.J., 3:200, 214, 220
Arzin, N., 7:181, 186
Asarnow, R.F., 1:175, 179, 189
Asberg, M., 8:131, 132, 137
Ashely, J., 8:56, 89
Ashikaga, T., 1:263
Asnis, G., 5:256, 271
Asnis, G.M., 8:254, 263
Athelstan, G.T., 9:39, 40, 58
Atkins, B.J., 9:178, 182, 191, 204
Atkins, M., 5:24, 38
Atkins, M.S., 4:119, 129
Atkinson, D.R., 9:186, 187, 188, 189, 198, 202, 204
Atkinson, P., 7:142, 148
Atkinson, R.M., 8:200, 201, 204, 205, 208, 213, 214, 215, 216, 220, 222
Aubin, F., 6:228, 238
Aubin, S., 6:228, 239
Auerbach, A., 2:87, 95
Austin, G.W., 5:205, 224
Austin, K.M., 10:40, 54, 55
Austin, N.L., 9:190, 207
Averill, S.C., 10:200, 202, 207
Avis, H., 8:4, 44
Axelson, J.A., 10:237, 246
Axline, V., 5:135, 149
Ayers, A.J., 9:128, 138
Ayers, W.H., 5:230, 246
Azim, F.A., 2:87, 92, 96
Azrin, N.H., 7:104, 127

B

Baarslag-Benson, R., 9:154, 157
Babor, T.F., 4:96, 105, 5:249
Bachman, D.L., 7:43, 44, 45
Bachman, J.G., 8:188, 195
Bachrach, H., 2:253, 259, 263, 264
Bachrach, L.L., 1:244, 260, 9:175
Backer, T., 10:59, 70
Backer, T.E., 8:17, 44
Badger, G.J., 7:177, 184, 185, 187
Baekeland, F., 2:261, 263
Baekland, F., 7:193, 210, 217, 228, 236
Baer, R.A., 7:156, 167
Bagarozzi, D.A., 6:2, 6, 7, 24
Bagnato, S.J., 5:7, 20
Bahr, H.M., 8:200, 201, 220
Bahr, S.J., 5:238, 246
Baike, E., 3:164, 173
Bailey, G., 4:116, 130
Bailey, G.W., 5:228, 246
Bailey, R., 4:116, 130
Baird, G.W., 6:37, 53
Baird, K., 6:41, 54
Bakal, D.A., 4:11, 22
Baker, A., 4:12, 32
Baker, E., 8:166, 170
Baker, H., 4:255, 259
Baker, L., 1:179, 185, 5:46, 47, 71, 72
Baker, M., 4:255, 259
Baker, S., 8:154
Baker, T.B., 7:218, 236
Balban, L., 1:51, 94
Baldessarini, R.J., 3:35, 46
Bales, B.F., 6:202, 217
Balick, L., 4:8, 22
Balint, E., 2:83, 93
Balint, M.P., 2:83, 93
Balk, D., 6:165
Ballenger, J.C., 8:131, 133
Balthazor, M.J., 5:56, 71
Baltrusch, H., 4:55, 66
Bamberger, P., 8:20, 44
Bandura, A., 4:15, 22, 5:135, 149, 225,
    6:174, 185, 7:176, 186, 8:68, 86
Banki, C.M., 8:131, 133
Bansen, S.S., 6:152, 162
Bar-Yam, M., 9:4, 15
Barbach, L., 6:230, 235
Barbach, L.G., 6:193, 213
Barber, J., 2:86, 94
Barbor, T.F., 8:66, 68, 69, 86, 88

Barcai, A., 5:12, 17
Barcus, M., 9:39, 59
Barefoot, J.C., 3:89, 90
Barker, J.C., 1:163, 167
Barker, R.L., 10:125
Barker, T.A., 7:100, 241
Barker, W.A., 3:233, 234, 236, 237
Barkley, R.A., 1:192, 193, 194, 197, 198,
    200, 201, 202, 204, 205, 206,
    207, 209, 5:42, 43, 47, 48, 49,
    52, 53, 55, 57, 58, 59, 71, 72, 74
Barlow, A., 1:174, 189
Barlow, D.H., 1:108, 115, 116, 4:14, 22, 29,
    70, 88
Barlow, E.L., 1:2, 28
Barlow, J.M., 2:31
Barnett, J.E., 6:201, 213
Barnett, L.W., 7:216, 237
Baron-Cohen, S., 1:174, 184
Barone, J.J., 7:157, 167
Barr, 1:43, 45
Barr, B.P., 4:6, 22
Barr, R.G., 5:56, 73
Barraclough, B., 8:126, 133
Barrager, E., 7:53, 61
Barrett, J., 3:234, 236, 237
Barrett, M.E., 8:100, 115
Barry, W.A., 6:203, 217
Bartak, L., 1:179, 184, 185, 189
Bartels, S.J., 8:275, 285
Barter, J.T., 5:256, 274
Barth, R.P., 7:172, 173, 177, 184, 188
Bartholet, E., 5:104, 120
Bartolo, R.D., 8:162, 173
Bartz, K.W., 6:61, 69
Baser, D., 3:35, 46
Basmajian, L.S., 4:10, 32
Basoglu, M., 1:2, 27
Bass, E., 4:134, 136, 137, 145, 146, 148
Basseches, M., 9:15
Bassuk, E., 5:80, 82, 83, 98
Bateman, D.A., 8:114, 116
Bateson, G., 2:145, 153, 161, 162, 6:32
Batson, C.D., 6:174, 186
Battjes, R.J., 8:170
Baucom, D.H., 6:226, 230, 233, 236
Bauer, L., 4:260
Baugan, A.S.J., 7:149
Baughman, T., 4:99, 108
Baum, M.S., 2:123, 141
Baumrind, D., 6:50, 53
Baxter, L.R., 1:40, 45, 46

Bayer, G., 8:35, 36, 44
Bayog, R.D., 7:108, 127
Beahrs, J.O., 1:55, 68, 85
Beale, D., 10:207
Beale, E.W., 1:76, 85
Beamesderfer, A., 6:24
Bean-Bayog, M., 1:16, 17, 24, 7:215, 236
Bear, D., 1:65, 82, 95
Beard, J.H., 1:243, 260
Beardslee, W.R., 5:18, 164, 169
Beardsley, M.M., 8:74, 90
Beattie, M., 7:99
Beattie, M.C., 8:16, 45
Beaty, A., 5:82, 98
Beaty, E.T., 4:10, 22
Beauchamp, T.L., 8:187, 194
Beaudett, M.S., 8:286
Beauvais, F., 8:162, 173
Beavers, W.R., 6:19, 24
Beavin, J.H., 2:154, 164
Bebbington, P., 1:261
Beck, A., 2:260, 263
Beck, A.T., 3:128, 129, 132, 133, 134, 139,
    140, 141, 142, 143, 144, 146,
    157, 166, 171, 184, 196, 204,
    218, 233, 238, 253, 262, 4:70,
    88, 159, 162, 163, 168, 174, 181,
    200, 5:130, 131, 132, 133, 149,
    263, 269, 6:24, 33, 225, 230,
    233, 236, 7:231, 236
Beck, N., 5:170
Beck, S., 5:81, 98
Becker, C.A., 7:100, 241
Becker, D., 5:249
Becker, J., 6:178, 187, 8:129, 134
Becker, R.E., 3:232, 234, 238
Beckett, R., 6:256, 266
Beckham, E.E., 2:91, 93, 3:141, 143
Beckham, G.C., 10:149, 158
Beckham, J.C., 3:89, 90
Beckner, C., 5:253, 273
Bedrosian, R., 5:142, 150
Beeder, A.B., 7:131, 144, 149
Begleiter, H., 4:99, 105, 7:225, 236, 240
Beidel, D., 5:5, 21
Beitchman, J., 5:24, 36
Beland, K., 5:36
Belkin, B.M., 8:249, 251, 265
Bell, R., 5:35, 38
Bellack, A.S., 1:241, 264, 8:270, 286
Bellecci, P., 8:204, 221
Belmaker, R., 1:231

Belsky, J., 2:196, 212
Belsky, J.K., 3:70, 90
Bemporad, J., 3:182, 185, 186, 187, 192,
    196, 234, 238
Bemporad, J.R., 5:164, 167, 169
Benda, C., 4:246, 259
Bender, M.E.S., 5:48, 77
Benfer, B., 10:207
Benjamin, L.R., 1:76, 85
Benjamin, R., 1:76, 85
Benkelfat, 1:43, 46
Bennefield, R.L., 9:80, 106
Benner, D.G., 1:63, 85
Bennet, L., 6:109, 114
Bennett, L., 7:13, 23
Bennett, L.A., 4:104, 105, 5:236, 246, 8:8,
    52
Bennett, W., 8:163, 170
Bennick, C.D., 4:8, 22
Benowitz, L.I., 3:35, 46
Benowitz, N.L., 7:41, 45
Benshoff, J.J., 10:62, 70
Benson, H., 4:2, 5, 6, 22, 23, 30
Bentham, J., 10:215, 231
Benthem, J.A., 4:8, 22
Bentler, B., 8:162, 173
Bentlor, P.M., 5:238, 248
Benton, M.K., 1:247, 260
Bentovim, A., 4:123, 130
Berenson, B.G., 8:167, 171
Berg, C.J., 7:156, 169
Berg, P., 6:194, 213
Berg, W.K., 9:111, 119, 124
Berger, P., 6:202, 213
Bergin, A., 2:251, 257, 260, 261, 263
Bergin, A.E., 10:22, 23, 33
Berglas, S., 4:96, 105
Bergler, E., 1:157, 163, 167
Bergman, A., 1:133
Bergman, S.J., 6:273, 277, 279, 283, 284
Berhman, R., 8:108, 114
Berkenstock, 2:194
Berkovitz, I., 5:180, 188
Berkowitz, A., 8:9, 45
Berkowitz, L., 6:174, 186
Berkowitz, R., 1:95, 247, 263
Berliner, L., 4:127, 129
Berman, A.L., 5:252, 254, 255, 257, 258,
    259, 267, 268, 269, 270
Berman, J.S., 3:119, 126, 5:93, 98
Bernal, G., 6:112, 114
Bernard, J., 6:274, 283

Berndt, E.R., 3:201, 220
Berne, E., 3:181, 196
Bernfeld, G., 5:48, 72
Bernier, J.E., 10:248
Bernstein, D.A., 4:4, 23
Bernstein, E.M., 1:60, 85
Bernstein, G.A., 5:3, 4, 5, 8, 10, 12, 17
Bernstein, J., 8:11, 23, 37, 45
Bernstein, P.P., 6:153, 162
Berreman, C., 4:23
Berry, C.A., 5:50, 72
Berry, G., 7:164, 169
Berry, J.W., 9:215, 216, 225
Berry, S., 1:76, 92, 3:221, 222
Berscheid, E., 6:195, 213
Bertilsson, L., 8:131, 137
Bertolucci, D.E., 8:251, 264
Besalel, V., 7:181, 186
Besedovsky, H., 3:16, 30
Besharov, D., 10:125
Best, C., 1:26
Besyner, J., 1:2, 28
Bettleheim, B., 2:6
Beutler, L.E., 2:91, 93, 8:164, 172
Beutler, L.F., 10:18, 22, 33
Beyer, J.M., 8:12, 34, 35, 45, 53
Bialos, D., 3:209, 219
Bialow, M.R., 3:157, 176
Bianchi, M.D., 5:11, 16, 165, 169
Bibring, E., 3:196
Bickel, W.K., 7:177, 179, 182, 184, 185, 187, 188
Biederman, J., 5:6, 17, 21, 49, 72
Biegel, D.E., 6:168, 170, 183, 186
Bienen, L.B., 4:115, 128
Bienenfeld, F., 6:55
Bienenfield, D., 8:201, 205, 206, 207, 212, 220
Bienvenu, J., 2:91, 96
Bierman, K.L., 5:130, 149
Biglan, A., 3:171
Bihari, B., 4:99, 105, 7:225, 236
Billings, A.G., 4:103, 104, 109, 7:227, 228, 236
Binder, J.L., 2:86, 87, 88, 91, 92, 93, 95, 97
Bingham, S.F., 8:124, 136
Binkoff, J., 4:18, 29
Binkoff, J.A., 7:239
Bion, W.R., 2:28, 30, 102
Birchler, G.R., 7:116, 127
Bird, H., 5:38
Birren, J.E., 2:204, 210

Birtchnell, J.A., 3:180, 181, 183, 184, 185, 195, 196, 197
Bishay, N., 6:266
Bishop, D.M., 10:152, 159
Bishop, D.S., 2:182, 190
Bishop, S., 3:141, 143
Black, A., 1:36, 46, 8:133, 134
Black, C., 4:77, 88, 8:9, 45
Black, H.R., 3:98, 109
Blackburn, I.M., 3:140, 141, 143, 233, 234, 236, 238
Blackson, T., 5:230, 248
Blackwell, G., 1:252, 263, 265
Blair, K., 1:249, 261
Blake, W., 1:12, 24
Blakely, C.H., 5:225
Blakeslee, S., 6:55
Blalock, J., 3:17, 32
Blanchard, E.B., 4:5, 6, 11, 12, 22, 23, 30, 32
Blanchard, J.J., 8:270, 286
Bland, J.S., 7:53, 61
Bland, K., 7:53, 61
Blankenship, K., 9:129
Blankfield, A., 8:251, 252, 253, 262
Blazer, D., 1:134, 2:194, 210
Blazer, D.G., 3:148, 149, 150, 155, 171, 175, 201, 218
Bleich, A., 5:254, 269
Bleuler, E., 6:249, 263
Bleuler, E.P., 3:34, 46
Bleuler, M., 1:243, 261
Blick, L.C., 5:35, 36
Blinder, M.G., 10:108
Bliss, E.L., 1:51, 63, 64, 85
Bloch, D., 2:161, 162
Bloch, J., 4:119, 131
Bloch, S., 2:103, 109, 119
Block, J., 5:249
Bloom, L.J., 4:18, 32
Bloomquist, H.K., 1:179, 185
Bloomquist, M.L., 5:69, 72
Blos, P., 5:184, 188
Blose, J.D., 8:22, 45, 48
Blose, J.O., 7:88, 99
Bluglass, R., 10:108
Blum, G.S., 5:116, 120
Blum, H.P., 2:233, 246
Blum, K., 4:100, 105, 7:226, 241
Blum, R.H., 4:250, 259
Blum, S., 8:9, 51
Blum, T.C., 8:10, 17, 18, 34, 35, 38, 45, 50, 51

Blume, S., 4:94, 110, 8:70, 86
Blumenthal, S.J., 5:252, 253, 255, 257, 269
Boccellari, A., 8:239, 242
Bodman, M., 5:230, 246
Boeck, M., 5:256, 271
Bograd, M., 10:185, 193
Bohannan, P., 6:77, 85, 96
Bohman, M., 1:185, 4:94, 98, 105, 106,
          8:124, 133
Bohn, M.J., 8:134
Boismare, F., 4:99, 106
Bok, S., 10:222, 231
Bolduc, E.A., 5:6, 21
Bolduc, P., 3:38, 49
Bolduc-Murphy, E.A., 5:17
Bolen, D.W., 1:162, 167
Bolla-Wilson, K., 3:41, 46
Bollerud, K., 8:95, 114
Bollman, S.R., 6:25
Bolton, B., 9:51, 59, 153, 156
Bolton, P., 1:179, 188
Bonagura, N., 5:76
Bonati, M., 7:154, 167
Bond, G.R., 3:219
Bongar, B., 5:12, 16
Bonk, J., 6:12, 24
Boon, S., 1:51, 85
Boone, S.E., 1:248, 265
Boor, M., 1:50, 86
Booth, G.H., 7:169
Booth-Kewley, S., 4:54, 55, 66, 67
Borchardt, C.M., 5:3, 4, 8, 17
Borcherding, B.G., 5:58, 74
Borders, D.L., 10:191, 193
Borders, L.D., 10:84, 94, 191, 194
Bordin, E.S., 2:187, 190
Borenstein, P.H., 5:225
Borg, S., 7:226, 236
Borkman, T., 1:240, 261
Borneman, E., 6:195, 213
Borus, J.F., 7:253, 255
Borysenko, J., 6:138, 144
Boscolo, L., 2:146
Boston, J., 3:41, 46
Bosworth, M.F., 8:201, 203, 204, 208, 222
Boszormenyi-Nagy, I., 2:147, 162, 6:75, 93,
          96
Bothwell, S., 3:206, 221
Botterbusch, K.F., 9:46, 58, 150, 156
Botvin, E.M., 8:166, 170
Botvin, G.J., 8:166, 170
Boucher, J., 1:173, 185

Boudreau, F., 7:245, 251, 255
Bouhoutsos, J., 10:196, 197, 200, 207
Bouhoutsos, J.C., 2:246
Boulenger, J.P., 7:160, 167
Boulos, C., 5:171
Boulos, L., 6:220, 228, 238, 239
Bourgeois, M.S., 3:153, 172
Bouton, M.E., 7:180, 187
Bowden, P., 10:108
Bowe, F., 9:238, 248
Bowen, M., 2:155, 156, 159, 160, 162, 3:190,
          197
Bowen, R.C., 5:11, 17
Bowers, M.D., Jr., 7:138, 139, 142, 148
Bowers, M.K., 1:75, 78, 86
Bowlby, J., 2:144, 162
Bowlby, J., 3:4, 5, 13, 6:195, 198, 214
Bowman, E.S., 1:50, 87
Bowman, S.L., 9:180, 200, 204
Bowyer, J.F., 7:146, 148
Boxill, N., 5:82, 98
Boyd, C., 7:187
Boyd, F.N., 6:119, 144
Boyd, J., 1:243, 256, 262, 4:173, 175
Boyd, J.H., 8:222
Boyd, S., 6:181, 187
Boyd, T.A., 1:180, 181, 187
Boyd, W.H., 1:162, 167
Boyer, L.B., 1:120, 132
Boyer, M.H., 5:19
Boyer, R., 8:135
Boyle, M.H., 5:11, 17, 170
Brace, K., 10:23, 31, 33
Bradley, B.S., 6:150, 163
Bradley, K., 1:77, 87
Bradley, S.J., 5:15, 17
Bradshaw, J., 4:75, 88
Brady, J.P., 5:132, 149
Brady, K., 8:248, 263
Braiker, H.B., 6:203, 214, 7:225, 240
Braiman, S., 5:173
Brammer, L.M., 9:19, 32
Branch, L.G., 7:216, 237
Brand, E., 3:169, 170, 172
Branden, N., 4:218, 219, 220, 221, 225, 227,
          234, 236
Brandon, T., 9:130, 131, 138
Brandon, T.H., 7:218, 236
Brandsma, J.M., 1:78, 86
Brandt, R.B., 10:215, 231
Branscomb, L.P., 4:185, 199
Bransford, J.D., 2:18, 27, 30

Brant, A.M., 10:212, 231
Brantly, D., 5:83, 98
Brasie, J., 5:38
Braswell, L., 5:69, 72, 138, 150
Bratter, B.I., 8:74, 86
Bratter, T.E., 8:74, 86
Braun, A.L., 8:37, 45
Braun, B.G., 1:50, 51, 54, 56, 62, 63, 69, 76, 77, 78, 81, 82, 86, 87, 89, 92, 95
Braverman, M., 1:174, 186
Bray, J., 6:17, 26
Bray, J.G., 4:135, 149
Breckenridge, J.N., 3:157, 168, 172, 177
Breckenridge, J.S., 3:140, 146
Breger, C., 4:15, 24
Breier, A., 1:253, 261, 263, 7:160, 167
Breit, M., 6:258, 264
Brennan-Quattrock, J., 5:100
Brenner, I., 1:74, 86
Brent, D.A., 5:159, 169, 249, 252, 253, 254, 264, 269, 270, 271
Brent, E.E., 4:102, 110
Breslau, N., 1:5, 24
Breuer,, 1:3
Briere, J., 4:116, 128, 134, 135, 137, 145, 146, 149, 5:24, 36
Bright, K., 1:2, 28
Brill, P., 7:239
Brinich, P.M., 5:104, 111, 112, 120
Brink, T.L., 3:172, 6:180, 189
Brismar, B., 8:56, 87
Brittingham, A., 8:4, 48
Britton, B.G., 5:56, 73
Bro-Rasmussen, F., 6:193, 217
Broadhead, W.E., 3:201, 218
Brodsky, A., 10:76, 94
Brodsky, M.D., 7:172, 187
Brodsky, S., 10:125
Brody, E.M., 3:66, 91, 6:170, 171, 174, 186
Brody, J.A., 8:200, 220
Brody, J.E., 6:37, 53
Brodzinsky, D.M., 5:109, 119, 121
Broening, H.W., 7:146, 148
Bromberg, W., 10:108
Bromet, E., 7:228, 236
Bromet, E.J., 3:201, 219
Bromfield, R., 5:180, 188
Brook, J.S., 4:103, 106
Brooke, V., 9:39, 59
Brooks, B., 4:116, 130
Brooks, D.K., 4:188, 199
Brooks, G., 1:263

Brooks, G.R., 4:10, 24
Brooks, L., 9:33, 193, 204
Broskowski, A., 7:245, 248, 255, 256
Broskowski, H., 8:205, 220
Bross, M.H., 8:10, 45
Brosse, R., 3:148, 171
Brouillard, M., 1:112, 116
Browder, D., 9:110, 120, 122, 125
Brown, D., 9:33, 180, 187, 191, 204
Brown, D.C., 3:160, 174
Brown, G.L., 8:131, 133
Brown, G.W., 3:228, 231, 238
Brown, H.S., 6:97
Brown, J., 8:134
Brown, K.W., 7:44, 46
Brown, L., 9:113, 125
Brown, L.K., 5:158, 169
Brown, R.H., 8:177, 194
Brown, R.V., 5:159, 169
Brown, S.A., 4:102, 106, 7:226, 236
Brown, T.A., 4:14, 22
Browne, A., 1:2, 24, 125, 132, 4:117, 118, 128, 134, 145, 149
Brownell, K.D., 8:87
Brubaker, E., 6:170, 172, 173, 186
Brubaker, T.H., 6:170, 172, 173, 186
Bruce, M.L., 3:69, 91, 201, 222
Bruce, M.S., 7:155, 159, 160, 161, 165, 167, 168, 169
Bruhnsen, K., 8:23, 46
Brunt, P.W., 7:142, 148
Bry, B.H., 8:162, 171
Bryant, D.M., 5:164, 170
Bryson, S.E., 1:179, 185
Bryson-Brockmann, W.A., 4:7, 27
Buchanan, A., 8:186, 194
Buchanan, C.F., 6:114
Buchanan, C.M., 6:38, 54
Buchbinder, J., 1:11, 27
Buck, O.D., 1:63, 86
Buckalew, L.W., 7:192, 210
Buckley, J., 9:119, 125, 10:58, 72
Buckman, J., 1:2, 28
Bucky, S.F., 8:9, 45
Budd, S.U., 1:239, 265
Budman, S.H., 7:245, 256
Budney, A.J., 7:177, 179, 182, 184, 185, 187, 188
Budziack, T.J., 8:69, 70, 73, 76, 77, 86
Bufe, G.M., 5:91, 98
Bugental, E.K., 9:19, 32
Bugental, J.F.T., 2:38, 45, 9:19, 32

Bukstein, O.G., 5:228, 244, 246, 247, 249, 7:10, 22, 24
Buller, P.F., 8:46
Bullock, R.C., 3:183, 197
Bunch, J., 8:126, 133
Buongiorno, G., 7:75, 85
Burch, Jr., E.A., 5:104, 122
Burden, H.W., 7:79, 83
Burk, J.P., 4:101, 106
Burke, J.D., 4:70, 88, 90, 7:249, 256
Burke, J.D., Jr., 8:222
Burke, P., 5:171
Burke, P.M., 5:3, 20
Burke, W.H., 8:56, 87
Burleson, J.A., 8:134
Burlew, L.D., 3:87, 91
Burmaster, D., 8:16, 53
Burnam, A., 8:246, 247, 260, 263
Burnham, A., 3:222, 4:94, 108
Burns, B., 2:194, 210
Burns, B.J., 2:213, 7:244, 249, 256, 257
Burns, C.I., 10:79, 94
Burns, D., 3:253, 262, 5:146, 150
Burns, D.D., 4:187, 199
Burns, G.L., 6:150, 162
Buros, O.K., 9:219, 225
Burrow, Trigant, 2:101
Burstin, K.J., 1:63, 87
Bush, P.W., 8:285
Busto, U., 8:256, 263
Butcher, J.N., 2:80, 95, 9:216, 225
Butler, R., 2:198, 204, 210, 3:83, 91
Butler, S., 4:134, 135, 136, 137, 142, 149
Butler, S.F., 2:91, 95
Butz, R.A., 4:135, 149

C

Caddell, J.M., 1:26
Caddy, G.R., 1:75, 87, 7:109, 126
Cadoret, R.J., 4:97, 106
Cafferata, G.L., 6:170, 189
Cairl, R.E., 6:172, 173, 177, 180, 188
Calder, P., 8:9, 46
Calderon, R., 5:171
Caldwell, A.B., 1:162, 167
Caldwell, J., 7:60, 61
Calfee, B., 10:125
Calhoun, K.S., 4:185, 199
Califano, J.A., 6:100, 105, 114
Calkins, D.R., 7:210
Callahan, W.J., 9:217, 231

Callanan, P., 2:123, 128, 138, 10:14, 40, 55, 65, 70, 187, 194
Callis, R., 10:76, 94
Calvert, W.R., 2:200, 213
Camara, W.J., 9:213, 225
Campanella, G., 8:255, 263
Campbell, D., 8:22, 46
Campbell, L., 4:18, 26
Campbell, M., 1:183, 185
Campbell, S., 5:130, 150
Campbell, S.B., 5:48, 72
Campbell, V.L., 9:215, 231
Campos, L.P., 9:213, 226
Canale, J.R., 4:260
Candarelli, A., 5:24, 38
Cannon, W.B., 4:41, 50
Cantor, M.H., 6:170, 171, 174, 177, 186
Cantwell, D., 1:179, 185, 5:46, 58, 77
Cantwell, D.P., 3:52, 63, 5:46, 47, 71, 72, 158, 169, 252, 253, 270, 6:52, 53
Caplan, G., 4:49, 50
Caplan, R.D., 3:202, 217, 218
Capone, D.M., 7:188
Capone, T.J., 7:188
Capparella, O., 3:174
Carattini, S., 7:167
Carboni, P.U., 3:174
Cardoret, T.J., 4:98, 106
Carey, G., 1:38, 46
Carey, W.B., 5:46, 72
Carkhuff, R.R., 8:167, 171
Carlisle, A., 2:204, 210
Carlson, C.R., 4:4, 7, 23
Carlson, E.B., 1:61, 87
Carlson, G., 5:156, 160, 172
Carlson, G.A., 5:81, 98, 154, 158, 169, 252, 253, 270, 6:52, 53
Carlson, J.G., 4:31
Carlson, P.V., 5:104, 123
Carlson, V., 4:28
Carman, J.S., 3:108, 110
Carman, M.B., 3:84, 91
Carmen, E., 1:2, 13, 14, 27
Carner, 2:194
Carpenter, J.S., 1:63, 87
Carpentier, N., 1:244, 261
Carr, R., 4:7, 28
Carrigan, S., 5:254, 273
Carrington, P., 4:4, 24
Carrington, P.C., 4:17, 28
Carroll, K.M., 7:175, 176, 187
Carroll, M.A., 10:168, 169, 170, 173, 178

Carroll, M.R., 2:123, 138
Carroll, R.A., 7:192, 211
Carter, J., 8:163, 171
Cartwright, D., 2:250, 251, 263
Casas, J.M., 9:217, 226, 10:236, 237, 238,
    244, 246, 248
Case, N., 8:129, 133
Case, W.G., 8:256, 266, 267
Casey, R.J., 5:93, 98
Cassavia, E., 5:36
Castaneda, A., 5:85, 98
Casto, S., 8:248, 263
Cataeno, R., 9:211, 226
Catalano, R., 8:162, 172
Catalano, R.F., 4:102, 108, 7:173, 189
Catherall, D.R., 2:166, 167, 187, 188, 190,
    191
Cattell, R.B., 4:28, 9:216, 217, 226
Caul, D., 1:76, 77, 78, 87
Caul, W.F., 5:42, 75
Cavell, T.A., 4:103, 106
Cayleff, S.E., 10:237, 246
Ceccin, G., 2:146
Celano, M., 5:29, 32, 34, 35, 37, 39
Centor, R.M., 5:256, 273
Cermak, T.L., 4:74, 75, 77, 80, 81, 84, 88
Cerny, J.A., 4:70, 88
Ceroni, G.B., 3:227, 238
Cerreto, M., 6:7, 25
Cessner, J., 8:56, 89
Chadsey, R.J., 9:119, 125
Chadwick, O.F.D., 5:172
Chait, R.M., 3:267, 280
Chalmers, D.T., 3:266, 277
Chaloff, J., 5:6, 21
Chambers, L., 4:7, 29
Chambers, W., 7:12, 23
Chambless, D.L., 8:164, 172
Chan, D.A., 7:227, 239
Chan, F., 8:56, 70, 79, 83, 87, 88, 89
Chancellor-Freeland, C., 3:27, 31
Chaney, E.F., 7:225, 239
Chang, G., 7:68, 69, 70, 74, 84, 8:136
Chang, P., 6:61, 69
Chang-Liang, R., 4:15, 24
Chapel, J., 5:50, 75
Chapman, C., 5:104, 120, 121
Chapman, N.J., 6:171, 188
Chapman, P.H.L., 7:89, 90, 91, 98
Chapman, T.F., 5:19
Chappel, J.N., 8:262, 263
Chappel, M.N., 4:9, 24

Charney, D.S., 3:278, 7:160, 161, 167
Charpentier, B., 3:28, 30
Chasnoff, I.J., 8:100, 101, 107, 108, 110, 114,
    115
Chaudhuri, S., 5:255, 273
Chavez, E.L., 9:216, 226
Chavkin, W., 8:110, 115
Cheatham, H.E., 9:180, 181, 192, 195, 206
Cheers, Y., 7:162, 168
Chen, J., 1:2, 28
Chernoff, G.J., 8:2, 46
Cherry, L., 10:59, 70
Cherukuri, R., 8:101, 115
Chesler, P., 6:38, 53
Chesney, M.A., 4:6, 8, 24, 27, 54, 67
Chess, S., 1:178, 185, 5:46, 72, 77
Chevron, E.S., 3:114, 125
Chiauzzi, E.J., 4:93, 7:204, 210, 221, 233,
    237, 8:66, 67, 87
Childress, A.R., 7:179, 180, 188, 227, 237
Childress, J.F., 8:187, 194
Chinman,, 1:95
Chodoff, P., 3:184, 197
Chodorow, N.L., 10:199, 200, 207
Chodorow, N., 6:273, 274, 283
Choppa, A., 9:149, 156
Chou, E.L., 9:189, 206
Christ, Jesus, 4:248, 249
Christiansen, B.A., 4:102, 106, 7:226, 236
Christie, K.A., 4:70, 90
Chrousos, G.P., 3:266, 277
Chu, J.A., 4:185, 186, 188, 189, 190, 192, 199
Chun, R.T., 9:92, 106
Chunn, J., 9:51, 59
Ciadella, P., 1:178, 179, 185
Ciborowski, P.J., 6:36, 37, 51, 53
Cicchette, D.V., 1:96
Cicirelli, V.G., 6:170, 186
Cimbolic, P., 5:14, 18
Ciompi, L., 1:243, 261
Claiborn, C.D., 4:16, 25
Clanton, G., 6:255, 263
Clark, A.J., 9:33
Clark, B.S., 1:179, 185
Clark, D.C., 3:209, 218, 219
Clark, D.M., 4:14, 24, 29
Clark, E.O., 3:154, 175
Clark, G., 8:230, 242
Clark, R.E, 8:285
Clark, S., 9:186, 187, 204
Clarke, C., 5:18
Clarke, E., 4:9, 27

Clarke, G.N., 5:166, 171
Clarkin, J.F., 3:220, 221, 4:76, 89, 5:254, 271
Clary, W.F., 1:63, 87
Claxton, S., 10:79, 95
Clayton, R.R., 5:230, 246
Cleary, P.D., 10:212, 231
Cleckley, H.M., 1:67, 96
Clemmons, D.C., 9:152, 157
Clemmons, R., 3:157, 176
Clifford, C.A., 4:97, 109
Clingempeel, W.G., 3:169, 170, 172, 6:51, 53
Cloninger, C.R., 4:94, 98, 105, 106, 5:230, 246, 8:120, 124, 133, 135
Cloninger, R., 8:256, 267
Clothier, F., 5:115, 121
Clum, G., 5:257, 273
Coates, T., 8:230, 244
Cobb, B., 6:150, 162
Cobb, J.P., 6:248, 263
Coccaro, E.F., 1:125, 132
Cocozza, J., 10:173, 178
Coffman, E.W., 2:123, 141
Coffman, G.A., 7:100, 241
Cohen, A., 8:171
Cohen, D., 3:172
Cohen, D.J., 5:172
Cohen, E., 10:59, 70
Cohen, E.D., 10:214, 217, 221, 222, 223, 224, 232
Cohen, H.J., 3:148, 150, 175
Cohen, H.L., 6:148, 164
Cohen, J., 3:218, 7:96, 98
Cohen, N., 3:32
Cohen, N.J., 5:46, 73
Cohen, S., 3:27, 31, 7:139, 148
Cohen-Sandler, R., 5:255, 256, 257, 270
Coke, J.S., 6:174, 186
Colan, N., 8:33, 36, 47, 51
Cole, N.S., 9:216, 226
Cole, P., 4:134, 149
Coleman, J.V., 7:253, 256
Coleman, M., 5:208, 209, 223
Coleman, N., 1:186
Coleman, S.B., 6:121, 144
Colerick, E.J., 6:177, 186
Coles, B., 7:57, 62
Colletti, G., 7:218, 237
Collier, M.T., 7:253, 256
Collin, S.J., 3:35, 36, 44, 46
Collingwood, T., 8:163, 164, 165, 166, 171, 172
Collins, B., 5:48, 78

Collins, F.L., 4:5, 26
Collins, J.F., 3:219
Collins, J.J., 8:47
Colonna, A.B., 6:165
Comas-Diaz, L., 9:188, 205
Condren, R., 7:188
Condron, M.K., 6:225, 237
Conger, R.E., 1:210
Conn, D.K., 3:44, 48
Conners, C.K., 1:197, 209, 5:42, 54, 73
Conney, A.H., 7:51, 61
Connolly, M., 10:62, 71
Connors, G.J., 7:105, 126
Conoley, J.C., 9:219, 221, 228
Conover, N., 5:269
Constantin-Page, L.D., 4:103, 106
Constantine, L.L., 6:257, 258, 263
Constantino, G., 9:216, 228
Conte, H.R., 5:254, 272
Conte, J.R., 4:117, 128, 5:34, 37
Conwell, Y., 8:206, 220
Conyne, R.K., 2:123, 138, 141
Cook, E., 2:122, 139
Cook, J.A., 3:203, 204, 219
Cook, R., 9:152, 157
Cook, S.W., 10:11, 16
Cookerly, J.R., 6:194, 214
Cooley, Charles, 2:100
Cooney, N.L., 5:249, 7:228, 239
Coons, P.M., 1:50, 51, 52, 56, 64, 65, 66, 77, 86, 87, 88, 4:119, 129
Cooper, A., 2:91, 94
Cooper, A.M., 3:226, 238
Cooper, J., 8:56, 89
Cooper, T., 5:172
Cooper, T.B., 5:164, 170
Coopersmith, S., 3:13, 4:222, 223, 237
Cope, D.N., 7:34, 41, 44, 45
Copeland, E.J., 10:244, 246
Copeland, Mary E., 1:215, 221, 231, 3:248, 252, 253, 262
Coppen, A., 3:107, 109
Copping, W., 5:164, 172
Corbet, M., 10:76, 95
Corbett, T., 5:225
Corbin, J., 6:189
Corcoran, C., 5:170
Corder, B., 5:183, 184, 188
Corey, G., 2:122, 123, 125, 127, 128, 135, 138, 10:6, 11, 14, 40, 44, 46, 47, 54, 55, 64, 70, 125, 184, 187, 192, 194

Corey, M., 2:122, 123, 127, 128, 135, 138, 3:85, 88, 91, 10:64, 70
Corey, M.S., 10:6, 11, 14, 40, 44, 54, 55, 64, 70, 187, 194
Corkery, J.M., 4:135, 149
Corn, R., 5:254, 271
Cornelius, J.R., 8:120, 121, 123, 124, 125, 126, 127, 128, 129, 133, 134, 136
Cornelius, M.D., 8:121, 125, 129, 133, 134
Cornes, C., 3:219
Corney, R.H., 3:234, 238
Correa, V.I., 9:182, 183, 205, 227
Corrigan, P.W., 1:240, 241, 261, 265
Corsini, R.J., 2:103, 119
Corthell, D.W., 9:235, 248
Coryell, W., 1:63, 81, 88
Costello, A., 5:5, 21
Costello, A.J., 5:269
Costello, C.G., 3:164, 172
Costello, E.J., 5:3, 6, 8, 11, 13, 17, 158, 169
Cotch, P.A., 4:23
Cotton, N.S., 4:95, 106
Cottone, R., 10:63, 64, 65, 70, 73
Cottrell, E., 7:217, 240
Coulter, M.L., 5:34, 37
Coulton, C., 6:168, 187
Courchesne, E., 1:178, 185
Coursey, R.D., 4:19, 31
Court, J.H., 9:217, 230
Courtois, C., 4:134, 136, 137, 145, 146, 149
Courtois, C.A., 4:120, 121, 126, 129
Coury, D.L., 5:86, 102
Covi, L., 3:143, 234, 238
Cowen, E.L., 4:104, 107, 6:47, 54
Cox, A., 1:179, 185
Coyne, J.C., 3:44, 49
Cramer, F., 5:183, 188
Cramer-Azima, F., 5:187, 188
Crary, B., 3:23, 30
Crawford, S., 5:256, 274
Creamer, V.A., 4:102, 106
Creasy, R.K., 8:103, 104, 105, 106, 107, 115
Creer, T.L., 4:28
Crepeault, C., 6:224, 225, 238
Cressler, D.L., 1:243, 262
Crewe, N.M., 9:39, 40, 58
Crits-Christoph, P., 2:86, 87, 90, 91, 92, 93, 94, 95
Crohn, M., 6:97
Cronbach, L.J., 10:149, 158
Cronghan, J., 8:120, 135

Cronin, J.K., 8:10, 45
Cronkite, R.C., 4:107, 7:114, 126
Croop, R.S., 7:74, 84
Cross, A.W., 8:190, 195
Cross, G.M., 7:64, 83
Cross, L.A., 5:104, 122
Cross, W.E., Jr., 9:189, 190, 205
Crouch, D.J., 8:12, 46
Crouch, E., 2:103, 109, 119
Crouse-Novak, M., 5:170
Crow, M.J., 6:258, 263
Crowley, T.Y., 7:178, 186
Crumley, F.E., 5:241, 246
Cruse, J.R., 4:75, 84, 88, 91
Cuellar, I., 9:212, 226
Culver, C., 8:187, 194
Culver, C.M., 10:30, 31, 33
Cummings, C., 8:68, 87
Cunningham, B., 4:250, 251, 255, 259
Cunningham, C., 5:35, 38
Cunningham, J., 8:87
Cupples, A., 7:100, 241
Cupps, T., 3:22, 30
Curan, D.K., 5:265, 270
Curl, R.C., 9:152, 153, 157
Curl, R.M., 9:119, 126
Curry, J.F., 5:264, 272
Curtis, E.C., 3:201, 219
Curtis, J.R., 8:220
Curtis, J.T., 2:90, 91, 97
Curulla, V.L., 5:207, 223
Custer, R.L., 1:155, 167
Cutler, R.B., 8:129, 135
Cytryn, L., 6:52, 54
Czarnecka, A., 7:226, 236
Czirr, R., 3:141, 146

D

Dackis, C., 7:226, 237
Dackis, C.A., 3:96, 101, 109, 8:129, 134
DaCosta, G., 5:36
Dahlstrom, W.G., 9:216, 226
Dalberg, C., 10:200, 207
Daley, D., 8:136
Daley, J., 7:198, 204, 210, 211
Dalhstrom, L.E., 9:216, 226
Daly, M., 6:252, 264
Daly, S., 7:149
Damgaard, J.A., 1:50, 88
Damon, J., 5:35, 38
Damon, L., 5:35, 37

Danek, M., 9:110, 126
Daniels, M., 3:222, 8:16, 53
Daniluk, J.C., 4:134, 135, 141, 146, 149, 150
Dantzer, R., 3:16, 30, 4:2, 24
Daoust, M., 4:106
Dare, C., 2:81, 96
Darlington, R.B., 9:217, 226
Daro, D., 4:116, 131
Davanloo, H., 2:83, 86, 91, 94
Davenport, A., 7:79, 83
Davidson, H.A., 10:108
Davidson, III, W.S., 5:225
Davidson, J., 1:2, 15, 24
Davidson, J.R.T., 3:209, 213, 219, 266, 277
Davidson, K.J., 6:225, 236
Davidson, R.J., 4:2, 21, 24, 31
Davidson, V., 10:200, 207
Davies, B., 6:150, 162, 163
Davies, J.M., 1:127, 132
Davies, M., 5:100, 172, 173
Davine, M., 5:46, 73
Davis, C., 1:5, 24, 9:211, 226
Davis, D.H., 1:76, 88
Davis, F., 5:182, 188
Davis, I., 8:236, 242
Davis, J.M., 7:40, 45
Davis, K.E., 7:244, 258
Davis, L., 1:231, 4:134, 136, 137, 140, 145,
        146, 148, 149, 9:125
Davis, L.J., 8:201, 221
Davis, M., 1:221, 231, 3:252, 253, 262,
        5:241, 247, 7:245, 254, 256
Davis, M.A., 7:68, 85
Davis, P., 4:103, 107
Davis, P.A., 5:265, 270
Davis, T.E., 10:54, 55
Davis, W., 6:107, 115
Davison, G.C., 5:149
Dawes, R.M., 10:26, 33
Day, N.L., 8:105, 115, 136
de Carufel, F., 2:91, 96
de Jong, R., 3:233, 234, 238
de Marneffe, D., 1:11, 27
De Miranda, J., 10:59, 70
de Misquita, P.B., 5:4, 18
de Perczel, M., 5:259, 270
De Silva, P., 6:258, 264
de Visser, L.A., 7:115, 125
de Vito, R., 1:77, 88
De Wit, H., 8:256, 264
Deakins, S., 1:247, 263
Dean, J., 5:84, 100

Debbane, E.G., 2:91, 96
Deblinger, E., 4:119, 129, 5:24, 37, 38
Decelles, P.G., 9:81, 106
Dehlin, O., 3:158, 171
Deinard, A.S., 6:61, 69
DeJong, A.R., 1:19, 25
Del Boca, F.K., 8:134
Delaney, D.D., 7:188
Delaney, W.P., 8:15, 46
Delbanco, T.L., 7:198, 210, 211
Delboca, F.K., 5:249
DeLecuona, J.M., 8:254, 263
Delgado, P.L., 3:278
Delgado, P.L., 7:35, 37, 45
D'Elia, L.F., 3:154, 175
DeMane, N., 3:220, 221
DeMaris, A., 6:63, 64, 66, 69, 70
DeMateo-Smith, R., 9:182, 183, 197, 205
DeMatteo, M., 8:163, 172
Demi, A.S., 6:149, 163
deMott, B., 2:12
Dempster-McClain, D., 6:175, 189
Den Boer, J.A., 4:70, 88
Denenberg, T.S., 8:7, 46
Denney, D.R., 4:8, 15, 24, 31
Denney, N.W., 4:29
Dennis, M., 3:35, 41, 47
Denzin, N., 8:20, 46
DePaulo, J., 3:263
DePauw, M.E., 2:127, 139, 10:76, 94
Derby, J.F., 3:86, 91
Deren, S., 8:84, 87, 105, 106, 107, 115
DeRisi, W.J., 8:277, 286
Dermody, E.W., 6:178, 188
Derrick, A.M., 5:253, 254, 273
Derry, M., 6:203, 218
Descartes, R., 1:2
Desmond, D.P., 7:217, 238
Dessonville, C., 3:172
Deutchman, D., 2:204, 210
Deventer, P., 9:125
Dew, M.A., 3:201, 219
Dewald, P.A., 5:149
Deykin, E.Y., 1:179, 186, 5:158, 159, 171,
        256, 270
Dial, J., 9:147, 149, 157
Diamond, B.L., 10:99, 107
Diamond, E.E., 9:218, 227
Diamond, R., 5:165, 172
Dibb, G.S., 6:122, 144
Dickerson, M.G., 1:155, 169
Dicks, H.V., 6:200, 202, 203, 214

DiClemente, C.C., 7:197, 199, 211, 212,
    8:78, 87, 89, 270, 276, 286, 287
Dies, K., 5:187, 188
Difiore, J., 5:256, 271
DiGiuseppe, R., 4:166, 173, 174, 175
Dileo, D., 9:115, 125
Dill, D.L., 1:87
Dilley, J., 8:239, 242
Dillon, C., 8:164, 172
Dilsaver, S.C., 5:15, 16
Dincin, J., 9:175
Ding, Y., 4:6, 27
Dinicola, V.F., 5:164, 172
DiNitto, D.M., 8:84, 90
Dittmann, J., 1:253, 261
Dittrich, J.E., 7:104, 125
Doan, R., 8:164, 172
Dobson, K.S., 3:140, 144
Docherty, J.P., 3:219
Dodson, F., 6:55
Dodson, W.E., 7:154, 169
Doell, S.R., 4:19, 26
Doherty, W.J., 6:36, 53
Doherty, W.L., 7:199, 210
Dolan, K., 8:230, 242
Dolinski, A., 5:173
Doll, M., 8:56, 88
Dollard, J., 2:6
Domino, E.F., 7:140, 149
Donahoe, C.P., 1:248, 265
Donahue, B., 7:181, 186
Donohoe, M., 8:230, 242
Donohue, R., 8:88
Donovan, D.M., 7:193, 212, 225, 226, 239,
    241
Dorans, N.J., 9:211, 212, 230
Dornbusch, S.M., 6:38, 54
Dorner, P., 5:104, 121
Dosning, R., 3:266, 279
Dostoevski, Fyodor, 1:156
Dotemoto, S., 5:48, 78
Doub, N., 4:27
Douglas, P.H., 10:212, 232
Douglas, R., 10:62, 71
Douglas, V.I., 5:43, 47, 56, 73
Douvan, E., 6:199, 214
Dow, M.G., 3:171
Dowd, E., 2:51, 61
Dowd, L.R., 9:235, 248
Doweiko, H.F., 8:4, 46
Dowling, C., 3:252, 262
Down, M., 3:140, 144

Downey, A.M., 5:254, 270
Downey, D.B., 6:63, 70
Downhill, J.E., 3:41, 46
Downing, C.J., 6:52, 53
Downing, M., 8:230, 242
Downing, R.W., 6:121, 144
Doyle, C., 7:99
Doyle, J.A., 6:272, 283
Doyne, E.J., 8:164, 172
Doyon, M., 10:62, 71
Draijer, N., 1:51, 85
Drake, R.E., 8:248, 254, 263, 285, 286
Drane, J.F., 10:19, 20, 33
Draper, E., 3:185, 186, 197
Drapkin, R., 2:123, 141
Dreikurs, R., 2:144
Dreisbach, R.H., 7:163, 167
Drew, C.J., 9:192, 205
Dreyfus, E.A., 6:78, 96
Driesbach, R.H., 7:167
Driscoll, M.S., 5:43, 73
Drucher, E., 6:120, 124, 145
Druley, K.A., 7:93, 99, 227, 239
Drummond, P.D., 4:11, 24
Drummond, R.J., 9:42, 59
Dryden, W., 4:155, 158, 171, 173, 174, 175
Du Canto, J.N., 6:78, 96
Dublin, J.E., 3:188, 197
Dubois, C., 5:171
Duffy, J., 4:260
Duffy, M., 2:202, 211
Duhl, B.S., 2:147, 162
Duhl, F.J., 2:147, 162
Dulcan, M., 5:269
Duncan, J., 2:123, 139
Duncan, P.W., 9:144, 157
Duncan, S.W., 6:162
Dunlap, L., 8:87
Dunlop, J., 8:208, 212, 220
Dunmeyer, S., 7:64, 85
Dunn, C.W., 9:181, 194, 205
Dunn, L.M., 9:216, 226, 216, 226
DuPaul, G.J., 5:53, 54, 57, 74
DuPont, C.M., 1:98, 106, 115
DuPont, R.H., 1:21, 25
DuPont, R.L., 1:98, 105, 106, 112, 115, 116,
    4:70, 83, 85, 89, 7:64, 74, 79, 83,
    150, 8:141, 150, 153, 154, 190,
    194
Duprau, J., 5:117
Dupree, L.W., 8:205, 208, 213, 214, 220
Duran, R.P., 9:211, 215, 226

Durell, J., 7:239
Durran, A., 10:248
Dusay, J.M., 3:193, 197
Dworkin, G., 8:187, 194
Dye, A., 2:123, 138
Dyer, W.W., 9:33
Dykhuizen, R.S., 7:142, 148
Dykman, R.A., 5:49, 71
D'Zurilla, T.J., 7:231, 237

E

Eadington, W.R., 1:167
Eames, P., 7:44, 46
Earls, F., 8:231, 244
Easson, W.M., 5:104, 112, 121
Eastham, J., 6:178, 187
Eaton, P., 5:258, 273
Eberlein-Vries, R., 1:247, 263
Eberly, R., 1:25, 28
Ebrahim, S., 3:35, 46
Eccles, J.S., 6:101, 114
Eccleston, D., 3:228, 231, 241
Eckman, T.A., 1:249, 252, 261, 263, 265
Ecton, R.B., 5:264, 270
Eddy, D.M., 5:267, 270
Edelbrock, C., 5:35, 36, 269, 7:11, 22
Edelbrock, C.S., 1:192, 197, 209, 5:48, 53, 54, 71, 72, 74
Edell, W., 5:249
Edelsohn, G.A., 5:34, 37
Edelstein, L., 6:165
Edgerton, J.W., 7:252, 256
Edgman-Levitan, S., 7:198, 211
Edvinsson, S.O., 1:185
Edwards, A., 3:29, 31
Edwards, E., 3:266, 278
Edwards, G., 8:126, 136
Edwards, K., 7:18, 24
Egan, G., 5:149, 10:84, 94
Egan, M.W., 9:192, 205
Egelko, S., 8:74, 87
Ehler, J., 8:126, 133, 134
Ehrman, R., 7:227, 237
Eiduson, B.N., 5:111, 112, 121
Einstein, E., 6:96
Eisdorfer, C., 3:148, 172
Eisen, J.L., 1:47
Eisen, L.E., 6:248, 265
Eisenberg, A., 8:153, 154
Eisenberg, D.M., 7:192, 210
Eisenberg, H., 8:153, 154

Eiser, J.R., 7:225, 238
Elderkiun, R., 4:99, 109
Elfner, L., 4:8, 22
Elia, J., 5:11, 16, 58, 74, 165, 169
Elkin, I., 3:140, 141, 144, 209, 213, 214, 219, 231, 238
Ellenberger, H.F., 1:83, 88
Ellers, B., 7:205, 210
Ellingboe, J., 4:96, 105
Ellingson, T., 8:287
Ellinwood, E.H., 7:173, 187
Elliott, L., 1:2, 28
Ellis, A., 2:48, 55, 61, 154, 260, 263, 4:154, 157, 159, 168, 173, 175, 5:130, 150, 6:233, 236
Ellis, B.G., 4:71, 89
Ellis, J., 5:50, 75
Ellis, T.W., 5:259, 270
Ellison, C.R., 6:192, 218
Ellison, J.A., 7:245, 256
Emener, W., 10:58, 71
Emerick, R.E., 1:240, 261
Emerson, P., 3:87, 91
Emerson, S., 10:79, 84, 85, 95
Emery, G., 4:70, 88, 5:130, 131, 132, 133, 142, 144, 149, 150, 263, 269
Emlen, A.C., 6:171, 188
Emrick, C.D., 7:92, 98
Endicott, J., 3:155, 172, 7:96, 98
Endman, M.W., 5:48, 72
Engdahl, B., 1:2, 16, 27, 28
Engdahl, F., 1:2, 25
Engel, G., 3:3, 4, 13
Engel, J., 1:241, 261
Engel, R.D., 4:6, 25
Engel, T., 6:97
Englesjgerd, M., 8:164, 171
Engstrom, A., 8:56, 87
Ennis, B., 10:168, 178
Enns, C.Z., 4:135, 136, 142, 149
Epstein, N., 6:226, 230, 233, 236
Epstein, N.B., 2:168, 182, 190
Epstein, S., 3:13, 7:13, 22
Erbaugh, J., 3:157, 171, 204, 218
Erfurt, J.C., 8:8, 17, 46, 47
Erickson, M.H., 1:78, 88, 2:67, 78, 146
Erickson, S.H., 10:9, 14
Ericson, P.M., 6:19, 24, 32
Erikson, E.H., 2:197, 211, 4:202, 206, 215, 250, 259, 5:184, 188
Erle, J.B., 2:259, 263
Eschelman, E.R., 1:221, 231, 3:252, 253, 262

Escobar, J., 1:264
Escoriheula, R.M., 7:189
Eshleman, S., 5:18
Estroff, T.W., 3:96, 106, 109, 5:229, 230, 246, 248
Eth, S., 1:16, 28, 264
Ettin, M., 2:100, 101, 119
Eunson, K.M., 3:141, 143
Evans, K.M., 9:189, 205
Evans, L., 3:266, 278, 9:234, 248
Everson, M.D., 5:34, 35, 37
Everstine, D.S., 10:4, 15
Everstine, L., 10:4, 15
Every, D.K., 8:23, 47
Ewart, C.K., 4:27
Ewing, J.A., 8:207, 221, 272, 273
Extein, I., 3:96, 101, 102, 103, 104, 106, 109, 111, 245, 262
Eyde, L.D., 9:212, 214, 226, 227, 228
Eysenck, H.J., 2:250, 263, 4:54, 55, 57, 60, 64, 66, 67, 68
Ezriel, H., 2:113, 119

F

Fabrega, H., 8:124, 133, 134
Fabro, S., 8:103, 104, 105, 108, 116
Fad-mina, J., 5:149
Fadden, G., 1:258, 261, 262
Fagan, J., 1:50, 60, 88
Fagerhaugh, S., 6:189
Fagg, J., 8:126, 134
Faherty, S., 5:35, 38
Fairweather, G.W., 1:243, 262
Faith, R., 3:24, 32
Falkowski, J., 3:184, 197
Falkowski, W., 7:181, 187
Fallahi, C., 5:170
Falloon, I.R.H., 1:243, 246, 254, 256, 258, 262
Faltz, B., 8:234, 240, 243
Falvo, D., 7:26, 27, 45
Fanaroff, A.A., 8:102, 103, 104, 105, 106, 107, 108, 115
Fanella, F., 7:217, 241
Fanning, P., 3:253, 262
Fanschel, D., 2:19, 30
Farabee, D.J., 8:10, 49
Faragher, E.B., 4:10, 32
Farber, B., 1:82, 93
Farber, B.A., 2:91, 96
Farberow, N., 3:120, 126

Farberow, N.L., 5:254, 258, 270
Farley, R.C., 9:51, 59
Farmer, M.E., 8:136, 247, 266
Farone, S.V., 5:17
Farrington, D.P., 5:206, 223
Fast, I., 3:185, 197
Fauci, A., 3:22, 30
Faulkner, L.R., 7:249, 256
Faure, N., 4:110
Fava, J., 8:16, 45
Fawcett, J., 3:209, 218, 219
Fedoroff, J.P., 3:48
Feehan, M., 5:20, 171
Feely, J.M., 4:17, 25
Fehrenbach, P.A., 5:225
Feibel, J.H., 3:35, 41, 44, 46
Feibelman, N.D., 1:20, 27
Feifel, H., 2:204, 211
Feigelman, W., 5:104, 121
Fein, D., 1:174, 178, 186
Feinberg, L., 10:248
Feinberg, T.L., 5:170
Feindler, E.L., 5:218, 219, 223, 264, 270
Feit, M.D., 7:181, 182, 189
Feldenkrais, M., 4:5, 25
Feldman, L.B., 2:168, 190, 6:269, 272, 283
Feldman-Summers, S., 10:196, 207
Feldstein, M., 10:196, 207
Felker, M.P., 8:216, 217, 218, 221
Felkins, B., 2:194, 212
Felsenfeld, N., 5:182, 189
Felton, D.L., 3:32
Fendrich, M., 5:159, 173
Fenichel, O., 1:156, 157, 167, 3:182, 197
Fennell, M.J.V., 3:233, 234, 238
Ferenczi, S., 2:83, 94
Ferguson, H.B., 5:164, 171, 172
Fernandez, P., 1:179, 185
Fernandez-Teruel, A., 7:189
Ferre, F., 7:189
Ferster, C.B., 3:163, 164, 172
Ficster, S.J., 3:219
Field, E.S., 9:150, 159
Field, J.E., 9:46, 59
Field, T.F., 9:46, 59
Figley, C., 1:5, 25
Figueroa, J.L., 4:11, 32
Figueroa, R.A., 9:218, 227
Filazzola, A.D., 8:166, 170
Fillit, H., 8:221
Fillmore, K.M., 4:104, 107
Filstead, W.J., 4:102, 107

Fine, C.G., 1:70, 72, 75, 88
Fine, H.J., 2:31
Fine, J., 8:246, 248, 249, 265
Fine, S., 5:166, 170
Fink, D., 1:67, 88
Fink, E., 7:99
Fink, M., 3:266, 279
Finkelhor, D., 1:2, 24, 125, 132, 4:114, 116,
        117, 118, 127, 128, 129, 134,
        145, 149, 150, 5:24, 28, 37
Finkelstein, R., 5:4, 19, 170
Finkelstein, S., 3:35, 46
Finkelstein, S.N., 3:201, 220
Finlayson, R.E., 8:201, 202, 209, 221
Finn, P.R., 4:100, 107
Finnell, K., 3:172
Finney, J.W., 4:107, 7:114, 126, 227, 239,
        8:201, 202, 221
Fiore, J., 6:178, 187
Firestone, P., 1:210
Fisch, R., 2:66, 70, 78, 6:198, 218
Fischer, B., 5:117
Fischer, G., 8:228, 233, 234, 235, 243
Fischer, J., 6:233, 236, 10:60, 73
Fischer, M., 1:192, 193, 209, 210, 5:48, 72
Fischhoff, B., 6:107, 115
Fischman, M.W., 7:151, 225, 240
Fish, L.S., 6:276, 283
Fish, R.C., 6:276, 283
Fishbein, M., 5:13, 14, 18
Fisher, J., 10:64, 71
Fisher, P., 5:38, 254, 273
Fisher, S.H., 3:34, 46
Fisher, W., 8:272, 278, 287
Fishkin, M.D., 7:142, 150
Fishman, H.C., 6:110, 115
Fiske, D., 2:251, 263
Fitting, M., 6:178, 187
Fitzenz, J., 8:21, 47
Fitzgibbon, J.J., 8:192, 194
Fixsen, D.L., 5:142, 150
Flach, F., 4:41, 50
Flanagan, C., 6:114
Flanigan, B., 4:260
Flaskerud, J.H., 10:213, 221, 232
Fleisher, W.P., 1:51, 95
Fleiss, J.L., 7:96, 98
Fleming, J.E., 5:159, 160, 170
Flinn, D.E., 3:185, 198
Flores-Ortiz, Y., 6:112, 114
Florio, L., 3:69, 91
Florio, L.P., 3:201, 222

Flynn, C.C., 9:120, 125
Flynn, J.M., 5:226
Flynn, T.H., 9:111, 124
Foa, E.B., 1:34, 41, 46, 47, 109, 116, 4:119,
        129, 5:24, 38
Fodor, I., 5:82, 99
Foerg, F., 7:177, 187, 188
Fogel, B.S., 3:71, 91
Folkman, S., 5:89, 99, 7:13, 22
Follette, V.M., 4:146, 150
Follette, W.C., 4:146, 150
Folstein, M.F., 3:35, 47, 154, 172, 7:18, 22
Folstein, S., 3:154, 172
Folstein, S.E., 7:18, 22
Fonagy, P., 5:63, 70, 74
Fontaine, M., 8:233, 243
Foote, A., 8:8, 17, 46, 47
Ford, J., 7:246, 256
Ford, M.R., 4:17, 25
Forehand, R., 6:36, 54
Forehand, R.L., 1:193, 199, 202, 209
Forer, B.R., 10:196, 207
Forest, J., 4:110
Forester-Miller, H., 10:54, 55
Forsell, C., 1:179, 186
Forth, A., 5:166, 170
Fortin, C., 6:220, 228, 239
Fossi, G., 8:255, 263
Foster, C., 7:210
Foster, S., 1:198, 210
Foster, S.L., 7:120, 127, 10:237, 247
Fotheringham, J.B., 1:178, 186
Fouad, N.A., 9:180, 198, 199, 205
Fountain, E., 4:260
Fowler, R.C., 5:241, 247, 253, 273
Fox, J.C., 7:244, 258
Foxx, R.M., 7:166, 168
Foy, D.W., 1:248, 265
Fradd, S.H., 9:211, 227
Framo, J., 6:92, 96
Framo, J.L., 6:198, 200, 214
Frances, A., 3:226, 238, 4:76, 89
Frances, A.J., 3:279
Frances, R.J., 8:270, 287
Francis, G., 5:8, 12, 19
Francke, L.B., 6:37, 41, 53
Frank, A.F., 1:120, 132, 240, 262
Frank, E., 3:209, 213, 219, 267, 269, 275,
        276, 278, 6:192, 214
Frank, H., 1:124, 133, 134
Frank, J., 4:185, 199
Frank, J.D., 5:149

Fransen, P., 4:244, 259
Fraser, R.T., 9:150, 151, 152, 154, 157
Frattura-Kamshoer, E., 9:125
Frawley, M.G., 1:127, 132
Frayn, D.H., 2:241, 246
Freedman, D.X., 7:138, 142, 148
Freedman, R.R., 4:7, 25
Freeman, A., 3:146
Freeman, B.J., 1:188
Freeman, R., 5:164, 165, 172
Fremouw, W.J., 5:259, 260, 263, 265, 270
French, M.T., 8:47
French, T., 2:66, 78
French, T.M., 2:83, 93
Frese, Fred J., 1:253, 262
Fretter, P.B., 2:91, 97
Freud, A., 5:184, 188
Freud, A., 8:177, 194
Freud, S., 1:3, 156, 167, 2:2, 6, 24, 26, 28, 29,
    30, 34, 80, 81, 83, 85, 94, 101,
    149, 162, 197, 211, 232, 238,
    246, 262, 3:180, 4:81, 89, 117,
    120, 6:253, 264
Frewer, L.J., 7:156, 168
Frey, D.H., 10:15
Fried, J., 5:172
Friedlander, A.H., 4:261
Friedman, H.S., 4:54, 55, 66, 67
Friedman, J.M., 6:192, 194, 214, 217, 221,
    222, 225, 227, 229, 233, 237
Friedman, L., 4:244, 259
Friedman, L.J., 6:200, 214
Friedman, M., 1:20, 21, 25
Friedman, R.C., 5:254, 271
Friedman, S., 6:257, 264
Friedrich, W.N., 5:24, 37
Frischholz, E.J., 1:76, 95
Fristad, M.A., 5:85, 88, 99
Fritz, G.K., 5:158, 169
Froese, A., 5:256, 271
Fromm-Reichman, F., 2:144, 162
Fry, P.S., 3:84, 91
Fry, W., 2:145
Fudge, H., 5:160, 170
Fuhrer, M.J., 9:39, 59
Fujiwara, S., 4:109
Fuller, B., 6:87, 96
Fuller, D., 5:209, 224
Fuller, G.D., 4:18, 25
Fuller, M., 10:196, 208
Fullilove, M.T., 4:135, 150
Fulop, G., 8:221

Futterman, D., 8:231, 243
Fyer, A.J., 5:6, 18, 19

G

Gabbard, G.O., 1:127, 129, 133, 2:234, 246,
    10:198, 201, 203, 204, 207, 209
Gabrielli, W.F., 4:96, 109, 5:104, 122
Gadlin, H., 6:200, 214
Gaffney, G.R., 1:179, 186
Gagnon, J., 6:222, 237
Gainey, R.R., 7:173, 189
Gaitz, C.M., 2:197, 211
Galanter, M., 8:74, 87
Gallagher, D., 2:198, 213, 3:156, 157, 166,
    167, 168, 169, 172, 173, 175,
    177
Gallagher, D.E., 3:140, 141, 144, 146
Gallagher-Thompson, D., 3:148, 160, 168,
    173, 176
Galletti, F., 7:167
Gantz, F.E., 3:160, 176
Gany, V., 9:85, 107
Garant, J., 2:91, 96
Garasky, S., 6:59, 66, 70
Garbarino, J., 6:179, 187
Garber, J., 5:142, 150, 154, 169
Garcia, J., 10:58, 72
Garcia, J.L., 6:168, 170, 177, 181, 187, 188
Garcia, R.E., 9:216, 225
Garcia, S.A., 8:111, 115
Garcia-Coll, C., 5:18
Garcin, F., 4:110
Gardner, K.R., 4:6, 18, 25
Gardner, R., 5:179, 188
Gardner, R.A., 5:116, 121
Gardner, W.J., 8:70, 88
Garfield, S., 2:251, 257, 260, 261, 263
Garfield, S.L., 2:196, 211, 7:192, 210
Garfinkel, B., 5:158, 173
Garfinkel, B.D., 5:5, 12, 17, 158, 170, 254,
    256, 271
Garland, A., 5:254, 273
Garland, J., 5:183, 188
Garmezy, N., 4:103, 107, 5:89, 99
Garner, D.M., 3:62, 63
Gartner, A., 1:240, 264
Gartner, J., 5:238, 247
Gartrell, N., 10:196, 197, 200, 202, 207,
    208
Gary, V., 8:164, 172

Garza, R., 9:183, 205
Gass, R., 8:163, 173
Gasser, R.D., 6:61, 70
Gastfriend, D.R., 8:261, 263
Gatens-Robinson, E., 10:64, 71
Gatewood, R., 9:213, 227
Gatsonis, C., 5:4, 19
Gatz, M., 2:194, 211
Gavaler, J.S., 7:225, 241
Gavin, L.A., 6:162
Gawin, F.H., 7:173, 187
Gay, P., 4:120, 129
Gaylin, W., 3:182, 197
Gazda, G.M., 2:141
Geary, C.A., 10:244, 247
Gelder, M., 4:14, 24
Gelder, M.G., 4:70, 89, 90, 5:20
Gelenberg, A.J., 7:35, 37, 45
Gelernter, C.S., 5:14, 18
Geller, B., 5:164, 170
Geller, G., 8:220
Gellhorn, E., 4:3, 25
Gemma, A., 3:174
Gendlin, E., 1:222, 231
Gendlin, G.T., 5:132, 151
Genest, M., 4:12, 32
Genshaft, J.L., 5:86, 102
Genthner, B., 8:164, 171
Gentile, C., 5:35, 39
George, L., 1:134
George, L.K., 2:197, 211, 3:148, 171, 201,
        218, 6:171, 177, 180, 186, 187,
        8:222
Gerardi, M.A., 4:11, 23
Gerardi, R., 1:12, 25, 4:23
Germanson, T., 7:227, 240, 8:120, 136
Gerrard, M., 4:24, 29
Gershaw, N.J., 5:67, 74, 76, 205, 223
Gershon, E.S., 3:52, 64
Gerson, R., 6:89, 97
Gerstein, L., 8:35, 36, 44
Gert, B., 8:187, 194
Gert, B., 10:21, 29, 30, 31, 33
Gerteis, M., 7:198, 211
Gerwirtzman, R., 5:82, 99
Gfroerer, J.S., 7:172, 187
Giampino, T.L., 5:76
Giannini, A.J., 3:98, 109
Gibbon, M., 7:12, 23
Gibbons, R.D., 3:219
Gibbs, J.C., 5:209, 223, 224
Gibbs, J.T., 5:254, 271

Gibson, F.M., 7:149
Gibson, G., 10:76, 95
Gibson, R.W., 2:196, 211
Gibson, S., 8:129, 134
Gil, E., 4:134, 145, 146, 150
Gilbert, G.S., 4:16, 25
Gilbert, M., 5:166, 170
Gilbert, M.S., 4:135, 149
Gilbert, P., 5:14, 21
Gilbert, R.M., 7:156, 168
Gilbride, D.D., 9:84, 106, 10:62, 71
Gilchrist, J., 4:28
Gilfillan, D., 7:217, 241
Gill, M.M., 5:149
Gill, S.J., 2:123, 138
Gillberg, C., 1:173, 174, 175, 178, 179, 180,
        184, 185, 186, 187, 189
Gillberg, I.C., 1:174, 178, 186
Giller, E.L., 3:209, 213, 219
Gillespie, H.G., 6:192, 193, 194, 197, 216
Gilliam, W.S., 5:4, 18
Gilligan, C., 4:206, 215, 6:272, 283, 8:195,
        10:199, 208
Gillin, G.S., 4:13, 25
Ginsberg, S.W., 2:145, 162
Gise, L., 1:2, 25
Gittelman, R., 3:111
Gittleman, R., 5:10, 11, 18, 81, 100
Glancy, L.J., 5:244, 246
Glaser, B.G., 6:189
Glaser, F.B., 7:227, 240
Glaser, I.B., 8:120, 136
Glasgow, M.S., 4:6, 25
Glass, D.R., 3:219
Glass, G., 2:252, 264
Glassock, J.A., 8:208, 218, 219, 221
Glatzer, H.T., 5:115, 121
Glaus, K.D., 4:8, 26, 27, 28
Glazer, W.M., 8:270, 287
Gleaton, T.J., 3:94, 108, 110, 7:133, 142, 143,
        149
Glenn, M.B., 7:44, 46
Glick, B., 5:196, 197, 205, 209, 210, 217,
        219, 223
Glick, I.D., 3:209, 215, 220, 221
Glow, P.H., 5:48, 74
Glow, R.S., 5:48, 74
Glueck, B., 4:19, 26
Glynn, S.M., 1:246, 264
Glynn, S.M., 3:203, 220
Gochros, H.L., 6:233, 236
Godard, S., 7:254, 256

Godman, M.S., 4:102, 106
Goettman, C., 1:50, 88
Goettsche, R.L., 3:98, 109
Goetz, D., 5:100
Gold, E., 5:24, 38
Gold, J.H., 4:202, 216
Gold, M., 9:111
Gold, M.S., 1:160, 167, 5:229, 246, 8:62, 88,
    129, 134, 154, 246, 249, 250,
    251, 253, 254, 255, 260, 261,
    263, 265, 266
Gold, M.S., 3:94, 96, 100, 101, 102, 103, 104,
    106, 108, 109, 110, 111, 112, 245,
    262, 7:66, 74, 78, 79, 83, 84,
    132, 133, 135, 142, 143, 149,
    172, 177, 188, 189, 226, 237
Gold, P.W., 3:266, 277
Goldberg, A., 4:188, 199
Goldberg, D.A., 2:259, 263
Goldberg, G., 7:79, 84
Goldberg, H., 6:272, 283
Goldberg, J.R., 10:186, 194
Goldberg, M., 8:100, 117
Goldberg, R.L., 1:124, 133
Goldbloom, D.S., 3:266, 278
Golden, C.J., 7:18, 22, 9:147, 157
Golden, E., 8:100, 115
Golden, G.K., 7:255, 256
Goldfarb, A., 2:201, 211
Goldfried, M.R., 3:150, 159, 173, 7:231, 237
Goldman, D., 8:135
Goldman, H.H., 7:247, 249, 256
Goldman, M.S., 7:226, 236
Goldman, R., 2:83, 96
Goldman, S.R., 9:220, 227
Goldner, V., 6:74, 96
Goldsmith, R.J., 8:253, 257, 258, 260, 263
Goldstein, A., 7:162, 168
Goldstein, A.P., 5:67, 74, 76, 196, 197, 205,
    209, 210, 217, 219, 223, 225
Goldstein, C., 5:270
Goldstein, G., 7:18, 22
Goldstein, J., 8:177, 194
Goldstein, M., 5:43, 46, 47, 48, 50, 51, 53,
    55, 57, 58, 59, 67, 74
Goldstein, M.G., 4:2, 6, 26, 30
Goldstein, S., 5:43, 46, 47, 48, 50, 51, 53, 55,
    57, 58, 59, 67, 74, 75
Goleman, D., 1:155, 167
Goleman, D.J., 4:21, 31
Gomberg, E.L., 8:200, 203, 221
Gomez-Schwartz, B., 5:24, 34, 38

Gonsiorek, J.C., 10:196, 200, 203, 208
Gonzales, L.R., 9:216, 230
Gonzales-Singh, E., 9:216, 226
Gonzalez, A.M., 4:18, 32
Gonzalez, S., 6:120, 135, 145
Good-Ellis, M., 3:220, 221
Goodall, P., 9:39, 59
Goodman, J.T., 1:210
Goodman, W.K., 3:266, 278
Goodnick, P.J., 3:104, 111
Goodrich, S., 1:134
Goodson, W.H.III, 10:196, 208
Goodwin, D.W., 4:98, 101, 107, 7:225, 237,
    8:9, 47, 77, 87
Goodwin, F., 1:231
Goodwin, F.K., 8:131, 133, 136
Goodwin, J., 1:51, 59, 89, 4:121, 129
Goodwin, J.M., 4:123, 129
Goodwin, L.R., 8:77, 84, 87
Googins, B., 8:33, 36, 47, 51
Gordis, E., 7:65, 68
Gordon, A., 4:103, 106
Gordon, D.A., 5:219, 223
Gordon, J., 4:153
Gordon, J., 7:122, 126
Gordon, J.R., 7:219, 221, 233, 238, 8:66, 68,
    87, 89
Gordon, L., 9:148, 157
Gordon, M., 1:200, 209, 5:55, 75
Gorkin, M., 2:236, 246
Gorman, J.M., 5:6, 15, 18
Gorman, J.R., 3:16, 31
Gossett, J.T., 6:19, 24
Gostin, L.O., 10:212, 231, 232
Gottesman, II, 1:38, 46
Gottfredson, L.S., 9:190, 192, 193, 194, 205
Gottfredson, M., 6:108, 114
Gould, R.E., 10:175
Gould, J., 1:178, 189
Gould, M., 5:38, 254, 273
Gould, M.S., 5:258, 271
Gould, R.E., 6:272, 283
Goulet, J., 1:244, 261
Grace, M., 1:7, 26
Gracin, L., 8:36, 51
Graeber, J., 8:70, 72, 88
Graham, D.L., 5:164, 170
Graham, J.R., 1:155, 162, 165, 168, 8:72, 88
Graham, M., 8:22, 46
Graham, P., 5:104, 121, 157, 172
Gravelle, K., 5:117
Graves, S., 4:195, 199

Grawe, K., 7:204, 211
Gray, M., 8:16, 53
Grayson, J.B., 1:41, 47
Greaves, G.B., 1:50, 58, 88, 89
Greden, J.F., 7:158, 163, 168
Green, B., 1:2, 4, 5, 7, 14, 25, 26
Green, C., 7:12, 23
Green, M.F., 1:242, 254, 262
Green, R., 6:193, 217
Green, S.L., 4:135, 150
Green, W.H., 1:183, 185
Greenberg, A., 1:163, 168
Greenberg, D., 3:119, 126
Greenberg, H., 1:157, 168
Greenberg, L., 4:188, 199, 5:55, 75
Greenberg, M., 10:196, 207
Greenberg, P.E., 3:201, 220
Greenberg, R., 3:132, 134, 143
Greenblatt, D.T., 8:256, 266, 267
Greene, B., 4:23
Greene, R.L., 9:217, 227
Greenfield, S., 3:221, 222
Greenhaus, J.H., 9:2, 15
Greenhill, L.L., 5:57, 75
Greenson, R.R., 2:81, 94
Greer, B.G., 8:56, 88
Gregory, J.C., 2:126, 141
Gregson, R.A.M., 7:225, 235
Greif, G.L., 6:58, 59, 60, 61, 62, 63, 64, 65,
        66, 69, 70
Greist, J.H., 1:44, 46
Grieger, R., 4:159, 173, 175
Griffiths, R.R., 7:156, 164, 168, 169
Grilo, G., 5:249
Grimes, J.W., 9:59
Grimley, L.K., 5:42, 75
Grispoon, L., 8:204, 221
Grisso, T., 10:149, 158
Grissom, G.R., 7:239
Griswold, P.P., 9:235, 248
Grochocinski, V.J., 3:219
Gropper, M., 7:172, 187
Gross, D.A., 3:96, 103, 104, 106, 111
Gross, D.R., 2:123, 140, 10:9, 15
Gross, M.D., 6:262, 264
Gross, R.H., 2:133, 139
Grossarth-Maticek, R., 4:54, 55, 57, 60, 67,
        68
Growick, B.S., 9:92, 106
Gruenewald, D., 1:62, 63, 67, 78, 89
Grunberg, F., 8:135
Grunebaum, H., 2:107, 119

Gruth, W.L., 8:56, 87
Gruzen, J., 6:174, 189
Guevremont, D.C., 5:53, 66, 74, 75
Gumaer, J., 2:123, 124, 139
Gunderson, J.G., 1:123, 124, 131, 133, 134,
        135, 240, 262
Gurling, H.M., 4:97, 109
Gurman, A.S., 6:203, 215
Guroff, J.J., 1:51, 94
Gustafson, D.J., 10:149, 158
Gustavson, K.H., 1:185
Guth, L., 10:80, 94
Gutheil, T.G., 10:150, 158, 206, 208
Guthrie, D., 4:145, 151, 8:164, 172
Gutierez-Mayka, M., 6:181, 187
Gutierrez, J.M., 10:236, 246
Guze, S.B., 4:98, 101, 107
Guzman, F., 10:76, 95
Gwyther, L.P., 6:171, 180, 187
Gysbers, N.C., 9:33

H

Haas, G.L., 3:220, 221, 8:133
Hackman, A., 4:14, 24
Hacob, B.R., 4:42, 51
Haenlein, M., 5:72, 75
Hagen, D.G., 3:202, 220
Hagerman, R., 1:179, 187
Hagner, D., 9:115, 125
Haizlip, T., 5:183, 188
Halbrook, M., 8:9, 49
Hale, A.E., 7:183, 187
Haley, G., 5:166, 170
Haley, J., 2:67, 74, 78, 145, 146, 153, 155,
        161, 162
Haley, J., 6:110, 114, 198, 215
Hall, A., 3:60, 64
Hall, C.P., 7:99
Hall, J., 5:99
Hall, J.A., 1:242, 262
Hall, K., 1:95
Hall, P., 1:89
Hall, R.C., 1:77, 89
Hall, R.C.W., 3:94, 95, 98, 100, 106, 107, 111
Halleck, S., 2:224
Halling, S., 4:260
Halpern, A.S., 9:39, 59
Halstead, R.W., 4:188, 199
Hamera, E., 1:264
Hamilton, J., 8:208, 220
Hamilton, M., 3:94, 111, 168, 173, 204, 220

Hamilton, P.J.S., 7:230, 240
Hamilton, S.B., 5:225
Hamilton, S.K., 7:100, 241
Hammeke, T., 9:147, 157
Hamon, M., 7:68, 84
Hampton, B.A.M., 7:165, 168
Hampton, J., 4:261
Hancock, S., 9:210, 228
Handelsman, M.M., 10:63, 71
Haney, T.L., 3:89, 90
Hanley, I., 3:164, 173
Hanley-Maxwell, C., 9:110, 112, 113, 125,
    126
Hanley-Peterson, P., 3:148, 173
Hanna, G., 5:58, 77
Hansen, J., 7:92, 98
Hansen, J.C., 4:135, 150, 8:37, 47
Hansen, V., 7:245, 256
Hanson, B., 3:213, 222
Hanyu, S., 7:141, 149
Harding, A.V., 4:9, 26
Harding, C.M., 1:243, 262, 263
Harding, P.S., 3:206, 222
Harding, S.S., 10:192, 194
Hardman, M.L., 9:192, 205
Hare, R., 10:19, 33
Harkavy-Friedman, J., 5:256, 257, 271
Harling, J., 4:9, 31
Harlow, H.F., 6:195, 198, 202, 215
Haroon, E.A., 3:35, 47
Haroun, A., 2:49, 52, 53, 61
Harp, H., 1:239, 265
Harpin, R.E., 3:233, 234, 239
Harrington, R., 5:160, 170
Harrington, S.S., 8:59, 88
Harris, E., 3:220, 221
Harris, G.A., 2:49, 60, 61
Harris, L., 9:81, 106
Harris, L.C., 9:226
Harrison, P.A., 5:244, 247
Harrison, W., 3:221
Hars, R., 8:163, 172
Hart, B., 5:142, 151
Hartl, E.M., 4:99, 109
Hartley, J.P., 4:9, 30
Hartocollis, P., 2:263
Hartwell, T.D., 8:18, 22, 27, 47
Harver, A., 4:8, 26, 28
Harvey, J.H., 10:26, 33
Harvey, R.B., 6:198, 215
Harvey-Krefting, L., 9:128, 139
Harwood, H.J., 8:11, 47

Harwood, S., 6:256, 266
Hassman, H., 3:266, 279
Hatfield, E., 6:174, 187
Hathaway, S.R., 1:9, 25, 7:11, 22
Hatsukami, D., 7:228, 237
Haub, C., 9:211, 226
Hauser, P., 5:51, 52, 75
Haverkamp, B.E., 4:134, 135, 141, 146, 149,
    150
Havranek, J., 9:46, 59
Hawkins, D., 8:192, 194
Hawkins, J., 8:162, 172
Hawkins, J.D., 4:102, 108, 7:173, 189
Hawkins, J.W., 5:252, 272
Hawkins, M.F., 3:159, 177
Hawkins, R.C., 4:19, 26
Hawks, B.K., 9:178, 201, 202, 206
Hawton, K., 3:41, 47, 8:126, 134
Hay, L.L., 3:255, 262
Hayashida, M., 7:68, 69, 74, 85, 89, 91, 99,
    8:137
Hayes, S.C., 3:159, 162, 164, 166, 171, 173,
    175
Hayghe, H., 8:18, 47
Haymann, G.M., 10:15
Haynes, S.N., 3:159, 174
Hays, J.R., 4:135, 149
Hays, R., 3:221, 222
Hayward, B., 7:188
Hazzard, A., 5:29, 34, 35, 37, 38, 39
Heafield, M., 7:56, 62
Healy, M., 2:122, 139, 10:186, 194
Healy, M.H., 5:252, 273
Heather, N., 7:109, 125
Hecht, M., 8:8, 48
Hechtman, L., 5:48, 49, 77, 78
Heczey, M.D., 4:8, 26
Hedberg, A., 4:18, 26
Hedges, L.E., 2:26, 30, 10:187, 194
Heeren, T., 5:257, 273, 7:100, 241
Heersema, P.H., 3:172
Hegedus, A., 7:18, 22
Hegedus, A.M., 7:225, 241
Hegegus, A.M., 4:100, 108
Heiman, J., 6:193, 215
Heiman, J.R., 6:192, 217, 221, 238
Hein, K., 8:231, 243
Heinemann, A.W., 8:56, 57, 58, 80, 81, 88
Heirich, M., 8:17, 47
Held, V., 6:276, 277, 282, 283
Hellerstein, D.J., 3:266, 278, 8:285, 287
Helmers, K., 1:60, 94

Helms, J.E., 9:178, 189, 190, 206
Helsel, W., 5:81, 99
Helsel, W.J., 5:9, 20
Helsing, K.J., 3:122, 125
Helwig, C., 5:46, 73
Helzer, J.E., 4:94, 108, 8:120, 134, 135, 246, 247, 249, 260, 263
Hemphill, D.P., 8:210, 222
Henderson, C., 4:94, 110, 8:9, 51
Henderson, J.B., 8:162, 172
Henderson, J.N., 6:181, 187
Hendricks, C.D., 3:150, 174
Hendricks, J., 3:150, 174
Henig, R.M., 5:109, 119, 121
Heninger, G.R., 3:278, 7:160, 161, 167
Henker, B., 5:48, 56, 78
Henley, G., 5:230, 243, 248
Henn, F.A., 3:266, 278
Henry, D., 5:24, 37
Henry, W.P., 2:87, 91, 92, 93
Heppner, P.P., 10:11, 16
Herbert, J.T., 9:180, 181, 192, 195, 206
Herbert, T.B., 3:27, 31
Herjanic, B., 7:12, 24
Herlihy, B., 2:122, 139, 10:8, 11, 15, 44, 46, 47, 53, 55, 184, 186, 192, 194
Herman, J., 10:196, 207
Herman, J.L., 1:67, 89, 123, 133, 4:134, 135, 136, 137, 142, 150, 185, 199
Herman, S.P., 4:121, 129
Hermansen, L., 4:98, 101, 107
Hern, K.L., 5:51, 75
Herr, E.L., 9:189, 205
Herr, J., 2:202, 211
Herridge, C.F., 3:94, 95, 111
Herridge, P., 3:110
Herrnstein, R.J., 5:104, 121
Hersen, M., 3:232, 234, 239, 5:4, 8, 11, 12, 19, 21
Hersey, P., 3:29, 31
Hershenson, D.B., 8:27, 48
Hertel, R.K., 6:203, 217
Herzov, L., 5:10, 18
Hess, A.K., 10:108, 148, 158
Hess, N.D., 1:75, 94
Hesselbrock, M.N., 8:68, 88, 124, 134
Hesselbrock, V.M., 8:68, 88
Hester, E.J., 9:81, 106
Hester, R.K., 7:88, 89, 99, 216, 239, 8:66, 68, 89
Hetherrington, E.M., 6:51, 53
Heumann, J.E., 9:65, 77

Hewer, R.A., 3:35, 49
Heywood, R., 4:98, 106
Hibbert, G., 4:9, 26
Hicks, G.J., 7:162, 168
Hicks, R.A., 7:162, 168
Higgins, J., 4:244, 260
Higgins, S.T., 7:177, 179, 182, 184, 185, 187, 188
Higgitt, A., 5:63, 74
Hilgard, E.R., 1:59, 89
Hill, J., 5:160, 170
Hill, S., 4:100, 108
Hill, S.Y., 4:99, 108
Hillemand, B., 4:106
Hillenberg, J.B., 4:5, 26
Hillman, L.S., 8:105, 106, 108, 116
Hilyer, J.C., 8:164, 172
Himmelhoch, J.M., 7:162, 169
Hindman, J., 5:33, 38
Hineline, P.N., 3:164, 174
Hingson, R.W., 7:100, 241, 8:258, 267
Hinrichsen, G., 2:194, 212
Hinrichsen, J.J., 8:203, 221
Hippocrates, 4:54, 5:278, 290
Hirschfeld, R.M.A., 3:183, 184, 197, 198
Hirschi, T., 6:108, 114
Hirshfeld, D.R., 5:6, 21
Hislop, I.G., 4:10, 27
Ho, H.H., 1:179, 187
Hoaken, P.C.A., 6:262, 264
Hobbs, T.R., 5:225
Hoberman, H.M., 5:158, 170, 254, 271
Hobson, R.P., 1:174, 187
Hochron, S.M., 4:2, 8, 9, 28
Hodges, W.F., 6:55
Hodgson, R.J., 1:31, 47
Hodson, C.A., 7:79, 83
Hoegerman, G., 8:100, 105, 106, 107, 113, 116
Hoelscher, T.J., 4:5, 27
Hoenigfeld, G., 3:169, 174
Hoeper, E.W., 5:170
Hoey, H., 3:266, 278
Hoff, R.A., 3:69, 91
Hoffman, C., 6:174, 186
Hoffman, H.J., 8:105, 106, 108, 116
Hoffman, I., 5:149
Hoffman, J.P., 8:4, 48
Hoffman, L.E., 6:225, 236
Hoffman, Lynn, 2:146, 147, 152, 163
Hoffman, M.L., 6:187
Hoffman, N.G., 5:244, 247, 8:191, 194
Hoffman, R.S., 3:95, 101, 111

Hoffmann, N.G., 3:112, 8:258, 259, 264
Hoffschmidt, S.J., 3:219
Hofman, A, D., 5:280, 290
Hofmann, A., 8:177, 194
Hogarty, G., 1:246, 263, 3:206, 221
Hogarty, G.E., 2:177, 190
Holahan, C.J., 3:83, 91
Holahan, C.K., 3:83, 91
Holcom, M.L., 8:2, 49
Holder, A., 2:81, 96
Holder, H.D., 7:88, 99, 8:22, 45, 48
Holland, J.L., 9:218, 221, 227
Hollander, M.A., 8:178, 196
Hollander, M.D., 6:248, 266
Hollender, M.H., 6:198, 215
Hollister, L.E., 8:129, 136
Hollon, S.D., 3:141, 144, 233, 239
Holloway, E.L., 10:79, 94
Holloway, H., 1:2, 28
Holm, H., 4:12, 32
Holmes, D., 7:34, 46
Holmes, R.D., 7:140, 149
Holmes, T.R., 4:202, 216
Holmgren, G., 1:185
Holroyd, J., 10:196, 207
Holroyd, K.A., 4:12, 32
Holsboer, F., 3:25, 31
Holt, L., 4:100, 109
Holt, M.M., 5:225
Holtzworth-Munroe, A., 3:141, 144
Holzer, C., 3:201, 222
Holzer, C.E., 3:157, 176
Holzer, M., 4:260
Holzman, P.S., 2:82, 96
Hong, G.K., 5:157, 170
Hood, J., 5:15, 17, 36, 256, 271, 6:63, 70
Hoon, P., 6:194, 215
Hooper, S.R., 1:180, 181, 187
Hoover, C., 1:37, 46
Hooyman, N.R., 6:176, 177, 187
Hoppe, C.M., 5:48, 77
Hopps, H., 3:163, 174
Hops, H., 5:166, 171
Horberg, L.K., 8:76, 90
Horevitz, R.P., 1:63, 78, 89
Horn, J., 7:10, 24
Horney, K., 2:11, 4:251, 260
Hornstein, N., 1:50, 51, 76, 82, 89, 90, 93
Horowitz, A., 6:170, 174, 188
Horowitz, J., 5:24, 38
Horowitz, M., 1:3, 5, 8, 25, 3:168, 174
Horowitz, M.J., 2:86, 88, 95

Horvath, A., 4:188, 199
Horvath, T.B., 1:134
Horwitz, L., 1:125, 131, 133, 2:258, 264
Hoshman, L.T., 5:205, 224
Hotaling, G., 4:134, 150
House, A., 3:35, 41, 47
Houseman, D., 5:257, 273
Houser, R., 9:179, 204
Howard, K.I., 5:184, 189
Howells, K., 4:159, 168, 175
Howie, J., 10:64, 71
Howland, J.S., 1:78, 90
Howland, R.H., 3:226, 228, 236, 239, 241
Howlin, P., 1:174, 184, 187, 188
Hoyme, H.E., 8:103, 104, 108, 116
Hoyt, L.A., 6:47, 54
Hrubec, Z., 4:97, 108
Hryvniak, M., 1:2, 25
Hsieh, C.C., 5:256, 270
Hsu, F.L.K., 6:201, 215
Hsuing, H., 7:75, 85
Hubbell, C.L., 7:142, 150
Huber, D., 4:12, 27
Huber, G., 1:243, 263
Huber, H.P., 4:12, 27
Hubert, C.E., 2:148, 163
Hubert, D.J., 2:148, 163
Huberty, C.E., 6:101, 114
Huberty, D.S., 6:101, 114
Hudson, J.I., 3:53, 64
Hudson, P., 2:122, 139
Hughes, C., 9:110, 111, 126
Hughes, D.C., 3:148, 171
Hughes, J.R., 7:27, 46, 177, 187, 188
Hughes, M., 5:18
Huguenin, P., 7:53, 62
Hulst, L.L., 4:8, 22
Humphreys, M.S., 7:156, 168
Hunt, W., 7:216, 217, 237
Hunter, J.O., 7:56, 62
Hunter, R., 1:37, 46
Hunter, W.M., 5:34, 37
Hurlbut, S.C., 8:286
Hurt, R.D., 8:201, 204, 205, 209, 210, 221
Hussain, R.A., 2:200, 212
Hussian, R.A., 3:160, 168, 174
Hutchings, B., 5:104, 122
Hutton, C.J., 6:150, 163
Huygens, I., 7:89, 90, 91, 98
Hwang, S.S., 3:200, 214, 220
Hyde, T.S., 5:16, 20

Hyman, S.E., 7:35, 38, 45
Hynd, G.W., 1:180, 181, 187, 5:51, 75

I

Ianni, P., 4:7, 25
Iasiello-Vailas, L., 7:199, 210
Ibrahim, F.A., 9:218, 227, 10:236, 237, 247
Ijiri, I., 4:109
Ikeguchi, K., 7:141, 149
Iles, S., 6:152, 163
Im, W., 6:258, 264
Imai, H., 7:141, 149
Imai, N., 7:141, 149
Imber, S.D., 3:219
Impara, J.C., 9:219, 221, 228
Incalzi, R.A., 3:150, 174
Ingersoll, B.D., 5:51, 75
Ingersoll-Dayton, B., 6:171, 188
Ingraham, K., 8:56, 57, 71, 88
Insel, T.R., 1:31, 37, 39, 42, 46, 47
Iqbal, N., 8:254, 263
Irwin, M.J., 5:197, 205, 223
Irwin, M.R., 8:125, 132
Irwin,M., 3:29, 31
Isenberg, S., 4:2, 28
Ismond, D.R., 7:156, 169
Israel, H., 7:162, 169
Ivey, A.E., 10:237, 247
Iwata, M., 5:218, 223
Iyengar, S., 5:172

J

Jackson, B., 4:18, 30
Jackson, D.D., 2:145, 149, 153, 154, 155,
        161, 162, 163, 164, 6:198, 215
Jacob, R.G., 4:6, 27
Jacob, T., 4:94, 100, 103, 104, 108, 110
Jacobs, S., 4:216
Jacobson, A., 1:2, 26
Jacobson, E., 4:3, 4, 10, 27, 5:140, 150
Jacobson, N.S., 3:141, 144
Jaffe, A.J., 7:68, 69, 70, 74, 84, 85, 8:136
Jaffe, J.H., 7:67, 83, 8:251, 264
Jalali, B., 7:228, 238
Jalow, P.I., 7:161, 167
James, J.E., 7:165, 168
James, O.F.W., 8:204, 222
Jamison, K.R., 1:231
Janata, J.W., 1:75, 90
Janoff-Bulman, R., 1:3, 26

Jansen, M., 3:202, 203, 218
Janson-Bjerklie, S., 4:9, 27
Janus, C.L., 6:222, 236
Janus, S.S., 6:222, 236
Jarrett, D.B., 3:219
Jarrett, P.J., 8:121, 133, 134
Jarrett, R.B., 3:171, 175, 209, 220, 4:8, 22,
        5:263, 271
Jarrett, R.B., 3:140, 142, 144
Jarvik, L.A., 3:150, 154, 174, 175
Jaspers, K., 6:243, 264
Jasso, R., 9:226
Jeffers, V., 4:19, 26
Jefferson, J.W., 3:100, 106, 107, 111
Jemerin, J., 5:187, 189
Jenigan, R.J., 8:3, 4, 50
Jenkins, A.E., 9:181, 206
Jennett, B., 9:144, 158
Jensen, G.D., 8:204, 221
Jensen, L., 3:88, 91
Jenson, W.R., 1:188
Jestor, B., 8:166, 171
Joanning, H., 6:110, 114, 115
Jobes, P.A., 5:252, 254, 255, 257, 258, 259,
        267, 268, 269
Joe, J.R., 9:186, 187, 207
Joffe, R., 2:115, 120
Johanson, C., 8:256, 264
John, K., 5:156, 169
Johnson, C., 7:79, 84
Johnson, C.R., 7:133, 134, 135, 149
Johnson, D.W., 8:218, 221
Johnson, F.A., 6:193, 217
Johnson, F.P., 8:218, 221
Johnson, H.G., 10:15
Johnson, J., 4:101, 108, 5:173, 6:163, 7:46
Johnson, J.R., 6:36, 55
Johnson, L.C., 4:13, 25
Johnson, L.D., 5:230, 247
Johnson, N.P., 8:37, 42, 52
Johnson, R., 7:12, 23
Johnson, S., 1:2, 28
Johnson, V.A., 7:104, 125
Johnson, V.E., 6:193, 206, 210, 216, 231,
        237
Johnson-Sabine, E.C., 3:53, 64
Johnston, D.W., 4:70, 90
Johnston, L.D., 8:188, 195
Jonas, E.A., 3:219
Jones, 4:260
Jones, D.C., 4:103, 106
Jones, E., 2:80, 95

Jones, G., 10:196, 207
Jones, H., 5:183, 188
Jones, J., 1:96, 3:87, 91
Jones, J.M., 7:172, 175, 180, 188
Jones, J.W., 8:42, 48
Jones, K.L., 8:108, 109, 116
Jones, L., 3:35, 47
Jones, L.R., 7:245, 257
Jones, R.R., 1:210, 5:195, 224
Jones, S., 8:243
Jones, S.B., 7:235, 240
Jones, Y., 5:208, 224
Jones-Barlock, A., 8:133
Jones-Brown, C., 1:2, 26
Jordaan, J.P., 9:19, 32
Jordan, J.S., 10:26, 33
Jordan, J.V., 6:269, 271, 277, 284
Jordan, L., 2:73, 78
Jorde, L., 1:188
Jorgensen, J., 9:125
Jorgenson, L., 10:196, 207
Joscelyne, B., 1:63, 85
Joseph, A., 9:217, 227
Joseph, K.S., 8:254, 263
Josepher, H., 8:74, 90
Josephson, S.C., 6:248, 266
Joshi, N., 5:256, 270
Joyce, S.A., 2:87, 92, 96
Judas, 4:248
Judd, L.L., 5:13, 18, 8:136
Jung, Carl, 2:3, 6, 197, 212
Jung, D., 7:12, 24
Jurich, A.P., 6:25
Jurish, S.E., 4:23

K

Kaczmarek, P.G., 4:144, 150
Kadden, R.M., 5:249, 7:228, 239
Kagan, J., 5:6, 10, 18, 55, 75
Kagle, J.D., 10:125
Kaij, L., 4:97, 108
Kaiser, W., 9:89, 106
Kaizer, S., 7:162, 168
Kalanthara, M., 8:254, 264
Kalas, R., 5:269
Kalikow, K., 5:173
Kalousek, D.K., 1:179, 187
Kaltreider, N., 3:168, 174
Kaminer, Y., 5:231, 241, 244, 246, 247, 249, 7:10, 22, 24
Kandaras, C., 5:183, 189

Kandel, D.B., 5:241, 247, 8:162, 174
Kang, S., 7:185, 188
Kanitz, B.E., 9:196, 207
Kanner, A., 5:11, 19
Kanner, L., 1:172, 187
Kant, I., 10:216, 232
Kanter, J., 5:91, 99
Kantor, D., 2:147, 162
Kaplan, A.G., 6:269, 284, 10:197, 208
Kaplan, B., 9:217, 227
Kaplan, D.M., 9:33
Kaplan, H.B., 8:207, 222
Kaplan, H.I., 10:149, 158
Kaplan, H.S., 2:168, 177, 190, 6:192, 193, 195, 206, 215, 220, 225, 228, 229, 231, 233, 236
Kaplan, J.D., 6:121, 144
Kaplan, L., 6:140, 145
Kaplan, R.F., 7:227, 237
Kaplan, S., 8:56, 88
Kaplan, S.L., 5:157, 170
Kappas, A., 7:53, 61
Karacan, I., 7:161, 169
Kardener, S.H., 10:196, 197, 208
Karno, M., 8:222
Karp, R.W., 4:100, 108
Kashani, J., 5:50, 75
Kashani, J.H., 5:3, 9, 18, 156, 157, 170
Kaslow, F.W., 6:74, 75, 76, 77, 78, 79, 85, 86, 89, 92, 93, 94, 95, 96, 97
Kaslow, J., 5:81, 101
Kaslow, N.J., 3:209, 221
Kastenbaum, R., 2:198, 212
Kates, W., 2:107, 119
Katic, M., 5:171
Katon, N.J., 4:116, 131
Katz, D., 8:205, 221
Katz, E.R., 5:12, 16
Katz, I.R., 3:150, 176
Katz, J., 10:176, 178
Katz, J.H., 10:237, 247
Katz, N.R., 1:242, 262
Kaufman, E., 6:145, 8:256, 264
Kaufman, K.F., 5:225
Kaufman, P., 6:145
Kaufmann, P., 6:101, 114
Kaufmann, P.G., 4:6, 27
Kavanagh, D.J., 1:245, 263
Kay, S.R., 8:254, 264
Kaye, K., 2:177, 190
Kazdin, A., 5:80, 81, 90, 91, 93, 99
Kazdin, A.E., 4:15, 27, 5:4, 8, 19, 21

Keane, T.M., 1:7, 8, 13, 15, 26
Kearl, G.W., 1:2, 28
Keelor, D., 4:100, 109
Keen, M., 8:88
Keener, J.J., 8:124, 134
Kegan, Robert, 9:2, 3, 6, 14, 15
Keissler, D., 2:250, 264
Keith, S.J., 8:136
Keith-Spiegel, P., 2:123, 140, 10:4, 11, 15,
    33, 80, 95, 196, 208
Keller, D.M., 6:173, 180, 188
Keller, D.S., 7:175, 187
Keller, M., 7:102, 125, 8:18, 48
Keller, M.B., 3:94, 112, 227, 239, 269, 278,
    5:164, 169
Keller, M.V., 5:4, 18
Kelley, D., 1:40, 46
Kelley, H.H., 6:203, 214
Kelley, J.T., 8:129, 136
Kellner, H., 6:202, 213
Kelly, C., 5:255, 272
Kelly, C.A., 7:100, 241
Kelly, G.A., 2:25, 30, 44, 45
Kelly, J., 5:20, 171, 6:37, 51, 55
Kelly, J.B., 6:78, 98
Kelly, K.W., 3:16, 30
Kelly, L.A.S., 6:225, 236
Kelly, S.D.M., 9:186, 187, 204
Kelman, H.C., 2:103, 115, 119
Kelman, S., 7:64, 85
Kelson, H.G., 4:7, 27
Kemp, J., 7:188
Kempler, W., 5:149
Kenardy, J., 3:266, 278
Kendall, P.C., 5:144, 150
Kendler, K.S., 5:18
Kendrick, D.C., 3:228, 239
Kennard, J., 3:183, 197
Kennedy, D., 7:227, 237
Kernberg, O., 2:251, 260, 264, 6:203, 216
Kernberg, O.F., 1:120, 121, 129, 133
Keskinen, B.A., 8:258, 266
Keso, L., 8:258, 259, 264
Kessler, L., 2:194, 213
Kessler, R.C., 1:104, 116, 5:18, 7:210
Kessler, S., 6:78, 97
Kett, J.F., 8:176, 194
Ketterer, B., 7:57, 62
Key, G.L., 9:128, 139
Keys, A., 3:52, 54, 64, 8:280, 286
Keysor, C.S., 5:58, 74
Khalsa, E., 8:287

Khantzian, E.J., 4:82, 83, 89, 7:219, 238,
    8:250, 257, 264
Khatami, M., 3:139, 145, 209, 220
Khuon, F., 1:11, 27
Kibbee, P., 4:100, 109
Kiesler, D.V., 5:132, 151
Kijima, T., 4:109
Killmann, P.R., 6:194, 218
Killorin, E., 6:12, 24, 25
Kilpatrick, D., 1:2, 26
Kim, M., 4:23
Kimmerling, G.F., 10:51, 55
King, A.C., 7:75, 85
King, C.A., 5:255, 256, 272
King, H.E., 5:35, 38
King, J., 5:172
King, J.C., 8:103, 104, 105, 108, 116
King, M.C., 10:149, 158
King, N.M., 8:190, 195
King, R., 5:172, 270
Kinney, J., 8:38, 48
Kinsbourne, M., 1:178, 187, 242, 254, 262
Kinsey, A.C., 6:222, 223, 237
Kirby, E.A., 5:72, 75
Kirby, P.C., 2:123, 132, 140
Kirisci, L., 7:9, 22, 24, 8:136
Kirk, H.D., 5:119
Kirschner, D., 5:104, 114, 115, 121
Kirshner, M.C., 8:248, 266
Kirtner, W., 2:251, 263
Kissin, B., 4:99, 105, 7:225, 236
Kitchener, K., 10:87, 94
Kitchener, K.S., 4:135, 136, 147, 150, 10:19,
    34, 40, 54, 55, 65, 71, 192, 194
Kitchur, M., 5:35, 38
Kivlahan, D.R., 7:106, 193, 212, 226, 241
Klagsbrun, F., 5:104, 122
Klatsky, A.L., 8:126, 134
Kleban, M.H., 6:174, 186
Kleber, H.D., 7:228, 238, 8:251, 252, 253, 264
Klein, D.F., 3:96, 111, 221, 266, 278, 279, 5:19
Klein, L., 10:58, 71
Klein, M., 10:58, 71
Klein, P., 5:67, 74, 205, 223
Klein, R.G., 5:4, 10, 11, 14, 15, 19, 56, 75, 76
Klein, R.H., 7:192, 211
Kleinman, A., 2:4, 16
Kleinman, C., 5:172
Klerman, G., 2:252, 264
Klerman, G.L., 3:114, 117, 125, 213, 222,
    228, 231, 234, 239, 241, 5:164,
    167, 169

Kline, J., 6:163, 7:252, 257
Kline, M.V., 1:67, 90
Kline, W.B., 2:141
Klonoff, E.A., 1:75, 90
Klosko, J.S., 4:181, 200
Kluft, R.P., 1:50, 51, 52, 53, 55, 56, 58, 60,
    62, 63, 64, 65, 66, 67, 68, 69, 70,
    71, 72, 73, 74, 75, 76, 77, 78, 80,
    81, 83, 84, 87, 90, 91, 92, 95, 96,
    4:119, 129
Knapp, R.J., 6:148, 163, 165
Knapp, S., 2:133, 139, 10:125
Kneale, T.A., 7:44, 46
Knee, D., 5:49, 72
Knell, S.M., 5:131, 135, 150
Knop, J., 4:96, 109
Knuppel, R.A., 8:102, 103, 116
Knutti, R., 7:155, 169
Kobayashi, R., 8:87
Koch, Ed, 10:175
Kochansky, G.E., 3:156, 174
Kocsis, J.H., 8:129, 135
Koehler, J., 1:2, 26
Koenig, H.G., 3:150, 155, 175
Koenigsberg, H.W., 1:133
Kofoed, L., 8:273, 280, 286
Kofoed, L.L., 8:201, 208, 214, 215, 220, 222
Kogan, E., 7:181, 186
Kohl, H., 8:163, 166, 172
Kohlberg, L., 5:219, 224, 8:195
Kohlenberg, B.S., 3:164, 173
Kohlenberg, R.J., 1:75, 92
Kohut, H., 4:82, 90, 255
Kolko, D., 5:270
Kolko, D.J., 5:159, 169, 252, 253, 264, 269,
    271
Kolodny, R., 5:183, 188
Kolvin, I., 1:173, 187
Koocher, G.P., 4:141, 147, 150, 10:11, 15, 33
Koplewicz, H.S., 5:11, 19
Koppel, D.B., 6:178, 187
Koppelman, J., 7:172, 175, 180, 188
Koranyi, E.K., 3:94, 95, 96, 111
Korella, K., 5:255, 271
Korman, M., 10:244, 247
Korn, R., 2:58, 61
Korn, S., 1:179, 185
Korner, P., 8:134
Kosberg, J.I., 6:168, 170, 172, 173, 177, 178,
    179, 180, 187, 188
Koscis, J.H., 3:226, 227, 228, 236, 239, 266,
    279

Kosky, R., 5:256, 271
Koss, M.P., 2:80, 95, 4:116, 131
Kosten, T.R., 7:225, 228, 238, 240, 8:251,
    252, 253, 264, 270, 280, 283,
    286, 287
Kostiniuk, A., 8:9, 46
Kotila, L., 5:258, 271
Kotses, H., 4:8, 26, 27, 28
Kottler, J., 2:126, 139
Kottler, J.A., 10:65, 73
Kovacs, M., 5:4, 19, 85, 99, 159, 170
Kovaks, M., 3:141, 144
Kozak, M.J., 1:34, 46
Koziol-McClain, J., 6:152, 164
Kraepelin, E., 3:34, 47, 269, 279
Kraines, G.A., 4:33
Kraines, S.H., 3:227, 229, 230, 236, 240
Kramer, J., 5:49, 76
Kramer, M., 8:222
Kramer, N., 6:120, 145
Krantz, D., 4:54, 67
Kranzler, H.R., 8:129, 134
Krasner, B.R., 2:147, 162
Krell, R., 6:153, 163
Krementz, J., 5:117
Krener, P., 4:121, 123, 129
Kristiansen, P., 8:11, 47
Kronfol, T., 3:25, 29, 31
Krueger, R., 3:27, 31
Krug, D.A., 1:183, 187
Krug, S.B., 4:16, 28
Krug, S.E., 1:155, 169
Ksir, C., 8:6, 50
Kubie, L.S., 1:78, 88
Kübler-Ross, E., 4:41, 50
Kübler-Ross, E., 2:204, 212, 6:39, 54, 148,
    149, 163
Kubos, K.L., 3:39, 49
Kuder, G.F., 9:218, 227
Kudler, H., 1:2, 24
Kuehl, B.P., 6:110, 115
Kuehnel, J., 7:115, 125
Kuehnel, T., 7:115, 125
Kuehnel, T.G., 1:263
Kuipers, L., 1:247, 261, 263
Kumin, I., 2:233, 235, 237, 241, 246
Kuperman, S., 1:179, 186
Kupfer, D.J., 3:209, 213, 219, 267, 269, 274,
    275, 276, 279, 5:252, 253, 255,
    257, 269
Kurcz, M., 8:131, 133
Kurpius, D., 10:76, 78, 81, 84, 86, 95

Kurtines, W., 9:230
Kutcher, S., 5:164, 171
Kutscher, R.E., 9:178, 206
Kuznetsov, O., 7:75, 85
Kvande, H., 7:226, 236
Kwentus, J.A., 4:13, 29
Kwok, L., 8:87
Kyle, E., 8:126, 136

L

L'Abate, L., 6:199, 202, 216, 217
Labov, W., 2:19, 30
Labriola, D.F., 7:74, 84
Lachar, D., 9:216, 226
Lacks, P., 4:13, 28
Lader, M.H., 7:155, 156, 159, 160, 165, 167,
        168, 169
LaFrombiose, T.D., 9:186, 187, 206, 10:237,
        247
Laird, S., 7:24
Laird, S.B., 4:99, 110
Lakin, M., 2:135, 140, 10:125
Lalonde, P., 1:244, 261
Lam, C.S., 8:89
Lamb, D.H., 2:133, 139
Lamb, H.R., 9:175
Lampert, C., 5:159, 173
Lampl-de Groot, J., 1:74, 92
Lance, J.W., 4:11, 24
Landau-Stanton, J., 6:141, 145
Landress, H.J., 8:100, 115
Lane, R.D., 6:262, 264
Lang, A.R., 4:101, 108
Langner, T., 4:253, 260
Langrod, J., 5:238, 248
Langs, R., 2:29, 30
Langs, R.D., 2:225
Lanning, W., 10:54, 55
LaPointe, C., 6:192, 193, 194, 197, 216
Lapouse, R., 5:49, 75
Larison, C., 8:4, 48
Larose, Y., 6:229, 239
Larson, D., 5:238, 247, 248
Larson, D.B., 5:247
Larson, S., 5:238, 247
LaRue, A., 3:154, 175
Lasky, R., 1:74, 92
Lasoski, A.M., 4:28
Last, C.G., 5:4, 8, 9, 10, 12, 14, 15, 19, 21
Latini, R., 7:167

Laumann, E., 6:222, 237
Lauritzen, L., 3:42, 46
Lavee, Y., 6:9, 25
Lavelle, J., 1:11, 27
Lavender, L., 10:58, 71
Lavori, P., 5:18
Lawrence, P.S., 3:168, 174
Lawton, M., 2:196, 212
Lawton, M.P., 2:194, 211, 3:150, 176
Lazarus, A.A., 5:149, 6:225, 237
Lazarus, L., 2:202, 212
Lazarus, R., 5:89, 99, 7:13, 22
Lazarus, R.S., 4:178, 180, 190, 200
Lazell, E., 2:101
Le Bon, G., 2:100, 101
Le Cann, A.F., 1:77, 89
Le Couteur, A., 1:184, 187
Leaf, P.H., 3:201, 222
Leaf, P.J., 3:69, 91
Leaff, L., 2:259, 263
Leal, A., 9:211, 227
Leary, T., 7:137
Lease, S.H., 8:43, 48
Leaton, G., 8:38, 48
Leber, W.R., 3:219, 7:226, 238
Lebowitz, B., 2:196, 212
Leckman, J., 5:172
Leckman, J.F., 5:5, 19
Leddick, G.R., 2:123, 138, 10:84, 94
Lee, A., 7:140, 149
Lee, C.C., 10:237, 238, 241, 244, 247
Lee, E.M.C., 1:178, 188
Lee, P.R., 8:11, 48
Lee, S., 3:44, 49, 10:59, 71
Leeman, L.W., 5:209, 224
Lefcoe, D., 6:199, 218
Leff, J., 1:247, 263
Legh-Smith, J., 3:35, 49
Lehman, A.F., 8:251, 264
Lehman, W.E.K., 8:2, 10, 15, 49
Lehrer, P.M., 4:2, 3, 4, 5, 6, 7, 8, 9, 11, 12, 13,
        15, 16, 17, 28
Leiblum, S.R., 6:192, 216, 221, 224, 225,
        227, 233, 237, 238
Leibowitz, R.E., 10:212, 232
Leifer, M., 4:260
Leigh, B.C., 7:226, 238
Leinman, P.H., 7:188
Lemay, A., 4:110
Lennox, R.D., 8:22, 48
Lentz, R., 1:243, 264
Leo, G.I., 7:227, 235, 240

Leon, I.G., 6:151, 163
Leonard, K., 4:104, 108
Leong, D.M., 8:23, 47
Leong, F.T.L., 9:184, 185, 186, 189, 199, 200,
    201, 206
Leong, G., 1:264
Lerman, H., 10:196, 207
Lerner, H.G., 6:269, 284
Lerner, M., 5:58, 77
Lesage, A., 1:244, 261
Lesage, A.D., 8:126, 135
Lesieur, H.R., 1:157, 168
Leslie, R., 10:187, 189, 194
Lestelle, V., 3:220, 221
Leung, B., 9:185, 186, 197, 200, 206
Leung, P., 9:179, 180, 207
Leung, S.A., 9:185, 207
Levenson, A., 2:194, 212
Levenson, J., 1:76, 92
Levenson, M.R., 3:148, 171
Levenson, S.M., 7:100, 241
Levin, R., 8:133, 134
Levin, S., 2:190
Levine, D.M., 8:220
Levine, J.L., 3:141, 145
Levine, S.B., 6:192, 216
Levinson, H., 4:34, 35, 36, 37, 38, 44, 50, 51
Levy, E.M., 3:27, 31
Levy, J.C., 5:158, 159, 171
Levy, K., 5:249
Levy, L.H., 3:86, 91
Lewin, K., 2:101
Lewin, L.M., 3:150, 162, 166, 175
Lewinsohn, P.M., 3:166, 172, 175, 5:158,
    159, 166, 171, 172
Lewis, A.B., 3:220, 221
Lewis, C.E., 8:120, 135
Lewis, I., 4:134, 150
Lewis, J., 6:178, 188, 10:76, 95
Lewis, J.A., 8:40, 49
Lewis, J.M., 6:19, 24
Lewis, M., 2:198, 210, 3:83, 91
Lewis, M.D., 8:40, 49
Lewis, R.A., 7:116, 127
Lewis, R.J., 4:8, 29
Lhuintre, J.P., 4:106
Li, T.K., 8:131, 135
Liberman, R.P., 1:238, 240, 241, 243, 246,
    249, 252, 254, 261, 262, 263,
    264, 265, 3:203, 220
Liberman, R.P., 7:115, 125, 8:277, 286, 9:175
Lichenstein, E., 8:87

Lichstein, K., 4:6, 29
Lichstein, K.L., 4:5, 27
Lichtenberg, P., 2:194, 212
Lidz, T., 2:155
Lieber, C.S., 7:56, 62
Lieberg, G., 1:95
Lieberman, J., 1:263
Liebowitz, M.R., 5:6, 18, 19
Liebowitz, N., 8:134
Lief, H.I., 6:192, 216, 223, 237
Liepman, M.R., 7:104, 126
Liese, B.S., 7:231, 236
Lifton, B.J., 5:104, 108, 110, 111, 113, 116,
    117, 119, 122
Lin, S., 7:193, 212
Lincoln, N.B., 3:35, 46
Lindahl, K.M., 6:162
Lindberg, C.E., 6:152, 163
Lindemann, E., 4:41, 44, 51
Linden, W., 4:3, 4, 7, 29
Lindholm, K.D., 9:218, 229
Lindseth, P., 4:19, 26
Lindy, J., 1:2, 7, 25, 26
Linehan, M., 5:265, 271
Ling, W., 7:172, 188
Links, P.S., 5:19
Linn, B.S., 3:88, 91
Linn, D., 4:261
Linn, M., 4:261
Linn, M.W., 3:88, 91
Linne, G.T., 6:109, 115
Linnoila, M., 8:8, 49, 126, 136
Linskey, A., 9:210, 228
Lion, J.R., 3:124, 126
Lipkus, I.M., 3:89, 90
Lipman, R.S., 3:140, 143
Lipowski, Z.J., 4:54, 67
Lipsey, J.R., 3:36, 39, 42, 47, 48
Lipsitz, J.O., 5:4, 19
Litman, G.K., 7:214, 215, 225, 238
Litman, R., 3:120, 124, 126
Litt, M.D., 5:249
Little, N.D., 9:51, 59
Litvak, S., 9:65, 69, 77
Litvin, S.J., 6:170, 174, 186, 188
Livermore, J.B., 5:111, 112, 121
Livingston, P., 8:84, 89
Livingston, R., 5:2, 9, 10, 11, 12, 18, 20
Lo, B., 10:196, 208
Lo, W., 1:46
Loar, L., 2:78
Localio, R., 10:196, 207

Lochman, J.E., 5:225, 264, 272
Locke, B.Z., 8:136, 222
Locke, H.J., 6:3, 24, 226, 237
Locke, N., 2:113, 119
Locke, S.E., 3:16, 31
Loder, J.E., 9:10, 11, 13, 16
Loeber, R., 5:230, 248
Loehlin, J.C., 4:97, 108
Loewenstein, R.J., 1:50, 61, 64, 74, 80, 81,
        82, 87, 92, 94
Loftus, E.F., 4:135, 142, 146, 150
Logsdon, R.G., 2:194, 213
Lohr, N., 5:182, 188
London, W., 3:245, 248, 251, 252, 258, 262
London, W.P., 4:100, 109
LoneWolf-Miller, D., 9:186, 187, 207
Loney, J., 5:48, 49, 76
Long, J.W., 3:246, 262
Long-Sutter, E., 8:9, 50
Longabaugh, R., 7:90, 99, 217, 238
Longnbaugh, R., 8:16, 45
Lonner, W.J., 9:215, 216, 228
Lonnquist, J., 5:258, 271
Lopez, J.F., 3:266, 277
LoPiccolo, J., 6:192, 193, 215, 216, 217, 221,
        222, 225, 227, 229, 233, 235,
        237, 238
LoPiccolo, L., 6:192, 193, 215, 216
Lopton, D.S., 7:188
Lotter, V., 1:175, 188
Lovaas, O.I., 1:183, 188
Lovett, S., 3:166, 175
Lowe, C.M., 10:18, 34
Lowenfeld, B.H., 1:155, 162, 165, 168
Lowenfels, A.B., 8:56, 89
Lowery, C.R., 6:38, 54
Lowery, S., 10:79, 95
Lowman, R.L., 10:82, 95
Loya, F., 9:216, 229
Loyer, M., 8:135
Lubkin, I.M., 6:172, 188
Luborsky, L., 2:86, 87, 90, 91, 95, 251, 253,
        260, 264, 6:198, 215, 7:10, 23,
        93, 96, 99, 227, 8:274, 286
Lucas, M.J., 6:178, 187
Lucignano, G., 10:59, 71
Ludolph, P., 4:119, 131
Ludwig, A.M., 1:78, 86
Luepker, R.V., 8:96, 116
Lugo, M., 2:18, 31
Lukens, E., 5:100
Lumeng, L., 8:131, 135

Lundervold, D.A., 3:150, 162, 166, 175
Lundwall, L., 2:261, 263, 7:193, 210
Lust, N., 5:84, 100
Lustbader, W., 6:176, 177, 187
Lustman, P.J., 3:209, 220
Luzzo, D.A., 9:181, 185, 207
Lyddon, W., 2:55, 61
Lydiard, R.B., 3:108, 110, 8:248, 263
Lynch, P.M., 4:10, 29
Lynch, S.K., 2:133, 140

M

Maack, L.H., 6:252, 265
Mabe, A.R., 10:214, 232
McAdoo, W.G., 8:9, 52
McAllister, J., 5:170
McAllister, R.J., 4:243
MacAlpine, I., 1:37, 46
McAUley, T., 7:99
McAuliffe, G.J., 9:4, 6, 16
McAuliffe, S., 5:48, 78
McBride, P.A., 8:131, 135
McBride, W.J., 8:131, 135
McBurnett, K., 5:58, 77
McCall, C., 5:34, 37
McCalley-Whitters, M., 4:100, 109
McCallum, M., 2:87, 92, 96
McCance-Katz, E., 8:280, 283, 286
McCandless, B., 5:85, 98
McCandless-Glimcher, L., 1:253, 264
McCann, B.S., 1:173, 188, 4:9, 17, 28
McCann, M.J., 7:172, 188
McCann, U.D., 7:142, 149
McCarrick, A.K., 8:251, 252, 264
McCarron, I., 9:147, 149, 157
McCarthy, B., 6:229, 231, 235, 237
McCarthy, B.W., 6:193, 194, 216, 217
McCauley, E., 5:3, 20, 171
McClaren, K.A., 6:194, 214
McClellan, A., 7:10, 23
McClellan, J.M., 5:20
Maccoby, E.E., 6:38, 50, 54
McConaghy, N., 1:163, 168
McConnell, S.G., 2:126, 141
McCorkle, L., 2:58, 61
McCormick, R.A., 1:155, 156, 158, 162,
        163, 165, 166, 168, 169
McCowan, C.J., 9:192, 204
McCown, D.E., 6:150, 163
McCoy, G.C., 4:5, 23, 32

McCrady, B., 7:89, 90, 99
McCrady, B.S., 7:109, 122, 126, 196, 204, 211
McCrainie, E.J., 3:184, 198
McCraken, S.G., 8:256, 264
McCullough, J.P., 3:230, 233, 234, 240
McCullough, L., 2:91, 96
McDavis, R.J., 9:178, 208, 10:245, 248
MacDonald, H., 1:174, 179, 188
MacDonald, M., 6:7, 25
McDonnell, K., 10:80, 94
McDougle, 1:44, 47
Mace, N.L., 6:179, 188
McEachran, A.B., 3:219
McElfresh, O., 4:102, 107
McElrath, D., 6:199, 203, 218
McEvoy, L., 4:94, 108, 8:125, 135
McEwen, B.S., 8:131, 135
McFall, M., 1:2, 27
McFall, M.E., 5:225
McFarlane, A., 1:2, 13, 26
MacFarlane, K., 5:35, 38
MacFarlane, W.R., 1:247, 263
McGarvey, B., 3:157, 175
McGaugh, J.I., 4:15, 24
McGee, M.B., 7:164, 169
McGee, R., 5:4, 6, 11, 12, 17, 20, 42, 47, 50, 76, 156, 157, 171
McGill, C.W., 1:243, 256, 262
McGinn, F., 10:64, 71
McGinnis, E., 5:67, 76
McGlashan, T., 5:249
McGlone, F.B., 8:205, 222
McGlynn, E., 3:221
McGoldrick, M., 6:89, 97
McGonagle, K.A., 5:18
McGovern, J.P., 4:83, 85, 89
McGovern, J.P., 7:64, 83, 8:141, 150, 153, 154
McGrath, P., 1:210
McGrath, P.J., 3:221, 8:129, 135
McGuire, M., 3:219
McGuire, T.G., 7:100, 241
McHugh, B., 3:154, 172
McHugh, P.R., 1:52, 93, 7:18, 22
McIntyre, J.W., 3:112
McIntyre, L.J., 10:125
MacIver, D., 6:114
Mack, J.E., 4:82, 83, 89, 90
MacKain, S.J., 1:252, 265
McKay, J., 7:105, 126
McKay, J.R., 7:217, 238

McKay, M., 1:221, 231, 3:252, 253, 262
McKenna, T., 4:95, 109, 8:9, 49
McKenry, P.C., 5:255, 256, 272, 274
McKeon, P., 8:162, 171
McKeown, S., 8:126, 134
McKinley, J.C., 1:9, 25, 7:11, 22
McKinney, W.J., 3:13
MacKinnon, R., 2:236, 246
McKnew, D.H., 6:52, 54
McKnight, S., 1:264
McKusick, L., 8:230, 244
McLachlan, J.F.C., 7:91, 99
MacLean, K., 7:217, 241
McLeer, S., 5:24, 37
McLeer, S.V., 4:119, 129, 5:24, 38
McLellan, A.T., 7:93, 96, 99, 217, 227, 237, 239, 8:274, 286
Maclennan, B., 5:182, 189
McMahon, B., 1:179, 186
McMahon, B.T., 8:89, 9:142, 151, 157
MacMahon, J., 8:166, 172
McMahon, P.P., 1:50, 60, 88
McMahon, R.J., 1:193, 199, 202, 209
McMahon, W.M., 1:188
McMichael, C.K., 7:79, 84
McNair, D.M., 3:156, 175
McNamara, J.J., 5:256, 270
McNeil, J.M., 9:80, 106
McNeil, D., 7:99, 217, 241
McNeilly, C.L., 4:135, 149
McNight, D.L., 3:171, 175
McQuie, H., 8:230, 242
Madanes, C., 2:146
Maddahian, E., 5:238, 248, 8:162, 173
Maddux, J.F., 7:217, 238
Madover, S., 8:234, 243
Maes, M., 3:31
Magni, G., 7:143, 150
Maguire, M.A., 3:140, 144
Magura, S., 7:173, 188, 8:74, 90
Maher, K.R., 4:9, 26
Maher, P.J., 8:133
Mahler, C.A., 2:130, 140
Mahler, J.C., 3:96, 112, 8:249, 251, 253, 255, 256, 257, 258, 265, 266
Mahler, M.S., 1:121, 133, 3:180, 190, 198
Mahoney, J.J., 8:11, 12, 50
Maiberger, R., 3:35, 47
Mainos, D., 6:189
Mairet, A., 6:243, 248, 249, 264
Maisto, S.A., 7:105, 116, 126
Major, L.F., 8:131, 133

Major-Kingsley, S., 2:123, 141
Maki, D.R., 7:26, 27, 45
Malamood, H.S., 4:23
Malamud, T.J., 1:243, 260
Malan, D.H., 2:82, 83, 84, 85, 86, 91, 95, 96
Malas, K., 1:2, 27
Maldonado-Colon, E., 9:219, 221, 228, 229
Males, M., 5:253, 272
Malgady, R.G., 9:216, 228
Malitz, F.E., 7:195, 212
Mallinger, A.G., 3:219, 7:162, 169
Mallinger, J., 7:162, 169
Mallory, R., 1:210
Malloy, P., 5:76
Malone, P., 6:17, 26
Maltz, D., 5:203, 206, 224
Mamelle, N., 1:178, 179, 185
Mammo, A., 7:202, 211
Mandell, J., 5:35, 38
Mandersheid, R.W., 8:251, 264
Manji, H., 7:36, 46
Mank, D., 9:125
Mank, S., 9:119, 125
Mann, J., 2:83, 84, 96
Mann, J., 2:103, 119
Mann, J.J., 3:279, 8:131, 133, 134, 135
Mannuzza, S., 5:19, 49, 76
Mantero-Atienza, E., 7:79, 84
Manuck, S., 4:54, 67
Marchand, A., 6:228, 239
Marchesano, D.R., 5:83, 100
Mardiros, M., 9:182, 183, 197, 207
Margraf, J., 4:14, 29
Marino, M.F., 1:135
Marion, R.L., 9:181, 207
Markel, H., 7:140, 149
Markman, H.J., 6:269, 284
Markowitz, J.C., 3:227, 228, 231, 236, 240
Markowitz, J.S., 3:221
Markowitz, P., 1:174, 186
Marks, C., 10:62, 72
Marks, E., 7:245, 256
Marks, I., 1:108, 116
Marks, I.M., 4:70, 90, 5:20, 6:248, 263
Marks, M., 6:258, 264
Marlatt, G.A., 7:122, 126, 219, 221, 229,
        233, 238, 8:66, 67, 68, 87, 89,
        164, 173
Marmar, C., 1:8, 25
Marmer, S.S., 1:74, 75, 93
Marriott, S.A., 5:218, 223
Marsella, A.J., 10:236, 247

Marsh, J.C., 7:143, 149
Marsh, L.C., 2:101
Marshall, J.R., 3:100, 106, 107, 111, 5:3, 13,
        20, 6:197, 216
Marshall, R.M., 5:51, 75
Marstellar, F.A., 5:164, 170
Martin, C., 5:230, 248
Martin, C.A., 7:64, 83
Martin, C.E., 6:222, 237
Martin, C.S., 5:228, 247
Martin, D., 2:139, 3:96, 112
Martin, F., 3:24, 32
Martin, J., 5:164, 171, 6:242, 265
Martin, J.K., 8:10, 15, 45, 49
Martin, L.Y., 5:19
Martin, M.F., 1:50, 55, 96
Martin, P., 3:157, 176
Martin, R.J., 8:102, 103, 104, 105, 106, 107,
        108, 115
Martin, W., 1:2, 27
Martin, W.E., Jr., 9:187, 207
Martinez, P., 5:75
Martinkowski, K.S., 3:86, 91
Martinson, R., 5:226
Marton, P., 5:171
Marx, J., 3:16, 31
Marzuk, P.M., 8:116
Masi, F.A., 8:9, 49
Maslow, A., 2:11, 15
Mason, B.J., 3:231, 234, 240, 279, 7:79, 84,
        8:129, 135
Mason-Brothers, A., 1:188
Massel,, 3:203, 220
Masson, J.M., 4:120, 129
Masterpasqua, F., 10:148, 158
Masters, W.H., 6:193, 206, 210, 216, 231, 237
Masterson, J.F., 1:120, 121, 122, 133, 134
Mastsakis, A., 1:224, 231
Matarazzo, J.D., 9:42, 59
Mathes, E.W., 6:256, 264
Matheson, L., 9:128, 129, 139
Mathews, A.M., 4:70, 90
Mathews, B., 8:9, 49
Mathews, K.A., 4:54, 67
Matochik, J.A., 5:75
Matsakis, A., 3:256, 263
Matson, J., 5:81, 99
Matson, J.L., 5:9, 20
Mattaini, M.A., 7:179, 188
Matte, B., 6:220, 221, 226, 228, 238, 239
Mattison, R., 5:46, 72
Mattison, R.E., 5:7, 20

Mattsson, A., 5:252, 272
Maudsley,, 1:39
Mavissakalian, M., 1:108, 116
Maxwell, D.S., 8:206, 223
May, J., 4:8, 22
May, Rollo, 2:37, 45
May, V., III, 9:138, 139
Mayberg, H., 3:45, 47
Mayer, J., 8:164, 172
Mayer, K.H., 10:212, 233
Mayfield, D., 8:255, 264
Maynard, H., 1:243, 262
Mayne, T., 4:28
Maza, P., 5:99
Meacham, A., 8:49
Meador, K.G., 3:150, 175
Meagher, R., 7:12, 23
Means, L.B., 7:172, 188
Mednick, S.A., 5:104, 122
Mee-Lee, D., 8:191, 194
Meeland, T.G., 1:155, 169
Meichenbaum, D., 4:12, 32, 5:145, 150,
        7:192, 193, 195, 199, 203, 207,
        211
Meichenbaum, D.H., 5:218, 224
Meinzer, A.E., 8:254, 264
Meisobov, G.B., 1:174, 183, 189
Meissner, W., 4:252, 260
Melacon, S.M., 3:164, 173
Melden, A.I., 8:181, 182, 195
Melia, R., 9:111, 125
Mellsop, G., 8:120, 136
Meloche-Kelly, M., 5:46, 73
Meloy, R., 2:49, 52, 53, 61
Melton, G.B., 8:191, 195, 10:156, 158
Meltzer, H., 7:39, 46
Menard-Buteau, C., 8:135
Menchetti, B.M., 9:120, 125
Mendelsohn, M., 3:157, 171, 204, 218
Mendelsohn, S., 5:254, 269
Mendelson, J.H., 4:96, 105, 8:250, 267
Mendes, H., 6:61, 70
Mendoza, D., 10:80, 94
Mendoza, D.W., 9:196, 207
Menke, E.M., 5:81, 82, 83, 84, 86, 91, 93,
        101
Menlove, F.L., 5:104, 122
Menninger, K.A., 2:58, 61, 82, 96, 240, 241,
        3:124, 126, 4:246, 260
Mensh, I.N., 10:196, 208
Mentari, A., 3:44, 49
Menustick, C.E., 8:202, 223

Mercer, W., 4:27
Mercer, William M., 8:19, 22, 24, 25, 27, 49
Meredith, B., 6:178, 188
Merikangas, K.R., 5:5, 19
Merrigan, D.M., 7:100, 241, 8:258, 267
Mersky, H., 1:52, 93
Mesmer, 2:100
Messersmith, C.E., 6:193, 217
Messing, M., 1:2, 28
Mesulam, M., 1:65, 82, 93
Metcalf, L., 7:199, 210
Metzger, D.S., 7:239
Meyer, Adolph, 3:34, 47, 4:202
Meyer, A.J., 8:162, 172
Meyer, D.J., 7:57, 62
Meyer, D.R., 6:59, 66, 70
Meyer, R.E., 7:68, 69, 70, 74, 84, 227, 237,
        8:68, 88, 124, 134, 135, 136
Meyers, C.P., 8:251, 264
Meyers, D.C., 4:222, 237
Meyers, J.K., 8:248, 264
Meyerson, A.T., 1:243, 264
Mezzich, A., 7:9, 22
Mezzich, J.E., 8:120, 121, 123, 127, 128,
        133, 134, 136
Mezzizh, A., 5:228, 247
Michael, R., 6:222, 237
Michael, S., 4:260
Michaels, S., 6:222, 237
Michels, R., 2:236, 246
Michienzi, T., 5:35, 39
Middlestadt, S.E., 5:13, 18
Midgley, C., 6:114
Mieckkowski, T., 8:100, 116
Mieczkowski, T., 7:187
Mihaly, L., 5:82, 100
Mikulincer, M., 4:42, 51
Miles, M.S., 6:149, 163
Milgrom, J.H., 10:196, 208
Milich, R., 5:48, 77
Milich, R.S., 5:48, 49, 76
Mill, J.S., 10:174, 178
Millard, R., 10:58, 59, 64, 65, 66, 72, 73
Mille, H., 6:120, 146
Miller, A., 3:32
Miller, B.A., 8:207, 222
Miller, J.B., 6:269, 271, 272, 274, 275, 284,
        10:199, 208
Miller, J.Y., 4:102, 108
Miller, K., 4:96, 105
Miller, K.E., 5:256, 272
Miller, L., 3:28, 31, 8:8, 49

Morris, P.L.P., 3:38, 43, 47
Morrisey-Adler, S., 4:19, 22
Morrison, J., 4:101, 109, 5:51, 76
Morrison, R.L., 1:241, 264
Morrissey, J.M., 5:280, 290
Morrow, R.D., 9:185, 207
Morse, R.M., 8:201, 204, 221, 222
Morten, G., 9:186, 204
Moses, E., 6:120, 146
Moskowitz, J., 8:162, 173
Moskowitz, J.A., 1:166, 168
Moss, G.R., 5:226
Moss, H.B., 4:99, 110, 5:230, 248, 8:131, 135
Moss, S.J., 5:3, 20
Mossberg, D., 7:226, 236
Most, R.B., 9:214, 227
Mott, F.L., 8:97, 114
Mowat, R.R., 6:252, 265
Mowatt, M.H., 6:55
Moynihan, D.P., 6:119, 145
Mrazek, P.B., 4:123, 130
Muenz, L.R., 4:27
Mueser, K., 8:270, 277, 286
Mueser, K.T., 1:246, 254, 264, 8:275, 286
Muffler, J., 5:238, 248
Mufson, L., 5:167, 171
Muha, D., 9:178, 201, 202, 206
Mule, S.J., 3:96, 112
Mulick, J.A., 5:86, 102
Mullan, H., 2:100, 101, 115, 119
Mullaney, P.A., 4:76
Mullen, P.E., 6:242, 243, 252, 255, 265, 266
Mullen, R., 6:110, 114
Muneyyirci, J., 3:266, 278
Munir, K., 5:49, 72
Munoz, R.A., 3:166, 175
Munro, A., 6:262, 265
Murgo, A., 3:24, 32
Murphy, D.L., 1:37, 46
Murphy, G., 5:256, 272
Murphy, G.E., 3:140, 141, 145, 209, 213,
    214, 215, 220, 8:125, 127, 135
Murphy, J., 4:261, 10:169, 178
Murphy, J.M., 8:131, 135
Murphy, L.L., 9:219, 221, 228
Murphy, P., 6:47, 54
Murphy, R.T., 7:217, 238
Murphy, T.J., 8:164, 173
Murray, D.M., 8:96, 116
Murray, E.J., 10:18, 22, 34
Murray, E.L., 6:225, 237
Murray, G.B., 3:44, 48

Murray, P.K., 7:27, 43, 46
Murray, R.M., 4:97, 109
Murrell, P.H., 10:79, 95
Murstein, B.R., 6:7, 25
Murthy, M., 4:110
Mussell, M.J., 4:9, 30
Musso, A., 4:23
Muzzolon, R., 3:174
Myers, D.M., 8:3, 50
Myers, J.K., 1:36, 47, 3:149, 177, 206, 222,
    8:222
Myers, K., 5:158, 159, 171
Myers, M.F., 4:216

N

Naber, G., 6:242, 266
Nacht, Sacha, 2:14, 16
Nadolsky, J., 9:142, 158
Nagel, L.S., 5:104, 122
Nagy, R., 1:12, 24
Nairne, K., 3:263
Nakao, K., 7:244, 257
Napolitano, D.M., 8:11, 47
Nasarallah, H.A., 4:100, 109
Nathans, S., 2:90, 97
Naylor, M.W., 5:256, 272
Neal, M.B., 6:171, 175, 188
Neal, N.R., 3:149, 176
Needle, R.H., 6:36, 53
Neff, D.F., 4:11, 23, 30
Neighbors, B., 6:36, 54
Neil, J.F., 7:162, 169
Neill, J., 6:197, 216
Neimeyer, R.A., 3:119, 126, 141, 145
Neims, A., 7:156, 169
Nekich, J., 4:107
Neligh, G., 7:247, 248, 249, 257
Nelson, B., 5:172, 8:126, 133
Nelson, C.B., 5:18
Nelson, D.W., 3:68, 92
Nelson, J.C., 5:172
Nelson, R.O., 3:159, 171, 175, 4:8, 22
Nemeroff, C., 3:25, 32
Nemiah, J.C., 1:52, 93, 3:184, 198
Nesdale, A.R., 5:226
Neubauer, P.B., 6:165
Neugebauer, R., 6:152, 163
Neukrug, E., 9:4, 16
Neukrug, E.S., 10:186, 194
Neuman, C.F., 7:231, 236
Nevo, I., 7:68, 84

Newby, R.F., 1:193, 210
Newcomb, M., 8:162, 173
Newcombe, M.D., 5:238, 248
Newcombe, R., 8:230, 243
Newfield, N.A., 6:101, 110, 115
Newlin, D.B., 4:96, 109
Newman, A.S., 10:95
Newman, C.F., 7:202, 203, 205, 211
Newman, J.P., 3:148, 176
Newman, L.M., 6:165
Newman, S., 3:86, 92
Newmeyer, J., 8:226, 236, 243
Niaura, R., 4:2, 6, 26, 30
Niaura, R.S., 7:227, 239
Nicholas, R.C., 4:97, 108
Nicholls, P., 8:126, 136
Nichols, N., 2:144, 147, 153, 158, 160, 163,
   7:226, 238
Nichols, S., 8:233, 243
Nicholson, N., 4:23
Nickman, S., 5:104, 118, 122
Niederehe, G., 2:196, 212
Nielsen, A.C., 3:157, 176
Nielsen, M.H., 6:193, 217
Nies, G., 3:157, 173
Nievod, A., 10:156, 159
Nigel, A.J., 4:18, 30
Nightingale, E.D., 8:192, 195
Nikkel, R.E., 8:281, 283, 286
Nirenberg, T.D., 7:239
Nixon, G., 2:87, 96
Noble, E.P., 4:105, 8:206, 223
Nobles, W.W., 8:101, 116
Noel, N.E., 7:109, 126
Noelker, L.S., 6:172, 189
Noordsy, D.L., 8:285, 286
Norcross, J.C., 7:197, 212, 8:78, 89, 270, 287
Nordin, S.R., 3:84, 91
Norin, F., 3:35, 46
Norlock, F.E., 7:210
Normand, J., 8:50
North, C.S., 1:253, 264
Norton, G.R., 1:51, 95
Nosek, M.A., 9:67, 69, 72, 73, 77
Notgrass, C.M., 4:145, 151
Novaco, R., 5:264, 272
Novaco, R.W., 5:218, 224, 226
Novak, C., 5:46, 73
Novak, D.E., 8:37, 45
Novello, A., 6:100
Novy, D.M., 9:194, 204
Nowinski, J., 8:154

Nuechterlein, K.H., 1:258, 264
Nunes, E., 3:221
Nunes, E.V., 8:135
Nunes-Dinis, M., 7:172, 173, 177, 184, 188
Nunez, J.F., 7:189
Nutter, D.E., 6:225, 237
Nyamathi, A.M., 10:213, 232
Nye, I., 8:184, 195

O

Oakland, T., 5:208, 223
Oberndorf, C., 2:251, 264
Obert, J.L., 7:172, 188
O'Brien, C., 7:10, 23
O'Brien, C.P., 7:68, 69, 74, 75, 85, 93, 99,
   179, 180, 188, 227, 237, 239,
   8:137, 274, 286
O'Carroll, R., 6:234, 238
Ocepek-Welikson, K., 8:135
O'Connor, P., 6:163, 8:164, 172
O'Donnel, J.O., 8:56, 89
Oetting, E.R., 5:238, 248, 8:162, 173
O'Farrell, T.J., 7:105, 108, 112, 116, 122,
   126, 127
Offer, D., 5:156–157, 172, 184, 189
Offord, D.B., 5:19
Offord, D.R., 5:11, 17, 104, 122, 157, 170
Ogata, S.N., 1:123, 134
Ogden, L., 9:128, 139
Ogden, R.L., 4:119, 130
O'Gorman, T.W., 4:98, 106
Ohlin, L.E., 5:206, 223
Olarte, S., 10:196, 207
O'Leary, K.D., 5:225
O'Leary, M.R., 7:193, 212, 225, 226, 239,
   241
O'Leary, S.G., 5:59, 71
Olgin, J.E., 7:68, 85
Oliver, P., 10:23, 34
Ollendick, T.H., 5:9, 13, 20
Olmedo, E.L., 9:216, 218, 228, 229
Olmstead, M.P., 3:266, 278
Olsen-Noll, C.G., 8:201, 203, 204, 208,
   222
Olson, D.H., 6:9, 11, 12, 13, 24, 25
O'Malley, P., 8:188, 195
O'Malley, S.S., 7:68, 69, 70, 74, 84, 85,
   8:130, 136
Omenn, G.S., 4:97, 108
O'Neil, M.E., 5:56, 73
Opalic, P., 2:103, 119

Oppenheim, A.N., 7:214, 225, 238
Oradei, D.M., 3:44, 48
Orav, E.J., 8:10, 53
Orlinsky, D., 7:204, 211
Ormont, L., 2:109, 120
Orne, M.T., 1:50, 57, 65, 78, 93, 94
Ornitz, E.M., 1:173, 188
Ornstein, P., 2:83, 93
Ornstein, R., 4:222, 237
Orozco, S., 9:210, 216, 225, 228
Ortega, M.J., 3:120, 126
Ortiz, A.A., 9:219, 221, 228, 229
Orvaschel, H., 5:3, 9, 18, 7:12, 23
Osgood, N.J., 8:206, 222
O'Shaunnessy, D.F., 7:149
Osher, F.C., 8:275, 286
Osherson, A., 1:76, 88
Osman, B.B., 5:57, 75
Ostrov, E., 5:184, 189
Ostrow, D., 8:231, 244
Ota, H., 5:82, 100
Ottati, V., 5:13, 18
Otto, M.W., 5:15, 20
Overall, J.E., 3:209, 219, 8:129, 136
Overholser, J., 5:158, 169
Owen, G., 10:22, 34
Owen, L., 3:172
Ozonoff, S., 6:162

P

Pace, S.K., 8:10, 45
Paddison, P., 1:2, 25
Padilla, A.M., 9:216, 229
Padilla, E.R., 9:216, 218, 229
Pagano, R.R., 8:164, 173
Page, R.D., 4:17, 30
Page, W.W., 1:16, 27
Palermo, D., 5:85, 98
Palkes, H.S., 5:47, 76
Palley, C.S., 8:162, 173
Pallmeyer, T.P., 4:23
Palm, E.A., 7:195, 212
Palmari, J.J., 4:16, 30
Palmblad, J., 3:29, 32
Palmer, T., 5:226
Pancheri, P., 9:216, 225
Pandina, R.J., 8:162, 171
Panos, A., 1:76, 94
Panos, P.T., 1:76, 94
Pape, D.A., 10:58, 71
Papolos, D.F., 3:66, 69, 92, 263

Papolos, J., 3:66, 69, 92, 263
Papp, P., 2:150, 163
Papp, Z., 8:131, 133
Paradise, L.V., 2:123, 132, 140, 10:54, 56
Parens, H., 3:180, 198
Parents, W.A., 10:216, 217, 233
Parham, T.J., 9:180, 190, 207
Parikh, R.M., 3:40, 42, 45, 48
Paris, B., 8:221
Paris, J., 1:124, 133, 134, 135
Parker, H.C., 5:59, 76
Parker, J.C., 4:16, 25
Parker, R.M., 9:110, 113, 114, 115, 116, 117, 118, 125, 126
Parker, W.M., 10:244, 247
Parkes, C.M., 3:122, 126
Parkinson, D.K., 3:201, 219
Parks, B., 7:204, 211
Parloff, M.B., 3:219
Parmalee, P.A., 3:150, 176
Parrot, W.G., 6:243, 265
Parry, A., 8:230, 243
Parson, T., 6:202, 217
Parsons, O.A., 7:226, 238
Partridge, F., 5:20, 171
Pasini, W., 6:224, 225, 238
Pask-McCartney, C., 5:197, 205, 223
Paskus, T.S., 8:286
Patel, C., 4:4, 30
Patick, D.L., 7:253, 256
Pato, M.T., 1:47
Patrick, K.D., 10:86, 95
Patterson, G., 2:161
Patterson, G.R., 1:193, 199, 200, 204, 205, 210, 5:195, 224, 226
Patterson, J.B., 9:119, 126, 10:58, 60, 62, 63, 64, 72
Patterson, L.E., 9:19, 23, 26, 27, 32, 33
Pattison, E., 4:249, 260
Pattison, E.M., 2:103, 120, 4:261
Patton, J., 4:261
Paul, G.L., 1:243, 264
Paulauskas, S.L., 5:4, 19, 170
Pauls, D.L., 1:38, 47, 5:5, 19
Pavlov, Ivan P., 1:3, 7:175, 188
Paykel, E., 5:81, 100
Paykel, E.S., 3:206, 213, 222
Peace, K., 8:120, 136
Pearsall, H.R., 3:96, 104, 110, 111
Pearson, E.S., 10:199, 208
Pearson, J., 6:38, 54
Pearson, R.E., 4:188, 200

Pedersen, P., 10:236, 237, 244, 247, 248
Pedraza, M., 7:239
Pedro-Carroll, J.L., 6:47, 54
Peele, S., 4:75, 90, 7:175, 188
Pekarik, G., 8:74, 89
Pekarkik, G., 7:192, 212
Pelcovits, M.A., 7:105, 126
Peleg, M., 7:214, 238
Pelham, W.E., 5:48, 56, 71, 76, 77
Pelletier, K.R., 4:2, 30
Pena, A., 4:55, 67
Pence, G., 10:175, 178
Penick, E.C., 8:124, 136
Penn, P., 2:147, 163, 6:10, 25, 31
Pennington, B., 1:174, 186
Pennock-Roman, M., 9:219, 221, 229
Pentland, B., 7:44, 46
Penzer, W.N., 8:21, 50
Peper, E., 4:9, 30, 32
Peplau, L.A., 6:195, 213
Pepper, B., 8:248, 266
Percudani, M., 3:274, 277
Perel, J.M., 3:209, 213, 219, 8:134
Perkins, H.W., 8:9, 45
Perkins, K.A., 7:218, 239
Perl, M., 3:150, 174
Perlin, M.L., 2:224, 225, 226, 227, 228, 229
Perlin, M.L., 10:173
Perloff, R., 9:213, 227
Perper, J.A., 5:254, 269, 270
Perrin, S., 5:8, 19
Perry, C., 8:162, 173
Perry, J.C., 1:133
Perry, R., 1:183, 185
Perry, S., 4:76, 89
Perry, S.W., 3:267, 279
Persky, T., 7:248, 253, 257
Person, E.S., 2:232, 233, 246
Peterfreund, E., 2:18, 22, 24, 26, 27, 31
Peters, C.P., 4:119, 130
Peters, J.E., 5:49, 71
Peters, K.G., 5:43, 73
Peters, R.K., 4:5, 30
Petersen, P.B., 1:188
Peterson, J., 6:172, 190
Peterson, J.J., 9:50, 59
Peterson, K.A., 1:264
Peterson, M., 7:188
Peterson, P.L., 7:173, 189
Petrila, J., 10:156, 158
Peyser, J., 3:220, 221

Pfeffer, C.R., 5:256, 272
Pfeiffer, C., 7:163, 167
Pfeiffer, E., 6:180, 189
Pfeiffer, G., 5:180, 188
Pfeiffer, S., 5:208, 223
Pharr, O.M., 4:19, 31
Phelan, J., 5:181, 189
Phibbs, C.S., 8:114, 116
Phillips, D., 6:52, 54
Phillips, E.L., 5:142, 150
Phillips, I., 5:187, 189
Phillips, J., 4:9, 31
Phillips, J.S., 5:226
Phillips, V.A., 6:19, 24
Phipps, C., 3:207, 220
Phipps, C.C., 1:249, 261
Phipps, E., 6:87, 97
Piaget, J., 4:181, 9:2, 11, 16
Pickens, R., 8:9, 49
Pickens, R.W., 4:95, 101, 109, 7:228, 237
Pickles, A., 5:160, 170
Pierattini, R.A., 7:27, 46
Pierce, J.L., 4:34, 38, 51
Piercy, F.F., 7:116, 127
Piercy, F.P., 2:144, 163
Pietrantoni, M., 8:102, 103, 116
Pigott, T.A., 3:266, 279
Pihl, R.O., 4:100, 107
Pike, F.H., 4:9, 24
Pikoff, H., 4:11, 31
Piliavin, J.A., 6:174, 187
Pilkonis, P.A., 3:219
Pilsbury, D., 4:9, 26
Pincus, H.A., 7:253, 257
Pine, F., 1:133, 5:114, 122
Pines, A.M., 6:256, 257, 258, 265
Pines, D., 6:151, 152, 163
Pingree, C., 1:188
Pinkham, L., 1:134
Pinsky, L., 10:212, 232
Pinsof, W.M., 2:166, 167, 168, 187, 188, 190, 191
Piper, R.E., 9:178, 190, 206
Piper, W.E., 2:87, 91, 92, 96
Pirie, P.L., 8:96, 116
Pisani, V.D., 3:219
Pisterman, S., 1:208, 210
Piuma, F., 9:111, 116, 117, 126
Plaut, T.F.A., 8:199, 222
Plescia-Pikus, M., 8:9, 50
Plotnikoff, N., 3:24, 32
Plumlee, A.A., 1:264

Plutchik, R., 5:254, 269, 272
Poikolanien, K., 7:228, 240
Pokorny, A.D., 8:207, 222
Poland, S., 5:265, 272
Polich, J.M., 7:216, 225, 236, 240
Pollack, M.H., 5:15, 20
Pollane, L., 6:6, 24
Pollio, H.R., 2:24, 31
Pollio, M.R., 2:31
Pollock, G.H., 6:151, 153, 156, 163
Pollock, M., 5:170
Pollock, V.E., 4:96, 109
Polonsky, S., 4:135, 150
Pomeroy, W.B., 6:222, 237
Ponterotto, J.G., 10:236, 237, 238, 244, 246, 248
Pope, H.G., 3:64
Pope, K.S., 2:123, 126, 131, 140, 234, 246, 10:2, 4, 5, 15, 42, 43, 56, 80, 95, 185, 194, 196, 208
Pope, S.K., 10:94
Pope, T., 8:18, 23, 50
Poppen, R.L., 3:164, 166, 176
Poresky, R.H., 6:25
Porjesz, B., 4:99, 105, 7:225, 236, 240
Porter, D., 4:5, 30
Porter, F.S., 5:35, 36
Porter, R., 1:253, 264
Portner, J., 6:9, 25
Post, R.M., 1:51, 94, 7:160, 167
Potash, A.C., 7:177, 189
Pottash, A.C., 3:101, 111
Pottash, A.L., 8:129, 134
Pottash, A.L.C., 7:226, 237
Potter, C., 9:72, 77
Potter, F.J., 8:47
Potter, J.F., 8:204, 222
Potter, W.Z., 7:36, 46
Powell, B., 6:63, 70
Powell, B.J., 8:124, 136
Powell, L., 5:35, 38
Power, P.W., 8:27, 48, 9:243, 248
Powers, S., 9:221, 229
Poythress, N.G., 10:156, 158
Prata, G., 2:146
Pratt, J., 2:100, 101
Preher, H., 4:68
Prendergast, D., 3:29, 31
Presig, R., 7:53, 62
Preskorn, S., 10:166, 178
Press, G.A., 1:178, 185
Preston, J., 7:46

Price, G., 7:79, 83
Price, J., 1:75, 94
Price, L.H., 1:47, 3:278
Price, R.H., 3:202, 218
Price, T.R., 3:35, 38, 39, 41, 43, 46, 47, 48, 49
Prien, R., 2:253, 264
Prien, R.F., 3:267, 269, 272, 273, 274, 275, 276, 279
Primoff, E.S., 9:214, 227, 229
Prindaville, G.M., 7:249, 257
Prinz, R.J., 4:95, 102, 111
Prior, A., 4:10, 32
Prochaska, J.O., 7:197, 212, 8:78, 89, 270, 271, 287
Procter, A., 7:163, 168
Protinsky, H.O., 6:101, 115
Proust, M., 6:257, 265
Pruitt, W.A., 9:243, 248
Prusoff, B., 5:156, 169
Prusoff, B.A., 3:206, 209, 213, 221, 222, 4:202, 216, 5:5, 19
Pruzinsky, E.W., 8:200, 203, 222
Pryzbeck, T.R., 8:120, 134, 246, 247, 249, 256, 263, 267
Puente, A.E., 9:211, 217, 229
Puig-Antich, J., 5:81, 82, 100, 172, 7:12, 23
Purisch, A., 9:147, 157
Purtill, J.J., 7:99
Purtillo, R., 10:59, 72
Putnam, F., 4:134, 149
Putnam, F.W., 1:50, 51, 52, 55, 60, 66, 69, 85, 87, 89, 94

Q

Quadry, M.J., 6:107, 115
Quan, H., 9:72, 77
Quay, H.C., 5:195, 224
Quaytman, M.S., 4:119, 130
Quillen, M.A., 4:8, 31
Quinn, W.H., 6:101, 103, 106, 110, 114, 115
Quitkin, F., 3:111
Quitkin, F.M., 3:209, 213, 221, 8:135

R

Rabin, A.S., 3:209, 221
Rabin, J., 7:217, 241
Rabinovich, H., 5:11, 16, 165, 169, 172
Rabins, P., 6:178, 187
Rabins, P.V., 6:179, 188
Rabkin, J.G., 3:221

Rabkin, L., 6:153, 163
Rachels, J., 10:19, 34
Rachman, S.J., 1:31, 36, 47
Radda, H.T., 8:74, 86
Radnitz, C.L., 4:11, 23
Rado, S., 3:182, 198
Radouco-Thomas, C., 4:110
Radouco-Thomas, S., 4:99, 110
Rae, D.S., 8:136, 222, 247, 266
Rafter, J.A., 7:64, 83
Rahe, R.H., 3:122, 126, 4:202, 216
Raimy, V., 5:149
Ralphe, D., 5:24, 38
Ralphe, D.L., 4:119, 129
Ramirez, L.F.G., 1:155, 158, 168, 169
Ramos, R.A., 9:213, 216, 229
Ramsey, P., 8:183, 195
Rand, A., 4:229, 237
Rando, T.A., 6:148, 149, 150, 164
Randolph, E., 1:246, 264
Rank, Otto, 2:6, 10, 11, 12, 83, 94
Rankin, H., 1:163, 168
Rankin, R.J., 9:215, 231
Rapee, R.M., 4:14, 22
Raphael, B., 3:38, 47
Raphaelson, A.H., 7:99
Rapoport, J., 1:31, 37, 40, 47
Rapoport, J.L., 5:52, 58, 74, 78, 7:156, 169
Rapp, S., 3:158, 176
Rappoport, J., 5:173
Rapport, M.D., 5:57, 74
Rasmussen, S.A., 1:37, 39, 47, 3:278, 6:248, 265
Rasmusson, A., 5:172
Ratican, K.L., 4:145, 151
Rausch, H.L., 6:203, 217
Rausch, L., 4:28
Ravart, Marc, 6:221, 226, 228, 239
Ravels, V.H., 5:241, 247
Raven, J., 9:217, 230
Raven, J.F., 9:217, 230
Rawson, N.S.B., 7:172, 173, 225, 238
Rawson, R.A., 7:177, 178, 181, 184, 188
Ray, O., 8:6, 50
Ray, R.S., 5:226
Raykel, E.S., 4:202, 216
Razzano, L., 3:219
Rea, W.J., 7:53, 62
Rea, W.S., 1:160, 167
Read, M.R., 8:124, 136
Reba, P., 4:9, 28
Reddon, J.R., 6:199, 218

Reding, M.J., 3:48
Redl, F., 5:182, 189
Reed, B.G., 8:108, 109, 116
Reed, K., 5:171
Reedy, R.G., 7:53, 61
Reever, K., 6:172, 190
Regier, D.A., 1:102, 116, 4:70, 88, 90, 8:120, 136, 199, 222, 247, 248, 249, 266
Rehm, L.P., 3:209, 215, 221
Reich, W., 2:12
Reich, W., 7:12, 24
Reichler, R.J., 1:178, 183, 188, 189, 5:16, 20
Reichlin, R.E., 2:204, 212
Reichlin, S., 3:28, 32
Reichman, W., 8:36, 51
Reid, J., 5:170
Reid, J.B., 1:210
Reid, J.G., 5:195, 224
Reid, L.D., 7:142, 150
Reik, T., 2:18, 28, 31
Reilly, D.M., 6:108, 115
Reilly, E.L., 8:129, 136
Rein, H., 7:50, 62
Reinhardt, J., 8:221
Reis, H., 1:74, 94
Reis, H.T., 6:174, 189
Reiss, D., 6:109, 114, 120, 138, 145, 7:13, 23, 8:8, 52
Reiss, D.A., 5:236, 246
Reiss, D.J., 2:177, 190
Reissman, F., 1:240, 264
Reitan, R., 7:18, 23
Reitan, R.M., 9:147, 158
Renaud, M., 1:244, 261
Rendell, J.R., 8:84, 87, 89
Renick, N.L., 8:166, 170
Renner, B.R., 1:183, 189
Renner, E., 7:53, 62
Resick, P.A., 4:185, 199
Resnik, R., 8:103, 104, 105, 106, 107, 115
Retschald, T., 8:163, 173
Reulbach, W., 8:231, 232, 243
Reuman, D., 6:114
Revelle, W., 7:156, 168
Reyes, J.R., 7:162, 168
Reynolds, C.R., 5:85, 86, 100
Reynolds, P., 5:258, 273
Reynolds, R., 8:163, 166, 171, 172
Reynolds, R.V., 4:12, 32
Reynolds, W., 5:81, 101
Reznick, J.S., 5:18

Rice, D.P., 7:64, 85
Rice, L.N., 2:21, 22, 23, 24, 31
Rich, C.L., 5:253, 273
Rich, G.L., 10:2, 15
Richards, C., 5:4, 19
Richards, D., 10:174, 178
Richardson, B.L., 10:237, 238, 247
Richardson, C.E., 7:248, 257
Richardson, F.C., 4:10, 24
Richardson, G.A., 8:105, 115
Richmond, B.O., 5:85, 86, 100
Richter, E., 6:165
Rick, G.R., 5:226
Rickard, W.H., 9:82, 106
Rickels, K., 3:266, 279, 8:256, 266, 267
Rickers-Ovsiankina, M.A., 9:217, 227
Riddle, M., 5:165, 172
Riddle, M.A., 3:209, 219
Ridley, C.R., 9:196, 207
Ridley, J., 6:258, 263
Riechler, R.J., 5:20
Rieker, P., 1:2, 13, 14, 27
Ries, R., 8:249, 259, 260, 266
Ries, R.K., 8:256, 266, 276, 287
Rifkin, A., 3:111
Rigali, J., 5:164, 165, 172
Rilke, R.M., 2:6
Rimland, B., 1:183, 188
Rinsley, D.B., 1:121, 122, 134
Rioch, M., 2:102, 114, 120
Rios, P., 1:179, 188
Risley, T.R., 5:142, 151
Risman, B.J., 6:61, 70
Ritchie, M.H., 8:37, 51
Ritvo, A., 1:179, 188
Ritvo, E.C., 7:79, 84, 8:129, 135
Ritvo, E.R., 1:173, 179, 188
Rivinus, T.M., 4:70, 90, 5:249
Rizzo, A.A., 7:218, 237
Roach, J.D., 7:156, 169
Robbins, D.R., 5:15, 16
Roberts, G.T., 10:79, 95
Roberts, H., 7:157, 167
Roberts, L., 8:287
Roberts, N., 5:171
Robertson, G.J., 9:214, 227
Robertson, I., 7:109, 125
Robertson, N., 8:198, 199, 223
Robin, A., 7:120, 127
Robin, A.L., 1:198, 210
Robins, E., 8:125, 135
Robins, L., 1:8, 14, 27

Robins, L.N., 5:5, 20, 8:222
Robinson, D., 5:172
Robinson, F.F., 3:88, 92
Robinson, G.E., 6:161, 164
Robinson, J., 6:175, 189
Robinson, L.A., 3:119, 126, 226, 235, 240
Robinson, R.G., 3:35, 38, 39, 40, 41, 43, 45,
    46, 47, 48, 49, 267, 276, 280
Robinson, S.E., 2:123, 140, 10:9, 15
Robitscher, J., 2:224, 226
Rock, D.L., 2:91, 93
Rockland, L.H., 1:120, 134
Rodgers, R.C., 10:155, 159
Rodgers, R.H., 6:75, 96
Rodichok, L.D., 4:22, 23
Rodman, J.L., 3:160, 176
Rodman, N.F., 8:47
Rodstein, E., 6:97
Roehling, P.V., 4:102, 106
Roessler, R., 10:61, 72
Roessler, R.T., 9:87, 106, 148, 158
Roffwarg, H.P., 3:209, 220
Rogers, Carl R., 2:11
Rogers, C.R., 5:132, 151
Rogers, L.E., 6:19, 24, 25, 32
Rogers, S.J., 10:23, 34
Rogers, W., 3:221, 222
Rogerson, J.S., 4:9, 24
Rogler, L.H., 9:216, 228, 10:242, 248
Rohde, P., 5:158, 159, 171, 172
Rohsenow, D.J., 7:239
Rohter, L., 6:38, 54
Rolf, J.E., 4:101, 108, 5:230, 247
Rolfs, R.T., 8:100, 117
Rolland, J.S., 6:127, 145
Rollins, C., 10:63, 64, 65, 71, 72
Rollins, D.E., 8:46
Rollins, S.A., 10:214, 232
Rollnick, S., 7:199, 201, 202, 209, 211, 8:30,
    50, 270, 276, 279, 280, 281, 282,
    286
Roman, M.A., 1:193, 210
Roman, P.M., 8:4, 10, 17, 18, 34, 35, 38, 45,
    50, 257, 266
Romano, J., 3:97, 112
Romano, M.D., 10:72
Rooney, A., 4:17, 28
Rosati, R., 9:85, 107
Rose, D., 1:2, 14, 27
Rose, G., 7:230, 240
Rose, G.D., 4:7, 31
Rose, T., 3:172

Rosen, H., 6:148, 151, 164, 165
Rosen, R.C., 6:192, 216, 221, 224, 225, 227,
        233, 237, 238
Rosenak, Y., 8:108, 109, 117
Rosenbaum, J.F., 5:6, 15, 17, 20, 21
Rosenbaum, M., 1:64, 83, 95, 2:100, 101,
        115, 119
Rosenberg, B., 2:103, 119
Rosenberg, M.L., 5:267, 270
Rosenberg, R., 5:81, 98
Rosenberg, S.D., 4:18, 31
Rosenberg, T., 5:170
Rosenfeld, A.A., 4:116, 130
Rosenman, R.H., 4:54, 67
Rosenthal, L., 5:182, 189
Rosenthal, M.K., 5:12, 17
Rosenthal, R.J., 1:157, 168
Rosenthal, R.N., 8:285, 287
Rosenthal, T.L., 4:5, 27
Rosner, R., 10:108
Ross, C.A., 1:51, 61, 69, 87, 95
Ross, D.C., 5:10, 21
Ross, D.M., 5:42, 50, 77
Ross, H.E., 7:227, 240, 8:120, 136
Ross, J., 1:109, 116
Ross, S.A., 5:42, 50, 77
Rosse, R., 1:2, 25
Rossman, E., 1:243, 260
Roszell, D., 1:2, 16, 27
Roter, D.L., 1:242, 262
Roth, D., 5:84, 85, 100
Roth, D.L., 4:16, 31
Roth, J., 5:18
Roth, M., 3:34, 49
Rothke, S., 2:115, 120
Rothlind, J., 5:43, 77
Rothschild, A.J., 3:25, 32
Rothweiler, H., 7:155, 169
Rotter, J.B., 5:149
Rounsavile, B., 1:96
Rounsaville, B., 8:136
Rounsaville, B.J., 3:114, 125, 7:68, 70, 74,
        84, 85, 175, 187
Rovner, B.W., 3:176
Rowe, J.O., 4:260
Roy, A., 8:126, 136
Roy, L., 3:228, 240
Rozal, G.G., 3:69, 91
Rubama, I., 5:197, 205, 223
Rubenstein, J.L., 5:257, 273
Rubert, M.P., 5:20
Rubin, C., 5:257, 273

Rubin, J., 1:180, 181, 187
Rubin, L., 5:80, 82, 83, 98
Rubin, S.E., 10:58, 59, 60, 61, 63, 64, 65, 66,
        71, 72, 73
Rubin, S.S., 6:149, 164
Rubinstein, D., 6:192, 214
Ruckpaul, K., 7:50, 62
Rudorfer, M.V., 7:36, 46
Rueda, R., 9:219, 230
Ruegg, R.G., 3:149, 176
Ruff, G., 1:26
Ruffins, S., 4:119, 131
Ruggieri-Authelet, A., 7:99
Ruiz, R.A., 9:216, 229
Rule, B.G., 5:226
Rund, B.R., 1:253, 264
Rundell, J., 1:2, 15, 28
Runeson, B., 5:253, 254, 273
Runtz, M., 4:116, 128, 145, 146, 149, 5:24, 36
Runyan, R.D., 4:103, 106
Runyon, D.K., 5:34, 37
Rusch, F.R., 9:110, 111, 126
Rush, A.J., 3:128, 139, 140, 141, 142, 144,
        145, 146, 220
Rush, A.J., 3:233, 234, 240, 5:130, 149, 263,
        269, 271
Russell, A.B., 4:116, 130
Russell, C.S., 6:11, 13, 25
Russell, D.E., 4:134, 135, 136, 137, 146, 151
Russell, D.E.H., 4:116, 130
Russell, M., 4:94, 95, 110, 8:9, 51
Russo, A.M., 1:162, 164, 167, 168
Rutan, J.S., 2:109, 120
Rutter, M., 1:173, 174, 175, 179, 180, 184,
        185, 187, 188, 189, 4:104, 110,
        5:2, 21, 89, 100, 157, 160, 170,
        172
Ryan, J., 8:10, 53
Ryan, M., 6:193, 217
Ryan, N., 5:159, 164, 172
Rychtarik, R.G., 7:199, 211, 8:276, 286
Rydberg, V., 8:56, 87
Ryglewicz, H., 8:248, 266

S

Saathoff, G., 1:2, 28
Sabalis, R.F., 5:104, 122
Sabo, A.N., 1:124, 133
Sabshin, M., 4:82, 90
Sachar, E.J., 3:267, 280
Sachs, G.S., 5:15, 20

Sachs, R.G., 1:50, 76, 77, 87, 92, 95
Sadavoy, J., 2:209, 213
Saddock, B.J., 10:149, 158
Sadoff, R.L., 10:108
Safran, J.D., 3:146
Sager, C.J., 2:158, 163, 6:74, 79, 89, 97
Saila, S.L., 7:228, 240
Sainsbury, P., 8:126, 133
St. Germaine, J., 10:185, 192, 194
Sakata, R., 9:179, 180, 207
Salaspuro, M., 8:258, 259, 264
Sales, E., 6:168, 186
Saligaut, C., 4:106
Salis, P.J., 7:169
Salkovskis, P.M., 4:14, 24
Sallis, R.E., 7:192, 210
Salloum, I.M., 8:120, 121, 123, 124, 125,
    127, 128, 129, 133, 134, 136
Salomone, P.R., 9:33
Salvato, F.R., 7:79, 84
Salvendy, J., 2:115, 120
Salyards, S.D., 8:12, 50
Salzinger, K., 3:166, 176
Samenow, S.E., 1:138, 141, 142, 143, 144,
    151
Samoilov, A., 5:171
Sampson, H., 2:88, 97
Samuels, J., 3:43, 47
Sanchez, R., 7:189
Sanders, C., 6:148, 164
Sanders, D.H., 1:243, 262
Sandler, J., 2:81, 96, 235, 246
Sandoval, J., 9:216, 230
Sandow, D., 9:119, 125
Sandrow, E., 4:248, 260
Sangl, J., 6:170, 189
Santa Barbara, J., 7:13, 23
Saposnek, D.T., 6:75, 98
Sargunaraj, D., 4:7, 8, 28
Sas, L., 5:35, 39
Satel, S.L., 7:225, 240
Satir, V., 4:77, 90
Satir, V., 2:145, 147, 155, 163, 202, 213
Satterfield, J.H., 5:48, 77
Sattler, H.A., 10:6, 15
Saul, L.J., 3:180, 198
Saunders, N.L., 4:23
Saunders, W., 1:2, 24
Saveanu, T., 5:84, 100
Saxe, G.N., 1:51, 95
Saylor, K.E., 1:112, 116
Schacht, T.E., 2:91, 92, 95

Schaef, A.W., 4:75, 90
Schaffer, N.D., 2:91, 97
Schaie, K.W., 3:67, 92
Schaller, J.G., 8:192, 195
Schaps, E., 8:162, 173
Scharff, D.E., 6:196, 217
Scharff, L., 4:23
Schaub, L.H., 4:17, 30
Schaughency, E.A., 5:43, 77
Schaumann, H., 1:175, 186
Schecter, M.D., 5:104, 109, 111, 119, 121,
    123, 7:142, 150
Scheidlinger, S., 5:176, 177, 180, 186,
    189
Scheier, I.H., 4:28
Schell, A.M., 5:48, 77
Schenk, L., 1:65, 82, 95
Schernan, A., 8:164, 172
Schiavi, R.C., 6:227, 238
Schifano, F., 7:143, 150
Schiff, H.S., 6:149, 150, 164
Schiller, E., 2:49, 52, 53, 61
Schinka, J.A., 7:12, 23
Schlatter, C., 7:155, 169
Schleifer, S., 3:26, 29, 32
Schlesinger, S.E., 8:76, 90
Schloredt, K., 5:171
Schmale, A., 3:3, 4, 13
Schmaling, K.B., 3:141, 144
Schmidt, M.J., 10:62, 73
Schmidt, S., 5:159, 165, 172
Schmiedenberg, M., 6:253, 265
Schmitt, A.P., 9:211, 212, 230
Schmitz, C.L., 5:83, 84, 86, 101
Schmitz, P.G., 4:2, 31
Schmitz, R.E., 8:202, 223
Schneider, H., 6:268, 284, 10:168, 178
Schneider, J., 3:160, 176
Schneider, P., 3:266, 278
Schneider, P., 6:268, 284
Schneider, R., 8:33, 36, 47, 51
Schneider, S., 4:14, 29
Schneier, F.R., 5:14, 21
Schnoll, S., 8:56, 88, 100, 105, 106, 107, 113,
    116
Schoener, G.R., 10:196, 200, 203, 208
Schonbrunn, M., 8:3, 53
Schonfel, L., 8:205, 220
Schoolar, J.C., 1:77, 89
Schooler, N., 3:206, 221
Schopler, E., 1:174, 183, 189
Schotte, D., 5:257, 273

Schottenfeld, R.S., 7:68, 69, 70, 74, 84,
        8:136
Schover, L., 6:221, 222, 235, 238
Schover, L.R., 6:192, 217
Schreiner-Engel, P., 6:227, 238
Schriner, K.F., 9:87, 106
Schroeder, H.E., 1:247, 260
Schroeder, L.O., 10:125
Schrott, H.G., 7:199, 210
Schubert, D.S.P., 3:44, 49
Schuchard, K., 7:133, 149
Schuckit, M.A., 7:82, 85, 225, 240, 8:124,
        125, 126, 132, 136, 248, 249,
        252, 255, 266, 267
Schuerman, J.R., 5:34, 37
Schulberg, H.C., 3:201, 219
Schulsinger, F., 4:98, 101, 107
Schultz, G.L., 10:237, 248
Schultz, R., 1:51, 95, 3:149, 176
Schulz, R., 6:168, 186
Schumm, W.R., 6:3, 25
Schuttler, R., 1:253, 261
Schwab, A.J., 8:84, 90
Schwab, J.J., 3:157, 176
Schwarts, C.E., 5:18
Schwartz, D.A., 3:185, 194, 198
Schwartz, E., 2:113, 120
Schwartz, G.E., 4:2, 21, 24, 31
Schwartz, I.M., 8:191, 195
Schwartz, J., 1:2, 25, 28, 95
Schwartz, L.L., 6:74, 78, 85, 97
Schwartz, R.H., 8:190, 195
Schwarz, R.M., 8:114, 116
Schwarz, S.P., 4:11, 23
Schweizer, B., 8:256, 266, 267
Schweizer, E., 3:266, 279
Schwitzgebel, R.K., 10:4, 15
Schwitzgebel, R.L., 10:4, 15
Schyler, D., 3:146
Scopes, J., 7:149
Scopetta, M.H., 9:230
Scott, J., 3:227, 228, 231, 233, 234, 240, 241
Scott, L., 2:123, 139
Scott, N.R., 7:160, 165, 167, 168
Searles, J.S., 4:97, 98, 110
Sedney, M.A., 4:116, 130
Sedvall, G., 7:226, 236
Seeley, J.R., 5:158, 159, 171, 172
Seeman, M.V., 6:253, 265
Seese, L.R., 5:252, 272
Segal, P.S., 2:87, 96
Segal, S.P., 7:246, 253, 257

Segal, Z.V., 3:146
Segraves, K.B., 6:220, 238
Segraves, R.T., 6:220, 238
Segreto, J., 4:28
Seibel, C., 2:51, 61
Seiden, R.H., 10:15
Seilhamer, R.A., 4:94, 103, 104, 110
Selekman, M., 6:103, 112, 115
Seligman, M.E.P., 3:83, 92, 7:193, 212
Sellers, B.M., 8:256, 263
Sellers, D., 3:219
Seltzer, M.L., 8:200, 223
Selvini-Palazzoli, M., 2:146, 163, 6:31
Selzer, M., 8:42, 51
Selzer, M.A., 1:133
Selzer, M.L., 8:71, 72, 90
Semlitz, L., 7:172, 188
Senturia, A.G., 5:111, 123
Settle, S.A., 6:38, 54
Seymour, R.B., 7:139, 140, 150
Shafer, M., 9:110, 126
Shaffer, D., 5:35, 38, 173, 254, 257, 258, 267,
        271, 273
Shaffer, H.J., 7:201, 212, 235, 240
Shafii, M., 5:252, 253, 254, 256, 273
Shagass, C., 1:40, 47
Shain, B.N., 5:256, 272
Shanas, E., 6:170, 189
Shaner, A., 1:16, 28, 264, 8:272, 287
Shapiro, 7:106
Shapiro, A., 4:6, 27
Shapiro, J.L., 2:123, 140
Shapiro, M.B., 2:20, 31
Shapiro, R.W., 3:94, 112
Shapiro, S.B., 2:123, 140
Share, D.L., 5:42, 47, 76
Sharrar, R.G., 8:100, 117
Shaughnessy, P., 10:11, 16
Shavit, Y., 3:24, 32
Shaw, B.F., 3:139, 140, 142, 145, 5:130, 149,
        263, 269
Shaw, K., 5:10, 12, 17
Shaywitz, B.A., 5:50, 72
Shaywitz, S.E., 5:50, 72
Shea, M.T., 3:219
Shea, V., 3:44, 48
Shearer, S.L., 4:119, 130
Shedler, J., 5:249
Sheeley, V.L., 10:8, 15
Shehan, I., 8:56, 89
Sheik, J.I., 3:158, 177
Shelly, C., 7:18, 22

Shelton, D., 6:133, 146
Shengold, L., 4:120, 130
Shepherd, I.L., 6:199, 217
Shepherd, J, N., 4:135, 149
Shepherd, M., 6:242, 265
Sher, K., 4:70, 90
Sher, K.J., 4:101, 102, 106, 110, 5:230, 247
Sherbourne, C.D., 3:205, 221
Sheridan, J.R., 8:12, 43, 51
Sheridan, M.J., 8:52
Sheridan, P.J., 4:105
Sheridan, S., 5:67, 77
Sherman, C.E., 7:75, 85
Sherman, P.S., 1:253, 264
Shernoff, M., 8:226, 227, 228, 244
Sherry, P., 10:76, 77, 79, 83, 95
Shertzer, B., 2:49, 61
Shih-Chao, H., 8:287
Shine, P., 7:160, 167
Shirlow, M.J., 7:164, 169
Shiro-Geist, C., 9:110, 126
Shneidman, E.S., 3:120, 121, 126
Shopland, S.N., 10:196, 209
Shorris, E., 9:211, 230
Shostrum, E.L., 9:19, 32
Shrout, P., 6:163
Shuman, D.W., 10:152, 153, 159
Sidwell, L.H., 7:249, 257
Siegel, B., 4:116, 130
Siegel, C., 7:193, 212
Siegel, L., 10:168, 178
Siegel, M., 10:3, 15
Siegelwaks, S., 10:54, 56
Siegler, I.C., 3:89, 90
Siepker, B., 5:183, 189
Sierles, R., 1:2, 28
Sifneos, P., 2:83, 86, 91, 97
Sigmon, S., 4:8, 22
Sigmon, S.T., 4:8, 31
Sigvardson, S., 4:94, 98, 105, 106
Sigvardsson, S., 5:230, 246, 8:124, 133
Silber, K., 5:104, 121
Silber, T.J., 8:176, 178, 180, 187, 188, 190, 195, 196
Silberfeld, M., 2:246
Silberman, E., 1:2, 28
Silberman, E.K., 1:51, 94
Silberschatz, G., 2:90, 91, 92, 97
Silberstein, S.D., 4:11, 31
Silk, K.R., 1:134
Silva, P.A., 5:4, 17, 20, 50, 76, 171

Silver, L.B., 5:2, 21
Silverglade, L., 10:79, 95
Silverman, C., 7:246, 257
Silverman, J.M., 1:125, 134
Simeon, J., 5:171
Simeon, J.G., 5:164, 172
Simmons, III, J.Q., 5:104, 123
Simmons, M., 5:29, 37
Simon, B., 10:196, 207
Simon, N.M., 5:111, 123
Simon, R., 2:161, 162, 8:254, 267
Simon, R.I., 10:108
Simons, A.D., 3:141, 145, 209, 220
Simpson, D.D., 8:2, 10, 49
Simpson, J.G., 7:142, 148
Simpson, S., 7:248, 257
Singer, B., 2:251, 264
Singer, M.T., 10:156, 159
Sink, J., 9:59
Sinyor, D., 3:35, 49
Sipkoff, M.Z., 8:19, 52
Siracusa, K., 4:23
Sisson, R.W., 7:104, 127
Sjostrand, L., 8:131, 137
Skaggs, S., 4:19, 26
Skinner, B.F., 3:162, 163, 166, 177, 7:174, 189
Skinner, H.A., 7:13, 23
Skodol, A., 6:163
Skorney, B., 8:208, 220
Slagle, P., 3:263
Slap, G.B., 5:255, 273
Slavson, S., 5:179, 189
Slawson, P.F., 3:185, 198
Sleator, E.K., 5:54, 77
Slikker, W., 7:146, 148
Sloan, R.L., 7:44, 46
Sloan, S., 6:202, 217, 8:163, 172
Slobogin, C., 10:156, 158
Sluzki, C.E., 2:167, 191
Small, A.M., 1:183, 185
Small, M., 7:188
Smalley, S.L., 1:175, 179, 189
Smallish,, L., 1:192, 209
Smallish, L., 5:48, 72
Smart, D.W., 9:180, 182, 183, 188, 191, 192, 198, 203, 207, 210, 215, 230
Smart, J.F., 9:180, 182, 183, 188, 191, 192, 198, 203, 207, 210, 211, 215, 230
Smart, R.G., 5:246
Smedes, L., 4:261

Smith, A., 7:18, 23, 9:42, 59
Smith, B.L., 1:264
Smith, C., 4:134, 150
Smith, C.C., 7:142, 148
Smith, D., 10:58, 71, 156
Smith, D.E., 7:139, 140, 144, 150
Smith, D.P., 7:172, 188
Smith, D.W., 8:102, 103, 117
Smith, E., 3:17, 32
Smith, E.J., 9:179, 181, 207, 10:248
Smith, G., 3:263
Smith, G.T., 4:102, 106
Smith, I.M., 1:179, 185
Smith, K., 4:9, 30, 5:253, 256, 274
Smith, L.G., 6:255, 263
Smith, M., 2:251, 252, 264
Smith, R., 1:2, 24
Smith, S.R., 10:159
Smith, T.L., 8:125, 132
Smith, W., 1:2, 28, 8:163, 172
Smull, M., 10:58, 72
Smyer, M.A., 2:194, 211
Snider, P.D., 10:12, 16
Snidman, N., 5:18
Snigel, J., 5:225
Snyder, D.K., 6:194, 213
Snyder, M., 10:26, 34
Sobell, L.C., 7:107, 127, 227, 235, 240
Sobell, M.B., 7:107, 127, 227, 235, 240
Socrates, 6:100, 10:19
Sode, S., 7:74, 85
Sollberger, J., 8:163, 173
Solnit, A., 8:177, 194
Soloff, P.H., 1:124, 134
Solomon, D.H., 8:206, 223
Solomon, M., 2:259, 264
Solomon, R.L., 7:174, 189
Solomon, S., 8:37, 52
Solomon, Z., 4:42, 51
Sonnenberg, S., 1:2, 13, 28
Sonnenstuhl, W.J., 8:15, 20, 39, 42, 44, 52,
    53
Sonnesshein-Schneider, M., 6:41, 54
Sotsky, S.M., 3:119, 126, 219
Soubrie, P., 8:131, 137
Souheaver, H.G., 10:62, 70
Soyka, M., 6:242, 266
Spanier, G., 6:4, 25
Spanier, G.B., 6:226, 238
Spar, J.E., 3:154, 175
Spark, G., 6:75, 93, 96
Sparr, L.F., 7:203, 212

Spaulding, W.D., 7:248, 257
Speed, N., 1:14, 25, 28
Spence, D.P., 2:18, 20, 21, 26, 31
Spence, M.A., 1:175, 179, 189
Spencer, E.D., 1:106, 115
Spencer, G.E., 8:9, 49
Spencer, J.H., 3:209, 215, 220, 221
Sperlich, P.W., 10:149, 159
Spiegel, D., 1:78, 95, 4:119, 130
Spiegel, R., 7:38, 46
Spielberger, S., 5:7, 21
Spinal-Robinson, P., 5:35, 39
Spinoza, B.D., 1:3
Spinweber, C.L., 4:13, 25
Spirito, A., 5:158, 169
Spiro, A. III, 3:148, 171
Spiro, K., 1:2, 27
Spitz, H.I., 7:181, 184, 189
Spitz, R., 3:4, 13
Spitz, S.T., 7:181, 184, 189
Spitzer, R.J., 1:8, 28
Spitzer, R.L., 3:155, 172, 7:12, 23, 96, 98
Sporakowski, M.J., 6:37, 53
Sprafkin, J.N., 3:150, 159, 173
Sprafkin, R.P., 5:67, 74, 76, 205, 223
Sprague, R.L., 5:54, 77
Sprenkle, D.H., 2:144, 163, 7:116, 127
Springer, C.J., 3:35, 41, 44, 46
Springer, E., 8:226, 227, 229, 244
Stabenau, J.R., 8:68, 88
Stacy, A., 8:163, 172
Stadler, H.A., 10:54, 56
Stall, R., 8:227, 230, 244
Stambul, H.B., 7:216, 236
Stanfield, James, 5:33, 38
Stanford, A.G., 8:210, 222
Stangel, W., 4:55, 66
Staniszewski, S., 9:85, 107
Stanley, E.J., 5:256, 274
Stanley, M., 8:131, 135
Stanton, M.D., 4:71, 91, 6:122, 123, 131,
    144, 146
Stapleton, J., 7:214, 238
Starch, R., 8:2, 52
Stark, K., 5:81, 101
Stark, M., 1:240, 265
Stark, M.J., 7:192, 193, 212
Starkstein, S.E., 3:38, 39, 41, 46, 48, 49
Starr, L.B., 3:39, 49
Starvynski, A., 3:119, 126
Stastny, P., 1:247, 263
Steadman, H.J., 1:156, 169, 10:172, 178

Stechler, G., 5:257, 273
Steele, H., 5:63, 74
Steele, M., 5:63, 74
Steele, P.D., 8:15, 47, 52
Stefano, J.J., 4:9, 24
Steffek, B., 4:23
Steffenbarger, R., 8:162, 173
Steffenburg, S., 1:175, 178, 179, 180, 187, 189
Steffert, B., 3:184, 197
Steidl, J.H., 7:228, 238
Stein, D.J., 6:248, 262, 266
Stein, J., 8:228, 243
Stein, L.I., 1:265
Stein, M., 3:32
Stein, N., 5:225
Stein, R.L., 7:91, 99
Steinberg, L., 6:49, 54
Steinberg, M., 1:59, 61, 89, 96
Steiner, K.M., 8:74, 86
Steinglass, P., 6:145, 7:13, 23, 8:8, 52
Steinhauer, P.D., 7:13, 23
Steinhauer, S.R., 4:99, 108
Steinmetz, J., 3:157, 172
Steinmetz-Breckenridge, J., 2:198, 213
Steketee, G.S., 1:41, 42, 47
Steltz-Lenarsky, J., 5:253, 273
Stensrud, R., 9:84, 106, 10:62, 71
Stephens, R., 7:217, 240
Steptoe, A., 4:9, 31
Stern, D., 4:103, 107
Stetson, B.A., 4:102, 106
Steuer, J., 3:167, 177
Stevens, A., 9:128, 139
Stevens, H.A., 6:152, 162
Stevenson, J., 5:104, 121
Steventon, G.B., 7:56, 62
Stevie, R.R., 8:37, 47
Stewart, A., 3:201, 221, 222
Stewart, J.W., 3:209, 213, 221, 226, 241, 8:135
Stewart, M., 4:101, 109
Stewart, M.A., 5:47, 51, 76
Stewart, S., 2:48, 61
Stiffman, A., 8:231, 244
Stiglin, L.E., 3:201, 220
Stimmel, B., 7:217, 241
Stirling, K.P., 7:165, 168
Stirtzinger, R., 6:161, 164
Stith, S.M., 9:201, 208
Stiver, I.P., 6:269, 271, 284
Stocker, H., 8:163, 173

Stokes, E.J., 8:220
Stokes, G., 7:164, 169
Stoller, E.P., 6:170, 189
Stone Fish, L., 4:188, 199
Stone, M.H., 4:120, 121, 124, 130
Stone, R., 6:170, 189
Stone, S., 2:49, 61
Stone-Washton, N., 8:155
Storr, A., 3:184, 198
Stott, D.H., 5:47, 77
Stout, R., 7:99
Stowell, R.J.A., 5:230, 248
Strachan, A., 1:246, 265
Strain, J., 8:221
Strauss, A.L., 6:172, 189
Strauss, C.C., 5:4, 8, 9, 19, 21
Strauss, J.S., 1:253, 261, 263
Strauss, M.A., 6:8, 25
Straussner, L.A., 8:24, 52
Stricker, G., 2:128, 140
Strober, M., 5:156, 159, 160, 164, 165, 172, 173
Stroebel, C., 4:19, 26
Stroebel, C.F., 4:17, 25, 7:227, 237
Strong, P., 4:17, 25
Strong, S.R., 10:18, 22, 34
Strupp, H.H., 2:86, 87, 88, 91, 92, 93, 97, 5:149
Stude, E.W., 8:61, 63, 64, 65, 66, 90
Stumphauzer, J., 5:226
Sturgeon, D.A., 1:247, 263
Subby, R., 4:75, 91
Suczek, B., 6:189
Sue, D., 9:200, 203, 208, 10:237, 244, 245, 248
Sue, D.W., 9:178, 186, 190, 196, 200, 203, 204, 208, 10:237, 248
Suinn, R.M., 4:15, 31
Sulik, L., 5:158, 173
Sullivan, H.S., 2:101, 144
Sullivan, M.E., 7:248, 249, 257
Sullivan, S., 5:46, 73
Suls, J.M., 4:23
Sumerel, M.B., 10:191, 194
Summerlin, M.L., 4:16, 22
Summers, K.J., 6:5, 19, 25
Summit, R.C., 4:124, 130
Sundberg, N.D., 9:216, 230
Sunderlin,, 8:166
Super, D.E., 9:12, 16
Supnick, J.A., 7:218, 237
Surrey, J., 6:277, 279, 283
Surrey, J.L., 6:269, 284

Susser, M., 6:163
Sutcliffe, J.P., 1:96
Svanum, S., 8:9, 52
Svedlund, J., 4:10, 32
Svendsen, P., 1:180, 187
Svikis, D., 7:228, 237
Svikis, D.S., 4:101, 109
Swain, M.A., 6:203, 217
Swanson, J.L., 9:178, 208
Swanson, J.M., 5:58, 77
Swartz, M., 1:124, 134
Swartzentruber, D., 7:180, 187
Swartzman, L., 4:9, 28
Sweeney, D.R., 8:129, 134
Sweeney, J., 3:279
Swenson, E., 2:134, 140
Swift, R.M., 7:75, 85
Sylvester, C.E., 5:4, 16, 20
Syvakic, D.M., 8:256, 267
Szalai, J., 5:171
Szapocnik, J., 9:212, 230
Szarek, B.L., 4:17, 25
Szasz, T., 8:178, 196
Szklo, M., 3:122, 125
Szymanski, E.M., 9:110, 112, 113, 117, 119,
    120, 122, 124, 125, 126

T

Tabachnick, B.G., 10:4, 15
Tabachnick, N., 3:185, 198
Tabachnik, B.G., 10:4, 15, 80, 95, 196, 208
Taber, J.I., 1:158, 162, 165, 167, 169
Tabrizi, M.A, 7:12, 23
Takacs, D., 5:83, 98
Takahashi, S., 8:131, 137
Talbott, M.M., 3:158, 177
Talbott, R.E., 1:254, 262
Talwar, N., 4:123, 129
Tamaklo, W., 3:44, 49
Tamerin, J.S., 8:250, 267
Tani, K., 8:131, 137
Target, M., 5:63, 74
Tarrier, N., 1:247, 265, 6:256, 266
Tarter, R.E., 4:99, 100, 108, 110, 5:230, 244,
    247, 248, 7:5, 9, 10, 18, 22, 23,
    24, 225, 241, 8:196
Tarvydas, V., 10:58, 65, 73
Tasto, D., 4:8, 24
Tatsuno, Y., 4:109
Taube, C.A., 2:194, 210, 213, 7:244, 257

Tavris, C., 4:167, 175
Taylor, A., 7:248, 257
Taylor, A.E., 4:23
Taylor, C., 3:44, 49
Taylor, C.B., 3:154, 177
Taylor, C.M., 6:61, 70
Taylor, K.L., 1:26
Taylor, M., 1:2, 28
Taylor, R.E., 2:141
Taylor, W.S., 1:50, 55, 96
Teague, G.B., 8:285, 286
Teare, M., 5:85, 88, 99
Teasdale, G., 9:144, 158
Teasdale, J.D., 3:233, 234, 238
Teasdale, T.W., 4:96, 109
Teders, S.J., 4:22, 23
Teevan, R.C., 4:22
Teismann, M.W., 6:256, 266
Teitelbaum, M., 6:109, 114
Telch, M.J., 4:14, 29
Telligen, A., 7:11, 24
Temkin, T., 7:246, 257
Temoshok, L., 4:68
Terestman, N., 5:46, 77
Teri, L., 2:194, 213, 3:149, 153, 167, 177
Teschendorf, R., 10:76, 95
Test, M.A., 1:265
Thacker, W., 7:246, 248, 249, 258
Thapar, A., 6:152, 164
Thapar, A.K., 6:152, 164
Thase, M.E., 3:142, 145, 219, 226, 233, 234,
    239, 241, 8:133, 134
Theimann, S., 10:196, 208
Thelen, M.H., 5:225
Thigpen, C.H., 1:67, 96
Thoenness, N., 6:38, 54
Thomas, A., 5:46, 72, 77
Thomas, C.W., 10:152, 159
Thomas, D., 9:146, 151, 158
Thomas, E.J., 7:104, 127
Thomas, F., 6:110, 114
Thomas, F.N., 6:115
Thomas, J.C., 7:16, 24, 217, 241
Thomas, J.C., 8:37, 42, 52
Thomas, M.B., 2:144, 148, 163
Thomas, R.E., 10:79, 95
Thomas, S.W., 9:55, 57, 59, 238, 243, 245,
    248
Thomas-Knight, R., 8:210, 223
Thomason, T.C., 9:187, 208
Thompson, A., 4:135, 136, 140, 151
Thompson, C., 2:10, 10:236, 246

Thompson, J.K., 4:11, 32
Thompson, L., 2:198, 213
Thompson, L.W., 3:140, 141, 144, 146, 148,
    156, 157, 168, 169, 172, 173,
    175, 177
Thompson, W.D., 3:206, 222
Thomsen, C.J., 10:26, 34
Thomson, J.B., 4:96, 109
Thoren, P., 8:131, 132
Thoreson, R.W., 10:11, 16
Thornby, J.I., 7:169
Thorndike, R.L., 9:216, 231
Thorson, J.A., 6:171, 189
Thrope, J.C., 5:280, 290
Tibbetts, V., 4:9, 32
Tiebout, H.M., 8:253, 257, 258, 260, 267
Tietz, N., 7:53, 62
Tiffany, S.T., 7:218, 236
Tilkin, J.M., 3:219
Tingelstad, J., 5:165, 173
Tinsley, H.E.A., 9:179, 208
Tinson, O., 3:35, 46
Tishler, C.L., 5:255, 272, 274
Tizard, J., 5:2, 21
Tobachnick, B.G., 2:123, 140
Tobena, A., 7:180, 189
Tobin, D.L., 4:12, 32
Tobler, N.S., 8:163, 173
Todak, G., 5:100
Todd, E., 4:261
Todd, T., 7:188
Todd, T.C., 4:71, 91, 6:103, 112, 115, 121,
    122, 123, 146
Tognoni, G., 7:167
Tolson, R.L., 8:201, 208, 214, 220, 222
Toman, W., 2:159, 163
Tomm, K., 10:186, 187, 194
Toneatto, T., 7:227, 235, 240
Tongue, R., 5:83, 101
Tooman, M.L., 9:90, 107
Torem, M., 1:87
Torkelson, N., 4:116, 131
Torras de Bea, E., 2:239, 246
Torres, D., 5:172
Torrey, E.F., 10:174, 179
Toth, R.F., 8:208, 214, 222
Toussieng, P.W., 5:104, 123
Townsend, A.L., 6:172, 189
Trachtenberg, M.C., 7:226, 241
Trainor, C.M., 4:116, 130
Traskman, L., 8:131, 132, 137
Trautman, P., 5:254, 273

Treaster, J., 8:230, 244
Tremaine, L., 7:246, 248, 249, 258
Trepper, T.S., 7:116, 120, 127
Trestman, R., 3:32
Tricamo, E., 3:221
Trice, H.M., 8:3, 12, 15, 34, 35, 39, 45, 53
Trickett, P.K., 1:60, 94
Trimble, J.E., 9:187, 206
Trotzer, J.P., 2:130, 141
Troughton, E., 4:98, 106
Trower, P., 5:14, 21
Truax, C.B., 5:132, 151, 10:18, 22, 34
Trudeau, K., 8:273, 287
Trudel, G., 6:220, 221, 225, 226, 228, 229,
    233, 238, 239
True, R.H., 10:15
Trueba, H.T., 9:220, 227
Truitt, R.B., 8:177, 194
Tsai, J., 7:142, 150
Tsai, L.Y., 1:179, 186
Tschler, G.L., 8:248, 264
Tse, C.K., 3:201, 218
Tsiu, P., 10:237, 248
Tsuang, M.T., 1:37, 47
Tuma, J.M., 5:93, 101
Tuomey, J., 5:172
Turgeon, L., 6:228, 239
Turk, D.C., 4:12, 32, 7:192, 193, 195, 199,
    203, 207, 211
Turkington, C., 6:151, 164
Turner, A., 9:181, 208
Turner, C., 6:120, 146
Turner, H., 2:201, 211
Turner, J.A., 8:201, 208, 214, 220, 222
Turner, P.E., 4:4, 32
Turner, S.M., 5:5, 21
Turner, V., 6:101, 116
Twemlow, S.W., 2:234, 246, 10:201, 203,
    209
Tyano, S., 5:254, 269
Tyler, J.M., 10:80, 94
Tymchuk, A.J., 2:123, 126, 141
Tyndel, M., 1:155, 169
Tyrala, E.A., 7:154, 169
Tyrer, P., 3:233, 234, 241
Tyrrell, B., 4:253, 260
Tyson, S., 1:50, 76, 90

U

Udvari-Solner, A., 9:111, 116, 117, 125, 126
Uhde, T.W., 5:14, 18, 7:160, 167

Uhlenhuth, E.H., 4:202, 216, 8:256, 264
Ullman, R.K., 5:54, 77
Ulrich, R.F., 8:133, 134
Uomoto, J., 9:147, 158
Uomoto, J.M., 3:153, 167, 177
Upchurch, D.W., 10:76, 81, 83, 85, 95
Ursano, R., 1:2, 7, 14, 28

V

Vaccaro, J.V., 1:263
Vaillant, G., 4:35, 36, 51
Vaillant, G.E., 6:121, 122, 146, 7:234, 241,
        8:216, 223, 256, 267
Valencia, R.R., 9:215, 231
Valley, M.M., 10:244, 247
Valzelli, L., 1:43, 47
van Benschoten, S., 1:50, 88
van der Hart, O., 1:50, 96
van der Kolk, B.A., 1:95, 133
Van Hessel, J.H., 4:18, 32
Van Hoose, W.H., 10:65, 73
van Pragg, H.M., 5:254, 272
Van Putten, T., 1:241, 265
van Ryn, M., 3:202, 218
VandeCreek, L., 2:133, 139, 10:31, 33, 125,
        196, 209
Vandergoot, D., 9:85, 87, 95, 107
Vandeusen, J., 4:103, 107
Vanier, C., 8:135
vanPraag, H.M., 1:231
Varley, W.H., 5:226
Varner, R., 2:200, 213
Vasquez, M.J.T., 10:5, 15, 42, 43, 56, 185,
        194, 196, 209
Vasquez-Nuttall, E., 10:248
Vaughan, V.C., 8:108, 114
Vaughn, B., 10:60, 73
Vauhkonen, K., 6:244, 266
Vaux, A., 5:48, 78
Velasquez, J.M., 4:103, 106
Velasquez, R.J., 9:217, 231
Veltkamp, L.J., 1:2, 27, 28
Veltman, G.C., 9:181, 194, 205
Verebey, K., 3:96, 112, 7:150
Verhoeven, W.M.A., 4:70, 88
Veronen, L., 1:26
Versani, M., 3:266, 280
Verwoerdt, A., 2:200, 213
Vestergaard, K., 3:42, 46
Vetter, H., 4:54, 55, 57, 67
Vetter, V.A., 2:126, 131, 140, 10:2, 15

Victor, B., 7:163, 168
Victor, G., 1:96
Victor, M., 3:34, 46
Villeponteaux, L., 1:26
Vinokur, A.D., 3:202, 218
Violato, C., 9:216, 231
Violette, K., 9:128, 139
Visher, E.B., 6:74, 94, 98
Visher, J.S., 6:74, 94, 98
Visintainer, P., 3:149, 176
Vitiello, B., 5:75
Voeller, K.K., 5:51, 75
Volberg, R.A., 1:156, 169
Volcher, A., 6:242, 266
Volk, R.J., 7:116, 127
Volpicelli, J.R., 7:68, 69, 74, 75, 84, 85, 99,
        8:130, 137
Von Hirsch, A., 10:173, 179
Vorters, D.F., 5:255, 273
Voss, C.B., 3:279
Vrana, S., 3:158, 176
Vriend, J., 9:33

W

Waals, V., 7:56, 62
Wachisen, B.A., 3:164, 174
Wachter, O., 5:33, 39
Wacker, D.P., 9:111, 124
Waddell, D., 4:9, 30
Wade, D.T., 3:35, 49
Wadsworth, B.J., 4:181, 200
Wager, S., 3:221
Wagner, A., 3:149, 177
Wagner, G., 6:193, 217
Wagner, J.D., 5:81, 82, 83, 84, 86, 91, 93,
        101
Wagner, R., 8:191, 196
Wagner, R.K., 5:56, 71
Wagner, W.G., 4:144, 150
Wagstaff, A.K., 2:23, 31
Wahlstrom, J., 1:185
Waite, D.S., 3:44, 48
Wakeling, A., 3:53, 64
Waldinger, R.J., 1:131, 134
Waldo, M.C., 3:209, 219
Walen, S.R., 4:173, 175
Walitzer, K.S., 4:102, 110
Walker, E.A., 4:116, 131
Walker, G., 6:132, 146
Walker, J.I., 1:19, 28
Walker, L., 6:97

Walker, M., 5:249
Walker, R.D., 7:193, 212, 225, 226, 239, 241
Wallace, B.C., 7:173, 175, 176, 184, 189, 217, 241
Wallace, C.J., 1:248, 249, 252, 263, 265
Wallace, D.H., 6:198, 217
Wallace, J., 7:241
Wallace, K.M., 6:3, 24, 226, 237
Wallach, M.A., 8:248, 254, 263
Wallerstein, J., 6:36, 37, 51, 55
Wallerstein, J.S., 6:78, 98
Wallerstein, R., 2:253, 259, 264
Walsh, B.T., 3:53, 64, 5:173
Walsh, D.C., 7:89, 100, 217, 241, 8:258, 259, 267
Walsh, E.M., 7:42, 46
Walsh, F., 1:123, 134
Walsh, J., 8:16, 53
Walsh, J.I., 3:266, 280
Walster, G.W., 6:174, 187
Walters, L.R., 8:187, 194
Waltz, M., 4:55, 66
Wanberg, K., 7:10, 24
Wang, J., 9:179, 204
Wang, M.H., 8:70, 88
Wapnick, K., 4:261
Ward, B., 5:171
Ward, C., 3:86, 92, 157, 171
Ward, C.H., 3:204, 218
Ward, D.E., 2:123, 138, 141
Ward, M.F., 7:204, 212
Ward-Ross, L.E., 9:234, 248
Ware, J., 3:205, 221, 222
Ware, J.E., 3:221
Waring, E.M., 3:233, 234, 241, 6:199, 203, 218
Waring, R.H., 7:56, 62
Warkentin, J., 6:202, 205, 218
Warlow, C., 3:41, 47
Warlow, K., 3:35, 47
Warner, R.W., Jr., 8:37, 47
Warner, V., 5:159, 173
Warren, G., 9:154, 158
Wartman, S.A., 7:195, 212
Washton, A., 8:155
Washton, A.M., 7:177, 189, 222, 242
Wasserman, E., 4:8, 29
Waterhouse, L., 1:174, 186
Waterman, A.S., 4:222, 237
Waterman, J., 5:35, 37
Waters, W.F., 3:159, 177
Watkins, C.E., Jr., 9:215, 231

Watkins, D., 2:49, 60, 61
Watkins, H.H., 1:68, 96
Watkins, J.G., 1:68, 96
Watkins, J.T., 3:139, 140, 145, 219
Watson, N.T., 7:75, 85
Watson, S.J., 3:266, 277
Watts, F.N., 2:18, 22, 27, 31
Watzlawick, P., 3:44, 49, 6:198, 218
Watzlawick, Paul, 2:66, 70, 73, 78, 145, 154, 155, 164
Waxman, H.M., 2:194, 213
Weakland, J., 2:66, 70, 73, 78, 145, 149, 155, 161, 162, 163, 202, 211, 6:198, 218
Weakland, R., 3:219
Wear, S., 10:164, 179
Weary, G., 10:26, 33
Weathers, P., 1:12, 24
Weaver, G.M., 1:95
Webb, C., 5:29, 34, 35, 37, 38, 39
Webb, D.O., 8:46
Weber, J., 2:259, 264
Webster, I., 1:210
Wechsler, D., 9:42, 60, 147, 159
Weddington, W.W., 7:174, 177, 184, 189
Weed, R.O., 9:150, 159
Weekes, C., 1:109, 110, 116
Weghorst, S.J., 6:252, 264
Wegscheider, S., 4:77, 91
Wegscheider-Cruse, S., 4:75, 84, 91
Wehman, P., 9:112, 126, 151, 157
Weiler, S.M., 6:192, 217, 221
Weinbaum, D.F., 7:203, 211
Weinberg, S.K., 4:115, 131
Weinberger, A., 4:181, 200
Weinberger, L.E., 2:133, 139
Weiner, C.L., 6:189
Weiner, I.B., 10:108
Weiner-Davis, M., 6:269, 284
Weinhold, C., 5:157, 170
Weinrach, S.G., 10:87, 95
Weins, A.N., 8:202, 223
Weintraub, B.D., 5:75
Weishaar, M.E., 3:166, 171
Weiss, A., 5:123
Weiss, C., 8:238, 244
Weiss, D., 1:8, 25
Weiss, G., 5:48, 49, 78
Weiss, J., 2:54, 55, 61, 88, 97
Weiss, M.E., 3:141, 145
Weiss, R.L., 6:5, 19, 25
Weissman, M., 3:206, 221

Weissman, M.M., 3:201, 202, 206, 209, 213,
   221, 222, 228, 231, 234, 241,
   4:70, 91, 5:5, 19, 156, 159, 167,
   169, 171, 173, 8:248, 264
Weissman, M.W., 3:114, 125
Weissmann, M.M., 3:149, 177
Weisz, G., 6:199, 218
Weitzman, L.J., 6:55
Welch, B., 7:79, 84
Welfel, E., 10:58, 73
Welfel, E.R., 9:23, 26, 27, 33
Weller, E.B., 5:85, 88, 99
Weller, R.A., 5:85, 88, 99
Wellner, Z., 7:12, 24
Wells, E., 8:162, 172
Wells, E.A., 7:173, 181, 189
Wells, K., 3:203, 205, 221, 222
Wender, L., 2:101
Wender, P.H., 5:42, 78
Wenig, P., 4:7, 25
Werner, E., 4:104, 110
Werner, E.E., 5:63, 78
Werry, J.S., 5:11, 21
Wesley, G., 10:168, 178
Wesolowski, M.D., 8:56, 87
Wessler, R.A., 4:173, 175
Wessler, R.L., 4:173, 175
West, D.J., 3:124, 126
West, L.J., 3:116, 120, 126, 8:8, 53, 206,
   223
West, M.O., 4:95, 102, 111
Westen, D., 4:119, 131
Westenberg, H.G.M., 4:70, 88
Westerlund, E., 4:134, 151
Westermeyer, J., 7:228, 242
Weston, D., 1:123, 134
Wetzel, R., 5:256, 272
Wetzel, R.D., 3:141, 145, 209, 220, 8:125,
   135
Wexler, H.K., 8:74, 90
Wexler, M., 2:81, 94
Whalen, C.K., 5:48, 56, 78
Wharff, E.A., 7:245, 256
Wheeler, E.G., 7:115, 125
Whelihan, W., 2:196, 212, 7:75, 85
Whiston, S.C., 10:79, 84, 85, 95
Whitaker, A., 5:157, 173
Whitaker, C., 2:147, 161, 164, 6:202, 205,
   218
Whitaker, D.S., 2:115, 120
Whitby, O., 7:162, 168
White, G.L., 6:243, 257, 266

Whitehead, C., 8:256, 267
Whitehead, W.E., 4:10, 32
Whiteman, M., 4:103, 106
Whiteside, L., 5:183, 188
Whitfield, C.L., 4:74, 91, 200
Whitman, B.Y., 8:120, 135
Whitmore, K., 5:2, 21
Whittinghill, J.R., 5:252, 253, 254, 273
Whorwell, P.J., 4:10, 32
Whybrow, P.C., 3:13
Wickman, R.E., 5:35, 39
Wickramaratne, P., 5:156, 159, 169, 171,
   173
Wicks, J., 6:163
Wienckowski, L.A., 7:245, 246, 258
Wiese, D., 4:116, 131
Wiesenthal, S., 4:261
Wiethholtz, H., 7:53, 62
Wigfield, A., 6:114
Wilbur, C.B., 1:73, 74, 78, 96
Wilbur, C.W., 1:51, 74, 75, 96
Wilcoxin, L., 4:15, 27
Wilder-Padilla, S., 8:9, 45
Wile, D.B., 6:202, 203, 218
Wiley, J., 8:227, 230, 244
Wilkes, T.C.R., 3:142, 146
Wilkins, J., 8:287
Wilkinson, S.M., 1:127, 129, 133
Willette, J., 9:211, 226
Williams, A.C., 7:56, 62
Williams, C.D., 3:148, 149, 171
Williams, D.M., 4:6, 27, 9:234, 249
Williams, G.T., 10:40, 55
Williams, J.B.W., 1:8, 28, 7:12, 23
Williams, M., 8:199, 207, 212, 213, 223
Williams, M.B., 4:134, 151
Williams, R., 3:88, 92
Williams, R.J., 4:210, 216
Williams, R.L., 7:169
Williams, S., 5:4, 17, 20, 50, 76, 171
Williams, T.A., 3:157, 176
Williams, V., 3:88, 92
Williamson, D., 6:17, 26
Williamson, D.A., 3:159, 177
Williamson, G.M., 3:149, 176
Willis, E.A., 6:193, 217
Wilner, R.S., 6:258, 264
Wilson, C., 10:58, 60, 64, 65, 72, 73
Wilson, D.G., 8:164, 172
Wilson, F.R., 2:141
Wilson, G.T., 8:87
Wilson, J., 1:2, 13, 14, 25, 28

Wilson, J.P., 8:9, 50
Wilson, J.Q., 5:104, 121, 206, 223
Wilson, L.L., 9:201, 208
Wilson, M., 6:252, 264
Wilson, P.H., 3:140, 146, 7:234, 242
Wilson, Reid R., 1:109, 116
Wing, L., 1:173, 174, 178, 179, 189
Winkelman, A., 4:23
Winkler, H.H., 8:12, 51
Winkler, K.J., 9:211, 231
Winnicott, D.W., 6:151, 164
Winokur, G., 4:98, 101, 107
Winsten, N., 4:100, 108
Winston, A., 2:91, 96
Winston, M.E., 10:218, 233
Winterberg, T.S., 5:104, 121
Winters, K.C., 5:230, 243, 248
Wise, P.S., 10:79, 95
Wisniewski, J.J., 5:86, 102
Witcher, W.C., 6:61, 69
Wittchen, H.U., 5:18
Wittrock, D.A., 4:5, 32
Wodarski, John S., 7:181, 182, 189
Wodarski, J.S., 6:7, 24, 9:211, 231
Wolberg, L., 2:87, 97
Wolberg, L.P., 10:77, 95
Wolf, A., 2:113, 120
Wolf, B., 9:192, 205
Wolf, K., 3:4, 13
Wolf, M.M., 5:142, 150
Wolfe, D., 5:35, 39
Wolfe, J., 1:12, 15, 25, 26
Wolfe, T., 4:244, 260
Wolfe, V.V., 5:35, 39
Wolff, E.A., 7:160, 167
Wolff, S., 1:174, 189
Wolfson, D., 9:147, 158
Wolin, S., 4:71, 91, 6:109, 114, 7:13, 23,
    8:145, 154
Wolin, S.J., 4:71, 91, 104, 105, 5:236, 246,
    8:8, 52, 145, 154
Wolkstein, E., 8:84, 89
Wollert, R., 1:240, 265
Wolpe, J., 4:15, 32, 5:138, 151
Wolpert, R.L., 5:267, 270
Wong, H., 10:58, 59, 65, 72, 73
Wong, N., 2:113, 114, 120
Wood, J.I., 1:76, 95
Wood, K.H., 3:53, 64
Wood, P., 4:102, 110
Wood, R., 5:226
Woodside, M., 4:94, 111

Woodson, P.P., 7:164, 168
Woody, G., 7:10, 23
Woody, G.A., 8:274, 286
Woody, G.E., 7:93, 96, 99, 227, 239
Woody, R.H., 10:125
Woolfolk, R.L., 4:3, 4, 5, 6, 7, 11, 12, 13, 15,
    16, 17, 28
Worchel, P., 9:128, 139
Worden, M., 5:229, 248
Work, H.H., 5:104, 123
Work, W.C., 4:104, 107
Worthington, E., 4:252, 260
Wozney, K., 1:51, 95
Wray, I., 1:155, 169
Wrenn, C.G., 10:238, 248
Wrich, J.T., 8:15, 17, 53
Wright, C., 7:67, 85
Wright, F.D., 7:231, 236
Wright, J., 6:230, 239
Wright, J.H., 3:142, 145
Wright, S., 6:262, 266
Wright, T., 10:58, 71
Wright, T.J., 9:178, 179, 182, 195, 204, 208
Wunder, J., 5:18
Wyatt, G.E., 4:134, 145, 146, 151
Wynne, L., 2:147, 154, 155, 164
Wyshak, G., 1:11, 27

Y

Yahraes, H., 6:52, 54
Yalom, I., 5:182, 183, 189
Yalom, I.D., 2:103, 109, 115, 120, 123, 141,
    3:74, 92
Yamaguchi, K., 8:162, 174
Yamane, H.K., 8:131, 137
Yanico, B.J., 8:43, 48
Yank, G.R., 7:244, 247, 254, 258
Yankrick, R., 8:23, 53
Yanow, M., 5:49, 78
Yarkony, G.M., 8:56, 80, 90
Yesavage, J.A., 3:158, 172, 177, 6:180, 189
Yeung-Courchesne, B.A., 1:178, 185
Yochelson, S., 1:138, 141, 142, 143, 144,
    151
Yoshida, M., 7:141, 149
Young, D., 5:253, 273
Young, D.W., 8:36, 51
Young, G.A., 4:28
Young, J., 9:85, 88, 107
Young, J.E., 4:181, 183, 200
Young, J.F., 7:167

Youngren, M.A., 3:166, 175
Yule, W., 5:157, 172

Z

Zaccardi, R., 6:152, 164
Zahn, T.P., 7:156, 169
Zahner, G.E.P., 7:245, 258
Zamble, E., 4:10, 29
Zametkin, A.J., 5:52, 75, 78
Zanarini, M.C., 1:123, 135
Zane, M.D., 1:110, 116
Zapata, A., 7:189
Zarit, J.M., 6:173, 190
Zarit, S., 2:200, 213
Zarit, S.H., 3:69, 76, 92, 153, 178, 6:172,
        173, 180, 189, 190
Zarkin, G.A., 8:47
Zasler, N.D., 7:44, 46
Zecker, S.G., 5:43, 73
Zeidner, M., 9:213, 219, 231
Zeiss, A.M., 3:166, 175
Zeitlin, H., 5:4, 21
Zelenak, J., 5:270
Zelinski, E., 3:157, 175
Zenk, R., 9:196, 207
Zentall, S.S., 5:48, 63, 78

Zetzel, E.R., 1:120, 135
Zhao, S., 5:18
Ziedonis, D.M., 8:270, 272, 273, 274, 277,
        278, 285, 287
Zilbergeld, B., 6:192, 193, 194, 218
Zimberg, S., 8:207, 208, 210, 213, 216, 224
Zimmer, L., 8:74, 89
Zimmerman, D., 5:219, 225
Zimmerman, J.P., 6:149, 164
Zimmerman, M.A., 1:155, 169, 7:245, 246,
        258
Zimmerman, R.R., 6:202, 215
Zinman, S., 1:239, 265
Ziskin, J., 10:108
Zisook, S., 3:149, 176, 209, 219
Zitrin, C.M., 5:10, 21
Zohar, J., 1:42, 43, 47, 48
Zubin, J., 4:99, 108
Zucker, K., 5:36
Zuckerman, M., 4:99, 111
Zukas, H., 9:65, 77
Zung, W.W.K., 3:157, 178
Zweben, A., 7:196, 199, 211, 8:276, 286
Zweben, J.E., 7:212
Zweig-Frank, H., 1:124, 134, 135
Zwerling, C., 8:10, 12, 53
Zwick, W.R., 7:239

Subject Index

A

A "Bill of Rights" for Supervisees (*table*),
    10:88
AA
    See Alcoholics Anonymous (AA)
Abandonment, 1:122
    of client, a type of negligence, 10:112–
        113
    fear of, 5:113
    type of relationship wound, 4:182
Abbreviations for Prescription
        Instructions (*table*), 7:33
ABC framework
    A stands for activating event, 4:156
    B stands for beliefs, 4:156
        irrational Belief (iB), 4:156, 157,
            158, 160, 162, 163, 164, 168,
            170, 171, 172, 173
        rational Belief (rB), 4:156, 157, 160,
            163, 164, 171, 172, 173
    C stands for consequences, 4:157
    cornerstone of rational-emotive
        therapy (RET) practice, 4:156
Abilities, identification of, 9:73–74
Abilities tests, 6:23
Abreaction, reexperiencing the wounging
        process, 4:188
Absenteeism, 3:203
    on-the-job, 8:13
    substance abusing employees and,
        8:12, 57
Absolute and Relative Problem Density
        Profiles of a 17-Year Old
        Woman (*figure*), 7:8
Absorption, of medications, 7:28–29
Abstinence, 8:253
    based model of treatment, 8:257–259
    from alcohol, rates of, 7:74
    from cocaine, rates of, 7:177
    from gambling, 1:166
Abuse
    See also Physical abuse; Sexual abuse;
        Verbal abuse

adult, 10:2
    cause for breach of
        confidentiality, 10:4, 7
    borderline patients with no history of,
        1:130–131
    child, 7:102, 10:2
        cause for breach of
            confidentiality, 10:4, 6–7
    emotional, 4:253
    reducing, 7:104
    reliability of memories of debated,
        1:51
    spouse, 7:102
    type of relationship wound, 4:182
Abuse reminder list, 5:27
Academic
    achievement, 9:149
    freedom, 10:2
    performance
        adopted child syndrome and, 5:107
        effects of Ritalin on, 5:57
        poor is risk factor for suicide,
            5:255
        relationship between childhood
            depression and, 5:83
Academic Performance and ADHD
        Rating Scales, 5:54
Acceptance
    and divorce, 6:39
    as stage of divorce, 4:212
Accessibility, 10:59
    of facilities, 9:52
Accidents, 3:255
    high rates with troubled employee,
        8:14
    industrial, 8:11
    on-the-job, 4:37
    plagued management for years, 8:13
Accommodations
    See Americans with Disabilities Act
        (ADA), reasonable
        accommodation and

Accountability, 10:78
  professional, 10:38, 39
Accreditation, CARF, requirements,
  9:134–135
Acculturation
  defined, 9:188
  inventories of, 9:212
  levels of, 9:188, 196, 211
Accuracy
  of recollections of childhood sexual
    abuse, 4:142, 144
  of recollections of incest, 4:120–121
Acetaldehyde, 7:66
  metabolite of alcohol, 4:96
Acetaldehyde dehydrogenase, 4:96
Acetaminophen (Tylenol), 7:42
Acetylcholine, 3:16
Acid
  See LSD
Ackerman Institute for Family Therapy,
  6:122
ACOAs
  See Adult children of alcoholics
    (ACOAs)
Acquired immunodeficiency syndrome
  See AIDS
ACTH
  See Adrenocorticotropic hormone
    (ACTH)
Acting out, 2:53, 238, 4:36, 5:111, 198,
  200
  by children with AIDS, 6:134
  characterizes adopted child
    syndrome, 5:105, 115
  example of, 6:14, 18
  interpretation of, 5:116
  sexual, 5:29, 33, 10:198
Action, 8:271, 282–283
Activity group training, for GAD, 5:12
Activity scheduling, 5:138, 142–143
Acupuncture, 7:192
  ear, 8:113
Acute stress disorder, 1:101, 5:5
ADA
  See Americans with Disabilities Act
    (ADA)
Adaptation
  in the development of autonomy, 3:2
  impact of stressful life experiences on,
    1:2
  to loss, 3:72, 73

  response, to stress in the workplace,
    4:41–42
  working, 3:8
Adaptational relevance, 3:116
Adaptive ability, 3:67
Adaptive styles, in etiology of depression,
  3:1–12
ADD
  See Attention deficit disorder (ADD)
Addict, label as, 8:66, 67
Addiction, 8:59
  See also Alcohol abuse; Alcoholism;
    Chemical dependence; Drug
    abuse; Stimulant abuse;
    Substance abuse; Tobacco
    abuse
  adolescent, 8:139–154
  alcohol, relapse rates, 7:217
  association between mood and, 8:250
  of caffeine, 7:164
  case study, 8:145–149
  cocaine, 7:133
  cognitive-behavioral treatment of,
    7:171–186
  relapse rates, 7:217
  commonality of, 8:96
  counseling, 8:209
  diagnosis of, 4:83
  elements of, 5:231–232
  etiologies of, 7:173–177
  great teacher of adolescents, 8:150
  has genetic component, 8:142
  heroin, 7:67, 75
    relapse rates, 7:217
  high levels of in children of
    immigrants, 6:122
  interagency collaboration in
    treatment of, 7:243–255
  learning from, 8:149–151
  motivational enhancement in
    treatment of, 7:191–209
  narcissism of, 4:82
  nicotine, relapse rates, 7:217
  overcoming, 4:85
  parental, 8:141–143
  reducing the risk of relapse in, 7:213–
    235
  risk for in co-dependents, 4:80
  severity of and treatment outcome, 7:95
  stigma of, 6:122
  willpower myth and, 7:223

Addiction Severity Index (ASI), 7:10, 93,
    96, 8:274
    (*table*), 7:94
Addictive cycle, 1:163
    for pathological gambler, 1:160–161
Addictive disorders, 3:60
    legal complaints against counselors
        treating, 10:118
    prevalence, 8:246
Addicts, 4:71, 74, 84, 86
    See also Co-dependence
    family members of, 4:73
    former, 6:124
    pathological attachment to is co-
        dependence, 4:87
Addison's Disease, 3:102, 5:162
ADHD
    See Attention-deficit/hyperactivity
        disorder (ADHD)
Adherence, 7:199
    to pharmacologic regimen, 7:31
Adjunctive techniques, to anxiety
        disorder therapy, 1:112–113
Adjustment disorder, 5:5, 253
Adjustment reactions, 4:117
Adolescence
    themes of, 5:184–185
    a western phenomenon, 8:176
Adolescents, 2:103, 108, 118, 3:142, 6:17,
        9:2, 3
    addiction in, 8:139–154, 247
        physical fitness for, 8:159–170
    African-American, 9:178
    aggression replacement training in,
        5:191–222
    as alcohol abusers, 7:120
    and alcoholism treatment
        information, 7:229
    antisocial behavior in, 4:102, 5:48, 49
    anxiety disorders in, 5:1–16
    Asian-American, 9:191
    at risk, 8:160
    with attention-deficit/hyperactivity
        disorder (ADHD), 5:48–49
    Child Behavior Checklist and, 7:11
    with chronic medical problems, 5:187
    "civil rights", 8:177
    date rape and, 5:33
    death of sibling and, 6:151
    definition of a minor, 5:280
    depression in, case study, 5:155

diagnosis and management of
    depression in, 5:153–168
with DID, 1:76
drug use, statistics, 7:133
Drug Use Screening Inventory and,
    7:9
Ecstasy and, 7:141
fears of, 5:3
from alcoholic families, 5:187
from minority groups, 9:178
group therapy for, 5:175–187
Hispanic, 9:178
HIV-positive, 8:232
incarcerated, 5:197–201
interviewing about substance abuse,
    5:237–239
involved in planning postdivorce
    future, 6:41
moral development in, 8:180–181
and peer pressure, 1:139–140
protecting the confidentiality of,
    5:275–290
raised by single fathers, 6:64
rules governing drugs, 8:144
school performance and, 7:14–15
senioritis and, 9:21
sex-for-money, 8:231
and sexual abuse, 4:117
sexuality in stepfamily of, 6:87
sexually abused, 5:187
Socratic view of, 6:100
substance-abusing, 6:99–113
    case study, 8:145–149
    evaluation and treatment of,
        5:227–245
suicidality in, 5:158–159, 251–268
Teen Addiction Severity Index and,
    7:10
themes at this stage of life, 8:161
those at highest risk of HIV, 8:231
threats to, 8:191
treatment of in cases of incest, 4:123
younger, 5:180–181
Adopted child syndrome, 5:103–120
Adoptees Liberty Movement Associates
    (ALMA) (*directory listing*),
    5:124
Adoption
    alcoholism and, 5:230
    periodicals
        Adoptalk, 5:126

Adopted Child, 5:126
Adoption Therapist, 5:126
Adoptive Families, 5:127
AdoptNet Magazine, 5:126
*American Journal of Adoption
    Reform*, 5:126
Chain of Life, 5:127
CUB Communicator, 5:127
Decree, The, 5:127
Geborener Deutscher, 5:127
People Searching News, 5:127
Roots and Wings, 5:127
resource directory, 5:124–127
Adoptions
    anonymity in encourages denial of
        feelings, 5:120
    chosen child story, 5:109
    closed, 5:104
    open, 5:104
Adoptive Families of America (*directory
    listing*), 5:124
Adoptive Parents Committee, The
    (*directory listing*), 5:124
Adoptive Parents for Open Records
    (*directory listing*), 5:125
Adrenal gland dysfunctions, 3:245
Adrenocorticotropic hormone (ACTH),
    3:16, 22, 25, 99
Adult Basic Learning Examination, 9:149
Adult Children of Alcoholics (ACOAs),
    8:9, 153 (*directory listing*), 4:86,
    8:156
Adult separation anxiety
    See Agoraphobia
Adult status, progression to, 3:192
Adults
    career reappraisal by, 9:12
    with history of ADHD, 5:49
    meaning and, 9:3
    in mid-career, 9:14
    older
        See Elderly
    panic disorder in, 5:15
    victimized as children, 5:24
    who were adoptees, 5:104, 119
Advertising, 9:104
Advil (ibuprofen), 7:42
Advocacy, 1:240, 9:202–203
Aerobic exercise, 4:5, 15, 16
Aesculapius, Greek god of medicine,
    4:82

Affection, 4:35, 38, 6:210–211
    needed for relationship quality, 6:213
    physical, 6:198
Affective disorders, 1:82, 3:98, 7:227,
    8:254–255
Affective illness
    may coexist with DID, 1:63
    OCD and, 1:38–39
Affective spectrum disorders, 3:60
Affirmations, 3:254–255
African Americans, 6:119, 9:179, 191
    adolescents, 9:178
    AIDS and, 6:133
    "Black self", 9:180
    case study of child sexual abuse,
        5:25
    case study of homelessness, 5:94–97
    characteristics, 9:180–182
    comorbid depression and alcoholism
        among, 8:124, 126
    in Crown Heights neighborhood of
        Brooklyn, 5:204
    higher arrest rates for youth, 5:193
    largest ethnic minority group in the
        United States, 9:180
    men, 8:247
        and sexual abuse, 5:34
    substance abuse assessment and, 8:72
    women, 8:113, 247
        drug choice in, 8:100
        drug use in, 8:98
Aftercare
    encouraged after formal treatment is
        ended, 8:141
    planning, 8:209
Age
    changes, 3:67
    differences, 3:67
Aged
    See Elderly
Agencies
    collaboration among in treatment of
        addictions, 7:243–255
    cooperation with other, 10:85
Aggression, 4:37, 79–80, 5:254, 256
    adolescent, psychology of, 5:193–196
    as a basic intrinsic drive, 4:35
    in child, responsible for difficulties,
        1:121
    complex response, 5:222
    defined, 5:192

depression and, 3:124–125
immaturity seen in, 5:195
physical, 5:195
skill deficiency seen in, 5:195
sociology of, 5:193
verbal, 5:195
withdrawal seen in, 5:195
Aggression replacement training (ART)
ethical and legal considerations,
5:221–222
multimodal response, 5:196
rehabilitation for aggressive youth,
5:191–222
research and efficacy, 5:196–210
Aggressive behavior, stress management
techniques for, 4:16
Aggressiveness, 7:11
Aging
three types
biologic, 3:66, 67
psychological, 3:66, 67
social, 3:67
Agitation, 1:82
in patients with DID, 1:62
severe, sign of potential suicide
3:258
Agoraphobia, 1:99, 100, 5:5, 6, 10, 12, 13,
7:35
Agranulocytosis, 7:39
AIDS, 1:4, 3:22, 121, 267, 5:162, 178, 7:132,
139, 172, 8:226, 10:2, 59
See also HIV
case study, 6:136–137, 138–140
client confidentiality and, 10:9–10,
213–214
case studies, 10:221–227
counseling sexually active clients
with, 10:211–231
course of
chronic phase, 6:128–129
crisis phase, 6:127–128
terminal phase, 6:129–130
death from, 8:237
dementia related to, 8:240
disclosure by patient with, 2:133
and discrimination, 6:134
family therapy interventions for,
6:117–144
goal of prevention, 8:229
mental impairment and, 6:129
neonatal, 8:106

and prejudice, 4:247
prevention, 6:143
reporting on, 10:49
seen as death sentence, 6:124
statistics, 10:212
AIDS Situational Distress Model, 8:233
Al-Anon, 4:71, 74, 83, 85, 86, 7:104, 110,
195, 8:29, 76, 141, 143, 145, 153
(*directory listing*), 8:156
Al-Anon Family Group Headquarters
(*directory listing*), 4:86
Alateen, 4:75, 85, 86, 8:76
(*directory listing*), 8:156
Alcohol, 5:15, 232, 241, 6:100, 101, 251,
260, 8:58, 59, 65, 98, 99, 105,
226, 270, 272
adolescents who abuse, ethical issues
in counseling, 8:175–193
alters biotransformation of many
drugs, 7:30
America's number one drug of
choice, 8:6
antipsychotic use and, 7:40
breath test (MOBAT), 7:107, 108
consumption and caffeine, 7:166
damages lining of intestines, 7:54, 56
dependence, features of, 8:122–123
detoxification
ability of liver and, 7:53
improved through nutrition,
7:49–61
effects of, 7:68
seven dwarves, 7:226
intoxication
decreased with naltrexone, 7:74
increased with lithium use, 7:38
most common teratogen, 8:102–104
naltrexone for treatment of
dependence on, 7:63–83
negative effects of with brain injury,
8:80
physical fitness programs reduce use
of, 8:166
reduced intake of can reduce panic
and anxiety, 1:113, 114
relapse rate from addiction to, 7:217
statistics, 8:199
stress dampening effect, 4:100
suppresses appetite, 7:50
use
with anxiolytics, 7:31

with benzodiazepines, 7:10
    discouraged after head injury,
        7:44
    statistics, 7:64
    withdrawal, 7:34, 8:111
Alcohol abuse, 3:58, 94, 96, 101–102, 258,
        4:37, 5:240
    See also Addiction; Alcoholism;
        Drinking; Drug abuse;
        Stimulant abuse; Substance
        abuse; Tobacco abuse
    genetic predisposition theory, 8:78
Alcohol, Drug Abuse, and Mental Health
        Administration, report on
        cost of alcoholism, 8:11
Alcohol metabolism, 4:96
Alcohol use disorders, 8:59, 61
Alcohol Use Inventory, 7:10
Alcoholic gene, 4:100
Alcoholics, 2:57, 108, 3:28, 102, 4:16, 17, 74,
        86, 8:66, 67
    abstinence in, 8:253
    See also Alcohol abuse; Alcoholism
    adult children of, 4:81, 8:9
    Americans with Disabilities Act
        (ADA) of and, 8:7
    children of, 6:109, 7:225, 8:9
    See also Adult children of alcoholics
        (ACOAs)
        adopted, 4:94
        adoption studies, 4:97–98
        caveats about research on, 4:103–
            104
        research findings on, 4:93–105
        resilience in, 4:104–105
        statistics, 4:94
        twin study, 4:96–97
    defined, 8:200
    depressed, 8:120
        clinical course, 8:125–126
        clinical features, 8:123–125
        defined, 8:121
        demographics, 8:126–127
        etiology, 8:130–131
        evaluation of, 8:128–129
        family history, 8:127–128
        future direction, 8:131–132
        stressors, 8:127
        treatment, 8:129–130
    familial, 7:225
    statistics, 8:199

Alcoholics Anonymous (AA), 1:112, 165,
        239, 2:201, 3:98, 4:70–71, 76, 83,
        85, 252, 5:178, 245, 265, 7:64, 79,
        90, 110, 111, 195, 216, 223, 8:29,
        66, 74, 77, 82, 140, 209, 215, 219,
        232, 235, 239, 257, 275, 283
    (directory listing), 8:156
    statistics, 8:262
Alcoholics Anonymous (book), 4:82
Alcoholism, 1:14, 17, 77, 103, 2:151, 200,
        5:230, 6:12, 14, 18, 100, 7:147,
        8:186
    See also Addiction; Alcohol abuse;
        Drinking; Drug abuse;
        Stimulant abuse; Substance
        abuse; Tobacco abuse
    behavioral model of, 8:210–211
    biological correlates, 4:95–100
    biopsychological correlates, 4:95
    case study, 7:107–108
    chronic, 4:97
    comorbidity with major depression,
        8:119–132
    costs of, 8:11
    defined, 8:198
    disease model of, 8:209–210
    early-onset, 8:198, 200–201, 213
    family, 8:201
        affected by, 8:8
    geriatric, 8:197–219
    guilt associated with, 7:74
    hereditary, 7:77
    inpatient and outpatient treatment
        contrasted, 7:87–98
    intermittent, 8:198, 201, 202–203
    late-onset, 8:198, 200, 201–202, 213
    legal trial concerning, 10:103
    lifelong affliction, 7:73
    marital and family therapy in
        treatment of, 7:101–125
    may be traumatic stressor, 1:16
    often comorbid with PTSD, 1:15
    P300 waves and, 7:225
    poor detection of in elderly, 8:206
    prevalence estimates, 4:94–95
    psychological correlates, 4:100–102
    relationship to poor nutrition, 7:50
    risk of relapse with, 7:64
    screening inventories and, 8:42–43
    self-medication diagnosis, 8:250
    social correlates, 4:102–103

and spinal cord injury, 7:32
spouse and, 7:104
statistics, 4:97–98, 8:246, 247
transmission across generations, 7:13
and traumatic brain injury, 7:32
types
type I, 4:98
type II, 4:98
Alcoholism therapists, 2:58
Alcoholism Treatment and Education
    Center (ATEC), 8:218, 219
Alienation, 5:254
of adolescents, 5:168
Alimony, 6:77, 85
maintenance, defined, 6:40
Allergies, 3:16, 18
to food, 3:245
to medications, 7:31
Alliance, therapeutic, 2:166, 187–188, 199
Allodi Trauma Scale, 1:10
Aloofness, countertransference reaction,
    2:236
Alpha-endorphin, 3:24
Alprazolam (Xanax), 5:14, 7:34, 147
and PTSD patients, 1:21
Alters
    See Personalities
Altruism, self-sacrificing, 6:277
Aluminum, poisoning, 3:104
Alzheimer's disease, 3:69, 71, 82, 86, 149,
    159, 160, 6:172, 179
support groups, 2:203, 209
Amantadine (Symmetrel), 7:39, 8:283
Ambivalence, 6:203
alcoholic's, 7:110–111
essential feature of process of change,
    7:201
in intimacy, 6:202
America, graying of, 8:219
American Academy of Child and
    Adolescent Psychiatry
    (AACAP), 4:121, 8:190
has developed guidelines on
    confidentiality, 5:279
American Academy of Pediatrics, mature
    minor doctrine adopted by,
    8:177–178
American Adoption Congress (AAC)
    (*directory listing*), 5:124
American Association of Counseling and
    Development, 2:122

American Association for Marriage and
    Family Therapy (AAMFT),
    2:126, 144
code of ethics, 10:188–189
guidelines for dual relationships,
    10:186
provision for guidelines for
    supervisors, 10:93
American Civil Liberties Union (ACLU),
    Joyce Brown case and, 10:175
American College Test (ACT), 9:212
American College Testing Program, 9:212
American Counseling Association (ACA),
    2:126
Code of Ethics, 10:40, 44, 46, 49, 188,
    189, 213, 236, 242
has developed guidelines on
    confidentiality, 5:279
American Group Psychotherapy
    Association, 2:122
American Handbook of Psychiatry (Arieti),
    4:244
American Personnel and Guidance
    Association, has developed
    guidelines on confidentiality,
    5:279
American Psychiatric Association (APA),
    has developed guidelines on
    confidentiality, 5:279
American Psychological Association
    (APA), 2:122, 123, 125, 126,
    251
founding of, 10:2
has developed guidelines on
    confidentiality, 5:279
must protect clients from harm, 10:8
record keeping guidelines, 10:12
requirements concerning breach of
    confidentiality, 10:4
American Society of Addiction Medicine
    (*directory listing*), 5:230
Americans with Disabilities Act (ADA),
    5:70, 9:84, 89, 98, 128, 138, 156,
    10:61–62
access to equal benefits, 9:51
based assessment process, 9:49
conditions covered under, 9:37
diagnosis of disability and, 9:36
direct threat, 9:54
essential functions and, 9:39, 48, 49
evaluation instruments and, 9:54–56

job analysis and evaluation, 9:50
major life activities and, 9:38, 45–47
    of 1990, 8:7
qualified individual with a disability,
    9:47–48, 50
reasonable accommodation and, 9:39,
    48, 50, 51, 71, 75, 151
    excerpt, 9:53
relevant strengths and limitations
    and, 9:39
reporting, 9:56–57
resources on (*table*), 9:61
substantial limitations and, 9:41–45,
    45–46
Title I, 9:36, 71, 74, 142
vocational assessment and, 9:35–58
working and, 9:45–47
Amino acids
    glutathione, 7:53, 57
    L-cysteine, 7:53, 57
    molybdenum, 7:57
    tyramine, 7:36
Amitriptyline (Elavil), 1:42, 3:272, 7:35, 38,
    10:114
Amnesia, 1:53, 60
    permissive, 1:77
    psycogenic, 8:252
    in traumatic brain injury, 9:144
Amobarbital, 1:65, 66, 77
Amoxapine (Asendin), 3:272, 7:36
Amphetamines, 7:41, 142, 8:58, 59, 61, 65
Amytal (Amobarbital), 1:77
An Algorithm For the Treatment of
    Depression (*figure*), 3:271
Anafranil (clomipramine), 3:272
    and PTSD, 1:21
Analgesics, 7:42–43, 8:205
    opioid, 7:76, 82
Analysis of Depressed Behavior (*table*),
    3:161
Angel dust, 8:61
Anger, 3:9, 4:35, 56, 125, 244, 6:5, 49, 129,
    151, 208–209, 227, 268, 278,
    280
    of adopted child, 5:108, 109, 110
    case study, 4:159–160, 160–161, 161,
        162, 164, 6:45
    conceptualizing problems of, 4:158–
        165
    as consequence of family caregiving,
        6:177
    control, 5:196, 198, 203, 206

    controlling with cognitive training,
        5:69
    a core emotion, 4:191
    counselors should not treat manic
        clients with, 1:226
    criminals and, 1:150
    and death of child, 6:149
    depression's link with, 3:88
    destructive aspects, 4:166
    and divorce, 6:39, 44–46
    from traumatic experience, 1:20
    hurt, 4:158
    management of, 5:264
    objects of
        interpersonal objects/life
            conditions, 4:159, 165
        others, 4:159–164
        self, 4:159, 165
    rational-emotive approach to
        management of, 4:153–174
    self-directed, 4:45
    stress management techniques for,
        4:16, 21
    suppression of, 4:55
    synonyms of, 4:157
Anger Control Training (ACT), 5:197,
    218–219
Anger Situations Inventory, 5:205
Anhedonia, 5:154, 156
Anitpsychotic drugs, 1:239, 241
Annihilation panic, 1:129–130
Annoyance, 4:166
    defined, 4:159
    refers to healthy negative emotion,
        4:157
Annsville Youth Center Project, 5:197–
    199
Anorexia nervosa, 3:266, 5:161, 7:36, 37,
    142
    See also Eating disorders; Starvation
    bulimic subtype, 3:58
    depression and, 3:51–63
    genetic contribution to, 3:55
    history of, 3:52–53
    obsessions and compulsions present
        in, 1:30
    restricting subtype, 3:54–56
Antabuse (disulfiram), 7:66, 67, 70, 108,
    111, 8:273
Antacids, 4:10
Antecedents of Self-Esteem, The
    (Coopersmith), 4:222

Anti-motion sickness medications, 5:68
Antibodies, 3:18
    anti CD3, 3:21
    immune responses involving, 3:17
    monoclonal, 3:27
Anticholinergic medications, 7:43, 44
Anticoagulants, 8:205
Anticonvulsants, 1:82, 2:200, 8:129
Antidepressants, 1:38, 42, 44, 82, 192,
        2:200, 3:232, 233, 5:163, 164,
        6:228, 261, 262, 7:33, 35–38, 42,
        43, 163, 8:129, 261, 283
    See also Medications; Pharmacotherapy;
        Selective serotonin-reuptake
        inhibitors (SSRIs); Specific
        names of medications;
        Tricyclic antidepressants
        (TCAs)
    for bulimic patients, 3:61
    for dysthymia, 3:236
    may take weeks to work, 3:245
    permit clients to function more
        efficiently, 3:12
    in post-stroke depression, 3:38, 42
    side effects, 3:272, 274, 7:35
    treatment considerations, 3:265–276
    used for eating disorders, 3:53, 62
    used in therapy for
        pseudoindependence, 3:11
    what they do, 3:266
Antidiabetics, 8:205
Antihistamines, 5:11
Antihypertensives, 5:57, 162
Antiobsessional drugs, 1:42, 44
Antiparkinsonian medications, 7:39
Antipsychotics, 2:200, 6:262, 7:33, 38–41,
        44, 163
Antisocial behavior, 5:48, 49, 195, 254
Antisocial personality disorder, 5:49, 7:15,
        227, 8:247, 248
    in veterans, 1:15
Antispastics, 7:43
Antiviral drugs, 10:212
Anxiety, 1:183, 222, 3:99, 100, 118, 4:5, 21,
        43, 158, 5:57, 159, 195–196,
        6:227, 228, 229, 257, 7:66, 76,
        96, 139, 144, 232, 8:250, 251,
        253, 255
    abuse-related, 5:26
    avoidance by OCD patient does not
        prevent, 1:31
    can be a useful feeling, 1:98

career decisions can evoke, 9:19, 32
    chronic, 5:10
    in COAs, 4:102
    a core emotion, 4:191
    counselor can alleviate, 9:172
    countertransference reaction, 2:236
    covered up by gambling, 1:154
    defined, 5:2
    distortions of, 4:80
    during divorce, 4:212
    and gamblers, 1:163
    helping children to manage, 5:27
    high levels of in poor children, 5:83,
        84
    in IBS patients, 4:10
    in incest victims, 4:118
    maladaptive, 1:98
    reduction after relaxation therapy,
        4:17
    substance abuse and, 8:94
    suppression of, 4:55
Anxiety disorders, 1:38, 197, 3:236, 4:14–
        16, 19, 5:156, 163, 7:33, 227,
        233, 8:239, 248, 255–256
    See also Panic disorder
    assessment, 5:7
    caffeine and, 7:153–166
    in children and adolescents, 5:1–16
    costs, 1:105
    definition of a cure for, 1:110
    etiology, 5:6–7
    goals of therapy, 1:105–108
    most prevalent of mental disorders,
        1:102
    organizations
        Anxiety Disorders Association of
            America, 1:117
        National Anxiety Foundation,
            1:117
        National Institute of Mental
            Health, 1:117
        Obsessive-Compulsive Disorder
            Foundation, 1:117
        Phobics Anonymous, 1:117
    recognition of, 1:99–102
    statistics, 1:102–105, 5:3, 4
    substance-induced, 5:5
    therapeutic approaches to, 1:97–115
Anxiety Disorders Association of America
        (ADAA) (*directory listing*),
        1:117
Anxiety management training, 4:15, 18

Anxiety triggers, 5:27
Anxiolytics, 7:31, 33, 159, 8:58–59
Anxious attachment, type of relationship wound, 4:182
APA
    See American Psychiatric Association; American Psychological Association
Apathy, 4:45, 9:168
Aphasia, 3:36
Aplastic anemia, Ecstasy and, 7:143
Apology, 4:244
Appetite, changes in, 3:36, 38
Applicant pool, 9:83
Applied behavioral analysis, 9:110–111
Applied relaxation training, 4:15, 18
Apprenticeship, 9:245
Aptitude, vocational, 9:149–150
Arguments, avoiding with clients, 2:69–70
Arizona State Psychological Association, 10:13
Arkansas Research and Training Center in Vocational Rehabilitation, 9:148
    (directory listing), 9:61
Arousal, sexual, 6:192, 225, 232
Arousal response, 4:42
Arrangement, of marriage, 4:204, 205
Arrangements for Receiving Personal Assistance Services Among Persons with Spinal Cord Injury (table), 9:68
Arsenic, poisoning, 3:104
ART
    See Aggression replacement training (ART)
Art, drawing used in therapy, 5:27, 32, 116
Art therapy, 1:77, 5:177
    for depression due to homelessness, 5:90
Arthritis, 3:88, 7:42, 56
Arylcyclohexylamines, 8:58
Asendin (amoxapine), 3:272, 7:36
Asian Americans, 9:179
    characteristics, 9:184–186
    referred to as "model" minority, 9:184
Asians, and alcohol metabolism, 4:96
Asperger's disorder, 1:172, 174, 177, 178, 181, 183
    case study, 1:181–182
Aspirin, 7:29, 42

Assertive community treatment (table), 1:245
Assertiveness training, 1:113, 115, 3:86–87, 4:11, 5:264, 6:182
Assessing Risk of Violence (table), 6:252
Assessing Therapeutic Response (table), 3:273
Assessment
    by rehabilitation specialist, unexpected results, 9:169
    defined, 9:235–236
    ecological, 9:113–114, 120
    facilitated by intake interview, 9:242
    formal evaluation strategies, 9:95–96
    functional, 9:38–41
        elements of, 9:40
    general, 9:114–118
    situational, 9:243
    specialized, 9:144–146
    for supported employment interventions, 9:120
    vocational, 9:198–199, 234
    work skills, 9:46
Assimilation, devalues cultural diversity, 9:201
Assistive technologists, 9:154
Assistive technology, 9:52, 246
Association of Labor-Management Administrators and Consultants on Alcoholism (ALAMCA), 8:17, 27
Association for Specialists in Group Work (ASGW), 2:122, 124, 125, 126
Assumptions, 2:24
    silent, 3:129, 130–131
Asthenia, 3:272
Asthma, 3:18, 5:240
    stress management techniques for, 4:8
"At risk", defined, 8:160
Atenolol (Tenormin), 5:14
Ativan (Lorazepam), 7:34, 147
Atonement, of sins, 4:248
Attachment, 3:12
    role of, 3:3–5
Attachment-separation, 3:8, 9
Attack, direct, theme of anger against others, 4:161–162
Attention, 4:100
    disorders of
        See Attention-deficit/hyperactivity disorder (ADHD)

evenly-suspended, 2:26, 28–30
free-floating, 2:26, 28–30
Attention deficit disorder (ADD), 1:126,
183, 5:42
persons with BPD having history of,
1:125
Attention deficit disorder with
hyperactivity, 1:194
Attention span, Ritalin and, 5:56
Attention-deficit/hyperactivity disorder
(ADHD), 4:101, 5:4, 10, 41, 156
See also Attention deficit disorder
(ADD); Hyperactivity
and behavior modification, 1:204
assessment, 5:52–55
biopsychosocial disorder, 5:69
building parent-child rapport, 1:201,
202
building parents' knowledge base,
1:200, 201
cause, 5:51–52
cognitive strategies, 5:68–69
common problem, 1:192
comorbidity disorders and, 1:198
definition, 1:193–198, 5:43, 45
delivering parental commands, 1:202–
203
development of social skills, 5:66–68
developmental course and
comorbidity, 5:46–49
diagnostic assessment, 1:199
diagnostic criteria
hyperactivity, 1:196
impulsivity, 1:196–197
inattention, 1:195–196
educational interventions, 5:59, 62–63
epidemiology, 5:49–51
handling future problems, 1:207–208
hyperactive-impulsive, 5:43
inattentive, 5:43
introduction, 5:42–43
managing behavior in public places,
1:206–207
medications for, 5:56–59
parent training for, 1:191–208
parenting skills, 5:63–66
questionnaires to diagnose, 1:197
treatment, 5:55–56
use of time-out with, 1:205–206
Attorneys
counselors' relationship with, 10:98
cross-examination and, 10:100

Autism, 1:178, 5:53
adults with, 1:180
causes, 1:178
common characteristics, 1:173
described, 1:172–173
diagnosis, 1:180–181
medical conditions coexisting with,
1:179
statistics, 1:179
treatment, 1:183–184
Autism Behavior Checklist, 1:183
Autistic disorder, 1:175–176
Autogenic training, 4:2, 3, 4, 5, 7, 8, 11, 19,
20
Autonomy, 3:2, 3, 190, 4:142, 143, 163, 221,
6:199, 8:161, 176, 185, 186,
10:58, 70
adolescent, 6:103
in chronic phase of AIDS, 6:129
client's right to, 4:139
male identity and, 10:199
moral principle of, 10:40–41
in multiple personalities, 1:56
strived for in life, 3:5
Aventyl (nortriptyline), 3:213, 270, 274,
5:57, 164, 7:35
Aversion therapy, 8:210
Avoidance, 1:109, 183, 5:26, 161
reduced in behavioral therapy, 1:107
source of disability in panic disorder,
1:100
Avoidant disorder, 5:2
Avoidant personality disorder, 5:13
Axis I, 1:63
Axis II, 1:63
Azidothymidine (AZT), 6:133, 10:212
AZT (azidothymidine), 6:133, 10:212

B

B cells, 3:18, 19, 20, 25, 26
Babies, born with HIV, 6:133
Baby Wolfpack, juvenile gang, 5:207
Baby-boom generation, 3:66
Babysitters, can provide information on
child's behavior, 5:8
Baclofen (Lioresal), 7:43
Bacteria, intestinal, 7:56
Bad seed, the, 1:138
Baggage, emotional, 6:86, 94
Bailey Developmental Scale, 8:107

Balance
    career questions and, 9:7–8
    institutional, 9:3, 4–6
    interindividual, 9:3, 6–7
    interpersonal, 9:3–4
Baltimore Health Systems, Inc., 7:253
Barbiturates, 7:34, 8:65
Barbor's model, of substance abuse, 8:68–69
Barriers, 9:150
    physical, 6:176
    relationship, 6:6–7
    to career opportunities, 9:193, 194
Barriers to patient collaboration in
        treatment (*table*), 1:242
Base-level functioning, 4:188
Basic Assumption groups, 2:102
Batterers, 2:60
Battle fatigue, 4:45
Bay Area Birthmothers Association
        (*directory listing*), 5:125
Baylor College of Medicine Research and
        Training Center on Spinal
        Cord Injury, 9:68
Beavers-Timberlawn Family Evaluation
        Scales (BTFES), 6:19–22, 32
    clarity of expression, 6:20
    closeness, 6:20
    empathy, 6:21–22
    global health-pathology, 6:22
    goal-directed negotiation, 6:20
    invasiveness, 6:20–21
    mood and tone, 6:21
    overt power, 6:19
    parental coalition, 6:20
    permeability of family members, 6:21
    range of feelings, 6:21
    responsibility for one's actions, 6:20
    unresolvable conflicts, 6:21
Beck Depression Inventory, 6:22
        (*appendix*), 6:33
Beck Depression Inventory (BDI), 3:157,
        158, 167, 168, 169, 170, 204
Bedwetting, 6:46
    in COAs, 4:101
Behavior
    avoidant, OCD characterized by, 1:31
    disorders, 5:42
    labeling of as maladaptive, ethical
        considerations, 9:196
    modification, 5:10
        abusive drinking and, 7:109, 119–
            120

and ADHD children, 1:204–205
    for substance abuse, 5:244
    patterns, assessment of, 7:11
    repetitive, 1:172, 176
    therapy, 2:7, 251, 3:114, 115, 4:2
        applicability to physical disease,
            4:62
        contrasted with cognitive therapy,
            3:140
        for depression due to
            homelessness, 5:90
        prolonging life with, 4:63–64
        to reduce chance of disease, 4:55
Behavioral
    approaches, to depression, 3:163–170
    assessment, 3:158–163
    family management, 1:246
    impairment, 4:100
    rehearsal, 7:116
    therapy, 8:277
        and anxiety disorders, 1:107
        intervention for PTSD, 1:21
        with OCD, 1:41–42
        as treatment for DID, 1:75
Behavioral Task Assignments (*appendix*),
        6:29–30
Behavioral Techniques (*table*), 3:136
Behaviorism, 2:6, 7
Behaviors, ritualistic, compulsions are,
        1:30
Beliefs
    irrational Belief (iB), 4:156, 157, 158,
        160, 162, 163, 164, 168, 170,
        171, 172, 173
    rational Belief (rB), 4:156, 157, 160,
        163, 164, 171, 172, 173
Beneficence, 8:176, 185, 191, 10:237
    moral principle of, 10:40, 41
Bennett Mechanical Comprehension Test,
        9:150
Benzodiazepines, 4:13, 5:11, 12, 14, 7:42,
        44, 147, 8:65, 111, 253, 256, 260,
        261, 280
    and alcohol use, 7:10
    and PTSD patients, 1:21
    side effects of, 7:34
    statistics, 8:247
Benztropine mesylate (Cogentin), 7:39
Bereavement, 3:86, 122, 8:127
    and AIDS, 6:131
Beta-blockers, 5:14
Beta-endorphin, 3:24

Betrayal, 5:28, 31–32
  type of relationship wound, 4:182
Better Safe Than Sorry (video), 5:33
Bettors, 1:157
Bias
  of counselors, 10:99
  cultural, 10:237, 238
  intentional, unethical nature of,
    10:149
Bibliotherapy, 1:112, 5:116
  See also Books; Self-help, literature
  adjunct to cognitive therapy, 5:146–147
  cautious use in suspected cases of
    sexual abuse, 4:142
  defined, 6:42
  erotic literature used in, 6:233–234
Bicultural, persons comfortable in two
    cultures, 9:201
Bilingualism, 9:202, 221
Bill of Rights, Fourth Amendment to, 10:3
Binge-purge, 3:58, 61, 62
  seen in bulimia nervosa, 3:56
Bioenvironmental factors, to late-life
    depression, 3:150–151
Bioenvironmental Factors (*figure*), 3:151
Biofeedback, 4:2, 6, 18, 20
  effects on hypertension, 4:7
  EMG, 4:8, 11, 12, 17, 18, 19, 20
  respiratory resistance, 4:9
  thermal, 4:7, 11, 20
  trachea noise, 4:9
  vaginal temperature, 4:8
Biological age, 3:67
Biological marker
  defined, 4:99
  types
    biochemical, 4:99
    morphologic, 4:99
    neurologic, 4:99, 100
    neurophysiologic, 4:99
    psychophysiologic, 4:99, 100
Biological ties, importance of, 6:91
Biopsychosocial, model of relapse, 7:221–
    222
Biotransformation, of medications, 7:28,
    29–30
Bipolar disorder, 1:82, 212, 2:201, 3:267,
    5:12, 154, 156, 160, 162, 164,
    166, 253, 7:233
  some DID clients are rapid-cyclers,
    1:64
  medications for, lithium, 7:37–38

Birth defects
  See Fetus, effects of Substance Abuse
    on
Birth order, 2:159
Birth trauma, 1:39
Birthparent Support Network (BSN)
    (*directory listing*), 5:126
Birthparent Support Network for Triad
    (*directory listing*), 5:126
Birthparents Connection (*directory listing*),
    5:125
Bismuth, poisoning, 3:104
Black Americans
  See African Americans
Blackouts, 1:53, 5:234, 235
  alcohol-related, 8:252
"Blacky" Pictures Test, 5:116
Blame
  for abuse, 5:29–31
  as stage of divorce, 4:212
Blindness, 9:112
Block determinants, 2:169
Blocks
  behavioral, 2:170
  interpersonal, 2:170
    resolving, 2:181–182
      case dialogue, 2:182–183
  intrapersonal
    resolving, 2:183–185
      case dialogue, 2:185–187
  problem-solving, 2:170
Blood, liver's role in cleansing, 7:56
Body dysmorphic disorder, 1:33
Body language, 2:155, 7:13
Body mechanics, 9:134
Body type, correlation with alcoholism,
    4:99
Body-building, 9:132
Bonding, poor family, 4:102
Bonds, emotional, sexuality as expression
    of, 6:196
Books
  See also Bibliotherapy
  dealing with adoption (*table*), 5:117
  self-help
    See self-help literature
  therapeutic use of
    See Bibliotherapy
Borderline personality disorder (BPD),
    1:63, 3:142, 4:117, 119, 127,
    134, 5:161, 254
  adolescents and, 1:123

case study, 1:125–126
causes of, 1:121–122
overlap and PTSD, 1:124
patients with no history of abuse or
    neglect, 1:130–131
psychotherapeutic considerations,
    1:126–131
psychotherapeutic strategies for,
    1:119–132
psychotherapy difficult with, 1:120
statistics, 1:123, 125
Boredom, 7:17
Boston Clinical Interview for PTSD, 1:12
Boston Collaborative Drug Surveillance
    Study, 3:102
Boundary violations, type of relationship
    wound, 4:182
Bowenian family therapy, 2:155–161
    techniques, 2:159–161
Boys
    and ADHD, 5:49, 50
    and child custody, 6:38
    do less housework, 6:64
    effects of divorce on, 6:37
    with feminine physiques, at higher
        risk for alcoholism, 4:99
    and gender identification, 6:273
    higher incidence of completed
        suicide, 5:158
    immature during early adolescence,
        5:181
    juvenile offenders, case study, 5:199–
        201
    more affected than girls with OCD,
        1:37
    robbery most violent crime
        committed by, 5:193
BPD
    See Borderline personality disorder
        (BPD)
Brady v. Hopper, 10:146
Brain
    degenerative changes in, 3:71
    dysfunction in recovering alcoholics,
        7:225
    and immune system interact, 3:16–17
    LSD and, 7:138
    naltrexone and, 7:78–80
    state of "new normal", 7:65
    traumatic injury to, 7:32, 41, 43–44
    tumors and depression, 3:100

Brain dysfunction, and ADHD, 5:52
Brain injury, 3:34
    location of, 3:39
    substance abuse and, 8:78–80
    traumatic
        See Traumatic brain injury (TBI)
Braine, Ecstasy and, 7:141–143
Brainstorming, 4:229, 7:232
Brazelton Neonatal Behavioral
        Assessment Scale, 8:108–109
Breach, in norms by adolescents, 6:101,
        102
Breathalyzer tests, alcohol, 8:272
Breathing, controlled, 4:5
Brecksville Veterans Administration
        Medical Center, treatment for
        gamblers, 1:164
BriefMAST, 8:207
Briquet syndrome, 1:63
Bromide, poisoning, 3:104
Bromocriptine (Parlodel), 8:283
Bronchodilation, 4:8–9
Brown, Joyce, homeless person, case of,
        10:175
Brownsville Neighborhood Youth Action
        Center, 5:204
Buckeye Youth Center, 5:210
Buddy systems, in group therapy, 7:183–
        184
Bufferin (aspirin), 7:42
Bulimia nervosa, 3:266, 7:35
    See also Eating disorders
    depression and, 3:51–63
    genetic contribution to, 3:55
    history of, 3:53–54
    implications for treatment, 3:60–62
    symptoms are egodystonic, 3:62
    unhealthy mood regulation in, 3:58
Bupropion (Wellbutrin), 5:14, 7:37, 8:283
Burnout, 4:45
    professional, 4:136
BuSpar (buspirone), 5:14, 7:34, 35
Buspirone (BuSpar), 5:14, 7:34, 35, 8:283
Bystander Equity Model of Supervisory
        Helping Behavior, 8:35

C

Caffeine, 5:12, 15, 7:41, 52, 53, 54, 8:58, 270,
        272
    anxiety disorder and, 7:153–166

consumption, statistics, 7:157
limits for depressed patients, 3:250
use of, 7:156–157
Caffeine, reduced intake can reduce panic
and anxiety, 1:113, 114
CAGE questionnaire, 8:207, 272, 273–274
Cairl v. State, 10:145
California, and laws governing duty to
warn, 10:142
California Department of Mental Health,
1:240
California Personality Inventory (CPI),
and the gambler, 1:163
California Supreme Court, *Tarasoff*
decision and, 10:133
Calories, 7:57
Camp, summer, for GAD, 5:12
Camp refusal, 5:9
Canadians, testing and, 9:216
Cancer, 3:16, 17, 88, 108, 6:168
caffeine and, 7:165
cigarette smoking and, 4:54
depression and, 3:100
diet and, 4:54
personality types prone to, 4:54
psychological factors in the treatment
of, 4:53–66
terminal, women and, 4:64
Candida, 5:51
Cannabis
See Marijuana
Carbamazepine (Tegretol), 5:166, 7:41, 44
and mania, 1:228
Carbohydrate, in diet, 7:53
Carcinoid syndrome, 3:99–100
Cardiac disease, 3:88, 121
Cardiovasculars, 8:205
Career
See also Jobs
behavior, risk factors, 9:190–195
choice of, 4:35, 9:2
case study, 9:6
impact of risk factors on, 9:193–
195
complicated decisions of, 9:18
decisions, evoke great deal of anxiety,
9:19
development, planning for, 9:95
dilemma, 9:8
dynamic understanding of, 9:2
maturity, defined, 9:185

phases of, 9:2
plays strong role in defining person,
9:19
reappraisal of, 9:12
case study, 9:13
Career Assessment Inventory, 9:148
Career counseling
client resistance to, 9:17–32
constructive developmental
perspective on, 9:1–15
defining objective of, 9:9–10
a development-enhancing activity, 9:14
impact of cultural diversity on, 9:177–
203
Career criminal, 1:144
Career Value Scale, 9:149
Caregiving
activities, 6:171–172
consequences of, 6:177–179
demographics, 6:170–171
efficacy of, 6:172–173
problems with, 6:174–177
to the elderly, overview of, 6:169–170
Caretakers, 6:123, 132
Caring, of counselors, 10:43
Carnegie Council on Adolescent
Development, 6:100, 8:163
Carotene, 7:51, 60
Case management, 6:183
for depression due to homelessness,
5:90, 91–93, 97
Case v. United States, 10:146
Catapres (clonidine), 5:14, 57, 162, 8:283
Catatonia, 2:108, 7:40
Catecholamine disorder, in gamblers,
1:160
Catecholamines, 3:16, 23, 29
Catharsis, 3:115
Causality, defined, 2:148
CD2 antigen, 3:22, 27
CD3 antigen, 3:22
CD4 antigen, 3:18, 21, 22, 23, 27, 28, 29
CD8 antigen, 3:18, 21, 22, 27, 28, 29
Cells of the Immune System (*table*), 3:19
Centers for Disease Control, role in
suicide prevention programs,
5:268
Cerebral infarcts, 3:267
Cerebral palsy, 9:112
Cerebrovascular accident (CVA)
See Stroke

Certification, for CRC-SAC, 8:85
Certified Employee Assistance
        Professionals (CEAP), 8:27
Certified in Vocational Evaluation, 9:241
Change
    case study, 2:36–37
    commitment to, 7:206–207
    considerations for therapists dealing
        with resistance to, 2:43
    divorce as stimulus for, 4:215
    fear of, 2:33–44, 9:19–20
    is to kill or to die, 2:44
    kind of a suicide, 2:44
    motivation for by criminal, 1:148–151
    stages of
        action, 7:197
        contemplation, 7:197
        maintenance, 7:197
        precontemplation, 7:197
        preparation, 7:197
    supporting, 9:23
    therapeutic, when it occurs, 2:83
    viewed as realignment, 2:5–6
    in the workplace, 4:41
Change Assessment Scale, 8:275–276
Chart For Depression Daily Warning
        Signs (figure), 3:249
Charting, 3:248
Charts
    Daily Warning Signs Chart for Mania,
        1:233
    Personal Daily Warning Signs Chart
        for Mania, 1:234
    Questions to Ask Physicians About
        Medication, 1:235
    Statement of Intent, 1:232
Checking, an OCD syndrome, 1:34, 35
Checklists, use of, 9:118
Chemical dependence, 4:70
    See also Addiction; Alcohol abuse;
        Alcoholism; Drug abuse;
        Stimulant abuse; Substance
        abuse; Tobacco abuse
    defined, 8:227
    is a family disease, 4:71
Chemotherapy, 4:64
Child abuse, 1:140, 3:255, 4:114, 5:256,
        6:176, 179, 10:2
    cause for breach of confidentiality,
        10:4, 6–7
    difficulties encountered in therapy of
        victims of, 1:129

history of in cases of DID, 1:59
    reporting, 5:285
    sexual
        See Sexual abuse of children
Child Behavior Checklist, 5:34–35, 53, 7:11
    for ADHD, 1:197
Child care, 6:61–63, 67
    as parenting task, 6:60
Child custody
    in a divorce, 4:210
    trial, 10:103
Child guidance movement, 2:145
Child protection movement, 4:114
Child protection system, 4:119
Child Sexual Abuse: A Solution (video), 5:33
Child support, 6:66, 77, 85
    defined, 6:40
Child welfare, doctrine, 8:177
Childhood
    aggression, 1:121
    antecedents of BPD, 1:121
    attachments during, 3:4
    of co-dependent person, 4:76
    dependence a normal feature of, 3:180
    excessive worry in, and correlation to
        anxious adults, 1:98
    molestation, 1:125
        See also Child abuse; Incest;
            Sexual abuse of children
    survivors, 4:133–148
    schizoid disorder of, 1:174
    separation and loss in, 3:3
    severe abuse in, 1:128
Childhood Attention Problems (CAP)
        Scale, 5:54
Childhood Autism Rating Scale (CARS),
        1:183
Childhood disintegrative disorder, 1:172,
        176, 177
Children, 2:103, 118, 3:142
    See also Adolescents; Infants
    adopted, psychopathology of, 5:103–
        120
    adult, as caregivers to elderly, 6:170
    aggression replacement training in,
        5:191–222
    of alcoholics
        See Alcoholics, children of; Adult
            children of alcoholics
            (ACOAs)
    anger in, 6:44–46, 49
    anxiety disorders in, 5:1–16

attention-deficit/hyperactivity
    disorder (ADHD) in, 1:192,
    5:41–71
autistic, 1:172–173
behavior-change agreements and,
    7:120
birth order of, 2:159
caffeine and, 7:156, 163
cognitive-behavioral play therapy
    used with, 5:129–149
commitment to, 6:92
confidentiality and, 10:170, 171–172
death of, 6:147–162
    case study, 6:153–157
decreases in CD4/CD8 ratio, 3:29
definition of a minor, 5:280
denial in, 6:42
with DID, 1:50, 60, 76
with disabilities
    African-American family and,
        9:181
    Asian-American family and, 9:185
    Hispanic family and, 9:183
disorders of, 1:172–184
of divorce, counseling, 4:210, 6:35–52
drinking by, 8:9
dying, 6:133
in family system, 6:10
fear of abandonment and, 6:46–47
grief in, 6:43
guilt in, 6:43–44, 49
of HIV drug users, 6:123
HIV transmitted to, 8:228
homelessness and depression in,
    5:79–97
hyperkinesis and, 7:163, 225
of immigrants, addiction in, 6:122
included in therapy of alcoholic
    parents, 7:116
inhibited, 5:6
need protection from further incest,
    4:119
number of in racial/ethnic groups,
    9:193
with OCD, 1:31, 37
and older persons, 3:85
need outside activities, 6:50
panic disorder symptoms in, 5:15
of parents with AIDS, 6:131–133
predate remarriage, 6:83–84
protecting the confidentiality of,
    5:275–290

with psychiatric needs, 7:245
and PTSD, case study, 1:17–19
raised by single fathers, 6:57–69
requirements for achieving healthy
    self-esteem, 4:222–223
resilient, 4:104–105
role of in causing trouble, 1:141
with schizophrenia, 2:145
school-phobic, 9:20
self-esteem in, 3:184
social skills program for, 5:67
substance abuse in, 4:102
transmission of HIV infection to, 6:124
who have AIDS, 6:133–134
Children of Alcoholics (COAs), 4:75, 83,
    85, 86
Children of Alcoholics Foundation
    (*directory listing*), 4:86
Children of Alcoholics Screening Test
    (CAST), 8:42, 43
Children of Alcoholics (USGPO), 4:104
Children's Depression Inventory (CDI),
    5:85
Children's Global Assessment Scale, 5:35
Children's Impact of Traumatic Events
    Scale-Revised, 5:35
Chiropractic therapy, 7:192
Chlordiazepoxide (Librium), 7:34
Chlorpromazine (Thorazine), 7:40
Choice, 2:41
    humans have, 2:38
Cholesterol, high, 4:59
Chores, division of in home, 6:61
Chrite v. United States, 10:144
Chromium, 3:21
Chronologic age, 3:67
Cigarettes
    See also Nicotine; Smoking; Tobacco
        abuse
    alter detoxification ability of liver,
        7:53
Cimetidine (Tagamet), 4:10, 7:155
Cinderella, 5:116
Circular Questioning (*appendix*), 6:31
Circular thinking, 2:148
Circumplex Model of Marital and Family
    Systems (CMMFS), 6:11
Cirrhosis, 4:99
Citalopram, 3:42
Civil rights movement, spawned laws
    against involuntary
    commitment, 10:174

Civilian Mississippi Scale, 1:10
Clarity, in mania, 1:227
Class of '45, elder-specific program,
    8:214–215, 216, 217
Classic conditioning, 7:175–176
Client-treatment matching, 7:2
Clients
    See also Patients
    abandonment of, 10:112–113
    adolescents as, 8:178
    with alcohol problem, 2:57
    rational-emotive approach for, 4:153–
        174
    anxious, 7:160
    bicultural, 9:201
    competence of, 10:168
    compliance with therapeutic regimen,
        4:5
    confidentiality and, 10:4–9
    court-ordered, 2:64
    culturally diverse, 9:177–203
    danger to, 10:7–9
    dangerous, 2:135
        failure to control, 10:122–123
    death of due to AIDS, 8:237
    deceptive reporting by, 7:9
    dependent, 3:186–187
    depressed
        checklist for use in working with,
            3:261–262
        immune status in, 3:25–28
        young, 3:275
    difficult, 2:47–60
        brief therapy with, 2:63–77
        case study, 2:71–72, 75–76
        defined, 2:65
        points to consider during
            treatment, 2:58–60
    with disabilities
        labor market for, 9:79–106
        placement practices for, 9:79–106
        psychological make-up of, 9:75
    distrustful, 3:11
    dying, 2:204
    dysthymic, 3:225–237
    education of, 7:204–206
    elderly
        See Elderly
    examination by medical specialist,
        10:26
    from drug programs, 2:49
    from prisons, 2:49

    guided by therapists in cognitive
        therapy, 3:133
    high-risk for dropping out of
        treatment, 7:202–203
    Hispanic, with disabilities, 9:209–224
    homosexual, case study, 2:241–242
    hypnotizability of, 4:6
    identification of, 10:82
        in EAPs, 8:39–40
    improper financial manipulation of,
        2:219
    individualized vocational evaluation
        plan (IVEP) for, 9:241
    intimidating, 2:52
    involuntary, 2:49, 55, 129
        participation by, defined, 2:130
    male, divorcing, 4:214
    management of dependency in
        depressed, 3:179–195
    manic
        how to treat, 1:226–227
        planning the day of, 1:225
        teaching self-help strategies to,
            1:211–230
    medications and, 7:25–26
    mentally ill, ethical dimension of
        treating, 10:161–178, 180–182
    mentally incompetent, 10:116
    mistrust by, 2:50
    monitoring of, 7:19–20
    neurotic, 2:233
    noncompliance in, 7:192–193
    overwhelmed by painful memories,
        4:136
    phobic, 4:16
    process of empowerment for, 9:53
    properties of speech, 2:18–19
    questioning about sexual orientation,
        8:228
    racially and ethnically diverse, ethical
        guidelines, 10:235–246
    readiness by, 9:238
    records of, 10:12–14
    with relationship wounds, 4:177–199
    relationship-imbedded, 9:11
    resistant to career counseling, 9:17–32
    right to autonomy, 4:139
    rights of
        constitutional, 2:221
        contractual, 2:221
        statutory, 2:221
    rules based on respect for, 10:23–32

with schizophrenia, 2:144, 145, 155,
  9:161–175
screening for group therapy, 2:128
selection criteria, 2:86–88
self-determination of, 10:21–22
sexual boundary violations against,
  10:195–206
  See also Sexual relationships with
    clients
sharing diagnosis of DID with, 1:62–
  63
socioeconomically deprived, 2:60
some with DID are bipolar, 1:64
with style of pseudoindependence, 3:12
successful, characteristics, 7:92
threats by
  See Duty to protect
as threats to confidentiality, 5:277
with traumatic brain injury,
  interviewing, 9:144
unhealthy transference problems
  with, 10:117–118
view of addiction, 7:201
violent, 2:52
voluntary, 2:65, 129
  participation by, defined, 2:130
vulnerability of, 10:11
welfare of, 10:20–21
willingness by, 9:238
Clients' Tasks in the Counseling Process
  (*table*), 4:187
Clinical Situations Usually Requiring
  Antidepressant
  Pharmacotherapy (*table*),
  3:268
Clinical Syndrome Associated with
  Cerebrovascular Disease
  (*table*), 3:37
Clinician-Administered PTSD Scale
  (CAPS), 1:12
Clomipramine (Anafranil), 1:42, 43, 44,
  3:272
  and PTSD, 1:21
Clonazepam (Klonopin), 1:82, 5:14, 7:41
Clonidine (Catapres), 1:39, 5:14, 57, 162,
  8:283
Clozapine (Clozaril), 7:39, 8:280, 283
Clozaril (clozapine), 7:39, 8:280, 283
Co-dependence, 4:69–87
  12-step programs for, 4:83
  arguments against, 4:75–76
  counselor, 8:153–154

defined, 4:73–74
diagnostic criteria for, 4:80–81
dynamic view of, 4:81–82
examples of, 4:76–77
implications for psychotherapy, 4:85–
  86
introduction, 4:70–73
roles in, 4:77–79
  impact of, 4:79–80
secondary, 4:84
treatment perspective, 4:83–84
Co-Dependents Anonymous (CoDA),
  4:75, 83, 86, 8:29, 153
  (*directory listing*), 4:86, 8:157
Co-workers, substance abuse and, 8:10
COAs
  See Children of Alcoholics (COAs)
Cocaine, 5:15, 6:101, 251, 7:41, 135, 8:58,
  61, 64–65, 97, 111, 251, 270
  abstinence, statistics, 7:177–178
  addiction, cognitive-behavioral
    treatment of, 7:171–186
  addicts, statistics, 7:133
  "crack", 7:172, 186
  employees and, 8:12
  physical fitness programs reduce use
    of, 8:166
  pregnancy and, 8:107–109
  relapse rate from addiction to,
    7:217
  statistics, 8:246, 247
  trends in prevalance (*table*), 8:98
  withdrawal, 5:242
Cocaine Anonymous, 5:245, 8:29, 76
  (*directory listing*), 8:156
CoDA
  See Co-Dependents Anonymous
    (CoDA)
Code of Ethics (ACA), 10:40, 44, 46, 49,
  188, 189, 213, 236, 242
Code of Professional Ethics for
  Rehabilitation Counselors,
  10:64, 65, 66, 67
Codeine, 7:42, 75
Codes of ethics
  See Ethics, codes of
Coercion, contrasted with temptation,
  10:169
Coercive
  escalation, 1:199
  interaction, 1:199
Cogentin (benzotropine mesylate), 7:39

Cognition, 4:154
    defined, 3:128
    evaluating validity of, 3:136–138
    leading to sexual desire disorders,
        6:225–226
    Piaget's theory of, 4:181
Cognitive
    abilities, evaluation of, 7:17–19
    difficulties, 1:173
    disorganization, 1:241
    evaluation, 3:152–154
    impairment, 3:153, 4:100
        depression and, 3:41
    interventions, 3:165
    rehabilitation, techniques of, 1:242
    remediation, 7:229–231
    restructuring, 4:11, 14
    skills
        development of in autistic
            children, 1:184
        difficulties with, 4:103
    style
        depressogenic, 1:165
        negative, 1:154
    theory, 3:166, 4:181
    training, 5:66, 69
    triad, 3:129–130
Cognitive Techniques (table), 3:137
Cognitive therapy, 2:55–56, 251, 253, 257,
        260, 261, 3:253–254, 4:2, 11, 12,
        13, 14, 15, 16, 20
    and anxiety disorders, 1:107
    based on cognitive model of
        emotional disorders, 5:131
    based on emotional model, 5:133
    brief and time-limited, 5:132
    for children with ADHD, 5:68–69
    contrasted with behavior therapy,
        3:140
    defined, 3:128
    for depression, 3:127–142
    for dysthymia, 3:233–234
    effectiveness of, 3:139–141
    focused approach, 5:130
    for homelessness, 5:90
    homework in, 3:138–139, 5:134
    intervention for PTSD, 1:21
    needs sound therapeutic relationship,
        5:132
    predicting response to, 3:141–142
    principles of, 5:131–134
    problem-oriented, 5:133

    for reactive jealousy, 6:253
    rely on inductive method, 5:133–134
    structured and directive, 5:133
    as treatment for DID, 1:75
    as treatment for gamblers, 1:166
    uses Socratic method, 5:132–133
    uses team approach, 5:132
Cognitive Therapy of Depression (Beck),
        3:253
Cognitive-behavioral
    interventions, 3:165
    model of relapse, 7:219–221
    stimulation, 6:182
    techniques, 8:257
Cognitive-behavioral play therapy
    See also Cognitive behavioral therapy
    cognitive therapy principles applied
        to, 5:131–134
    compared with traditional play
        therapies, 5:135–136
    introduction to, 5:130
    properties of, 5:134–135
    special issues, 5:147–148
    techniques, 5:138–147
        activity scheduling, 5:138, 142–
            143
        bibliotherapy, 5:146–147
        cognitive change strategies,
            5:144–145
        contingency management, 5:138,
            140
        coping self-statements, 5:145–146
        extinction and differential
            reinforcement, 5:138, 141–142
        positive reinforcement, 5:138, 140
        recording dysfunctional thoughts,
            5:143–144
        self-monitoring, 5:138, 142
        shaping, 5:138, 140
        stimulus fading, 5:138, 140–141
        systematic desensitization, 5:138–
            140
        time-out, 5:138, 142
    use of with young children, 5:130–131
Cognitive-behavioral therapy, 1:114, 192,
        2:255–256, 257, 260
    See also Cognitive behavioral play
        therapy
    for adolescent depression, 5:166
    for anxiety disorders, 1:108–111
    application to elderly, 2:200
    for cocaine addiction, 7:171–186

for GAD, 5:12
for sexual abuse, 5:24
for suicidal clients, 5:263–264
as treatment for specific phobias, 5:14
Cognitive-Behavioral Treatment For
Social Phobia (*table*), 5:15
Cognitive-developmental theories, 9:1–3
Cohesion, 2:135, 6:13, 14
Cohort, defined, 3:67
Collaboration
barriers to, 7:248–249
defined, 7:244
history of, 7:246–247
interagency, in addiction treatment,
7:243–255
models, 7:252–254
successful, 7:249–252
Collaborative empiricism, 3:133
Collaborative Perinatal Study, 8:103
College
choice of fields of study in, 9:11, 11–12
environment, 9:4
College Board, 9:212
Color
people of
See also Minorities
economically disadvantaged, 6:119
underrepresentation in descriptive
studies, 6:59
Columbus, Ohio, case study of poverty
and depression, 5:83–91
Coma, in traumatic brain injury, 9:144
Comic books, as sexual abuse prevention
materials, 5:33
Commands
alpha, 1:202
appropriate, 5:64
parenting, delivering, 1:202–203
Commission on Accreditation of
Rehabilitation Facilities
(CARF), 9:129, 130, 134, 135,
235, 241
Commission on Certification of Work
Adjustment and Vocational
Evaluation Specialists
(CCWAVES), 9:235, 241
Commission on Rehabilitation Counselor
Certification (CRC), 8:84,
10:39
Commission on the Review of the
National Policy Toward
Gambling, 1:155

Commitment, involuntary, 10:173–176
Common Symptoms of Depression (*table*),
3:244
Commonly Used Antipsychotics and
Their Side Effect Profiles
(*table*), 7:40
Communication, 5:264, 6:9, 19, 20, 21, 22,
173, 278, 280
See also Listening; Speech
ability of, 4:181
about adoption, 5:109, 113
about death, 6:161
in addiction treatment, 7:204
assessment of skills in, 9:242
as assistance need category, 9:73
beneficial skill to teach to clients, 9:53
between parent and child, 5:144
blocked, 6:150
breaches in, 6:103
by expert witnesses to jury, 10:106
by therapists, with divorcing parents,
6:42
can account for variance in vocational
decisions, 9:235
clients' motivation for may be
ambivalent, 2:18
and COAs, 4:101
confidential, 5:285
difficulties in common in co-
dependency, 4:79
direct, Asian Americans and, 9:186
family, 5:163
fostering in therapy with elderly,
2:203
good, 7:195
honest and open if self-esteem is high,
4:221
inadequate, 7:116
of information through referral
questions, 9:239
in interpersonal psychotherapy, 5:167
needed for relationship quality, 6:213
needed with suicidal client's
physicians, 5:262
nonverbal, 6:210
open and regular in combined
therapy, 2:111
part of strategic planning, 9:101
part of successful promotions, 9:103–
104
part of supported employment, 9:121
poor, 5:168

privileged
    and confidential, 5:279
    defined, 10:3
skills, 6:182
    couples therapy to improve, 6:258
    deficits in, case study, 6:268
    lacking in alcoholic families, 7:112
    teaching, 7:116–120, 122, 125
    training, 6:230
    in therapy groups, 3:74
    validation and, 9:244–247
    verbal, 6:271, 9:198
    written, 2:74, 129, 9:144
Communication skills, aberrations seen in
    autism, 1:180
Communications
    technology, black box concept of, 2:154
    theory, 2:146
    therapy and theory, 2:155
Communications family therapy, 2:153–
    155
Community
    integration, 9:110
    outreach, 9:198
    resources of, 6:141, 142, 183–184
Community Adjustment Rating Scale,
    5:205, 206
Community Reinforcement Training for
    Families, 7:103
Community-Based (Aftercare) Project,
    5:201–204
Comorbidity
    See Depression, major, comorbity
        with alcoholism; Substance
        abuse, comorbidity in
    types of stressors and, 1:13–15
Compassion, a core emotion, 4:191
Competency, 10:77
    case study, 10:150–156
    defined, 10:149
    to counsel, defined, 10:148
Competition, pervades all layers of job
    market, 9:84
Complaints, counselors and, 10:111
Complementarity, 2:90
Complex skill acquisition, 3:167, 168, 169–
    170
Compliance
    See also Noncompliance
    client's, 4:5
    confused with motivation, 7:224
    defined, 7:195

effected by structure of treatment,
    7:203
    of pharmacologic regimen, 7:31, 193
    treatment, known as adherence, 7:199
Complications in Opioid-Dependent
    Pregnancies (table), 8:112
Comprehensive Teacher's Rating Scale,
    5:54
Compulsions, 1:101, 4:80, 5:232
    See also Obsessive-compulsive
        disorder (OCD)
    defined, 1:32
    OCD clients without, 1:109
    present in a variety of
        psychopathologic conditions,
        1:30
Computed tomography scan, 10:101
Computers
    as risks to client confidentiality, 5:281–
        284
    used for testing, 9:137
Concanavalin A (conA), 3:21, 25, 26
Concentration
    difficulty in, 3:36, 155, 5:11
    inability for, 4:204
Conceptual orientation, of therapists,
    3:114
Concerned United Birthparents (CUB)
    (directory listing), 5:124, 126
Conditions That Promote Aggression
    (table), 5:192
Conduct disorder, comorbid with ADHD,
    1:198
Conduct disorders, 4:117, 5:10, 43, 48, 106,
    107, 156, 163, 254
    immaturity and, 5:195
Confidence, 3:5, 6
Confidentiality, 2:65, 127, 129, 131, 132,
    133, 4:138, 141, 147, 8:40, 184–
    185, 189, 9:223, 10:2, 59, 83, 91
    See also Disclosure; Information;
        Privacy
    breached, 2:221–222
    case study, 5:282
    clients with HIV and, 10:213–214
    in combined therapy, 2:111
    computer issues, 5:281–284
    concerns about, 5:163
    defined, 5:278–279
    exceptions to, 5:279–281
    governed by Title 42 of Federal
        Regulations, 10:122

in group therapy, 5:181–182
honored in aggression replacement
  training, 5:221
inform adolescent client about, 5:161
measures to protect, 5:284–285
mentally ill client and, 10:169–173
protecting that of children and
  adolescents, 5:275–290
in therapy with adopted children,
  5:118
threats to, 5:276–278
violations of, 2:219
when to breach, 10:4–9, 172, 219–221
Conflict resolution, 5:261, 6:29
Conflicts, 2:85, 6:13, 14, 16
avoiding in group therapy, 2:121–137
between sexes inevitable, 6:272
core, 2:83
dynamic, 2:81
in elderly couple, 6:182
expression of, 6:276
family, 4:102
  extreme, 6:106
  incest, 6:198
internal, 2:113, 4:122
intrapsychic, 2:81, 88, 258, 259
marital, 4:103
  and gender identification, 6:269
  and sexual dysfunction, 6:194
nonzero sum negotiation strategies,
  6:19, 20
parent-child, 6:14
poor ability to manage, 7:12
result from stress, 6:138
suppression of, 6:275
unresolvable, 6:21
Conflict Tactics Scale (CTS), 6:8–9, 28
Conflicts
Confrontation,
constructive, 8:34, 9:27
existential, 2:40
Congruence, person-job, assessment of,
  9:116
Conjoint therapy, 6:258
Connectedness, 6:272
women's capacity for, 6:273
Connecticut Mental Health Center
Alcohol Treatment Unit, 7:70
Outpatient Clinic, 8:273
Conners Questionnaire, for ADHD,
  1:197
Conscience, 4:43

Consciousness
case study, 4:225
encouraging, 4:225
level of, 4:224
stream of, 3:130
Consensual validation, 2:135
Consent, 8:184, 185–186
informed, 10:5, 79, 115–116
  conditions for obtaining, 10:169
  morally valid, 10:167–169
Consequences
for children with ADHD, 5:64
defined, 3:161–162
self-defeating negative, 4:157
self-enhancing negative, 4:157
Conservation-withdrawal, 3:4
Constipation, side effect of some
  medications, 1:229
Constitution, interpretation of, 10:3
Constructive development
assessing, 9:9
career counseling and, 9:1–15
institutional balance, 9:3, 4–6
interindividual balance, 9:3, 6–7
interpersonal balance, 9:3–4
neo-Piagetian theory of, 9:2–3, 15
Constructive Thinking Inventory, 7:13
Consumer
hidden victim of substance abuse,
  8:12
of supported employment, 9:119
Consumer advocacy, 10:62, 65
Consumer Employment Screening Form,
  9:146
Consumerism, growing movement of,
  1:239
Contemplation, 8:271, 281
Content
latent, 2:19, 22
manifest, 2:19–22
Contested divorce, defined, 6:40
Contingency management, 5:138, 140,
  7:178–179
Continuity, our well-being requires, 2:42–
  43
Contract
contingency, 7:179
disulfiram, 7:108, 122
no-suicide, 5:260–261
as part of treatment of substance
  abusers, 5:244–245
sobriety trust, 7:106

therapeutic, 4:138–140
    written behavioral, 7:106, 125
Control, 4:135
    excessive, 3:9–10
Controlled Substance Act (1985), 7:141
Conviction, defined, 4:173
Convulsive disorders, 7:34
"Cookers", 8:226, 229
Cooperation, building, 2:67–68
Coping, 2:258, 3:3, 5:27
    autoplasmic modes, 2:260
    case study, 4:180
    with grief, 6:161
    inability during divorce, 4:204
    mechanisms, 3:57, 4:181, 7:111, 226
    process, outcomes, 4:180
    self-statements, 5:145–146
    skills, 4:2, 18, 41, 45, 5:91, 257, 6:49, 51,
            159, 181, 8:82, 167, 9:27
    fewer in COAs, 4:101
    learning new in treatment of DID,
            1:70
        maladaptive, 3:228
    poor, 1:107
    recovery and, 8:68
    therapy, 7:70, 125, 221, 230
    strategies, 5:93
    styles, 2:257, 4:38
    may mediate stress response, 5:89
    tools for in poverty-stricken family,
            6:119
    with trauma of recollections of sexual
            abuse, 4:140
    two forms
        emotion-focused, 4:178, 180
        problem-focused, 4:178, 180
Coping With Depression (Beck &
        Greenberg), 3:134
Copper, 7:51, 60
    poisoning, 3:104
Core conflict relationship theme, 2:90
Core Emotions (*table*), 4:191
Core symbols, 7:115–116
Cornell Medical Index, 7:54
Coronary heart disease (CHD)
    cigarette smoking and, 4:54
    diet and, 4:54
    psychological factors in the treatment
            of, 4:53–66
Corrective emotional experience, 2:66,
        83
Corticosteroids, 5:162

Corticotropin, 3:99
Corticotropin-releasing hormone (CRH),
        3:22, 23, 25
Cortisol, 3:16, 25, 26, 29, 102, 103, 5:7
Costs
    EAPs and, 8:21–24
    health care, as concern of elderly, 3:82
Cotherapy, 5:182
"Cotton", 8:226
Coumadin (warfarin), 3:43
Council Care Senior Adult Day Care
        (ADC), 3:85
Council for Equal Rights in Adoption
        (CERA) (*directory listing*),
        5:124
Counseling
    See also Therapy
    alcohol and drug, 9:135
    approaches to the difficult client
        cognitive therapy, 2:55–56
        emotive, 2:54–55
        strategic, 2:56–57
    behavioral for older adults with
            depression, 3:147–171
    career
        See Career counseling
    and exercise, 3:87
    formats with older adults, 3:170
    group
        See Group therapy
    plan, 3:187
    in post-stroke depression, 3:42
    special concerns for older adults,
            3:73–74
    therapeutic aims, 3:186
    three-stage model of, 9:23–28
        case study, 9:25–26, 28–31
        commitment to action, 9:27–28
        in-depth exploration, 9:25–27
        in relationship wounds, 4:186–192
        initial stage, 9:23–24
    traditional, ineffectiveness with
            minority population, 9:179
Counselors
    See also Mental health professionals;
            Psychologists; Psychothera-
            pists; Therapists
    as advocates for minority clients,
            9:202–203
    bilingual/bicultural, 9:223
    biopsychosocial model of relapse and,
            7:221–222

called on to testify in court, 10:98
career
   can help with transition and
      transformation, 9:8
   as information providers, 9:10
   response to challenges of diverse
      populations, 9:195–199
   self-appraisal of personal world
      views, 9:195–196
   tasks of, 9:15, 32
   tend to shortchange first phase of
      counseling, 9:24
certification for, 8:84–85
certified in vocational evaluation,
   9:241
co-dependence of, 8:153–154
correction of errors in clinical
   judgement, 10:26
credentials, 10:82–83, 101
credibility, 10:99, 105
dealing with drinking during
   treatment, 7:110
discrimination on part of, case study,
   10:238–243
duty of disclosure, 10:225–227, 227–230
duty to protect, 10:127–138
ethical considerations for, 8:175–193
ethical dimensions of treating
      mentally ill by, 10:161–178
function of, 9:169
important to dependent clients, 3:187
must be sensitive to diversity, 10:47–
   49
must exercise best judgement in
      evaluation, 7:10
need empathy, 7:203
need to show caring feelings to
      dependent client, 3:188
parental image of, 3:191
power of means more ethical
      responsibilities, 10:18
practicing beyond scope of
      competency, 10:118–119
preventing lawsuits against, 10:109–
   124
primary intervention agent in disease
      model of relapse, 7:218
rehabilitation, 9:120, 153
   guidelines for, 9:71–76
   increasing job complexity for,
      10:61–63
   plan of action by, 9:90–95

preparing to deal with ethical
   dilemmas, 10:57–70
service-based focus, 10:62
should consider acculturation
   influences, 9:188
role in 12-step programs, 8:150–151
role in selecting group members, 3:77
separation from, 3:188, 189
sexual boundary violations and,
   10:195–206
shortcoming of, 7:19–20
should avoid instruments that screen
   clients out of jobs, 9:55
should possess knowledge of
   pharmacology, 7:26
substance abuse, 8:239
teaching of communication skills by,
   7:116
training sites, 10:86
values of
   and clients' self-determination,
      10:22
   influence counseling goals, 10:18
   views on old age, 3:73, 74
Counter-ritual, 1:35
Counteridentification, 1:73
Countertransference, 1:131, 2:92, 198,
   5:182–183, 8:276, 10:45, 78–79,
   86, 186, 187, 197
   therapist's reactions to erotic
      transference feelings, 2:235–
      237
County Alcohol Detoxification Unit
   (Wisconsin), 8:217
County of Buckingham (England), 1:258
Couple Contract/Fulfillment Record
   (*figure*), 7:121
Couples
   childless, 6:168
   cognitive therapy for, 3:139
Couples therapy, 6:258, 259
   mutuality in, 6:267–283
   for reactive jealousy, 6:253
   for the remarriage family, 6:93
   sex therapy and, 6:193
Court system, 6:110, 112
   navigating, 6:61, 66
Courts, involvement of in cases of school
   refusal, 5:10
"Crack babies", 7:172
"Crack" cocaine, 8:64, 100, 101
Crack Cocaine Epidemic (1991), 8:101

Craving
    of cocaine, 7:174, 176
    naltrexone blocks that of alcohol,
        7:74
Craving Scores (*figure*), 7:71
Crawford Small Parts Dexterity Tests,
        9:150
CRH
    See Corticotropin-releasing hormone
        (CRH)
Crime, 5:228, 7:217
    criminals and their feelings of, 1:145
    neighborhoods with, 3:151
    psychological factors, 1:140–142
    sociological explanations for, 1:138–
        140
    statistics, 5:193
    substance abuse and, 7:132
Criminal
    behavior, 1:144–148
        and genetics, 1:142
        psychological factors, 1:140–142
    career, 1:144
    and change, helping to motivate,
        1:148–149
    characteristic of the, 1:144–148
    inadequate parenting and the,
        1:140
    intelligence of the, 1:145
    personality, 1:137–151
        concept of, 1:143–144
    psychosis and the, 1:142
    rejection of mainstream, 1:139
    thinking patterns of the, 1:144
    who is according to the law, 1:138
    youth, 5:197–201
Criminal justice system, 4:119
    free will basis of, 2:222
Criminologists, 6:108
Crisis, in social drama, 6:101–102
Crisis clinics, community, 5:267
Crisis in Homelessness, The (government
        publication), 5:80
Crisis intervention, 3:115
    for homelessness, 5:90–91, 97
    with suicidal client, 5:259–263
Critical-evaluative level, of ethical
        consideration, 10:19
Criticism, type of relationship wound,
        4:182
Cross-examination
    bias in, 10:156

counselors task concerning, 10:100,
        102, 105
Crossroads: Critical Choices for the
        Development of Healthy
        Adolescents (CCAD), 6:100
Crying, 6:268
    child's, 6:43, 47
    in COAs, 4:101
Crystallization, of problem focus, 2:85
CT scans, 1:40
Cued recall, 2:29
Cues, use of, 9:118
Cultural diversity, impact on career
        counseling, 9:177–203
Culture
    and emotional expressions, 4:35
    shared, 9:179–180
Culture-Fair Intelligence Test, 9:217
Cumulative adoption trauma, 5:113
Cushing's disease, 5:162
Cushing's Syndrome, 3:102
Custodial parent, defined, 6:40
Custody, 6:37–38
    cases, 6:58
    conflicts, confidentiality and, 5:287,
        289
    glossary of terms (*table*), 6:40–41
    joint, 6:58
        legal, defined, 6:40
        physical, defined, 6:40
    shared, 6:58
    sole, 6:62
        defined, 6:40
    split, defined, 6:41
    worry about losing, 6:66
Cybernetics, 2:153
Cyclical maladaptive pattern (CMP), 2:88,
        89, 90
Cyclothymia, 3:267, 8:251, 5:154
Cylert (pemoline), 5:56
Cytochrome P-450, 7:53, 57, 60
    detoxification enzyme, 7:50
Cytokines, 3:20, 21

D

Daily Record of Dysfunctional Thoughts
        (*table*), 3:135
Daily Warning Signs Chart for Mania
        (*chart*), 1:233
Dance therapy, 5:177

Danger
  at job site, 9:54
  cause for breach of confidentiality,
    10:4, 7–9
Dangerousness, question of predictivity
  of, 10:135
Dantrium (dantrolene), 7:43
Dantrolene (Dantrium), 7:43
Darvocet (propoxyphine), 8:80
Date rape, 5:33
Dating, after divorce, 6:64–65, 68
Daughters
  adolescent, 6:64
  raised by fathers, 6:63
Davis v. Lhim, 10:144
Day care, incest in, 4:116
Day treatment center, 9:163
Daydreaming, 6:51
  See also Dreams
Deafness, 9:112
Death, 6:106, 8:204
  acceptance of, 6:130
  acetaldehyde and, 7:66
  adolescent, suicide second common
    cause of, 5:252
  AIDS and, 6:124
  of a child, 6:147–162
    case study, 6:153–157
  communication about, 6:161
  concept of, 5:159
  desire for, 4:56
  due to alcohol-related traffic
    accidents, 8:203
  due to tricyclic antidepressants, 5:165
  Ecstasy and, 7:140, 144
  of family member, as risk factor for
    separation anxiety disorder,
    5:10
  from addiction, 8:149
  grief as reaction to, 3:6
  of hospital and nursing home
    patients, 3:121
  impending, 2:204
  inevitability of, 6:129
  of loved one, 3:154
  memorial rituals needed for, 6:161
  as negative life event leading to
    relapse, 7:227
  by overdose, naltrexone prevention
    of, 7:67
  of parent, 6:95, 141
  in patients with eating disorders, 3:62

  planning for, 6:126
  post-stroke depression and, 3:43
  predictors of, 3:88
  preparation for in HIV, 8:235
  rates in older adults, 3:69
  at raves, 7:131
  single fathers and, 6:59, 62
  of spouse, 2:201, 6:95
    dating after, 6:64
  of spouse a stressful event, 4:202
  and stress, 1:4, 6:135
  thoughts of, 3:36, 155, 5:154
  tied to adolescent suicide, 5:256
  as traumatic event, 1:2, 4
  using bibliotherapy in event of, 5:146–
    147
Death penalty, issue of power struggle in,
  2:216
Deaths From Cancer and CHD According
  to Personality Type:
  Heidelberg Study (*figure*),
  4:58, 59
Deaths From Cancer and CHD According
  to Personality Type: Yugoslav
  Study (*figure*), 4:58
Deaths From Cancer and Other Causes in
  Control, Placebo, and
  Therapy Subjects: Short
  Individual Therapy (*table*),
  4:63
Decision tree, 7:4, 21
Decision-Tree Approach to Assessment
  (*figure*), 7:5
Decision Tree for Matching Patients with
  Either Inpatient or Outpatient
  Treatment for Alcoholism
  (*figure*), 7:97
Decision making, diverse models of,
  10:64–65
Decker v. Fink (1980), 2:227
Defeat depression, 3:184
Defendants, therapists as, immunity of,
  10:140–141
Defense mechanisms, 4:43, 1:14
  acting out, 4:36
  displacement, 4:36
  exhibited in the workplace, 4:36
  passive-aggressive behavior, 4:36
  projection, 4:36, 43
Defenses, 2:257
  dissociative, 1:63
Defensive strategies, 4:35

Delayed gratification, 8:161
Delinquency, 6:132, 8:160, 192
 juvenile, 5:193
Delinquency Cases by Offense (*table*),
  5:194
Delirium, 3:43, 5:240
Delirium tremens (DTs), 3:103, 7:95, 96
Delusional disorder, 6:253, 8:252
Delusions, 1:16, 3:142, 7:40, 146, 8:61, 128,
  251
 case study, 6:262
 of infidelity, 6:242, 247, 261
Dementia, 3:107, 153, 167
 AIDS-related, 8:240
 Alzheimer's type, 3:70
 cerebral vascular, 3:70
 chronic, 2:203
 comorbid with depression, 3:150
 defined, 3:69
 of depression, 3:41
 in Huntington's disease, 3:105
 senile, 3:25
Demerol (Meperidine), 7:42
Demographic Information on Children
  and Families (*table*), 5:87
Denial, 1:3, 2:114, 4:70, 80, 6:158, 8:151
 about adoption, 5:110, 112–113, 119,
  120
 about substance abuse, 5:236
 at the heart of addiction and co-
   dependence, 4:86
 in divorce, 4:203, 212, 6:39
 in elderly alcoholics, 8:206–207
 first reaction children experience, 6:42
 in HIV diagnosis, 8:233–234
 mechanism of false forgiveness,
   4:253
 of mortality, 6:127
 in patients with addictions, 7:192
 primary characteristic of alcoholism,
   8:212
Denmark, adoption studies in, 4:98
Depakene (valproic acid), 1:228, 7:41
Depakote (divalproex, Valproate), 1:229,
  5:166, 7:41
Department of Transportation, law
  governing commercial
  vehicle operation, 8:7
Dependence
 in adolescents, 5:185
 an adaptive style, 3:7–9

defined, 3:180, 4:39
excessive, 5:159
interpersonal, 4:39–40
on medication, 7:32
normal, 3:180
oral type, 3:182
pathological, 3:180, 181–182
relationship between depression and,
  3:182–184
two components
 closeness, 3:183
 lowerness, 3:183
Dependency, 4:35, 36, 43, 9:166
 needs for as reason for marriage,
  4:204–205
Depersonalization, 7:139
Depressants
 central nervous system, 5:162
 what they do, 8:251
Depression, 1:10, 81, 98, 106, 123, 166, 183,
  222, 2:108, 135, 261, 4:80, 5:4,
  13, 24, 195, 233, 240, 241, 256,
  263, 6:9, 22, 51, 149, 158, 181,
  227, 228, 229, 242, 259, 7:66,
  96, 140, 144, 221, 232, 234,
  8:204, 205, 239, 247, 253, 9:166
 abandonment, 1:122
 adaptive styles in, 3:1–12
 in adolescents, 5:153–168, 8:162
  statistics, 5:157–158
  treatment, 5:162–168
 in adults, 5:10
 after divorce, 6:39, 47–48
 aggression and, 3:124–125
 agitated, 7:35
 anaclitic, 3:4
 atypical, 1:82, 7:36
 behavioral counseling for elderly
   patients with, 3:147–171
 bipolar, 3:142
 can generate jealous preoccupations,
   6:252
 case study, 6:48, 5:155
 in cases of irrational beliefs, 4:158
 checklist, 3:154–155
 in children, 5:81–83, 6:36
 chronic
  See Dysthymia
 in COAs, 4:102
 coexisting with DID, 1:63–64
 cognitive therapy for, 3:127–142

common after head injury, 7:43
confounding factors associated with,
   3:28–29
   dietary changes, 3:28
   heavy drinking, 3:28
   heavy smoking, 3:28
   medications, 3:28
   sleeplessness, 3:28
as consequence of family caregiving,
   6:177
debilitating for older adults, 3:90
defined, 3:163, 164
dependency and, 3:179–195
distinguished from PTSD, 1:21
due to homelessness, 5:79–97
during divorce, 4:204, 212
dysthymic
   See Dysthymia
eating disorders and, 3:51–63
in elderly
   See Depression, in older adults
factors causing, 5:80
in gamblers
   See Gambler, depressive
group counseling for elderly patients
   with, 3:65–90
high levels of cortisol in some clients
   with, 3:25
in IBS patients, 4:10
and immune system, 3:15–30, 6:138
in incest victims, 4:118
major, 5:12, 154, 157, 253, 7:37, 233
   comorbidity with alcoholism,
   8:119–132
   medically based causes of, 3:244–
   246
and miscarriage, 6:152
misdiagnosing of physical illnesses
   as, 3:93–108
OCD reveals symptoms similar to,
   1:38–39
in older adults, 2:201, 6:180
   diagnosis, 3:151–163
   difficulty of diagnosis, 3:69–71
   statistics, 3:68–69
panic disorder comorbid with, 5:15
post-stroke, 3:33–45
   duration, 3:38–39
   symptomatology, 3:36–38
principles in psychotherapy for,
   3:113–125

in prisoners of war, 1:16
psychopathology of
   essential elements
      cognitive triad, 3:129–130
      logical errors, 3:129, 132
      silent assumptions, 3:129,
      130–131
reactive, 3:2
reduced by aerobic exercise, 1:112
related to PTSD in veterans, 1:15
relationship between dependence
   and, 3:182–184
restoration of work capacity in
   persons with, 3:199–218
scales, 3:155, 156, 157, 158
severe, 5:57
severity of and work capacity, 3:216
stress management techniques for,
   4:16–17
symptom rather than disease, 3:114
symptoms, alleviating, 3:243–262
symptoms can mimic those of
   dementia, 3:70
vulnerability to, 3:132–133
work-related, 4:45
Depression Guideline Panel, 3:210, 213,
   267, 270
Depression Scale of the Nurses'
   Observation Scale for
   Inpatient Evaluation, 3:169
Depression Workbook: A Guide to Living
   with Depression and Manic
   Depression (Copeland), 1:215,
   221, 3:253
Depressive disorders
   common in adolescents, 5:154
      statistics, 5:159–160
   related to anxiety disorders, 5:3
Deprivation depression, 3:184
Derealization, 7:139
Desensitization
   for gambling patients, 1:163
   techniques
      genital, 6:230–231
      nongenital, 6:230–231
   in therapy, 1:110, 111
   of traumatic scene to jealous person,
   6:256
Desipramine (Norpramin, Pertofrane),
   1:42, 3:44, 274, 5:56–57, 164,
   7:35, 8:111, 283

Desire
  defined, 6:192
  sexual, 6:192
Desoxyn (methamphetamine), 5:56, 7:141
Despair, 4:45, 248, 6:129
Destiny, 2:37
Desyrel (trazodone), 3:42, 272, 7:36
"Detach with love", admonition for
    counselors, 8:154
Determining the Significance of a Limited
    Function (*table*), 9:44
Detoxification, 3:98, 5:241, 8:278
  home program, 6:110
  improved through nutrition, 7:49–61
  inpatient contrasted with outpatient,
    7:87–98
Development, described, 9:3
Developmental disorders, 9:221
Dexamethasone, 3:35
Dexamethasone suppression test (DST),
    1:39
Dexedrine (dextroamphetamine), 5:56
Dextroamphetamine (Dexedrine), 5:56
Diabetes, 2:255, 3:18, 88, 100–101, 5:162, 240
Diagnosis
  aid to successful therapy of elderly,
    2:200–205
  of disability, 9:36
  of mental illness, 10:166
Diagnostic Criteria for Caffeine
    Intoxication (*table*), 7:158
Diagnostic Interview for Children and
    Adolescents (DICA), 5:243,
    7:12
Diagnostic Interview Schedule, 1:36
Diagnostic Interview Schedule for
    Children (DISC), 5:243
Diagnostic Specificity and Treatment
    Planning, series, 2:253–254
Diagnostic and Statistical Manual of
    Mental Disorders
  See DSM; DSM-I; DSM-II; DSM-III;
    DSM-III-R; DSM-IV
Diarrhea, 3:99
  in IBS patients, 4:10
Diary, used in suspected cases of DID,
    1:59
Diazepam (Valium), 2:220, 7:27, 34, 43,
    147, 8:80
Dictionary of Occupational Titles (U.S.
    Department of Labor), 9:46,
    128, 138

DID
  See Dissociative identity disorder
    (DID)
Diet
  See also Fat; Food; Eating disorders
  an adjunctive technique for anxious
    clients, 1:112
  changes in due to depression, 3:28, 29
  detoxification, 7:53–54, 57, 60
  foods for substance abusers to avoid,
    7:56
  healthy, balanced needed for bulimic
    patients, 3:61
  high-complex carbohydrate indicated
    for manic clients, 1:229
Dietary guidelines, for depressed clients,
    3:248, 249
Dieting, 5:15
  in anorexia nervosa, 3:54, 60
Differences Between Cognitive-
    Behavioral Play Therapy and
    Traditional Play Therapies
    (*table*), 5:137
Differential Aptitude Test, 9:150
Differentiating the Adopted Child
    Syndrome From Conduct
    Disorder (*table*), 5:106
Differentiation, 3:190
  of self
    interpersonal, 2:157
    intrapsychic, 2:157
Diflunisal (Dolobid), 7:42
Dilantin (phenytoin), 5:51, 7:29, 41
Dilaudid (hydromorphone), 7:42
Dilemmas
  ethical, 10:163
    case study, 10:59–60, 221–227
    confidentiality types, 10:170
    rehabilitation counselors and,
      10:57–70
    seven-step approach to, 10:54
    statistics, 10:2
Dimenhydrinate (Dramamine), 5:68
Dinnerstein v. United States (1973), 2:134
Direct Comparisons of Medication,
    Psychotherapy, and Placebo
    in Five Contributing Projects
    (*table*), 3:214
Disabilities
  See also Americans with Disabilities
    Act (ADA)
  assessment and evaluation of, 9:37

assessment of views about, 9:197
child's
    African-American family
        response to, 9:181
    Asian-American family response
        to, 9:185
    Hispanic family response to,
        9:183
diagnosis of, 9:36
employment needs of clients with,
    9:80–82
finances and, 9:70
full integration of persons with into
    society, 9:58
level of need and, 9:71
limited employment opportunities
    due to, 9:64
mild, 9:119, 223
Native American reaction to, 9:187
pride and, 9:70
qualified individual with, defined,
    9:47–48, 50
severe, 9:40, 111, 223, 236, 242
    workers with, 9:113, 115
statistics, 9:65, 80–81
substance abuse and, 8:55–86
    statistics, 8:56–57
transportation to work site and, 9:70
vocational evaluation of Hispanic
    clients with, 9:209–224
Disappointment, a core emotion, 4:191
Disasters, 3:255
Disclosure
    See also Confidentiality; Information;
        Privacy
    full, and rehabilitation of criminals,
        1:149
    of recollections, 4:126
Discrepancies, between job/task
        requirements and individual
        characteristics, 9:117–118
Discrimination, 9:191, 10:242
    against AIDS victims, 6:134
    in counseling relationship, 10:237
Disease
    addiction as powerful, 8:149
    approach to diagnosis, 7:194
    autoimmune, 3:16, 18
    infectious, role of psyche in, 3:16
    influence of stress on, 4:2
    model of alcoholism, 8:209–210
    model of relapse, 7:218

psychosomatic approach to
        explaining presence of, 4:54
    substance abuse as, 8:66–67, 74
Disease consciousness, formation of,
    1:253
Diseases
    contagious, fatal
        reporting on, 10:49–50, 213–214
        See also AIDS; HIV
    sexually transmitted, 4:119
*Diseasing of America: Addiction Out of
    Control* (Peele), 4:75
Disequilibrium, 4:42, 1:3
Disgust, a core emotion, 4:191
Disorders
    See also Specific types of disorders
    mental
        prevalence of (*table*), 1:103
        self-management approaches for,
            1:237–260
Displacement, 4:36
Disruptive behavior disorders, 5:159
Dissociation, 1:14, 50
    ego-dystonic, 1:60
Dissociative disorder, 1:197
Dissociative Disorders Interview
        Schedule (DDIS), 1:61
Dissociative Experience Scale (DES), 1:60–
    61
Dissociative identity disorder (DID),
        1:49–84, 4:117, 119, 127, 134,
        10:27
    See also Personalities; Personality
        disorders
    background, 1:50–52
    case studies and statistics, 1:83–84
    characteristics of, 1:52–54
    in children, 1:50
    coexisting syndromes, 1:63–66
    definition and description, 1:52–58
    diagnosing, 1:58–63
    formerly known as multiple
        personality disorder, 1:50
    hospitalization of clients with, 1:79–80
    host, presenting, and original
        personalities, 1:56
    hypnosis and, 1:61–62
    medications for, 1:80–82
    modalities of treatment, 1:74–84
    number of personalities in, 1:55
    overlap and BPD, 1:124
    signs of, 1:58–59

therapist's reactions to working with,
  1:72–74
treatment of, 1:66–72
types of personalities in, 1:54–58
Distance, 4:40
Distortions, cognitive, 6:225
Distribution, of medications, 7:28, 29
Disulfiram (Antabuse), 7:66, 67, 70, 108,
  111, 8:129, 273
Ditropan (oxybutynin), 7:43
Divalproex sodium (Depakote), 7:41
Diversity, 10:78, 80–81
  ACA *Code of Ethics* and, 10:49
  case study, 10:238–243
  cultural, 10:236
    impact on career counseling,
      9:177–203
  ethics and, 10:235–246
Divorce, 2:113, 118, 5:7, 10, 6:106, 202,
  7:102, 124
  See also Remarriage families
  and change in family structure, 6:168
  contested, defined, 6:40
  counseling children of, 6:35–52
  economic, 6:77, 85
  effects on child, case study, 6:38–39
  legal, 6:77, 85
  money and, 6:85–86
  parental, 1:22
  psychological stages
    acceptance, 6:39
    anger, 6:39
    denial, 6:39
    depression, 6:39
    guilt, 6:39
    resentment, 6:39
  reality in today's world, 6:52
  single fathers and, 6:58, 59
  stages of, 4:212
  statistics, 6:74
  therapy of clients undergoing a,
    4:201–215
  tied to adolescent suicide, 5:256
  uncontested, defined, 6:41
  using bibliotherapy in event of, 5:146–
    147
Divorce monologue technique, 6:51
Docusate calcium (Surfak), 7:43
Dolobid (diflunisal), 7:42
Dolophine (methadone), 8:111
Domination

case study, 6:275
  as manifestation of sexism, 6:274–
    276
Dopamine, 1:44, 3:99, 5:52, 7:37, 39, 67, 68,
    78, 226
  D2 receptor, alcoholic gene, 4:100
Doriden (glutethimide), 8:65
Doses, therapeutic, 3:270, 272
Double bind theory, 2:145
Doxepin (Sinequan), 3:272, 7:35
Dramamine (dimenhydrinate), 5:68
Dread, 6:280
  defined, 6:279
Dreams, 2:113, 5:116
  See also Daydreaming
  abuse-related, 5:26
Drinkers, nonproblem, 7:227
Drinking
  See also Alcohol; Alcoholism
  abusive, 7:102, 103, 105, 109
  during treatment, 7:110–111
  problem, 8:15
    defined, 8:199
    effects of on elderly, 8:203–206
  social, 4:97, 7:75, 106, 110
  stress-induced, 4:101
Drives
  and career choices, 4:35, 36
  innate
    aggression, 4:35
    sex, 4:35
  instinctual, 4:43
Drug abuse, 1:103, 3:58, 94, 96, 101–102,
    258, 6:18, 36, 37, 251
  See also Addiction; Alcohol abuse;
    Alcoholism; Chemical
    Dependency; Stimulant
    abuse; Substance abuse;
    Tobacco abuse
  in families, 6:120–123
  hallucinogenic, 7:129–148
  intergenerational pattern of, 6:105
  integrative approach for evaluation
    and treatment, 7:1–21
  statistics, 4:70, 7:132–136, 8:56
  treatment services are missing link,
    7:136
Drug Abuse Screening Test (DAST), 8:273
Drug dealers, 5:239
Drug Enforcement Agency (DEA), 7:134
Drug offenders, 2:60

Drug reactions, due to improper
    treatment, 2:219
Drug screen, 5:239, 240, 245
Drug use, intravenous, 6:121, 123
Drug Use Screening Inventory (DUSI),
    5:243
Drug Use Screening Inventory (DUSI-R),
    7:5, 6, 8, 9, 19, 20, 21
Drug-Free Workplace Act (1988), 8:6–7
Drug-testing
    mandatory, 8:5
    preemployment, 8:12
Drugs
    See also Medications; Pharmacotherapy
    alter detoxification ability of liver,
        7:53
    analgesics, 7:42
    classes of, 8:58–59
    concentration, 7:28
    detoxification, improved through
        nutrition, 7:49–61
    function, 7:28
    history of usage, 7:154
    illicit
        See also Drug abuse; Substance
            abuse
        prevalence of (*table*), 8:97
    interactions, 7:31
    multiple, use of, 7:10
    nomenclature of, 7:27
        brand name, 7:27
        chemical name, 7:27
        generic name, 7:27
    side effects, 7:30–31
    variations in choice of, 8:99–102
"Dry drunk", 7:222, 8:253
DSM, 2:254, 4:244
    See also DSM-I; DSM-II; DSM-III;
        DSM-III-R; DSM-IV
DSM-I, addiction in, 8:246
DSM-II, addiction in, 8:246
DSM-III, 1:65
    addictive disorders in, 8:246
    and age of onset of autism, 1:173
    alcoholism and depression in, 8:120
    AXIS I diagnosis and, 7:227
    criteria for substance use disorders,
        4:70
    definition of hypoactive sexual desire
        disorder, 6:220
    diagnosis of post-stroke depression

and, 3:36
    label of ADHD, 1:193–194
    and PTSD symptoms of Vietnam
        veterans, 1:9
DSM-III-R, 1:10, 11, 12, 14
    addictive disorders in, 8:246
    clinical interview for PTSD, 1:8–9
    comparative criteria for PTSD (*table*),
        1:6–7
    criteria for psychiatric disorder
        leading to suicide, 5:253
    Structured Clinical Interview for, 7:12
    substance abuse disorders in, 7:9
DSM-IV, 3:100, 101, 104, 167
    addictive disorders in, 8:246
    and adopted child syndrome, 5:105
    alcohol dependence in, 8:122–123
    and attention-deficit/hyperactivity
        disorder (ADHD), 5:42
    brief psychotic disorders and, 6:247
    bulimia nervosa and, 3:56
    comparative criteria for PTSD (*table*),
        1:6–7
    contains detailed descriptions of
        anxiety disorders, 1:99
    criteria for adolescent substance
        abuse, 5:230–231
    criteria for Asperger's disorder, 1:177
    criteria for childhood disintegrative
        disorder, 1:177
    criteria for DID, 1:53
    criteria for major depression, 3:149–
        150
    criteria for major depressive disorder,
        3:59
    criteria for PTSD, 1:5
    criteria for ruling out physical illness,
        3:94
    decision rules for differential
        treatment, 3:154
    definition of depression, 3:267
    definition of hypoactive sexual desire
        disorder, 6:220, 221
    definition of pathological gambling,
        1:155
    definition of personality trait
        disorders, 4:74
    description of jealousy, 6:249
    description of manic episode, 1:212–
        213
    diagnosis of anxiety disorders, 5:5

diagnosis of dementia, 3:69
diagnosis from part of information
    released to insurance
    companies, 10:5
diagnosis of post-stroke depression
    and, 3:36
diagnostic criteria for depression, 5:154
differential diagnosis of depression,
    3:98
distinction between abuse and
    dependence, 8:199
Generalized anxiety disorder in, 7:157
hallucinogen persisting perception
    disorder in, 7:140
label of ADHD, 1:193–194
label for depressive symptoms, 5:81
major depressive disorder and, 8:121–
    122
    See also DSM-IV, criteria for major
    depressive disorder
paranoid personality disorder noted
    in, 6:244
personality disorders, 4:81
pervasive developmental disorders
    and, 1:175
substance abuse
    as defined in, 8:94
    disorders and, 8:58–59
substance dependence in, 8:251
substance use disorder and, 8:271
three phobias described in, 5:12–13
types of anorexia in, 3:58
and types of attention-deficit/
    hyperactivity disorder
    (ADHD), 5:43
use of standard deviation as
    classification tool in, 9:42
DSM-IV Criteria for Attention-Deficit/
    Hyperactivity Disorder
    (table), 5:44
DSM-IV Criteria for Substance Abuse
    (table), 8:62
DSM-IV Criteria for Substance
    Dependence (table), 8:60–61
DSM-IV Criteria for Substance
    Intoxication (table), 8:63
DSM-IV Diagnostic Criteria for Mental
    Retardation (table), 9:43
Dual diagnosis relapse prevention
    (DDRP), 8:270, 277–278, 280,
    285
Dual relationships, 10:2, 78, 79–80

case study, 10:117–118
    Code of Ethics (ACA) and, 10:50–51
    defined, 10:184, 190
    examples of, 10:184
    minimizing the risk, 10:192–193
    toward a consensus in thinking,
        10:183–193
    warnings against, 10:10–12, 185
Dual sensory impairment, 9:110
Duke University Center for the Study of
    Aging and Human
    Development, 6:180
Duress, consent given under, 10:169
Duty to protect, 10:127–138, 172, 173, 218–
    219
    ethical dilemma of, case studies,
        10:221–227
Dyadic Adjustment Scale, 6:3–4, 27, 226
Dyadic Adjustment Scale Scores for Mr.
    and Mrs. Smith (table), 6:5
Dynamic conflict
    See Dynamic hypothesis
Dynamic hypothesis, 2:80, 81
Dynamic psychotherapy, 3:234
Dysfunctional families, 2:146
Dyslexia, 1:126
Dysmenorrhea
    See also Menstruation
    defined, 4:8
    stress management techniques for, 4:8
Dysmorphic disorder, 1:33
Dysphoria, 1:79, 81, 82, 160, 161, 3:55, 61,
        149, 159, 162, 6:227, 7:174
    and gamblers, 1:159
    in homeless children, 5:83
Dysthymia, 2:252, 253, 3:217, 225–237,
        266, 267, 5:12, 154, 157, 159,
        165, 253, 8:252
    clinical aspects of, 3:227–229
    contrasted with major depression,
        3:228
    defined, 3:226
    mild and chronic, 3:226
    psychosocial therapies in, 3:225–237

E

EAP
    See Employee assistance program
        (EAP)
EAPA

See Employee Assistance Professional
Association (EAPA)
Eating disorders, 1:33, 2:103, 4:134, 5:156,
8:68
See also Anorexia nervosa; Bulimia
nervosa; Obesity
death in patients with, 3:62
depression and, 3:51–63
relationship to mood disorders, 3:63
Eccentricity, contrasted with mental
illness, 10:165
Echo, mythological character, 4:82
Ecological, defined, 9:113–114
Ecstasy, 3:102, 7:130, 131, 132, 133
also known as MDMA, 3:102
description, 7:140–144
signs of overdose, 7:144
treatment, 7:144, 146–148
ECT
See Electroconvulsive therapy (ECT)
Eczema, 7:56
Education
continuing, 10:38
protection against lawsuits,
10:119
of depressed clients, 3:247
in ethics, 10:63–69
of patients, 7:204–206, 228–229
Educational group interventions, for
elderly caregivers, 6:181–182
EEG
See Electroencephalogram (EEG)
Effect of Prophylactic Behavior Therapy
on Cancer-Prone and CHD
Probands (*table*), 4:61
Effects of MDMA Use (*table*), 7:145
Effects of Psychoactive Substances (*table*),
5:233
Effexor (venlafaxine), 3:61
Ego, 2:7, 80, 233, 4:43, 222, 5:229
boundaries, 4:245
control, 1:163
dystonic, 3:118
fragmentation, 2:117
function, 1:127
ideal, 4:35, 38, 39, 43, 5:229
defined, 4:37
derived from bonds of childhood,
3:5
identity, 4:206
observing, 3:60
poor, 2:105

states, 3:181, 193
strength, 1:63, 68, 74, 120, 2:9, 117, 257,
258, 4:209, 6:199, 200
support, 4:45, 6:93
talking to well part of, 9:166
weakness, 2:258, 259
Elavil (amitriptyline), 1:42, 3:272, 274,
7:35, 38, 10:114
Elder abuse, 6:179
Elderly, 2:103, 108, 118
able to benefit from psychotherapy,
2:194
alcoholism and, 8:197–219
statistics, 8:204–205
assessment of, 6:180–181
barriers to effective mental health
services to (*table*), 2:197
case study, 2:205–208, 208–209, 3:73
categorizing, 3:66–68
current approaches to therapy with,
2:193–210
depressed
behavioral counseling for, 3:147–
171
group counseling for, 3:65–90
devalued by society, 3:89
diagnosis as aid to successful, 2:200–
205
dying, 2:204
family caregiving of the, 6:167–185
fastest growing age group, 2:194, 209
as former child abuser, 6:176
as former spouse abuser, 6:176
late-life functional impairment of,
2:200, 201–203
medications and, 7:27
minimal impairment of, 2:200, 204–
205
more diverse than alike, 3:68
myths regarding mental illness in
(*table*), 2:195
"old old", 3:68
organic brain impairment of, 2:200,
203
reasons for low rate of psychotherapy
in, 2:196–198
recurrent functional impairment of,
2:200–201
represent a varied age group, 2:197
statistics, 2:194, 3:66
stroke in, 3:34
syllabus for life review (*table*), 2:205

those susceptible to depression, 3:71–
72
underserved in mental health care,
2:194
"young old", 3:68
Elderly Recovery Group (Wisconsin),
8:216–217, 218
Electric-shock aversion therapy, 1:163
Electrocardiogram, 3:43
Electroconvulsive therapy (ECT), 3:44,
116
Electroencephalogram (EEG), 4:99,
10:101
in patients with OCD, 1:40
Electromyographic biofeedback (EMG),
4:8, 11, 12, 17, 18, 19, 20
ELISA kit, to measure cytokines, 3:21
Elliot & Fitzpatrick (*directory listing*),
9:61
Embarrassment
fear of, 1:100–101
of manic clients, 1:228
EMG
See Electromyographic biofeedback
(EMG)
Emotional cutoff, 2:158
Emotional reactions
disturbed, 4:154
heightened level of in middle stage of
counseling, 4:190
Emotional reserves, 3:192
Emotional triangles, 2:156, 157
Emotional withholding, type of
relationship wound, 4:182
Emotions
core (*table*), 4:191
management of, 7:233–234
Emotive approaches, therapy style, 2:54–55
Empathy, 6:21
advanced level statements of, 9:25
defined, 2:66
mutual, 6:277, 279
Employability, personal assistance and,
9:69–71
Employee Assistance Professional
Association (EAPA), 8:17, 27
(*directory listing*), 8:28
Employee assistance program (EAP),
7:79, 217, 8:3, 16
basic components
accountability, 8:25–26
employee orientation training,

8:26–27
evaluation, 8:27
identification of treatment
resources, 8:26
intake and referral, 8:26
policy statement, 8:25
procedures for case finding, 8:25
program marketing, 8:26
record keeping, 8:27
supervisor training, 8:26
defined, 8:17
developing skills for, 8:31–32
economic benefits of, 8:21–24
external vendors and, 8:19
facets of, 8:16–27
integration into an organization, 8:24
referrals to, 8:37–38
staffing, 8:27
statistics, 8:9, 17–18, 22–24, 33, 35, 38
survey to decide involvement with,
8:28–31
types of
capitated program, 8:19
consortium, 8:20
fee-for-service, 8:19
fixed fee-for-service, 8:19
internal/in-house, 8:18–19
labor organization-based, 8:19–
20
professional organizations, 8:20
using strategy of, 8:32–39
wave of the future, 8:20
Employee Assistance Society of North
America (EASNA), 8:27
(*directory listing*), 8:28
Employee-assistance programs, 3:217
Employees
absenteeism and, 8:12
alcoholic, 8:11
characteristics of substance abusing,
8:12–15
help-seeking by, three stages, 8:42
personal problems and, 8:2
Employers
the Americans with Disabilities Act
(ADA) does not place all
burden on, 9:52–53
application of marketing strategies
by, 9:97–105
attitudes about personal problems in
the workplace, 8:2
educating about diversity, 9:202

implications of substance abuse for,
8:10–12
legal requirements of, 8:6–7
options for, 8:15–16
placement services for, 9:84–87
role in dealing with troubled
employees, 8:33–37
Employers' Comparison of Disabled
Workers with Other Workers
(*table*), 9:88
Employment
Americans with Disabilities Act
(ADA) and, 9:36
competitive, 9:112
depression's impact on, 3:201–202
history, patients', 9:170
lack of opportunity in, 1:138
loss of, 4:44
models
place-train, 9:86, 96
place-train-maintain, 9:86
needs of clients with disabilities,
statistics, 9:80–82
part-time, 9:52, 81, 154
sheltered, role of, 9:165
and single father, 6:62
supported, 9:109–124
core features, 9:111–113
history, 9:110–111
planning, 9:121
quality components of, 9:118–124
training procedures for, 9:122
Empowerment, 9:53
of depressed clients, 3:247
Empty-nest syndrome, 2:201
Enabler, co-dependent role, 4:77–78
Encephalitis lethargica, 1:39
Enclaves, 9:112
dispersed, 9:112
Encounter groups, 2:13, 100, 102
End goal development, 10:19
Endocrine disorders, 3:107
in gamblers, 1:160
Endocrine gland dysfunctions, 3:245
Endorphins, 3:16, 24, 4:99, 8:166
and exercise, 3:87
lack of in alcoholics, 7:226
mediation, 7:74
Endoscopy, 4:10
Energy, productivity and, 9:71
English as a second language, 9:197
Enkephalins, 3:16, 24

Environment
interaction of PTSD client and, 1:23
shared, 6:88
Environmental assessment, 9:99–100, 116
Environmental events, may contribute to
depression, 3:151
Envy, a core emotion, 4:191
Enzymes, detoxification, 7:50
Epidemiologic Catchment Area (ECA),
1:102, 3:69, 201, 8:120, 247
study to determine prevalence of
OCD, 1:36
Epidemiologists, 4:66
Epilepsy, 5:162
in autistic children, 1:175, 179
temporal lobe, 1:39, 64, 65
Epinephrine, 3:23, 24, 99, 5:6
EQUIP, 5:209–210
Equitable (fair) distribution of property,
defined, 6:41
Erection, 6:193
Ergonomics, 9:133–134
Eros, 2:7
Erotic transference
defined, 2:232
interpretation of, 2:243
statistics, 2:234
steps in therapeutic management of
(*table*), 2:234
therapeutic approaches to, 2:231–
245
therapists' need for consultation with
colleague, 2:245
Esalen, 2:14
Escape, as reason for marriage, 4:204, 205
Eskalith
See Lithium (Eskalith Lithane)
Essential Guide to Prescription Drugs
(Long), 3:246
Est, 2:14
Ethanol
See Alcohol
*Ethical Case Management Practices Training
Program* (Rubin, Millard,
Wong, & Wilson), 10:65, 66–67
Ethical Considerations in Treating the
Mentally Ill: Two Case
Studies (*appendix*), 10:180–182
Ethical Guidelines (EGs) (*table*), 10:220
Ethical Guidelines for Group Counselors
(ASGW), 2:122, 129
Ethical Guidelines for Group Counselors

(Association for Group
Work), 3:76
Ethical practices, in group therapy, 2:121–
137
*Ethical Practices in Rehabilitation Training
Modules* (Rubin, Wilson, et
al.), 10:65, 67, 68–69
Ethical Principles of Psychologists (APA),
2:122
*Ethical Principles of Psychologists and Code
of Conduct* (APA), 10:2, 76, 82,
167, 188, 189
Ethical reasoning, 10:58
Ethical rules
defined, 10:19
for disclosure of confidential
information, 10:227–230
Ethical Rules (ERs) *(table)*, 10:228–229
Ethical Standards (AACD), 2:122
Ethical Standards (ACA), 10:45
pro bono service according to, 10:51
Ethical Standards Casebook (Callis, Pope, &
DePauw), 10:76
Ethical theory
defined, 10:20
described, 8:182–184
Ethicists, in agreement of principle to "do
no harm", 4:146–147
Ethics
aspirational, 10:39, 40, 47
codes of
are living documents, 10:187
as catalysts for improving
practice, 10:37–55
excerpts from, 10:189
limitations, 10:43–45
living documents, 10:45–53
making them work, 10:53–55
consequential, 8:183
of counseling adolescent substance
abusers, 8:175–193
defined, 10:148
deontologic, 8:183
insanity pleas and, 10:147–157
issues of in treating drug abusing
pregnant women, 8:113–114
Kantian, 10:216–219
in labeling a behavior as maladaptive,
9:196
mandatory, 10:39, 40
multiculturalism and, 10:235–246
self-development, 8:183

teaching decision making in, 10:63–69
treatment of mentally ill and, 10:161–
178, 180–182
utilitarianism, 10:214–216
in working with survivors of sexual
abuse, 4:134–148
Ethnicity, roles and, 9:4, 8
Ethyl alcohol
See Alcohol
Euphoria
from alcohol, 7:68
from cocaine, 7:174
Evaluation
computerized, 9:137
decision-tree approach to, 7:4–19
dual-language testing, 9:222
intermediate, 9:153–154
job-site, 9:243, 244
of substance abuse, integrative
approach to, 7:1–21
vocational
defined, 9:235
effective use of, 9:233–247
of Hispanic clients with
disabilities, 9:209–224
of traumatic brain injury clients,
9:141–156
Evaluation Design for the ART Community
Project *(table)*, 5:202
Evening Primrose Oil, 5:68
Events, stressful, 1:4
Ex-spouses, 6:77, 93
Ex-wife, 6:61
including in therapy sessions, 6:68
relationship with, 6:65–66
Exaggeration, to reshape client's
perception, 2:56
Example of a Fitness Program Schedule
(table), 8:165
Examples of Affirmations *(table)*, 3:254
Examples of Behavioral Techniques in
Cognitive-Behavioral Play
Therapy *(table)*, 5:139
Examples of Cognitions From the
Automatic Thoughts
Questionnaire *(table)*, 3:129
Examples of Cognitive Techniques in
Cognitive-Behavioral Play
Therapy *(table)*, 5:141
Examples of Stages of Moral
Development *(table)*, 8:181
Exchange Orientation Inventory, 6:7–8, 27

Excretion, of medications, 7:28, 29
Executive Caravan, surveys on EAPs,
    8:17–18
Exercise, 8:209
    aerobic, 4:5, 15, 16
    useful in anxious clients, 1:112,
        114
    alleviates depression, 3:252
    benefits, 8:164
    in HIV positive clients, 8:236
    increases endorphins, 3:87
    model of work hardening, 9:132–133
    positive benefit, 3:118
Exhaustion, 1:39
Existential Conditions of Being (*table*),
    2:39
Existential continuity, 3:116
Expectations, 2:40
    by company of employees, 4:38
    gender-related, 6:270–272
    of persons with schizophrenia, 9:167–
        168
    in remarriage, 6:89
    unrealistic by criminals, 1:147
Experiments, conducted in cognitive
    therapy, 5:134
Expert witness
    contrasted with standard witness,
        10:98
    testimony, ethical and legal issues,
        10:97–107
Exposure therapy, 4:16
Expressiveness, 6:13, 14
Extinction, 5:138, 141–142, 7:179–181
    enhancing, 7:183
Exxon Valdez, alcohol consumption and
    accident, 8:2

F

Factors, conditions in occupations, 9:2
Failure
    feelings of in divorce, 4:214
    type of relationship wound, 4:182
Fair Labor Standards Act, 9:112
Faith, needed to counter hopelessness,
    4:45
Familial tremor, 4:100
Families
    addiction in, 4:75
    alcoholic, 4:102, 6:12
    chemically dependent, 6:12, 105–108

    of criminals, 1:141
    drug-using, characteristics of, 6:120–
        123
    dysfunctional, 4:74, 123, 128
    educating, 1:244–245
    inner-city, affected by AIDS, 6:117–144
    with schizophrenia, 2:149
    traumatized, 1:71
Families Adopting Children Everywhere
    (FACE) (*directory listing*),
        5:125
Families Anonymous (*directory listing*),
        8:157
Family
    of addicted adolescent, 8:141–143
    adjustment, 7:13–14
    adoptive, and communication about
        adoption, 5:109
    African-American, 6:119
    alcohol treatment and, 7:101–125
    alcoholic, teenagers from an, 5:187,
        8:201
    blended, defined, 6:75
    caregiving, of elderly, 6:167–185
    cocaine treatment and, 7:184–186
    cohesion, 5:93
    conferences, 6:94
    conflict, extreme, 6:106
    design, ideal, 6:11–12
    diagnostic testing, 6:1–23
    disharmony, 6:178
    dynamics, 4:145
    dysfunctional, 2:148, 149, 5:228, 264
        with drug abusing adolescents,
            examples, 6:104–105
    effects of ADHD child on, 5:65
    effects of substance abuse on, 8:8–9
    of elderly alcoholic, 8:213
    as enablers to drug user, 6:123
    environment conducive to suicide,
        5:255–256
    extended, 6:201
    greater than the sum of its parts, 2:150
    heritage of nonalcoholic behavior,
        4:105
    hero, co-dependent role, 4:77, 78
    hierarchical with Hispanic
        Americans, 9:182
    history, 5:7
    history of in depressed alcoholics,
        8:127–128
    history of suicide, 5:159

homeostatic system, 2:148, 149
honor, held high in Asian Americans,
     9:184
intervention, and safe sex counseling,
     6:143
interventions, 1:76
interviews, 4:119
involvement in rehabilitation process,
     9:200
networks relied on in African-
     American community, 9:181
nuclear, 2:154, 6:201
as option for personal assistance,
     9:65–66
of origin, 6:17, 18, 280, 281
as part of backup network, 9:76
participation in treatment, 8:209
planning, and task execution, 6:30
poorly functioning, 2:150
projection process, 2:156, 158
psychologists, 6:23
reluctance to change, 2:146
remarriage, understanding and
     treating, 6:73–95
responsibilities, 9:192–193
rituals, limited, 6:106, 108
roles
     inappropriate, 6:112
     incongruent, 6:107
setting limits within, 8:143–145
single-parent, 6:38, 58
size, small, as risk factor for
     separation anxiety disorder,
     5:10
support, 6:13
systems, 6:13, 93
     and drug behavior, 6:102–109
     theorists, 6:120–121
treatment model, 6:109–113
treatment programs for, 8:76
values, 6:16, 177
violence in, 5:228
Family Adaptability and Cohesion Scales
     III (FACES III), 6:9–12, 28
Family Adaptability and Cohesion Scales
     III (FACES III) Scores for the
     Smith Family (table), 6:9
Family Assessment Measure, 7:13
Family Environment Scale (FES), 6:13–17,
     28, 7:13
     personal growth dimension, 6:13–14
     relationship dimension, 6:13

systems maintenance dimension, 6:14
Family Environment Scale (FES) Profile
     (figure), 6:15
Family Institute of Chicago, 2:168
Family Profile Report (table), 6:4
Family Systems Therapy (table), 6:111
Family therapy, 2:148, 3:44, 115, 6:22, 46,
     47
     See also Marriage therapy
     for adolescent depression, 5:166
     for chemical dependence, 4:71
     communications theory of, 2:153–155
     conceptual development of, 2:147–
          148
     contraindicated in adopted child
          syndrome, 5:117
     conventional, and AIDS, 6:134, 135–
          141
     in curbing adolescent drug abuse,
          6:99–113
     death of child and, 6:147–162
     development of, 2:145
     of elderly, 2:202
     for history of incest, 4:123
     for homelessness, 5:90
     with inner-city families affected by
          AIDS, 6:117–144
     need for theory, 2:151–153
     other family members in, 2:166
          conflicting goals of, 2:167
     problem-centered approach to
          interviewing in, 2:165–189
     problem-centered model, 2:167–168
     rationale for, 2:151
     for suicidal adolescents, 5:265
     techniques
          boundaries, 2:153
          challenging, 2:152
          circular perspective, 2:153
          enactment, 2:152
          interpersonal intensity, 2:153
          joining, 2:152
          linear perspective, 2:153
          maintenance, 2:152
          mimesis, 2:152
          reframing, 2:152
          tracking, 2:152
          unbalancing, 2:153
     theories and applications, 2:143–161
Family trees, also called genograms,
     6:140
Fantasies, 2:113

of adopted child, 5:108
Fantasy, 6:201–202
  sexual, 6:224–225, 233–234
Fat, in diet, 3:29, 7:53
  See also Food; Diet; Eating Disorders
Fathers
  See also Parents
  awarded custody of children, 6:38
  children raised by contrasted, 6:63
  as incest perpetrators, 4:118
  self-employed, 6:62
  single
    characteristics of, 6:59–60
    families headed by, 6:57–69
    statistics, 6:58
Fatigue, 3:155, 6:229
  in IBS patients, 4:10
Faulty attributions, 6:225
Fear, 1:99, 100, 4:43, 5:2, 3, 6, 6:227
  See also Phobias
  of abandonment, and divorce, 6:46–47
  and AIDS, 6:118
  an impediment to therapeutic
    alliance, 4:124
  of becoming independent, 9:22
  of becoming trapped, 9:22–23
  of body sensations, 4:14
  by dying child, 6:133
  of change, 2:33–44
  of confrontation, 4:209
  and criminals, 1:145–146
  of disclosure, 4:126
  of failing to satisfy significant others,
    9:21
  of fatness, 3:59
  gender differences and, 4:125
  of greater responsibility, 9:21–22
  of growing up, 3:192
  in incest victims, 4:118
  of intimacy, 4:218
  of lack of ability, 9:20–21
  of medications' side effects, 3:246
  normative, 5:13
  of public speaking, 5:13
  of recollection of sexual abuse not
    being believed, 4:142
  of retaliation, 4:142
  of school, 9:20
  of school in COAs, 4:101
  of separation from parents, 6:150
  of uncertainty, 9:23
Federal Substances Act, 7:42

Feedback, 2:150, 4:190, 7:116, 207–208
  loops, self-regulating, 2:149
Feeling Good (Burns), 3:253
Feeling Yes, Feeling No (National Film
  Board of Canada), 5:36
Feelings
  children's, 6:43, 68
  after a divorce, 6:38–39
Fellatio, 4:115
Female orgasmic disorder, 6:220
Fenfluramine (Pondimin), 1:183
Fertility, as source of self-respect, 6:143
Fetal Alcohol Study Group, 8:102
Fetal alcohol syndrome (FAS)
  characteristics of, 8:102
  statistics, 8:103
Fetus, effects of substance abuse on,
  8:102–109
Fibercon, 7:43
Fidelity, 10:58
  moral principle of, 10:40, 42
Fight-flight response, 4:9, 41
Figueiredo-Torres v. Nickel, 10:120, 124
Finances
  disabilities and, 9:70
  needs associated with, 9:91
Financial
  planning, 6:89
  problems with elderly caregiving,
    6:175
Finkelhor's model, of childhood sexual
  abuse, 5:28–34
Firearms, 5:267
Firesetting, 5:106
First fear, 1:100
First National Conference of Co-
  Dependency, 4:74
Fit
  between company and individual,
    4:39, 44
  judging, 4:46
Fitness program
  See Physical fitness
5-hydroxyindoleacetic acid (5-HIAA),
  1:42, 43, 3:100, 8:131
5-hydroxytryptamine receptors, 7:138
Fixation, at child level, 3:192
Flashbacks, 4:136, 1:6, 101
  LSD use and, 7:139, 140
Flexibility, 4:46
  in some families, 6:120
Flip-Flops, Cartwheels, and High-Tops

(Spinal-Robinson &
    Wickham), 5:35
Florida Couples and Family Institute, 6:79
Fluoxetine (Prozac), 1:42, 44, 3:59, 272,
    5:14, 57, 164, 7:36, 44, 8:129
    and OCD, 1:21
Fluphenazine decanoate (Prolixin
    Decanoate), 1:255, 8:280
Flushing, of upper body, 3:99
Fluvoxamine (Luvox), 1:42, 44, 3:272, 7:36
    and OCD, 1:21
Flying, fear of, 1:99
Focus group, 9:105
Focusing, 1:220, 222–223
Folate, 3:105
    deficiency, 3:106, 107
Folie à deux, 1:67
Follow-up, after treatment for DID, 1:71
Follow-up support, 9:86, 94–95, 247
Food
    See also Fat; Diet; Eating Disorders
    fear of, 5:13
Forgetfulness, in DID, 1:53, 59
Forgiveness, 4:243–259
    case study, 4:254–255, 256–258
    dangers of premature, 4:253–258
    obstacles to, 4:250–252
    psychodynamics of, 4:250
    psychological dimensions of, 4:249–250
    theological aspects of, 4:247–249
Formaldehyde, 8:272
Forms
    See also Scales, questionnaires, and
        inventories
    assessment, 9:39–40
Foster care, 8:101
    incest in, 4:116
Fragile X chromosome, 1:179
Framingham Heart Study, 7:157
Freedom, loss of, 2:50, 51
Frequency of Rearrest by Condition
    (table), 5:204
Frustration
    a core emotion, 4:191
    low frustration tolerance (LFT), 4:159,
        161, 164, 165
    theme of anger at others, 4:159–161
Fugues, 1:64, 65, 79
Fun, needed by depressed clients, 3:258
Functional assessment, 9:38–41
    problems of, 9:40–41
Functional wholeness, 3:116

Functioning
    base-level, 4:188
    disruption in
        phases
            disorganization, 4:42
            initial impact, 4:42
            recovery, 4:42
            reorganization, 4:42
Funding
    for personal assistance, 9:68–69
    under Title I of ADA, 9:74
Furr v. Spring Grove State Hospital, 10:145
Fury, synonym of anger, 4:157
Fusion, 1:68, 83, 84, 2:156, 158, 3:190

G

G6 PDase deficiency, 3:108
GABA
    See Gamma-aminobutyric acid
        (GABA)
GAD
    See Generalized anxiety disorder
        (GAD)
Gallup poll, of illegal drug use, 8:2
Galt Visiting Scholar Model, 7:254
Gam-Anon, 1:165
Gambler
    depressive, 1:154, 158–159, 161, 162,
        163, 166
        catecholamine changes in, 1:160–
            161
    narcissistic, 1:154, 159–160, 165
    pathological
        clinical management of, 1:161–166
        personality of, 1:156–158
        upper-class, plays stock markets,
            1:156
Gambler's Anonymous (G.A.), 1:164, 165,
    4:252
Gambling, 8:68
    casino, 1:156, 159
    of novelist Dostoevsky, 1:156
    pathological, 1:153–166
        addictive cycle in, 1:160–161
        defined, 1:155
        statistics, 1:155–156
        treatment of, 1:163–164
Game theory, 2:153
Gamma-aminobutyric acid (GABA), 5:6,
    7:67, 8:250
Gandianco v. Sobol, 10:121, 124

Gangs, 5:204–207
  See also Peer groupings
  Baby Wolfpack, 5:207
  Lo Lives, 5:207
Gardner Adoption Story Cards (Gardner),
    5:116
Gay Men's Health Crisis (GMHC), 6:141
Gender
  differences, 6:268
    between patient and therapist,
      4:125
    in workplace and social life, 6:282
  discrepancies, 6:270
  identification, 6:268
  source of sexism, 6:273–274
  role
    expectations, 6:250
    orientations, 6:16
General paresis, 3:106
General systems theory, 2:153
Generalization, as part of therapy, 5:147
Generalized anxiety disorder (GAD),
    1:101, 109, 5:5, 11–12, 7:157,
    159, 8:252
  statistics, 5:11
  stress management techniques for,
    4:14–16
  symptoms, 5:11
Generations Together, 3:85
Genetics, and criminal behavior, 1:142
Genetics of Alcoholism (USGPO), 4:100
Genograms, 2:160
  resource, 6:140–141
Geriatric
  See Elderly
Geriatric depression
  See Depression, in older adults
Geriatric Depression Scale (GDS), 3:158,
    6:180
Germany, study of stress and mortality,
    4:57
Gerontologists, 2:198, 204
Gerontology Alcohol Project (GAP),
    8:213–214
Gerontophobia, 2:198
Gestalt therapy, 2:13, 260, 3:115
Girls
  and ADHD, 5:49, 50
  aggravated assault most violent crime
    committed by, 5:193
  anxiety disordered, 5:4
  and child custody, 6:38

effects of divorce on, 6:37
  in gangs, 5:204
  and gender identification, 6:273
  less affected than boys with OCD,
    1:37
  more mature during early
    adolescence than boys, 5:181
  more suicide attempts among, 5:158
  raised by fathers, 6:63
  specific phobia more common in, 5:13
Glasgow Coma Scale, 9:144, 155
Glaucoma, 3:43
Global Assessment Scale, 7:96, 1:243
Glossary of Custody Terms (*table*), 6:40–
    41
*Glover v. The Board of Medical Quality
    Assurance*, 10:114, 124
Glucocorticosteroids, 3:16, 17, 22
Glutathione, 7:53, 57
Glutethimide (Doriden), 8:65
Goals
  clients' for change, 4:165
  company, 4:40
  counseling
    ethical considerations in
      development of, 10:17–32
    rules in development of, 10:24–32
  family, 6:110
  group therapy, 2:129
  identification of, 10:82
  incompatibility, 10:24
  individual therapy, 2:129
  life, 9:193
  orienting treatment toward, 5:135
  setting, 9:196–198, 200–201
  vocational, 9:96, 194, 197
  work, 9:115, 136, 146, 150
"Goodness of fit," 10:85
Gordian Group (*directory listing*), 7:5
Gordon Occupational Checklist II, 9:148
Grandparents, 6:110
Granulocytes, 3:18
Gratification, autonomous, 3:185
Great Smokies Diagnostic Laboratory,
    7:52
Greece, ancient, and group therapy, 2:100
Greeks, ancient, psychosomatic approach
    to explaining disease, 4:54
"Gregory K", case of child custody, 6:38
Grief, 3:6–7, 122, 231, 4:41, 6:128, 181
  See also Mourning
  acceptance of, 3:123

associated with PTSD, 1:20
cessation of medications for, 3:123
coping with, 6:161
death of child and, 6:149
and divorce, 6:43
due to child loss, 6:148
felt by adopted child, 5:109, 110
from child separated from incestuous
    parent, 4:122
and homelessness, 5:89
lingering, 6:160
resolution, 3:86
Group development
phases of
    active phase, 3:80–81
    initial, 3:79–80
    termination phase, 3:81
Group dynamics, 2:148
Group therapy, 2:99–118, 3:44, 115, 234,
    4:229, 6:182, 8:212
for adolescent depression, 5:166
for adolescents, 5:175–187
cautious use in suspected cases of
    sexual abuse, 4:142
for cocaine addiction, 7:181–186
cognitive, 2:115
combined with individual therapy,
    2:109–113, 5:180
confrontive, 2:115
curative influences of, 3:74, 76
dangerousness and legal liability,
    2:132–135
defined, 2:124
for depressed alcoholics, 8:129
for depressed older adults, 3:65–90
for depression due to homelessness,
    5:90
with DID, 1:76–77
dynamics of elderly groups, 3:76–79
efficacy of, 2:103–104
elder-specific contrasted with mixed
    age, 8:215–216
of elderly, 2:202
ethical and legal issues, 2:121–137
    minimizing the risks, 2:136–137
everything brought into, 2:107
existential, 2:115
factors necessary to effect change
    altruism, 2:103
    catharsis, 2:103
    corrective recapitulation, 2:103
    existential factors, 2:103

group cohesiveness, 2:103
imitative behavior, 2:103
imparting of information, 2:103
installation of hope, 2:103
interpersonal learning, 2:103
socializing techniques, 2:103
universality, 2:103
four structure types
group psychotherapy, 5:177
human development and training
    groups, 5:177–178
self-help and mutual help, 5:178
therapeutic groups, 5:177
with gamblers, 1:165
group termination issues, 2:135–136
growth-centered, 2:124
for history of incest, 4:123
initiation issues, 2:127–129
inpatient, 3:168–170
interpersonal, 2:115
medications used with, 2:115–116
moral education (ME) groups, 5:219–
    221
for older white males, 3:72
ongoing counseling issues, 2:129–132
outpatient, 3:166–167
phases of group development
    termination, 5:184
    working phase, 5:183–184
problem behaviors during, 5:185–187
psychoanalytic, 2:113–114
and PTSD, 1:20
purpose, 5:178
regression in, 2:117–118
relationship wounding and, 4:198
for patients with schizophrenia, 1:250
selecting patients for, 2:107–108, 134–
    135, 5:179–180
    case study, 2:108–109
for sexually abused children, 5:35
study, 4:61–62
for suicidal patients, 5:265
supportive, 2:115
time commitment, 2:106
widely used for inpatients and
    outpatients, 2:102
works, 2:103
Groups
assertiveness, 3:76
elderly
    types of
        assertiveness training, 3:86–87

bereavement, 3:86
counseling and exercise, 3:87–89
educational/therapeutic,
    3:82–83
intergenerational, 3:84–86
life review, 3:83–84
psychodrama, 3:84
exercise, 3:76
gender selection, 3:78
inclusion of married and singles, 3:78
reminiscence, 3:83
support
    See Support groups
Growth hormone, blunted response to
    clonidine, 1:39
Growth therapists, 2:11
Growth therapy
accentuates the positive, 2:9
an open system, 2:10–11
contrasted with repair therapy, 2:1–16
danger of solipsism, 2:12
emphasis towards iconoclasm, 2:13–
    14
emphasizes potential for self-
    actualization, 2:9
focuses on individuality, 2:13
has goal of profound change, 2:12–13
key points, 2:1
leans toward vitalism, 2:11–12
open and flexible, 2:10
seeks self-actualization, 2:12–13
Guidance, defined, 8:180
Guidance counselors, 6:23
Guidelines for Release of Confidential
    Information (*table*), 5:286, 287
Guidelines for the Training of Group
    Psychotherapists (AGPA),
    2:122
Guidelines for Treating Suicidal
    Adolescents (*table*), 5:266
Guilt, 1:39, 222, 4:39, 43, 45, 158, 209, 244,
    252, 5:29, 30, 31, 257, 6:49, 51,
    151, 174, 226, 229, 260, 281,
    8:207, 234
and AIDS, 6:118, 133
with alcoholics, 7:74, 111
associated with PTSD, 1:20
by gambler, 1:158
by manic clients, 1:228
and caring for elderly relative, 6:170
case study, 6:43–44
a core emotion, 4:191

death of child and, 6:149
and divorce, 6:39
low levels of in aggressive youth,
    5:195
and miscarriage, 6:152
others' still acknowledged after
    forgiveness, 4:255
perpetrator and, 10:152

H

Halcion (triazolom), 4:13
Haldol (haloperidol), 8:280
Hale v. Portsmouth Receiving Hospital
    (1975), 2:226
Halfway houses, 8:74
Hallucinations, 1:16, 53, 71, 72, 3:142,
    5:232, 240, 7:40, 43, 96, 138–
    140, 8:61, 128, 251
in DID, 1:64
reduced by use of antipsychotics, 7:38
Hallucinogen persisting perception
    disorder
    See Flashbacks
Hallucinogenic drugs, 3:102
trends in use, 7:129–148
Hallucinogens, 5:232, 8:58, 61, 61–63, 270
Haloperidol (Haldol), 1:44, 8:280
Halstead-Reitan Neuropsychological Test
    Battery, 7:18, 9:147
Hamilton Depression Rating Scale, 3:25,
    26, 27, 42, 168, 169, 170, 204,
    209, 216, 217
Hand-wringing, in Rett's disorder, 1:176
Handbook of Psychotherapy Research
    (Garfield & Bergin), 2:251
Handwriting, difference in seen in DID,
    1:55
Hangover, drug, 4:13
Hansel and Gretel, 5:116
Happiness
    a core emotion, 4:191
    high self-esteem as predictor of, 4:222
Harm, principle of not causing, 4:135,
    136–137
Harvard Trauma Questionnaire (HTQ),
    1:11
Hasenei v. United States, 10:146
Hate, 4:35, 246
    synonym of anger, 4:157
Hazelden Clinic (*directory listing*), 4:86
Headache, 5:11

Headaches, 4:5, 1:82
  migraine, 4:12, 21
  muscle-contraction, 4:19
  severe, as sign of DID, 1:58
  stress management techniques for,
    4:11–12
  tension, 4:12, 21
Health, assessment of, 7:11–12
Health care
  adolescent, 8:189
  modern, centered on individualism,
    6:109
  professionals, must assess child's
    potential for self-destruction,
    5:89
  team, 3:245
Health maintenance organizations
  (HMOs), 2:103, 118, 3:82, 83
HealthComm International (*directory
  listing*), 7:57
Healthy living groups, 8:278
Hearing impairments, 9:112, 221
Heart attacks, and panic disorder, 1:105
Heart disease, 6:168, 1:106
Heart rate, rapid, 4:96
Heaven v. Pender, 10:139
Heavy metal poisoning, 3:104
Hedonism, 8:183
Heights, fear of, 1:99
Held overly responsible, type of
  relationship wound, 4:182
Helpers, a personality in DID, 1:57
Helping Hands Program, 8:218, 219
Helplessness, 3:83
Hepatitis, 3:105
Hepatitis B profile, 5:239
Hermeneutics, 2:253
Heroin, 7:65, 75, 76, 78, 226, 8:105–107
  addiction and overdoses, role of
    naloxone in, 7:67
  relapse rate from addiction to, 7:217
  statistics, 8:246, 247
Hero's journey, counseling motif, 4:185–
  186
Heuristic, CMP is used as, 2:88
High blood pressure
  See Hypertension
High-school, drop-out rates, 9:178, 191
Hillside Strangler Case, malingering and,
  1:65
Hippuric acid, 7:52

Hirsutism, 7:41
Hispanics, 9:179, 191
  See also Latinas; Latinos
  adolescents, 9:178
  characteristics, 9:182–184
  concept of deity, 9:217
  culture, 10:242
  defined, 9:211
  designation, 9:220
  with disabilities, 9:209–224
  drug and alcohol addicts, 8:247
  least acculturated ethnic group,
    9:182
  strong family unit in, 9:183
Histamine, 3:99
History taking, 1:69
  in assessing jealousy, 6:250–252
  in sex therapy, 6:203–205
HIV, 3:100, 5:239, 282, 6:118
  See also AIDS
  confidentiality and, 10:9, 171, 213–
    214
  case studies, 10:221–227
  counseling chemically dependent
    persons with, 8:225–242
  counseling sexually active client with,
    10:211–231
  drug use as precipitant of, 6:120, 123–
    125
  model for adjusting to diagnosis of
    stages
    acceptance, 8:235
    crisis, 8:233–234
    preparation for death, 8:235
    transition, 8:234–235
  prevention, 6:142–143
  reporting on, 10:49
  residential treatment centers for,
    8:235–237
HMOs
  See Health Maintenance
    Organizations (HMOs)
Hobbies, benefits of, 2:76–77
Holidays, 6:89
Holmes v. Wampler, 10:145
Home detoxification program, 6:110
Homeless Children Interview Schedule,
  5:85
Homeless Children Interview Schedule-
  Mother Version, 5:85, 86
Homelessness, 5:79–97

See also Poverty
case study, 5:94–97
Columbus, Ohio studies of
    depression and, 5:83–91
mentally ill clients and, 10:175–176
statistics, 5:80
Homeostasis, postulated, 2:4–5
Homework
    in cognitive therapy, 3:138–139, 5:134
    for dysthymic patients, 3:234
    as part of therapy, 7:112, 115, 231
    in rational-emotive therapy (RET),
        4:173
Homicide
    criminal, 5:193
    ideations, 8:128
    juvenile, 8:101
    victims, 8:149
Homosexual
    See also Lesbians; men, homosexual
    concerns, gay bashing as product of,
        5:186–187
    longings, 2:239
    relationships, 6:168
Honesty, value in adoption, 5:119–120
Hope, 6:126, 129
    a core emotion, 4:191
    needed by homeless family, 5:92
    parental, will empower child with
        ADHD, 5:66
    remind clients of its existence, 3:247
Hopelessness, 5:154, 161
    a core emotion, 4:191
    in dysthymic patients, 3:227
    experienced by suicidal adolescents,
        5:263
Hopewell v. Adibempe, 10:146
Hopkins Symptom Checklist, 1:11
Hormones
    immune system and, 3:16
    neuroendocrine, 3:22
        depression and, 3:24–25
Hospice, 2:205, 3:122, 6:184
Hospitalization, 2:259
    See also Inpatient treatment
    adolescent, 8:191
    of chemically dependent clients with
        AIDS, 8:238–239
    of depressed alcoholics, 8:128–129
    of depressed patients, 3:247
    of elderly, 2:202

phone calls by patients to therapists
    may head off, 1:130
    of patients with schizophrenia, 1:246
    statistics, 1:243
    of substance abusers, 5:240–244
    of suicidal adolescent, 5:262–263
    for treatment of DID, 1:79–80
Hospitals
    day, 6:184
    prevalence of depressed older adults
        in, 3:150
Hostels, elder, 3:82
Hostility, 2:21, 22, 4:244, 6:208–209, 268,
    278
    aimed at adoptive parents, 5:115
    in incest victims, 4:118
Housework, 6:61–62, 67
    as activity of caregiver to the elderly,
        6:171
    as parenting task, 6:60
*How to Maintain and Enhance Your
    Rational-Emotive Therapy
    Gains* (Ellis), 4:173
Human
    Existential Conditions of Being (*table*),
        2:39
    five givens of being
        action, 2:38
        choice, 2:38
        embodiment, 2:38
        finitude, 2:38
        separate-but-relatedness, 2:38
Human immunodeficiency virus (HIV)
    See HIV
Human Potential Movement, 2:260
Human service matrix, 7:246
Human Service Matrix (*figure*), 7:247
Humans, social nature of, 6:195
Humor, 5:264
Humoral responses, 3:17
Huntington's Disease, 3:104–105
Hurt, a core emotion, 4:191
Hydromorphone (Dilaudid), 7:42
Hygea, daughter of Greek god
    Aesculapius, 4:82, 83
Hyperactivity, 8:102, 5:42
    See also Attention-deficit/
        hyperactivity disorder
        (ADHD)
    in ADHD, 1:193, 196
    in COAs, 4:101

common in gamblers, 1:162
Hyperadrenalism (Cushing's Syndrome),
  3:102
Hyperkinetic syndrome, 1:193
Hyperparathyroidism, 3:103–104
Hypersomnia, 8:252
Hypertension, 3:88, 4:5, 5:232
  stress management techniques for,
    4:6–7
Hyperthyroidism, 5:12
Hypertriglyceridemia, 8:204
Hyperuricemia, 8:204
Hypervigilence, 4:80
Hypnosis, 1:65, 66, 74, 75, 78
  cautious use in suspected sexual
    abuse cases, 4:142
  as diagnostic tool for DID, 1:61–62
  as evaluation of patients with DID,
    4:119
Hypnotherapy, 1:77–78, 3:115, 4:10
Hypnotics, 1:81, 8:58
Hypnotizability, of clients, 4:6
Hypoadrenalism (Addison's Disease),
  3:102–103
Hypochrondriasis, 1:33, 7:36
Hypocrisy, 4:231
Hypoglycemia, 3:103, 8:204
Hypomania, 3:99
Hypoparathyroidism, 3:103–104
Hypotension, orthostatic, 3:42
Hypothalamic-pituitary-adrenal (HPA)
  mediators, 3:22, 24, 25, 27
Hypotheses, 2:189
  linear, 6:138
  systematic, 6:139
  systemic, defined, 6:135
  testing of by therapist, 2:169, 5:114–145
  thoughts as, 3:138
Hypothyroidism, 3:105, 245, 267, 5:51, 162
  in some cases of gambling, 1:162
Hysteria, 4:117
Hysterical personality disorder, case
  study, 2:243–245

I

*I Can't Get Over It: A Handbook for Trauma
  Survivors* (Matsakis), 1:224,
  3:256
Iatrogenic factors, in treatment of DID,
  1:67
Ibuprofen (Advil, Motrin), 7:42

Id, 2:7
  strengths, 2:9
IDEA
  See Individuals with Disabilities
    Education Act (IDEA)
Idealization, 6:203
Ideation
  disturbed, 5:111
  suicidal, 5:158, 159, 234, 241, 252
Ideational content, 5:107–108
Identification, mechanism of false
  forgiveness, 4:253
Identified patient (IP), 2:148, 149, 6:10, 11,
  14
Identity, 2:40, 41
  adopted child's quest for, 5:108–110
  death of child and, 6:149
  establishment of, 3:189–191
  feminine, 6:178
  formation of, 4:84
  racial and ethnic, 9:188–190
  regaining sense of in a divorce,
    4:211
  search for, 8:161
  self, female, 10:199
Idiosyncratic toxicities, 7:30–31
Illiteracy, functional, defined, 9:44
Illness
  approach to diagnosis, 7:194
  medical
    impact of stress on, 4:53–66
    stress-related, 4:80
  as stress event, 6:135
Imcompetence, child's, 5:63, 64
Imipramine (Tofranil), 1:44, 2:253, 3:175,
  213, 274, 275, 276, 4:14, 5:56,
  164, 7:35
Immaturity, 5:195
Immigrants, 9:178
Immune Changes in Depressed Patients
  (*table*), 3:26
Immune function
  altered, 7:56
  changes in caused by stress, 1:23
Immune system, 3:88, 4:65
  depression and, 3:15–30, 6:138
  function of, 3:17
  overview of, 3:17–20
Immunity, cell-mediated, 3:17
Immunocompetence, measurements of,
  3:20–22
Immunoglobulin

IgA, 3:18
IgD, 3:18
IgE, 3:18
IgG, 3:18
IgM, 3:18
Immunologists, 4:66
Immunosuppression, 3:23
Impairment
    affective work, 3:209
    functional, 3:206, 209
        statistics, 3:200–202
    measures of affective, 3:206
    work
        classifying, 3:206, 207
        tools for assessing, 3:203–210
Impartiality, level of, in mental health
        professional, 10:99
Impulse control, 1:125, 2:71
Impulse disorder, 4:80
Impulsivity, 4:99, 5:42, 111, 159, 254, 257,
        7:11
    in ADHD, 1:194, 196
    Ritalin and, 5:56
In-laws, 6:89, 93
In-vivo mitogen test, 3:21
Inattention, 5:42, 56
    in ADHD, 1:194, 195–196
Incapacitated, defined, 10:7
Incentives, provided by rehabilitation
        programs for employers, 9:85
Incest, 1:125, 2:233, 4:145, 6:18, 87, 121,
        122, 198
    See also Child abuse; Childhood
        molestation; Sexual abuse of
        children
    association with mental disorders,
        4:116–118
    boundaries in therapy, 4:125–126
    defined, 4:115
    epidemiology, 4:115–116
    exploration of history of, 4:123–124
    feminist model of treatment, 4:122
    goals of treatment, 4:122–123
    homosexual, little information on,
        4:114–115
    indications for treatment, 4:121, 122
    legal requirement for reporting, 4:119
    prevention of mental disorders in
        cases of, 4:127
    psychoanalytic model of treatment,
        4:122
    shared experience in group therapy

        for DID, 1:77
    statistics, 4:116
    syndrome, 4:122, 127
    therapeutic approaches for patients
        with history of, 4:113–128
    therapy to help deal with, 1:113
    treatment methods
        family therapy, 4:123
        group therapy, 4:123
        individual therapy, 4:123
    treatment outcomes, 4:126–127
    validity of reports of, 4:120–121
Income
    See also Wages
    low, and depression, 5:82
    needs associated with, 9:91
    of persons with disabilities, 9:81
Incoordination, 4:100
Independent living, 9:246
    movement, 9:67
Inderal (propranolol), 5:14, 7:44
Individual therapy
    for adolescent depression, 5:166
    combined with group therapy, 5:180
    for depression due to homelessness,
        5:90
    of elderly, 2:202
    for separation anxiety disorder, 5:10
    for suicidal adolescents, 5:265
    used for sexual abuse cases, 5:35
Individual Work-Related Expenses
        (IWRE), 9:154
Individualism, tradition of in modern
        health care, 6:109
Individuality, seen in growth therapy,
        2:13
Individualized Vocational Evaluation
        Plan (IVEP), 9:241
Individuals with Disabilities Education
        Act (IDEA), 5:70
Individuation, 3:190
Industrial revolution, 6:200
Infants
    anxiety in, 5:2
    with difficult temperaments, 5:46
    morbidity and mortality, 5:228
Infarcts, hemispheric, 3:38
Inference chaining, 4:168
Inferences, 4:170
Infidelity, 6:243, 251, 256, 258, 262
    delusions of, 6:242, 247, 261
Influence of Neuroendocrine Hormones

and Transmitters on
Lymphocyte Function (*table*),
3:23
Information
communicated through referral
questions, 9:239
confidential, 10:2–3, 169–173
See also Confidentiality; Disclosure;
Privacy
ethical guidelines for disclosure
of, 10:219–221, 227–230
guidelines regarding release of,
5:285–287
timely, needed by rehabilitation
specialist, 9:137
used to make decisions, 9:82
Information for Prospective Group
Members (*table*), 3:77
Informed consent, 2:132, 10:79
conditions for obtaining, 10:169
defined, 2:128, 4:135, 10:5, 115
Inhalants, 5:232–233, 240, 8:58, 61, 65–66,
272
Inhibition, 5:159
Injury, self, 3:58
Innocence, not recaptured after
forgiveness, 4:255
Inpatient programs, for pathological
gamblers, 1:164
Inpatient treatment, 7:201, 217
See also Hospitalization
of alcoholism, 7:87–98
caffeine consumption and, 7:163
medication compliance in, 7:31
Input, components of supported
employment, 9:119
Insanity
acquittal, issue of power struggle in,
2:216
defense, 1:141
jealous, 6:243
pleas, ethics and, 10:147–157
traumatic, 3:34
Insight, 1:250, 2:82, 91, 114, 3:119
See also Triangle of insight
criminals and, 1:148
failure to apply by criminal client,
1:150
forgiveness after major, 4:251
goal in repair therapy, 2:6
and higher-level borderline patients,

1:131
little displayed by narcissistic
gambler, 1:154
patients' concerning family
interactions, 3:78
resentment major deterrent to, 4:244
retained by patients with OCD, 1:31
stimulated by sentence-completion
program, 4:232
therapy, 3:115
three major in rational-emotive
therapy (RET), 4:172
Insomnia, 3:28, 29, 100, 7:36, 37, 66, 161–
162, 225, 8:252
See also Sleep, disturbances in
chronic, 4:13
in IBS patients, 4:10
often a symptom of relapse, 1:248
rebound, 4:13
sleep-onset, 4:19
stress management techniques for,
4:12–14, 21
Institute for Personality and Ability
Testing, 9:148
Institute for Rational-Emotive Therapy
(*directory listing*), 4:174
Institute for Rehabilitation and Research,
9:73
Institutionalization, 6:174, 183
of elderly, costliness, 6:168
Instruction, systematic, 9:111
Instrumental Activities of Daily Living,
6:180
Instrumental goal development, 10:19
Instruments, assessment
See also Scales, questionnaires, and
inventories
findings must be analyzed with
caution, 7:9
Insurance, liability, no psychologist
should be without, 10:9
Insurance companies, as threats to
confidentiality, 5:277, 278
Integration, 1:67, 68, 70, 83
Integration-resolution, 1:70
Integrity
defined, 4:230
one of the guardians of mental health,
4:232
practice of, 4:230–232
Intelligence

criminals and, 1:145
employability and, 9:69
Intelligence quotient
  See IQ
Intelligence tests, 6:23
  See also IQ
Interactions
  parent-child, 6:196–198
  case study, 6:207–208
Interagency collaboration, in addiction
    treatment, 7:243–255
Intercourse, 5:32
  incest and, 4:115, 118
  means of HIV transmission, 10:212
Interdependence, 4:36, 39
  criminals have no concept of, 1:147
Interdependency, 6:199
Interferon, 3:20
Intergenerational groups, 3:84–86
Interleukin-2, 3:20
Intermittent explosive disorder, 8:252
International Society for the Study of
    Dissociation, 1:50
International Society for the Study of
    Multiple Personality and
    Dissociation, 1:50
Interoceptors, 3:160
Interpersonal deficits, 3:231
  dynamics, 10:42–43
  therapy, 2:253
Interpersonal psychotherapy (IPT), 3:232,
    234
  for adolescents (IPT-A), 5:167
  treatment for dysthymia, 3:230–232
Interpretation
  useful technique, 9:26
  useful in group therapy, 2:114
Intervention
  confusion in choosing strategies for,
    2:167
  forward-looking, 2:67
  ordered in hierarchical structure,
    2:169–170
  strategies, problem-centered
    approach, 2:167
  structure, in action, 2:170–187
Interventions
  behavioral counseling, 3:165–166
  cognitive, 3:165
  cognitive-behavioral, 3:165
  instructional, 9:117

to reduce discrepancies, 9:118
Interviewers, errors by, 2:20
Interviewing
  assessment of skills in, 9:242
  case dialogues, 2:171–173, 174–176,
    178–181, 182–183, 185–187
  passive therapists can lose control
    during, 2:166
  problem-centered approach to, 2:165–
    189
Interviews
  drug-facilitated, 1:77
  exit, 9:244
  initial intake, 9:196–198, 242
  structured, 3:155, 162
  subject-object, 9:9
  videotaped, 1:77
Intimacy, 6:213
  differing views of, 6:271
  in marriage, 6:198–203
  sexual, 6:227
Intoxication, 5:231
  alcohol, 1:53, 7:38, 74
  caffeine, 7:158
  substance, 8:59
Intravenous, administration of
    medication, 7:29
Introject, soothing-holding, 1:122, 129
Introversion, 1:31
Intuitive understanding, defined,
    10:19
Inventories
  See Scales, Questionnaires, and
    Inventories
Involuntariness, in therapy, 2:49, 129
Invulnerability, personal, 1:3
Iowa, alcoholism study in, 4:98
IP
  See Identified patient (IP)
IPAT Anxiety Scale, 4:16
IPT
  See Interpersonal psychotherapy
    (IPT)
IQ, 8:103, 107, 9:214
  See also Intelligence tests
  low, may indicate low acculturation,
    9:222
  ranges, 9:42
Iron, 7:60
Irrational, defined, 4:155
Irritable bowel syndrome (IBS), 7:56

stress management techniques for,
    4:10–11
Isocarboxazid (Marplan), 3:213
IV drug abuse, 8:226
IVEP
    See Individualized Vocational
        Evaluation Plan (IVEP)
IWRE
    See Individual Work-Related
        Expenses (IWRE)

J

Jablonski v. United States, 10:144
Jaundice, and Ecstasy in younger
    patients, 7:142
Jealous Reactions (Normal Range) (*table*),
    6:244
Jealousy
    assessing, 6:249–253
    case study, 6:247–248
    clinical management of, 6:241–263
    common clinical problem, 6:263
    a core emotion, 4:191
    excessive, 6:243
    fait accompli, 6:243
    managing, 6:253–262
    morbid, 6:262
    nondelusional, 6:248
    obsessive, 6:248–249
    pathologic, 6:242
    reactive, 6:253
        normal, 6:243–244, 254–255
        pathologic, 6:244–247
    romantic, 6:242
    suspicious, 6:243
    symptomatic, 6:247–249
Jesus Christ
    dying on the cross, 4:249
    and forgiveness, 4:248
JIST Works, Inc. (*directory listing*), 9:61
Job
    analysis, 9:133
    coach, 9:113, 118, 152, 153
    development, 9:96–97
    environmental analysis, 9:54
    function, 9:48
    loss of, 2:113
    match, conditions for, 9:116–117
    modifications, 9:118
    restructuring, 9:52, 118
    search, should be intensive, 9:93, 93–

94
    seeking skills, 9:88–89
    sharing, 9:165
    sites, 9:120
        evaluation, 9:243, 244
Job Accommodation Network (JAN),
    9:145, 154
    phone number, 9:52
Job market, employability and, 9:69
Job performance, 8:3, 14
Jobs
    See also Career
    changing, 9:18, 172
    entry-level, 9:162, 167
    low-pay, 9:166
    occupational information on, 9:46
Johns Hopkins Phipps Psychiatric
    Service, 3:55
Johnson Institute, 7:104
Joint National Committee on Detection,
    Evaluation, and Treatment of
    High Blood Pressure, 4:6
Journaling, 1:220, 223
Judas, betrayal of Jesus, 4:248
Judges
    in custody cases, 6:38
    legal, 2:223
Jure v. Raviotta, 10:119, 124
Jurors, 2:223
Justice, 10:58, 70
    moral principle of, 10:40, 42
    theories of, 10:87
Juvenile delinquency, statistics, 5:193

K

Kansas Marital Adjustment Scale, 6:3, 27
Kantian ethics, 10:216–219, 230
Kaposi's sarcoma, 10:212
Kaslow's integrative model, 6:93
Katz Index of Activities of Daily Living,
    6:180
Kiddie Schedule for Affective Disorders
    and Schizophrenia, 7:12
Kidnapping
    dreams of by adoptee, 5:117
    fear of, 5:2
Kidneys, excretion of drugs by, 7:29, 30
Killers, 1:146
Kissing, 4:115
Klonopin (clonazepam), 1:82, 5:14, 7:41
Knowledge, defined, 4:173

Koch, Ed, treatment of mentally ill
   homeless and, 10:175
Kosberg's Cost of Care Index, 6:180

L

L-cysteine, 7:53, 57
Lab tests, important component of
   evaluation, 3:108
Labor market
   for clients with disabilities, 9:79–106
   demand side, 9:84
   knowledge of needed, 9:47
   not entered by many patients with
      schizophrenia, 9:168
   supply side, 9:84
Laboratory tests, 7:3, 8:71, 209
   for evaluating liver function, 7:52, 77
   MOBAT, alcohol breath test, 7:107,
      108
Lack of structure, type of relationship
   wound, 4:182
Landau v. Warner (1961), 2:220, 221
Language
   bias, 9:220–223
   and children with ADHD, 5:46, 47,
      63
   of clients may be ambivalent or
      vague, 2:18
   common, commitment to in
      Hispanics, 9:182
   deficits, 1:173
      pragmatics, 1:174
      semantics, 1:174
   delays in development of, 1:176, 180
   "I", 2:160
   preferences, 9:188, 197, 201, 212
   Spanish, 9:211, 215, 219
Late-life functional impairment, of
   elderly, 2:200, 201–203
   drug use in, 8:98
Latinas
   See also Hispanics; Latinos
   AIDS and, 6:133
Latinos, 9:220
   See also Hispanics; Latinas
Law
   cases of sexual misconduct, 2:220–221
      Landau v. Warner, 2:220, 221
      Roy v. Hartogs, 2:220
      Zipkin v. Freeman, 2:220
   issues of and the mental health

profession, 2:217–222
tort, reluctance to provide remedies
   for emotional injuries, 2:217
Laws
   and confidentiality, 5:280
   violations of, statistics, 5:193
Lawsuits, prevention of, techniques,
   10:109–124
Lazarus (1991) Model of Coping (*figure*),
   4:179
Lead, poisoning, 3:104
Learning disabilities, 1:126, 248, 5:10, 42,
   47, 69, 243, 9:37, 10:61
Learning disorders, 5:156
Learning style, Zentall's instructional
   model, 5:63
Learning Style Inventory, 9:215
Leedy v. Hartnett, 10:145
Left-handedness, increased in alcoholics,
   4:100
Legal counsel, 6:69
Legal issues
   expert witness testimony, 10:97–107
   in group therapy, 2:121–137
Legal process, of divorce, 4:210–211
Legal requirement
   to report incest, 4:119
   to report sexual abuse, 4:135, 140
Legal separation, defined, 6:41
Legitimation, of schism, 6:102
Lesbians, 8:231
   See also Homosexual
Lethality, evaluated in suicide risk, 3:120
Letter, as follow-up to clients, 2:74
"Letter to the Offender", 5:31
Leukocyte, 3:27
Levinson Institute, 4:34, 49
Lexical leakage, 2:21
LFT
   See Low frustration tolerance (LFT)
Libido
   lack of, 3:105
   loss of, 3:38
Librium (chlordiazepoxide), 7:34, 8:65
Life, prolonging with behavior therapy,
   4:63–64
Life review, in elderly group work, 3:83
Life review group, syllabus for (*table*),
   2:205
Life skills, fitness program, 8:166
Life support, 6:130
Light, full-spectrum, 3:251–252

Limits, setting, 2:4
Linear thinking, 2:147
Linkage
    See Collaboration
Lioresal (baclofen), 7:43
Lipari v. Sears, Roebuck & Co., 10:8, 144
Lipoprotein cholesterol, 7:77
Listening
    See also Communication; Speech
    active vs. passive strategies, 2:26–30
    cues to alert therapists, 2:23
        assumptions and preoccupations,
            2:24–25
        conjunctions of adjectives, 2:25
        evaluative terms, 2:25
        frequency of topics, 2:25
        frequency of words, 2:25–26
        moments of unintelligibility, 2:23–
            24
        movement and posture, 2:23
        novel metaphors, 2:24
        particular content categories,
            2:26
        sequence, 2:24
        slips of the tongue, 2:24
        voice quality, 2:23
    key points, 2:17
    processes in psychotherapy, 2:17–31
    rules for, 2:22
    strategies, risks in, 2:21–22
Listening With the Third Ear (Reik), 2:18
Literacy, multicultural, 10:241, 243–245
Literature, erotic
    See Bibliotherapy
Lithane
    See Lithium (Eskalith Lithane)
Lithium (Eskalith
        Lithane), 1:82, 228, 256, 2:200, 3:107,
            5:164, 166, 7:37, 44, 8:261
    and mania, 1:228
Litigation
    explosion of, 2:217
    malpractice, 2:218
Liver
    function in detoxification, 7:51, 54
    method to evaluate function, 7:52–
        53
Living will, 6:130
*Living Without Depression and Manic
        Depression* (Copeland),
        1:221
Lo Lives, juvenile gang, 5:207

Locke-Wallace Marital Adjustment Test,
    6:3, 5, 27, 226
Locus of control, 4:6, 9:197
Logical errors, 3:129, 132
    arbitrary inference, 3:132
    magnification, 3:132
    minimization, 3:132
    overgeneralization, 3:132
    personalization, 3:132
    selective attention, 3:132
Loneliness, 4:78, 8:205, 208
    a core emotion, 4:191
    in divorce, 4:204, 211, 213
Lorazepam (Ativan), 7:34, 147
Loss, 4:181
    adaptation to, 3:72, 73
    of appetite, 6:150
    associated with AIDS, 6:121
    of child due to death, 6:147–162
    common cause of depression, 3:2
    of control, 6:181
        in substance abusers, 5:232
    dealing with, 4:41
    in divorce, 4:203
    of employment, 4:45
    experience in childhood, 3:3
    fear of, 6:256
    grief as response to, 3:6
    of homes, 5:82
    identifying, 6:158
    of kin systems, 6:122
    in late-life, 3:150
    mourning, 4:190
    personal, 3:255
    prenatal, 6:160
    some persons sensitive to, 3:7
    unresolved, 6:159
    vision and hearing, 3:78
Lost child, 4:81
    co-dependent role, 4:77, 78
Lotteries, 1:154, 156
Love, 3:195, 4:35, 6:181, 227, 231
    See also Marriage, Relationships
    expectations of in marriage, 4:214
    hunger for, 3:188
    needed by depressed clients, 3:257
    problems with, 2:234
    as reason to marry, 4:204, 206
Love addict, 3:182
Lovesick therapist, 10:201
Lovesickness, defined, 10:201
Low blood pressure, due to acetaldehyde,

4:96
Low frustration tolerance (LFT), 4:159,
	161, 164, 165
Loyalties, divided, 6:91
LSD, 3:102, 5:232, 240, 7:141, 144, 8:61, 62
	decline in usage in 1960s, 7:137–138
	description, 7:136–140
	experimentation, 7:134
	trends in use of, 7:129–148
Ludiomil (maprotiline), 7:35
Luminal (phenobarbital), 5:51, 7:32, 41
Luria-Nebraska Neuropsychological
	Battery, 7:18, 9:147
Luvox (fluvoxamine), 3:272, 7:36
	and OCD, 1:21
Lying
	by gamblers, 1:161
	compulsive, by criminals, 1:144, 145
	pathologic, 5:106
Lymphocytes, 3:18, 22, 23, 24, 27
Lymphokines, 3:20
Lysergic acid diethylamide
	See LSD

M

MacAndrew Alcoholism-Revised Scale
	(MAC-R), 8:71, 72
McCarron-Dial Work Evaluation System,
	9:147, 149
MacCormick Youth Center Project, 5:199–
	201
McIntosh v. Milano, 10:8
McMaster model, of problem-centered
	family therapy, 2:168
Macrophages, 3:20, 21, 22, 24, 27
Magnesium, 7:51, 1:183
	poisoning, 3:104
Magnetic resonance imaging (MRI), 3:45
Mainstream, rejection of by criminals,
	1:139
Maintenance, 8:271, 283–284
Major depressive disorder, 8:121, 1:33
	symptoms, 8:122
Major life activities, 9:39–40
	Americans with Disabilities Act
		(ADA) definition of, 9:38
Making and Keeping Friends (Sheridan),
	5:67
*Makris v. The Bureau of Professional and
	Occupational Affairs*, 10:119,

124
Maladaptive interpersonal pattern,2:91
Maladaptive Schemata Categorized Into
	Six Domains (*table*), 4:184
Male erectile disorder, 6:220
Malingering, 1:65–66, 106
Malnutrition, in children, 3:29
Malpractice suits, 2:217, 10:119, 128
	See also Lawsuits
Managed care, 4:198
	as threats to confidentiality, 5:277
Management, of collaborative treatment
	efforts, 7:251
Management of Drug Withdrawal During
	Pregnancy (*table*), 8:112
Manganese, 7:51, 60
	poisoning, 3:104
Mania, 1:82, 222, 5:241, 7:38, 8:247, 255
	description of, 1:212
	early warning signs, 1:217–218
	early warning signs (*table*), 1:218
	increased at certain times of day,
		1:227–228
	sample charts to assist in teaching
		self-help for, 1:232–235
	and seasons, 1:228
	self-help strategies for clients with,
		1:211–230
	signs of, 1:213
	techniques to alleviate early warning
		signs of (*table*), 1:220
Manic, what to do when becoming (*table*),
	1:219
Manic-depressive disorder, 1:212, 3:116
Mannerisms, in autistic disorder, 1:176
Mantra, 4:15, 20, 21
	defined, 4:4
MAO
	See Monoamine oxidase (MAO)
MAOIs
	See Monoamine oxidase inhibitors
		(MAOIs)
Mapping, 1:69
Maprotiline (Ludiomil), 7:35
Marathon groups, 2:102
Marijuana, 3:102, 5:232, 7:131, 133, 136,
	147, 173, 8:58, 62, 98, 99, 105,
	111, 226, 253, 270
	physical fitness programs reduce use
		of, 8:166
	statistics, 8:246, 247
Marital

discord, 3:141
problems, 3:255
therapy, 3:115
Marital Attitude Survey, 6:226
Marital and family therapy, in treatment
    of alcoholism, 7:101–125
Marital Interaction Coding System III
    (MICS III), 6:19
Market research, 9:104–105
Marketing
    components
        environmental assessment, 9:99–
        100
        implementation, 9:102–104
        strategic planning, 9:100–102
    techniques, use of, 9:97–105
Marplan (isocarboxazid), 3:213
Marriage
    See also Divorce, Love; Relationships;
        Remarriage
    break-up of
        See Divorce
    conflict in, 4:103
    dependency in, 3:8, 9
    diagnostic testing of, 6:1–23
    dissolution of
        See Divorce
    early stages of, 4:206–207
    expectation of lasting nature, 4:203
    expectations, case study, 6:270–271
    ghosts from prior, 6:84, 93
    hostility in, case study, 6:208–209
    and loss of child due to death, 6:147–
        162
    as "patient", 6:205–206
    process, 6:201
    reasons for
        arrangement, 4:204, 205
        desire for a child, 4:204, 205–206
        escape, 4:204, 205
        love and completion of self, 4:204,
        206
        pregnancy, 4:204, 205
        security and dependency needs,
        4:204–205
        social pressure, 4:204, 205
        unconscious needs, 4:204, 206
    sexual character in, case study, 6:195–
        196
    as system, case study, 6:209–210
Marriage therapy, 2:50, 6:52

    See also Family therapy
    theories and applications, 2:143–161
Mascot, co-dependent role, 4:77, 79
Mastery
    defined, 2:66
    one concept of work therapy, 9:167
Mastery technique, 3:57
Masturbation, 5:32, 185
    excessive, 5:33
Matching Families Figures Test, 5:55
Maternity leave, 4:207
Mathematics, and children with ADHD,
    5:47, 63
Mature minor doctrine, 8:177
Maturing out, 4:104
Mayo Clinic, Alcoholism and Drug
    Dependence Unit (ADDU),
    8:201, 209
Mazindol (Parlodel), 8:283
MDMA
    See Ecstasy
Meals-On-Wheels, 6:183
Meaning
    and adults, 9:3
    perception of lack of by elderly, 2:204
    reconstruction of, 9:10
    of speech, 2:19–22
Meaningfulness, 2:40
Measurement Domains of the Revised
    Drug Use Screening
    Inventory (table), 7:7
Medicaid, 6:183, 9:69
Medical evaluation, 3:245
    of physical illness, 3:99–107, 151–154
Medical illness
    See Physical illness
Medical Outcomes Study, 3:201, 205
Medication Agreement (table), 8:241
Medication Chart for Treating Attention-
    Deficit/Disorders (table),
    5:60–61
Medication management module, 1:248
Medications
    See also Antidepressants;
        Benzodiazepines; Drugs;
        Monoamine oxidase
        inhibitors (MAOIs);
        Pharmacotherapy; Selective
        serotonin reuptake inhibitors
        (SSRIs); Specific names of
        medications; Tricyclic

antidepressants (TCAs)
for ADHD, 1:192; 5:56–59
along with social skills training for
schizophrenia, 1:246–247
antianxiety, 6:228
antidepressants, 6:228, 261, 262
antihypertensive, 4:6
antipsychotics, 6:262
anxiolytic, 4:15
case study, 2:116
for clients with HIV and substance
abuse, 8:239–240
cold, 5:15
defined, 7:27
and DID, 1:80–82
immune response affected by, 3:28, 29
indicated for certain signs and
symptoms, 2:115–116
and OCD, 1:42–44
over-the-counter, 8:205
placebo-like responses to, 1:64, 81
prescription, 8:82, 272
can cause psychopathological
symptoms, 3:102
psychotropic, 2:200
and PTSD, 1:20
side effects, 2:219, 7:26, 30–31
fear of, 3:246
need to be discussed, 2:115
to stabilize manic clients, 1:228–230
as treatment for autism, 1:183
used in rehabilitation settings, 7:25–45
and work capacity, 3:213–215
Medications That Can Mimic Depression
(*table*), 3:152
Medicine
holistic, 2:13
model of linear causation of
disorders, 2:147
Meditation, 4:4, 5, 6, 7, 15, 16, 20
Eastern, 4:2
transcendental, 4:19
Western, 4:2
Megabrush, defined, 8:17
Megavitamins, 5:68
Meier v. Ross General Hospital (1968), 2:134
Melancholia, 4:54
Mellaril (thioridazine), 10:114
Memories, 4:125, 142
anxiety-provoking, 5:26
defense mechanisms used as

protection from, 1:14
painful may emerge as hallucinations,
1:72
personalities as guardians of, 1:57
of relationships, 4:178
reliability of debated, 1:51
repressed, debate over, 4:146
Memory
accurate, 4:142
evocative, 1:122
short-term, 4:100
weaknesses in, 1:173
Memory loss
due to dementia, 3:153
in elderly, 3:70
Men
African-American, 8:247, 9:193
bisexual, 8:226, 231
statistics, 8:227
as caregivers to elderly, 6:170
with disabilities, 9:80
Hispanic, 8:247, 9:193
historically dominant to women, 6:274
homosexual, 8:226, 231
See also Homosexual
statistics, 8:227
low sexual desire and, 6:192
male self-identity and, 10:199
sex drive in, 6:222
young, as survivors of traumatic
brain injury, 9:149
Menninger Clinic, 2:155, 240
Menninger Foundation, 2:250
Psychotherapy Research Project,
2:253, 258
Menninger Treatment Interventions
Project, 1:125
Mens rea, a guilty mind, 10:152
Menstruation, 5:32
painful
See Dysmenorrhea
Mental disorders
See Disorders, mental; Specific names
of disorders
Mental Health Act (1963), 7:246
Mental health professionals
See also Counselors; Psychologists;
Psychotherapists; Therapists
distanced from world of work and
organizations, 4:34
insufficiently familiar with 12-step

programs, 4:83
often unequipped to deal with
  physical illness, 3:96
required to take courses on incest,
  4:114
should not violate client's right to
  autonomy, 4:139
Mental illness
characterized, 10:165, 165–166, 168
chronic, 9:110, 112, 221
defined, 10:164
ethical considerations in treating, case
  studies, 10:180–182
Mental Measurements Yearbook (Buros),
  9:219
Mental Research Institute (MRI), 2:145
model in brief strategic therapy, 2:70–
  73
  benefits, 2:73
model in brief strategic therapy
  (*table*), 2:71
Mental retardation, 9:37, 110
fetal alcohol syndrome leading cause
  of, 8:102
Meperidine (Demerol), 7:42
Mercury, poisoning, 3:104
Mescaline, 7:142
MET
  See Motivational enhancement
  therapy (MET)
Meta-analysis
of social skills training, 1:247
statistical method, 2:252
Metabolic rates, 7:30
Metabolic Screening Questionnaire, 7:54
  (*figure*), 7:55
Metabolism, of trauma, 1:70
Metabolites, defined, 7:50
Metachlorophenylpiperazine, 1:43
Metacommunications, 2:145
Metal poisoning, 3:104
Metaphors, novel, 2:24
Methacholine (Provocholine), 4:9
Methadone, 7:75, 76, 78, 192, 8:63, 105–
  107, 229, 237–238
  (Dolophine), 8:111
Methamphetamine (Desoxyn), 7:141, 5:56
Methods Time Measurement (MTM), 9:47
Methylphenidate (Ritalin), 3:44, 5:56–59
Mexican Americans, 9:182, 211
  See also Hispanics; Latinas; Latinos
Michigan Alcoholism Screening Test

(MAST), 8:42, 43, 57, 71, 72,
  200, 207, 273
Microcephaly, 8:102, 108
A Midcourse Review (DHHS), 8:160
Mikkelsen v. Salama, 10:123, 124
Milan group, 6:31
Millon Behavioral Health Inventory, 7:12
Millon Clinical Multiaxial Inventory,
  9:148
Mind, immune system can influence,
  3:16–17
Minerals, 7:53, 57
Mini-Mental State Examination, 3:154,
  7:18
Minimal brain dysfunction, previous
  term for ADHD, 1:193
Minimal impairment, of elderly, 2:200,
  204–205
Minnesota Model, 4:75
inpatient treatment to overcome
  denial, 4:70
Minnesota Multiphasic Personality
  Inventory (MMPI), 1:9, 6:14,
  7:11, 8:72, 9:148, 211, 217, 218
  Dependency Scale of, 3:183
  and the gambler, 1:162–163
Minnesota Multiphasic Personality
  Inventory-2 (MMPI-2), 1:9
Minor
considered incompetent, 10:116
defined, 5:280, 10:6
emancipated, defined, 10:6
Minorities, 6:119
  See also Color, People of; Specific
  minority groups
AIDS and, 6:133
characteristics and world views of,
  9:179–187
ethnic, 9:178
racial, 9:178
support groups and, 6:181
Miscarriage, 6:151–152
Misdiagnosis
lawsuits filed alleging, 10:120–122
of physical illnesses as depression,
  3:93–108
statistics, 3:95, 96
why it exists, 3:96–98
Mississippi Scale for Combat-Related
  PTSD, 1:9–10
Mississippi Scale-Hostage Version, 1:10
Mistrust, 4:39

an impediment to therapeutic
    alliance, 4:124
by adopted child, 5:109, 110
by clients in therapy, 2:50, 51, 4:126
Mitogens, 3:21, 24, 29
MMPI
    See Minnesota Multiphasic
        Personality Inventory
        (MMPI)
Mnemonics, useful to enhance treatment,
    7:208–209
MOBAT, alcohol breath test, 7:107, 108
Mobile work crew, 9:112
Modeling, 5:136, 263, 6:211, 7:116
    technique used in cognitive-
        behavioral play therapy, 5:135
    used with aggressive youth, 5:211, 213
Modifications
    to enhance work speed, 9:244
    to work environment, 9:51
Modular Arrangement of Predetermined
    Time Systems (MODAPTS),
    9:47
Molybdenum, 7:57
Money
    divorce and, 6:85–86
    in marriage, 4:209
Monitoring
    continued, of patients with
        schizophrenia, 9:171
    of supported employment programs,
        9:123
Monitoring the Future Study (Youth
    Indicators), 6:101
Monkeys, Harlow's research with, 6:202
Monoamine oxidase inhibitors (MAOIs),
    1:44, 82, 3:44, 53, 213, 7:35, 36
    side effects, 5:14
Monoamine oxidase (MAO), low levels in
    persons at high risk for
    alcoholism, 4:99
Monocytes, 3:20
Monomania, jealous, 6:243
Mononucleosis, 3:105
Mood disorder, 6:228, 262
    substance abuse and, 8:94
Mood disorders, 1:197; 3:45, 227, 266, 269,
    5:154
    eating disorders as variants of, 3:53
    obsessions and compulsions present
        in, 1:30
    relationship to eating disorders, 3:63

support system of people
    knowledgeable about, 1:216
Mood ratings, 3:163
Mood swings, 5:236
    in gamblers, 1:157, 161, 162
Moral, model of relapse, 7:218, 219
Moral development, adolescent, 8:181–
    182
Moral discomfort, 10:18
Moral Education (ME), 5:197, 207, 208,
    219–221
Moral principles
    autonomy, 10:40–41
    beneficence, 10:40, 41
    fidelity, 10:40, 42
    justice, 10:40, 42
    nonmaleficence, 10:40, 41
Moral reasoning, 5:201, 219
Morality, views of, 10:21
Morally valid consent
    See Consent, morally valid
Morphine, 7:75
Mother-infant symbiotic state, longing to
    return to, 2:242
Mothers, 3:194
    See also Parents
    awarded custody of children, 6:38
    of BPD patients, 1:121, 122
    children raised by, 6:63
    dependency on, 3:185
    of drug users, 6:121
    involved in counseling sessions, 3:189
    referred to as "the ONE", 3:186
    and relation to child's self-esteem,
        3:184
    role in psychodynamic formulations,
        1:124
    separation from, 3:188
    of sexually abused children, 5:34
    single, 6:59, 67
        and poverty, 6:60
    substance abusing
        See Pregnancy
Motivation, 4:232
    of caregivers to elderly, 6:173–174
    contrasted with compliance, 7:195–
        197, 224
    of the criminal personality, 1:148–149
    five stages of, 8:271
    lack of, 7:192–193
    substance abuser and, 8:270–271
Motivation-Based Dual Diagnosis

Treatment Model, 8:270
Motivational Enhancement Therapy Manual
(book), 8:276
Motivational enhancement therapy
(MET), 7:197, 199–200, 235,
8:270, 276–277
Motor retardation, 3:203
Motrin (ibuprofen), 7:42
Mount Zion research team, 2:90
Mourning, 4:190, 212, 6:130
See also Grief
connected with loss of important
figure, 2:240
unresolved, in divorce, 6:94
Movement therapy, 1:77
Movies, dealing with adoption (*table*),
5:117
MRI
See Magnetic resonance imaging
(MRI)
Multiaxial Problem-Oriented Diagnostic
System for Sexual
Dysfunctions, 6:192, 222
Multiculturalism, ethics and, 10:235–246
Multidimensional Personality
Questionnaire, 7:11
Multidirectional partiality, 6:93
Multigenerational projection system,
2:156, 158, 160, 161
Multigenerational theory (Bowen), 2:155–
161
Multiple personality disorder
See Dissociative identity disorder
(DID)
Multiple sclerosis (MS), 3:105, 5:162, 6:261
"Multiproblem family", 6:119
Murder, 3:124, 5:200
of adoptive parents by adoptees, 5:114
Muscles
relaxation, 4:2, 4, 15
tension in, 4:3
Music, relaxing, for stress management,
4:5
Music therapy, 1:77
Mutual, defined, 6:269
Mutual-aid groups, 4:84
Mutuality
contrasted with reciprocity, 6:276–278
in couples therapy, 6:267–283
therapeutic strategies for, 6:278–279
Myasthenia gravis, 3:18
Myelopathy, 3:107

Myers Briggs Type Indicator, 9:215

N

NA
See Narcotics Anonymous (NA)
Nafazodone (Serzone), 7:36
Nakkula, 3:85
Nalmefene, 7:79
Naloxone (Narcan), 3:24, 7:67
Naltrexone (ReVia), 8:130, 273
costs, 7:80
dosage, 7:76–77
FDA approval of, 7:68
liver and, 7:77–78
side effects, 7:76
for treatment of alcohol dependence,
7:63–83
Naltrindole, 7:142
"Name That Touch Game", 5:32
Naprosyn (naproxen), 7:42
Naproxen (Naprosyn), 7:42
Nar-Anon Family Group (*directory
listing*), 8:157
Narc-Anon, 8:29
Narcan (Naloxone), 3:24, 7:67
Narcissism, 4:82, 84, 6:259
Narcissistic blows, 2:202
Narcissistic disorder, 1:63
Narcissus, myth of, 4:82
Narcosynthesis, 3:115
Narcotic, defined, 7:42
Narcotics Anonymous (NA), 4:71, 85, 5:178,
245, 265, 7:147, 8:29, 76, 96, 232,
235, 239, 283, 5:178, 245, 265
(*directory listing*), 8:157
quote, 8:111
Nardil (phenelzine), 3:213, 5:14, 7:36
National Adoption Information
Clearinghouse, 5:118
(*directory listing*), 5:124
National Alliance for the Mentally Ill,
2:201
National Anxiety Foundation (*directory
listing*), 1:117
National Association for Social Workers,
2:126
National Board for Certified Counselors,
10:39
National Center on Child Abuse and
Neglect, 4:116
National Clearinghouse for Alcohol and

Other Drug Information,
8:276
directory (*appendix*), 8:158
National Commission on Testing and
Public Policy, 9:213
National Committee on Schools, 6:100
National Committee to Prevent Child
Abuse, 4:115
National Comorbidity Survey (NSC)
(*table*), 1:104
National Council on Alcoholism, estimate
on losses to businesses, 8:11
National Council on Disability, 9:81
National Council on Self-Help and Public
Health, 1:240
National Education Association, 2:102
National Highway Traffic Society
Administration (NHTSA),
8:203
National Household Survey on Drug
Abuse, 8:4
National Institute on Aging, projections,
9:82
National Institute on Alcohol Abuse and
Alcoholism (NIAAA), 5:231,
7:64, 102, 8:6, 16, 57, 199
National Institute on Disability and
Rehabilitation Research, 8:58
National Institute on Drug Abuse
(NIDA), 7:130, 134, 8:96
National Institute of Education, definition
of functional illiteracy, 9:44
National Institute of Health's
Hypertension Pooling Project,
4:6
National Institute of Mental Health, 1:36,
102, 2:252, 5:51, 8:164
(*directory listing*), 1:117
National Longitudinal Study of Youth, 8:98
National Narcotics Intelligence
Consumers Committee
(NNICC), 7:134
National Organization for Birthfathers
and Adoption Reform
(NOBAR)(*directory listing*),
5:125
National Research Council Commission
on Behavioral and Social
Sciences, 8:192
National Research Council Twin Registry,
4:97
National Umbrella Network of the

Adoption Reform Movement
(*table*), 5:124–127
Native Americans, 9:179, 191
characteristics, 9:186–187
little known about career behavior of,
9:187
Natural killer (NK) cells, 3:19, 21, 23, 24,
27, 28, 29
Nausea, 3:272
due to acetaldehyde, 4:96
in IBS patients, 4:10
Need/value structures, 2:40–42
Needles, 8:229, 230
HIV from sharing, 8:226
Needs
affiliative, 4:37
social, 4:37
Neglect
of children, 5:256
type of relationship wound, 4:183
Negligence, 2:220
professional, 10:110
defined, 10:111
types
client abandonment, 10:112–
113
failure to control dangerous
client, 10:122–123
failure to obtain informed
consent, 10:115–116
misdiagnosis, 10:120–122
practicing outside scope of
competency, 10:118–119
sexual relationship with
clients, 10:119–120
unhealthy transference
relationships, 10:117–118
unorthodox treatments,
10:113–114
"Negro Family: The case for National
Action, The" (Moynihan),
6:119
Neo-Kraepelinians, 2:4
Nervous system, damage to, 7:56
Nervousness, 5:233
Network link intervention, 6:141
example, 6:142
Network of Mental Health Clients, 1:240
Network of support, building a, 2:76–77
Networks
kin, 6:140
large family, 6:120

support, 6:134
Neuroendocrine system, interaction of
    immune system with, 3:22–24
Neurofibromatosis, 1:179
Neuroleptic therapy, 1:250
Neuroleptics, 8:261, 274
Neuropeptides, 3:24
Neuropsychological testing, 7:17–19,
    9:147
Neuropsychologists, 9:150
Neuroses, 2:258
Neurotic depressive reaction, 3:116
Neurotoxicity, 7:132, 142, 146
Neurotransmitters
    See Serotonin
New Jersey Coalition for Openness in
    Adoption (directory listing),
    5:125
Newlyweds, 4:206
Niacin, 3:107
Nicoderm, 8:283
Nicorette, 8:283
Nicotine, 5:15, 241, 8:58, 247, 270, 272, 274
    See also Cigarettes; Smoking; Tobacco
        abuse
    abuse, 3:101
    physical fitness programs reduce use
        of, 8:166
    relapse rate from addiction to, 7:217
    replacement patch, 8:283
Nightmares, 1:101
    about separation, 5:9
    by gamblers, 1:158
    in COAs, 4:101
    and PTSD, use of alcohol to suppress,
        1:15
Nihilism, therapeutic, 2:53
Nitrates, 8:226
NK cells
    See Natural killer (NK) cells
Noise, 2:22
    fear of loud, 1:172
Noncompliance, 7:192–193, 199, 200, 208
    See also Compliance
    child's, 5:63, 64
    defined, 7:196
    serious problem, 1:241
Nondiscrimination, Code of Ethics (ACA)
    and, 10:47
Nonmaleficence, 10:58, 237
    moral principle of, 10:40, 41
Norepinephrine, 5:6, 52, 8:250

Normalization, primary tenet of, 9:110
Norpramin (desipramine), 1:42, 3:44, 274,
    5:56–57, 164, 7:35, 8:283
North American Council on Adoptable
    Children (NACAC) (directory
    listing), 5:125
Nortriptyline (Aventyl, Pamelor), 1:42,
    3:42, 43, 44, 213, 270, 274, 5:57,
    164, 7:35
Not guilty by reason of insanity (NGRI),
    10:148, 150, 157
    case study, 10:150–156
Nuclear family emotional system, 2:156,
    157, 158
Null cells, 3:18, 19
Nurses, needed for depressed homeless
    children, 5:91
Nursing homes, 2:194, 3:121, 149
    residents, psychodrama and, 3:84
Nutrient Composition of the Two Base
    Powdered Meal Supplement
    Products (table), 7:58
Nutrients, 7:51
Nutrients Appropriate for Those
    Undergoing Detoxification
    (table), 7:51
Nutrition
    and AIDS, 6:118
    improved detoxification through,
        7:49–61
Nutritional disorders, 3:107

O

Obesity, 7:234
    See also Eating disorders
Object-relations theory, 6:195
Objectivity, 3:190, 10:155
Observation, as behavioral assessment
    method, 3:162–163
Observational Measures (appendix), 6:32
Obsessional disorder, 6:251
Obsessional neurosis, former name of
    OCD, 1:30
Obsessions, 1:101, 5:116
    See also Obsessive-compulsive
        disorder (OCD)
    defined, 1:32
    present in variety of
        psychopathologic conditions,
        1:30
Obsessive-Compulsive Disorder

Foundation, Inc. (*directory listing*), 1:117
Obsessive-compulsive disorder (OCD), 1:21, 101, 109, 2:260, 3:98, 266, 5:5, 6:248, 249, 253, 260, 7:35, 37, 234
See also Compulsions; Obsessions
affective illness and, 1:38–39
a chronic disorder, 1:44
diagnosis, 1:30–33
DSM-IV definition of (*table*), 1:32–33
genetics and, 1:37–38
neuropsychologic findings, 1:39–40
new findings, 1:29–45
no significant cultural differences, 1:37
prevalence, 1:36–37
rehabilitative treatment, 1:40–44
symptoms
checking, 1:34–35
primary obsessional slowness, 1:35–36
pure obsession, 1:35
washing, 1:34
therapeutic rapport, 1:44–45
Obsessive-compulsive
personalities, and hypoactive sexual desire, 6:227
traits, 2:201
Obsessive-compulsive psychotics, 1:31
Obsessive-compulsive rituals, 4:218
Occupational therapists, 6:185, 9:133, 134, 145, 154
Occupational therapy, 1:76, 5:177, 9:137
Occupations
See Career; Jobs
OCD
See Obsessive-compulsive disorder (OCD)
O'Connor v. Donaldson, 10:176
Office of National Drug Control Policy, 4:70
Ohio Department of Youth Services, 5:209
OJT
See On-the-job training (OJT)
On Liberty (Mill), 10:174
On-the-job training (OJT), 9:92, 93
Operant conditioning, 7:174–175
for autistic children, 1:183
Operant-behavioral therapy, application to elderly, 2:200
Opiate receptors, 3:24

Opiates, 5:241, 8:61, 63–64, 105–107, 253
Opinions, objective, 10:155
Opioids, 7:67, 68, 75, 78, 8:58, 61, 63–64
defined, 7:42
Oppositional-defiant disorder, 5:12, 43, 48, 156
comorbid with ADHD, 1:198
Optimism, 2:53
Optimist, hopeless, 2:53
Oral contraceptives, 5:162
Orality, 3:182
Orap (pimozide), 6:262
Organic brain impairment, of elderly, 2:200, 203
Organic brain syndrome, 3:142
Organizational consulting firms, 4:49
Orgasm, 6:192, 232
female orgasmic disorder, 6:220
Origins (*directory listing*), 5:126
Orphan Village (*directory listing*), 5:124
Osteoporosis, 8:204
Ostracism, type of relationship wound, 4:183
Others, expectations of, 2:89
Outcome expectancy, 8:68
Outcomes
studies of, 1:242–243
therapeutic, unpredictable nature of, 2:261
Outpatient family therapy, 6:112
Outpatient treatment
adherence to medication regimen in, 7:31
of alcoholism, 7:87–98
with naltrexone, 7:68
Outreach, 9:198
Ovaries, polycystic, 3:108
Overanxious disorder, 5:9, 12
Overdose, 8:186
Overeaters Anonymous, 4:252
See also Eating Disorders; Food
Overprotection, type of relationship wound, 4:183
Oversensitivity, 6:259
Overwork, 3:255
Oxazepam (Serax), 7:34
Oxybutynin (Ditropan), 7:43
Oxycodone (Percocet, Percodan, Tylox), 7:42
Oxygen-free radicals, 7:50, 51

P

P300 waves, 4:99
Pain, 4:34
  abdominal, 5:11
  associated with PTSD, 1:20
  of attachment-separation problems,
    3:8
  chronic, 7:41
    stress management of, 4:12
  coital, 6:220
  emotional associated with some
    interpersonal relationships,
    4:178
  locating sources of, 4:46
  medications to alleviate, 7:42–43
  opioids and, 7:76
  of recollection of sexual abuse, 4:142
Pain-in-living, 3:185, 186
Paired associate learning, 5:58
Palmer v. The Board of Regents in Medicine,
    10:117, 124
Palo Alto groups, 2:145
Palpitations, 5:2
Pamelor (nortriptyline), 1:42, 3:42, 170,
    213, 270, 274, 5:57, 164, 7:35
Panacea, daughter of Greek god
    Aesculapius, 4:82, 83
Pancreas, cancer of, 3:100
Panhypopituitarism, 3:105
Panic, 7:139, 147
  annihilation, 1:129–130
Panic attacks, 1:81, 3:100, 5:5, 6
  symptoms, 1:99
Panic disorder, 1:99, 100, 109, 3:98, 266,
    4:16, 5:5, 6, 14, 7:35, 37, 159,
    161, 234, 8:247, 251
  See also Anxiety disorders
  distinguished from PTSD, 1:21
  and heart attacks, 1:105
  stress management techniques for,
    4:14
  substance abuse and, 8:94
  and suicide, 1:105
Paradox, therapeutic therapy in couples
    therapy, 6:258
Paranoia, 3:10, 5:232, 6:260, 7:139
Paranoid disorder, 2:201
Paranoid illness, 6:247
Paraphilia, 1:33
Pardon, 4:244
Parent-child alienation, 5:157

Parent-neonate relationship, 8:178
Parental Attribution Scale, 5:35
Parental consent, 8:185
Parental Reaction to Incest Disclosure
    Scale, 5:35
Parental splitting, in organizations, 4:36
Parenting, tasks of, 6:60–66
Parents
  See also Fathers; Mothers
  abusive, 1:128
  of ADHD child, outline of training,
    1:198–207
  adoptive, 5:112, 114, 115, 116, 118
    qualities needed in, 5:120
  agoraphobic, 5:5
  with AIDS, 6:131–133
  alcoholic, 7:116
    See also Alcoholics, children of
  of autistic children, 1:184
  becoming, 4:207
  birth, curiosity about by adoptee,
    5:108, 117
  conflict with, 5:255
  counseling of, 5:10
  of criminals, 1:141
  custodial, 6:37–38, 50
  and death of child, 6:147–162
  defined, 6:40
  of dependent person, 3:191
  depressed, 5:11
  desire to reunite, 6:48–49
  divorced and confidential
    information, 5:280–281
  elderly, 3:85
  guidance training, 5:168
  guidelines for raising children with
    healthy self-esteem, 4:222–223
  of hyperactive children, 4:101
  as incest perpetrators, 4:118
  informing, 10:170
  interviewing about adolescent
    substance abuser, 5:235–237
  investment in keeping client weak,
    3:194
  parental sovereignty and, 8:177
  psychiatric disorders in, 5:236
  response to stress, 5:6
  role of in adolescent drug abuse,
    6:108–109
  role in psychodynamic formulations,
    1:124
  as security, 6:46

single, fathers as, 6:57–69
skills in dealing with ADHD children,
    5:63–66
skills training, 5:168
of substance abusing adolescents,
    8:143–145
substance-abusing, 7:172
tend to underreport depression in
    adolescents, 5:160
as a threat to confidentiality, 5:277
troubled, 6:107–108
underestimation of children's anxiety,
    5:3
Paresthesia, 5:2
Parkinson's disease, 7:56
Parlodel (bromocriptine), 8:283
Parnate (tranylcypromine), 1:44, 7:36
Paroxetine (Paxil), 3:59, 272, 5:14, 57,
    7:36
Participation
    family, 6:110
    part of normalization, 9:110
    part of strategic planning, 9:101
Partnership, therapists need with clients,
    2:68
Passive-aggressive behaviors, 4:36, 158
Paternalism
    case study, 10:30–31
    defined, 8:186, 10:30
    justified, 8:187, 188
    therapist's, mentally ill client and,
        10:166
    toward children, 10:171–172
Paternity leave, 4:207
Pathologic Jealous Reactions (*table*), 6:245
Patient, identified
    See Identified patient (IP)
Patient Personality Characteristics vs.
        Worker Personality
        Characteristics (*table*), 9:131
Patients
    See also Clients
    abusing hallucinogenic drugs, 2:108
    alcoholic, 6:14
    borderline, with no history of abuse,
        1:130–131
    BPD, with neurophysiologic
        impairment, 1:126–127
    cancer, terminally ill, 6:39
    depressed, hospitalization of, 3:247
    elderly, 3:65–90, 147–171
    gender differences of, 4:125

with history of incest in childhood,
    4:113–128
less interested in insight, 1:131
mentally ill institutionalized, 2:218
with OCD, may be misdiagnosed,
    1:37
with psychiatric illness,
    responsibilities of, 10:166
psychotic, 2:108
with PTSD and schizophrenia
    present, 1:16
records of, 5:282–284
retarded, 2:108
with schizophrenia, self-management
    approaches for, 1:237–260
sociopathic, 2:108
terminally ill, 2:204–205, 3:121, 4:65
"three", 6:205–206
who are in a crisis, 2:110
Pavlov's experiments, 7:175
Paxil (paroxetine), 3:59, 272, 5:14, 57, 7:36
PCP
    See Phencyclidine hydrochloride
        (PCP)
PDD
    See Pervasive developmental
        disorders (PDD)
Peabody Individual Achievement Test
    (PIAT), 9:149
Peabody Picture Vocabulary Test (PPVT),
    9:216
Pease v. Beech Aircraft Corporation, 10:141
*Peck v. Counseling Service of Addison
    County*, 10:136, 145
Peer
    affiliation, 7:14
    counseling, 1:220, 221–222, 3:256,
        10:60
    EAPs and, 8:20
    groupings, 5:176
        See also Gangs
    loss, 5:257
    pressure, 8:161, 1:139
        increases in substance abuse,
            5:234
    relationships, 7:16–17
        children with ADHD and, 5:66–
            68
    status, Ritalin and, 5:56
    support, 2:206, 8:212
        lack of, 5:254
Peers, 6:104

adolescents seek sense of belonging
with, 6:103
Pemoline (Cylert), 5:56
Penicillin, psychiatric treatment, 3:106
Penn Psychotherapy Project, 2:253
People v. Burnick, 10:141
People v. Poddar, 10:138
Peper's technique, of trapezius EMG
biofeedback, 4:9
Peptic ulcer
Caffeine and, 7:155
stress management techniques for,
4:9–10
Percentage of First-Time Mothers who
Smoked Cigarettes, Drank
Alcohol, or Smoked
Marijuana During Pregnancy
(*table*), 8:99
Perception, alteration of by LSD, 7:138
Perceptual disorders, 1:173
Perceptual distortion, in anorexia
nervosa, 3:59
Percocet (oxycodone), 7:42
Percodan (oxycodone), 7:42
Perfectionism, type of relationship
wound, 4:183
Performance, work, impaired by
depression, 3:202–203
Performance anxiety, 5:7, 14
Performance feedback, 5:211
used with aggressive youth, 5:215–
216
Perkins v. Dean, 10:117, 124
Perpetrator, of sexual abuse, normal
feelings toward, 5:27
Persecution, fears of, 1:13
Person-centered therapists, 2:54
Personal assistance
adequacy assessment of, 9:72
categories of needs, 9:73
defined, 9:64–65
key to employability, 9:63–76
options
barter/multiple assistants, 9:66
family, 9:65–66
family/hired assistant, 9:66
full-time assistant, 9:66
institution, 9:66
shared provider, 9:66
spouse/family, 9:66
rating of options, 9:67–68
statistics, 9:65, 68

three levels
minimal, 9:65
moderate, 9:65
extensive, 9:65
Personal Assistance Satisfaction Index,
9:72
Personal Authority in the Family Systems
Questionnaire (PAFS-Q),
6:17–18, 28
Personal Daily Warning Signs Chart for
Mania (*chart*), 1:234
Personal Experience Inventory (PEI),
5:243
Personalities
See also Dissociative identity disorder
(DID)
alter, in DID, 1:55, 57, 61, 64, 68, 69, 71
child-like, in DID, 1:57
differences between in DID, 1:55–56
number of in DID, 1:54–55
Personality
cancer-prone, 4:55
co-dependence as disorder of, 4:74
criminal, 1:137–151
disease-prone, 4:55
disorders of, 6:259
masochistic, 2:258
dominant, 3:181, 182
drug-prone, 4:103
employability and, 9:69
host, 1:56
hysterical, 2:108
maladaptive styles of, 3:7–11
maturity of, challenged in marriage,
6:200
measures of useful in family
assessment, 6:2
obsessive-compulsive, and
hypoactive sexual desire,
6:227
original, 1:56
paranoid, 6:246
passive-aggressive, 5:196
patient, 9:130
presenting, 1:56
testing, and the gambler, 1:162
Type 1, increased risk of cancer
mortality, 4:55–56, 57, 60
Type 2, increased risk of heart infarct,
4:56, 57, 60
Type 3, average survival rate, 4:56
Type 4, increased survival rate, 4:56

Type C, 4:55
unified, goal in treatment of DID,
    1:68
worker, 9:130
Personality development, theories of, 9:2
Personality disorders, 1:197, 3:141, 4:74,
    81, 84, 5:15, 8:256
    narcissistic, 2:258
Pertofrane (desipramine), 1:42, 3:274,
    5:56–57, 164, 7:35, 8:111
Perturbation, evaluated in suicide risk,
    3:120
Pervasive developmental disorders
    (PDD), 1:171–184, 197
    common characteristics, 1:173–175
    definition, 1:172
    early descriptions, 1:172–173
    epidemiology, 1:178
    etiology, 1:178–180
PET scan
    See Positron emission tomography
        (PET scan)
Petersen v. State of Washington, 10:8, 145
Pharmacology
    basic knowledge of needed by
        counselors, 7:26
    of caffeine, 7:155
    defined, 7:27
    medical, 7:27
        analgesics, 7:42–43
        anticholinergics, 7:43, 44
        anticonvulsants, 7:41–42
        antispastics, 7:43
Pharmacotherapy, 1:238, 246, 260, 2:253,
    259, 261, 3:114, 119–120, 140,
    236, 4:14
    See also Antidepressants;
        Benzodiazepines; Drugs;
        Monoamine oxidase
        inhibitors (MAOIs); Selective
        serotonin reuptake inhibitors
        (SSRIs); Specific names of
        medications; Tricyclic
        antidepressants
    for adolescent patients with
        depression, 5:165
    for anxiety disorders, 1:113–115
    in chronic depression, 3:226
    complex field, 7:44
    for depressed child, 5:93
    in DID, 1:80–82
    for insomnia, 4:13–14

for mania, 1:228–230
naltrexone and alcohol dependence,
    7:63–83
in OCD, 1:42–44
in PTSD, 1:20, 21
for separation anxiety disorder, 5:10
to treat pathological gamblers, 1:166
Phencyclidine hydrochloride (PCP),
    5:232, 7:141, 8:58, 61
Phenelzine (Nardil), 3:213, 5:14, 7:36
Phenobarbital (Luminal), 5:51, 7:32, 41
Phenytoin (Dilantin), 5:51, 7:29, 41
Philadelphia Veterans Affairs Medical
    Center, Substance Abuse
    Unit, 7:69
Phobias, 1:81, 100, 2:261, 5:12–14
    See also Fear; Specific names of
        phobias
    sexual, as cause for hypoactive sexual
        desire disorders, 6:227
    simple, 5:12
    social, 5:2, 3, 4, 5, 13, 15, 7:15
    specific, 5:12–13
    statistics, 5:13
    stress management techniques for, 4:15
Phobic disorders, 1:31
Phobics Anonymous (*directory listing*),
    1:117
PHPD
    See Posthallucinogen perceptual
        disorder (PHPD)
Physical abuse, 1:123, 127, 4:253, 6:122
Physical fitness
    in adolescent substance abuse
        treatment, 8:159–170
    organizational factors, 8:169–170
    programming factors, 8:167–169
    staff factors, 8:169
Physical illness
    can cause or worsen symptoms of
        mental illness, 3:97
    can induce depression, 3:98
    depressive symptoms as part of, 3:200
    misdiagnosing of as depression, 3:93–
        108
Physical Illnesses That Can Mimic
    Depression (*table*), 3:153
Physical testing, 9:136
Physical therapists, 6:185, 9:132–133, 134,
    145, 150, 154
Physical therapy, 9:137
Physician's, 6:185

as threats to patient confidentiality, 5:276

Physician's Desk Reference (Medical Economics Co.), 3:246, 7:45

Physician's Desk Reference for Non-Prescription Drugs (Medical Economics Co.), 7:45

Phytohemagglutinin (PHA), 3:21, 24, 25, 26

Picker/Commonwealth Program for Patient-Centered Care, 7:198–199, 208

Pilot testing, 9:105

Pimozide (Orap), 6:262

Pinocchio, 5:116

Pittsburgh Initial Neuropsychological Testing System, 7:18

Pity pot, the, 1:112

Placement, 9:245
    awareness of inequities in system of, 9:203
    models, 9:151–152
        client-centered placement, 9:83
        competitive placement, 9:83, 84
        enclaves, 9:112
        individual, 9:112
        mobile work crew, 9:112
        selective placement, 9:83
        supported placement, 9:83, 84
    practices, literature review, 9:95–97
    practices for clients with disabilities, 9:79–106

Placement Services (*table*), 9:86

Plagiarism, 10:2

Plan for Achieving Self-Sufficiency (PASS), 9:154

Plan diagnosis, 2:90

Planning, for depressed clients, 3:258

Play
    imaginative, delay in seen in autistic children, 1:176
    themes of, 5:116

Play therapy
    See also Cognitive-behavioral play therapy
    compared with cognitive-behavioral play therapy, 5:135–136
    for depression due to homelessness, 5:90–91
    for GAD, 5:12

Pneumocystis carinii, 10:212

Poddar, Prosenjit
    See People v. Poddar; Tarasoff v. Board of Regents of University of California (1976)

Poisoning, heavy metal, 3:104

Pokeweed mitogen (PWM), 3:21, 25, 26

Polypharmacy, defined, 3:152

Polysubstance dependence, 8:59

Pondimin, 1:183

Pornographic filmmaking, 8:231

Porphyria, acute intermittent, 3:108

Porphyrias, 3:267

Positive Peer Culture, 5:209

Positron emission tomography (PET scan), 1:40, 3:45

Postconcussion syndrome, 3:106

Postfusion therapy, in DID, 1:82–83

Posthallucinogen perceptual disorder (PHPD), 7:139

Postnuptial agreements, 6:78

Posttraumatic stress disorder (PTSD), 1:101, 106, 224, 2:118, 3:266, 4:76, 117, 119, 127, 185, 5:5, 24, 161, 7:140, 8:95
    an update on, 1:1–24
    assessments for, 1:8–12
    case study, 1:17–19
    defined, 1:5–8
    future research, 1:22–23
    historical review, 1:2–5
    model, 5:25–26, 27, 28
    treatment issues, 1:19–23
        cognitive-behavioral, 1:19
        pharmacotherapeutic, 1:19
        psychoanalytic, 1:19

Posttreatment Work Impairment, Symptom Remission, and Treatment Duration (*table*), 3:212

Posture, 2:23

Potency, 2:40, 41, 43

Poverty, 1:138, 6:118, 120, 143, 8:191, 192, 9:183, 1:138
    See also Homelessness
    of ethnic persons with disability, 9:191
    higher with Hispanics, 9:182
    persons with disabilities living in, 9:81
    and single mothers, 6:60
    study of Columbus, Ohio, 5:83–91

Power

of counselors, 10:18, 42–43
differential in supervisory
relationship, 10:90–91
imbalances of in therapeutic
relationships, 2:215–223
struggle, 2:216
of supervisors, 10:83
Powerlessness, 5:28, 33–34
Powers of Psychiatry, The (Robitscher),
2:216
Preconscious, 2:29
Precontemplation, 8:271, 279–281
Pregnancies, unwanted, 6:36
Pregnancy
alcohol use and, 8:102–104
caffeine and, 7:155
complications in opiod dependent
(*table*), 8:112
loss of child during, 6:151–152
marijuana use and, 8:105
as reason for marriage, 4:204, 205
as stress event, 6:135
substance abuse and, 8:93–114
teen, 5:178, 228
test, 5:239
tobacco use and, 8:104–105
withdrawal during, 8:111–113
(*table*), 8:112
Prejudice, freedom from, 4:163
Prenuptial agreements, 6:78, 79
Preparation, 8:271, 281–282
Preschoolers, 5:2, 130–131
Pressure, to marry, 4:204, 205
Prevention, of stress in the workplace,
4:49
*Prevention Resource Guide: Children of
Alcoholics* (USGPO), 4:101
Pride, 6:181
a core emotion, 4:191
disabilities and, 9:70
Primal Scream therapy, 2:260
Primary mood disorders, 5:154
Primary obsessional slowness, an OCD
syndrome, 1:35–36
Principles, defined, 10:20
Prisoners of war, 1:2, 16
Privacy, 4:163, 10:3
client's right to, 10:169
defined, 10:216
Privilege, waiving of by client, 10:6
Pro bono services, 10:42

Ethical Standards (ACA) and, 10:51
Pro-banthine (propantheline bromide),
7:43
Pro-male bias, 6:38
Probability of Functional and Affective
Work Impairment as a
Function of Observer-Rated
Severity of Depression (*table*),
3:216
Problem
anger, 4:167
emotional, secondary, 4:169
sharing of, 9:24
solving, approaches to, 9:2, 122–123
Problem density scores, 7:6, 8
Problem identification assignment, 6:29
Problem maintenance structure, 2:168
Problem solving, 6:9, 7:118, 119, 120, 125,
231–232
Problems
conceptualized in cognitive therapy,
5:133, 263
developing solutions, 2:173–174
case dialogue, 2:174–176
externality of clients', 2:50, 51, 52
implementing solutions, case
dialogue, 2:178–181
MRI approach to solution of, 2:70–73
must be identified in therapy, 2:59,
170–171
case dialogue, 2:171–173
as reference point of therapist
interventions, 2:168
Procainamide (Procan), 3:43
Procan (procainamide), 3:43
Productivity, 9:71
occupational, depression's impact on,
3:201
Profanity, 5:195
Professional disclosure statements, 10:38
Professional Practice Act, 10:119
*Professional Standards for the Training of
Group Workers* (ASGW), 2:122
Professionals, sexual abuse by, 4:119
Programmed confrontation, 7:104
Progressive relaxation, 4:2, 3–4, 5, 11, 12,
13, 14, 15, 20
Prohibition, The, 7:131
Project MATCH, 7:235
Project Return Clubs, 1:240
Project for the Study of Schizophrenia

(Bateson), 2:145
Projection, 4:36
  of parental attributes to boss, 4:43
Projective identification, 2:114
Prolactin, 6:221
Prolixin Decanoate (fluphenazine
    decanoate), 1:255, 8:280
Promiscuity, 5:106
Promises, by counselor, should be kept,
    10:27–28, 58
Propantheline bromide (Pro-banthine),
    7:43
Property Crime Index, 5:193
Propoxyphene (Darvocet), 8:80
Propranolol (Inderal), 1:82, 5:14, 7:44
Proprioceptors, 3:160
Prosocial Gang Project, 5:207–207
Prostitution, 5:239
  used to obtain drugs, 6:122
Protease inhibitors, 10:212
Protect, duty to
  See Duty to protect
Protein, in diet, 7:53
Protriptyline (Vivactil), 7:35
Provocholine (methacholine), 4:9
Proximate cause, 10:112
Prozac (fluoxetine), 3:59, 272, 5:14, 57, 164,
    7:36, 44
  and OCD, 1:21
Pseudodementia, 3:41
Pseudoindependence, 3:8
  antidepressant medication for, 3:11
  method of adaptation, 3:10–11
Psilocybin, 7:141
Psuedo-incest, 6:87
Psychache, 3:121
Psychiatric disorders, in suicide victims,
    5:253–254
Psychiatrist
  interaction with rehabilitation
    counselor, 9:173–174
  questions by concerning vocational
    referrals, 9:169
  timing of vocational referral and, 9:170
Psychiatrists
  board certified, help of, 10:121
  expert witness and, 10:101
Psychiatry, descriptive, 4:114
Psychoanalysis, 2:14, 253, 256, 257, 261,
    3:114, 4:114, 120
  common indications for, 2:258, 259
  follows laws, 2:7

in groups, 2:113–114
  is analysis of resistance, 2:34
  reconciliation with behaviorism, 2:6
Psychoanalysts, 2:54
Psychoanalytic psychotherapy, 1:74–75
Psychoanalytic theory, and basic drives,
    4:35
Psychodrama, 2:144, 3:84, 115
Psychodynamic therapies
  application to elderly, 2:200
  short-term, 2:79–93
    historical background, 2:80–83
    treatment focus, 2:88–90
Psychodynamic therapy, 5:167
Psychodynamics of Family Life (Ackerman),
    2:146
Psychoeducation, 3:229, 236
  and AIDS, 6:134–135
Psychological age, 3:67
Psychological contract, 4:38
  defined, 4:38–39
Psychological disorders, 9:221
Psychological scarring, 5:159
Psychologists, 4:66, 6:185, 9:134
  See also Counselors; Mental health
    professionals;
    Psychotherapists; Therapists
  clinical, 6:168
  confidentiality and, 10:4
  family, 6:23
  school, 6:23
  should not practice without liability
    insurance, 10:9
  as threats to patient confidentiality,
    5:276
Psychology
  competency in, 10:149
  contemporary cognitive, 2:27
  current ethical issues in, 10:1–14
  experimental, 2:253
  forensic, 10:147–157
  slow to address ethics in supervision,
    10:94
Psychopathology, 2:27
  conflict models of, 1:122
  psychotherapy not panacea for all,
    2:254
Psychopathology of Everyday Life (Freud),
    2:149
Psychopharmacology, 3:116, 7:27
  antidepressants, 7:35–38
  antipsychotics, 7:38–41

anxiolytics, 7:33–35
Psychoses, 1:42, 142, 227, 2:128, 261,
   4:117
   hysterical, 1:81
   often anticrime, 1:142
Psychosis, 3:99, 247, 8:61, 65
   affective, 6:253
   difficulty in diagnosing with
      prevalence of drug abuse,
      3:102
   induced by bupropion, 7:37
   organic, 6:242
   substance abuse and, 8:94
   toxic, 5:240, 7:139
Psychosocial prenuptial accord, 6:79
Psychostimulants, notorious for inducing
      jealous reactions, 6:251
Psychotherapists
   See also Counselors; Mental health
      professionals; Psychologists;
      Therapists
   functions of contrasted with
      rehabilitation counselors,
      9:169
   make distinction between manifest
      and latent content, 2:19–22
   may need to play role of abuser
      during therapy, 1:128
   need to read between the lines, 2:20–21
Psychotherapy, 4:84, 7:201, 244, 9:172
   See also Counseling; Specific types of
      therapy
   of the absurd, 2:147
   for adolescent depression, 5:166–168
   with borderline patients, 1:127, 131
   brief, 3:115
   brief history of, 2:250–254
   for bulimic patients, 3:61, 62
   and cancer patients, 4:64
   for clients with dysthymia, 3:226, 234
   for clients with HIV, 8:240
   compared with medication, 3:214
   conclusions regarding efficacy of,
      2:261–262
   contractual agreement in is needed,
      1:129
   criteria for classifying, 3:114–115
   dealing with difficult clients during,
      2:47–60
   defined, 2:256–257
   for depressed alcoholics, 8:129
   for depression, principles in, 3:113–

125
   for divorce, 4:215
   dynamic, 4:62
   efficacy of, 2:249–262
   elderly able to benefit from, 2:194
   of elderly groups, 3:76
   emergency, 3:115
   establishing in treatment of DID, 1:69
   experiential, 6:195
      case study, 6:211–212
   of gamblers, 1:161–166
   gestalt, 6:195
   for grief and mourning, 3:122–124
   group, 2:99–118
      defined, 5:177
      ethical and legal issues of, 2:121–
         137
      guidelines for with elderly, 2:198–200
   holds individual responsible for own
      behavior, 4:76
   individual, 8:209
   integrating types for dysthymia,
      3:234–236
   integrative, 3:116
      elements in, 3:117–119
      is client centered, 3:117
   listening processes in, 2:17–31
   outpatient, 8:233
   principles of in treating dysthymia,
      3:229
   psychoanalytic, treatment in DID,
      1:74–75
   psychodynamic models, 4:213
   resistance to, 7:192
   role of forgiveness in, 4:252
   short-term expressive, 2:259
   symptom-based, 6:228
   traditional, should not be staple of
      treatment, 6:112
   as treatment of anxiety disorders,
      1:111
   a vital part of a multimodal
      treatment, 2:2
   working with self-esteem in, 4:217–
      236
Psychotic disorder, 1:197
Psychotropic substances
   See Drugs
PTSD
   See Posttraumatic stress disorder
      (PTSD)
Puberty, panic disorder developing after

onset of, 5:14
Public offenders, 2:60
Public relations, 9:103
Public speaking, fear of, 1:99, 101, 5:13
Puerto Ricans, 9:182, 211
Pulmonary disease, 3:121
Pure obsession, an OCD syndrome, 1:35
Purpose, defined, 4:229
Purposefulness, practice of living with,
4:229–230
Pyromania
See Firesetting

Q

Quality assurance, 10:59
Quality of object relating, 2:87
"Question of Family Homeostasis, The"
(Jackson), 2:145
Questionnaires
See Scales, questionnaires, and
inventories
Questions, hypothetical, asked during
trial, 10:105–106
Questions to Ask Physicians About
Medication (*chart*), 1:235
Quid pro quo
financial, 6:178
none in ideal situation, 6:277
a reciprocity, 6:276
Quinidine, 3:43
Quinine, 8:105

R

Race, vocational counseling and, 9:177–
203
Racial identity
stages
conformity/preencounter, 9:189
dissonance/encounter, 9:189
integrative awareness, 9:190
internalization, 9:190
resistance/immersion, 9:189
Racism, 1:138, 9:183
Radioimmunoassays, enhance ability to
measure neuroendocrine
mediators, 3:30
Rage, 4:35, 122, 244, 245, 5:254, 6:5
dissociated, 5:114
ego-disruptive, 4:254
as stage of divorce, 4:212, 214

synonym of anger, 4:157
Rancho Scale, 9:144
Rand 36-Item Short-Form Health Survey,
3:205
Rand Report, 7:216
RAP
See Recovering From Abuse Project
(RAP)
Rape, 1:2, 4, 77, 5:193, 200
date, 5:33
often synonymous with incest, 4:115
therapy to help deal with, 1:113
Rapid eye movement (REM), 1:39, 4:13
Rapport, 3:117–118
therapeutic, is necessary for OCD
treatment, 1:44
Rapprochement, 1:121
Rates of Patients Without Relapse (*figure*),
7:73
Rating Various Arrangements for
Receiving Personal
Assistance (*table*), 9:67
Rational, defined, 4:155
Rational Recovery, 8:76
(*directory listing*), 8:157
Rational-cognitive therapy, and criminal
behavior, 1:150
Rational-emotive theory, 4:155, 170
Rational-emotive therapists, 2:55
Rational-emotive therapy (RET), 2:154,
6:233
12-step treatment sequence, 4:165–
173
ABC framework, 4:156–157
for anger management, 4:153–174
basic principles, 4:154–155
goals, 4:154, 155
major musts, 4:157–158
training, 4:174
Rational-Emotive Treatment Sequence
(*table*), 4:166
Rationality, 10:168
defined, 4:155
Rationalization, 9:168
Raves, 7:130, 141
all-night dance parties, 3:102, 7:131–
132
Raynaud's disease, 4:19
behavioral treatments for, 4:7
defined, 4:7
surgery for, 4:7
Reaction formation, mechanism of false

forgiveness, 4:254
Reading comprehension, Ritalin and, 5:56
Reading-Free Vocational Interest
    Inventory, 9:148
Reality coaches, 2:77
Reality testing, 2:135
Reality therapy, 3:115
Rearrest
    See Recidivism
Reasonable accommodations
    See Americans with Disabilities Act
    (ADA), reasonable
    accommodation
Reassurance, 3:117, 118
Rebound neural excitation, 7:65
Recall
    of childhood events, inability of in
        DID, 1:59
    cued, 2:29
    problems with, 3:154
Recency criteria, for caffeine intoxication,
    7:158
Receptivity, and rehabilitation of
    criminals, 1:149
Recidivism, 7:52
    defined, 5:203
    rearrest as index for, 5:206
    study, 5:208
Reciprocity
    contrasted with mutuality, 6:276–278
    negative, 6:5, 6
    positive, 6:5, 6
    social, lack of in pervasive
        developmental disorders,
        1:177
"Recommendations to Physicians
    Practicing Psychoanalysis"
    (Freud), 2:28
Reconciliation, 4:249
    See also Forgiveness
    defined, 4:244
    forgiveness does not necessarily bring
        about, 4:258
Reconstituted families, defined, 6:75
Record keeping, 10:2
    related to confidentiality, 10:12
Records
    ABC, defined, 3:163
    patient's, 5:282–284
The Recovery Book (Mooney, Eisenberg, &
    Eisenberg), 8:153
Recoupled families, defined, 6:75

Recovering From Abuse Project (RAP),
    5:34
Recovery, 3:269
    defined, 7:215
    from addiction, 6:124
    goal of, 1:260
    "Recovery, Inc., The", 1:240
Recovery
    manic client's responsibility for own,
        1:215
    possible for co-dependent, 4:87
    relationship between work and, 9:163
Recreation and leisure, 7:17
Recurrence, 3:215, 268, 269
    rates, 3:275
Recurrent functional impairment, of
    elderly, 2:200–201
Referral
    appropriate patients for, 9:169–170
    preparing for, 9:238–239
    timing of, 9:170, 173
        example, 9:174
    writing questions for, 9:239–240
Reframing, 2:155, 6:208
    case study, 6:206–207
    defined, 6:206
    jealousy, 6:256
Refugees, 9:178
Regression, 6:207–208, 9:166
    in group therapy, 2:117–118
Rehabilitation, 1:244
    counselors
        See Counselors, rehabilitation
    and the criminal, 1:148
    engineering, 9:52, 145
    functional assessment and, 9:38–41
    head trauma, 10:59
    plan, developing a, 9:90–95
    programs
        for employers, 9:84–87
        use of marketing techniques in,
            9:97–105
    substance abuse on outcomes of,
        8:56–58
    vocational, 1:259
        with diverse clients, 9:195–199
        of patients with schizophrenia,
            9:161–175
Rehabilitation Act (1973), 9:36, 74
Rehabilitation Act Amendments, 9:113
Rehabilitation counseling, 8:84–85, 86
Reinforcement, 3:161, 162, 164, 165

negative, 5:64
positive, 5:64, 138, 140
social, 5:215, 216
    developing, 1:203–204
Reintegration
    of separately connected adolescents,
        6:113
    of social group, 6:102
Rejection, 3:255
    feelings of in divorce, 4:203
    hypersensitivity to, 5:108
    invited or expected by child with
        adopted child syndrome,
        5:107, 115
Relapse, 3:94, 141, 149, 215, 268, 269, 274,
        276, 8:278, 281
    defined, 7:69, 214–215
    hospitalization for, 8:129
    methods to reduce rates of, 1:260
    models of
        biopsychosocial, 7:221–222
        cognitive-behavioral, 7:219–221
        disease, 7:218–218
        moral, 7:218
        self-medication, 7:219
    mythology, 7:222–224
    prevention, 5:147–148, 163, 7:20, 120,
        122, 123
        model of substance abuse, 8:67–68
    reducing the risk of, 7:213–235
    risk of with alcoholism, 7:64, 66, 67
    risk factors, 5:242, 7:224–228
    statistics, 7:69–70, 79
    symptoms that predict, 1:248
Relapse Rates (*figure*), 7:72
Relatedness, 2:40
Relational impasse, 6:279–280
Relationship Between Depressive
        Symptoms and Bulimia
        Nervosa (*table*), 3:57
Relationship Communication Coding
        System (RCCS), 6:19
Relationship wounds
    assessment and treatment of, 4:177–
        199
    case study, 4:192–197
    three stages of counseling, 4:186–192
Relationships
    See also Marriage
    between two dependent persons
        unstable, 3:195
    consulting, 10:81

counselor-adolescent
    types
        active-passive, 8:178
        guidance-cooperation, 8:179
        mutual participation, 8:179–
            180
    counselor-defendant, 10:101
    damaged, reestablishment of, 4:244
    dual
        See Dual relationships
    healthier if self-esteem is higher, 4:221
    humans need a network of, 2:41
    needed by humans, 6:195
    supervisory, 10:79–81
    therapeutic, power imbalances in,
        2:215–223
Relationships Between Affective
        Disorders and Anorexia
        Nervosa (*table*), 3:56
Relaxation, 1:220, 221, 3:252–253, 260,
        5:264
    muscle, with alcohol, 4:100
    postural, 4:5
    response, 4:2, 3
    skills, 7:232
Relaxation and Stress Reduction Workbook
        (Davis, Eschelman, &
        McKay), 1:221, 3:253
Relaxation therapy, 4:6, 7, 9, 11, 16, 17
    methods of, 4:2–3
        autogenic training, 4:4
        meditation, 4:4
        other procedures, 4:5
        progressive relaxation, 4:2, 3–4, 5,
            11, 12, 13, 14, 15, 20
Relaxation training, 1:113, 115
    for depression due to homelessness,
        5:91
    for GAD, 5:12
    as treatment for specific phobias,
        5:14
Reliability
    internal, 7:3, 4
    interrater, 7:3
    test-retest, 7:3
Relief, a core emotion, 4:191
Religion
    Christian, 4:248
    criminals and, 1:145
    and forgiveness, 4:247–249
    Jewish, 4:248
Religious melancholy, former name of

OCD, 1:30
Religious orthodoxy, as cause for
    hypoactive sexual desire,
    6:227
REM sleep
    See Rapid eye movement (REM)
Remarriage, 6:65, 106
    See also Marriage
    defined, 6:76
    statistics, 6:74
Remarriage families
    See also Divorce
    case study, 6:80–83
    composition, 6:76–77
    course of treatment, 6:89–94
    incest in, 6:87
    themes in treating, 6:83–89
    understanding and treating, 6:73–95
Remission, 3:215, 269, 272, 7:10
    rates, 3:213
Reorganization, 3:117, 119
Reorientation, 2:2
Repair therapy
    contrasted with growth therapy, 2:1–
    16
    insight is often the goal of, 2:6
    key points, 2:1
    nine characteristics, 2:3
        aims for client's social
            acceptability, 2:8
        fault-centered, 2:3
        leans toward regularized training
            for its practitioners, 2:8–9
        postulated homeostasis, 2:4–5
        realistic goals and standards, 2:7–
        8
        subscribes to gradualism and
            change, 2:5–6
        use of mechanistic paradigm,
        2:6
        uses limits and controls, 2:4
        variety of views about
            humankind, 2:7
Reparenting, 1:78
Replacement child, 6:151
Report, evaluation, content of, 9:56–57
Repression, 1:14
Reproduction, women's identification
    and behavior related to
    capacity for, 6:274
Research Society on Alcoholism, 8:102
Research Triangle Institute, 8:18

Resentment, 4:244, 6:5, 88, 95, 227
    and divorce, 6:39
    synonym of anger, 4:157
Resilience, 4:41, 45, 46, 222
    child's, 5:46, 70
    in COAs, 4:104–105
    low if self-esteem is low, 4:220
Resistance, 2:34, 42, 48, 10:187
    allegory describing, 2:34–35
    an attempt to refrain from checking in
        OCD, 1:35
    client, to career counseling, 9:17–32
    defined, 2:48
    erotic transference is a, 2:238–239
    iatrogenic, 2:54
    patient, factors in, 7:193–195
    problem of the therapist, 8:280
    stage of racial identity, 9:189, 197
Resistance, 4:122
Resolution, as stage of divorce, 4:212
Resolve, Inc. (*directory listing*), 5:125
Resources on the ADA (*appendix*), 9:61
Resources for Adoptive Parents (*directory
    listing*), 5:125
Respect, 4:38
    for client's best interest, rules based
        on, 10:24–29
    for client's ethnic/racial differences,
        10:245
    for client's self-determination, rules
        for, 10:29–32
    for client's welfare, indispensable,
        10:20, 21
    for cultural differences, 9:201
        must be communicated, 9:223
Respite, defined, 6:184
Respite care, 2:203, 208
Response, treatment, 3:269
Response cost, 5:65
Responses
    cognitive, 3:160
    overt, 3:160
    overt motor, 3:160
    physiologic, 3:160
    verbal, 3:160
Responsibility
    criminal, 10:149
    personal, 4:227–228
Restraint, of manic clients, 1:226
Results of the Combined Five-Site ECA
        Study (*table*), 8:248
RET

See Rational-emotive therapy (RET)
Retardation, 1:173, 176, 194
Reticuloendothelial system, 3:18
Retrovirus, 3:22
Rett's Disorder, 1:172, 176
Rett's syndrome, 1:179
Revelation, 3:117, 118–119
Revenge, 4:246, 252
ReVia (naltrexone), 8:273
    for treatment of alcohol dependence,
        7:63–83
Revised Children's Manifest Anxiety
    Scale (RCMAS), 5:7
Revised Classification of Jobs (Field & Field),
    9:46
Revised Consumer Employment
    Screening Form, 9:146
Reward structures, group, 7:181–183
Reward system, attention-deficit/hyper-
    activity disorder (ADHD) as
    dysfunction of, 5:42
Rewards, for children with ADHD, 5:64
Reynolds Manifest Anxiety Scale, 5:85,
    88
*Reynolds v. National Railroad Passenger
    Corporation*, 10:123, 124
Rheumatoid arthritis, 3:18
Right to die, 3:120–122
Right(s)
    adolescent, 8:191–192
    defined, 8:183
Rights, violation of as trigger for anger,
    4:163
Rights and Goods (Held), 6:282
Rigidity, 3:7
    of structure, type of relationship
        wound, 4:183
Risk management, four-step process,
    10:110
Risk taking, OCD therapy built around,
    1:41
Risperdal (risperidone), 7:39–40, 8:280,
    283
Risperidone (Risperdal), 7:39–40, 8:280,
    283
Ritalin (methylphenidate), 3:44, 5:56–59
Rites of passage, 6:108, 112
    adolescent, lacking in American
        culture, 6:103
    few exist in our culture, 6:106
Robbery, 5:193, 200
Robert Wood Johnson Foundation, 7:132,

136
Rodriguez v. Bethlehem Steel Corporation,
    10:140
Roebuck v. Smith, 10:114, 124
Role
    caretaking, 6:121
    conditioning
        female, 6:270
        male, 6:269
    conflicts, 10:77–78
    confusions, 10:186
    examples of inherent duality in,
        10:191
    expectations, 6:272
    models, 6:50, 67
        paucity of single fathers as, 6:60
    playing, 6:258
    reversal, 6:258
    sex, dual relationship issues and,
        10:197–199
    transitions and disputes, 3:231
    wife's, viewed as subordinate, 6:275
Role models, positive, 4:104
Role playing, 5:211, 217, 7:118, 8:218
    by sexual abuse victims, 5:33
    in cognitive-behavioral therapy, 5:136
    for GAD, 5:12
    used with aggressive youth, 5:213–215
    useful to children, 5:138
Roles
    change after death of child, 6:149
    of co-dependents, 4:77–79
        enabler, 4:77–78
        family hero, 4:77, 78
        lost child, 4:77, 78, 81
        mascot or baby, 4:77, 79
        scapegoat, 4:77, 78, 81
    expectations of, 9:4
    family, 6:107, 112, 7:123
    gender, 6:175
    in marriage, 4:207
Rolfing, 2:14
Roman Catholicism, 9:183
Rorschach Inkblot Test, 9:217
Rosenfeld v. Coleman (1959), 2:226
Rowland v. Christian, 10:139
Roy v. Hartogs (1976), 2:220
Rubella embryopathy, 1:179
Rule, transgression against as a theme of
    anger against others, 4:163–
    164
Rules

for guiding goal development in
    psychotherapy, 10:23–32
moral, well-defined, not possible in
    counseling, 10:177
Runaways, families with an ascent in
    deviant behavior, 2:149
Running away, 5:106, 116, 255, 6:36

S

Sadness, 6:243
    after divorce, 6:47–48
    a core emotion, 4:191
Safety, job, 9:54
Sample Authorization for Release of
    Confidential Information
    (*table*), 5:288
Sample Confidentiality Statement (*table*),
    5:283
Sample Daily Schedule for
    Interdisciplinary / Vocational
    Model (*table*), 9:135
Sample Day Plans (*table*), 3:259
Sample Diet, Days 1 Through 4 (*table*),
    7:59
Sample Information for Patient
    Information Brochure (*table*),
    5:284
Sample Items From the Dysfunctional
    Attitudes Scale (*table*), 3:131
Sample Record Sheet of Daily Caring
    Behaviors (*figure*), 7:113
Sanorex (mazindol), 8:283
SAS
    See Social Adjustment Scale (SAS)
SAS-Based Criteria For Affective Work
    Impairment (*table*), 3:211
SAS-Based Criteria For Functional Work
    Impairment (*table*), 3:210
Scales, questionnaires, and inventories
    See also Forms; Instruments,
    assessment; Screening
    instruments; Standardized
    tests
Academic Performance and ADHD
    Rating Scales, 5:54
Addiction Severity Index (ASI), 7:10,
    93, 96, 8:274
Adult Basic Learning Examination,
    9:149
Alcohol Use Inventory, 7:10
American College Test (ACT), 9:212

Anger Situations Inventory, 5:205
Bailey Developmental Scale, 8:107
Beavers-Timberlawn Family
    Evaluation Scales (BTFES),
    6:19–22, 32
Beck Depression Inventory (BDI),
    3:157, 158, 167, 168, 169, 170,
    204, 6:22
Bennett Mechanical Comprehension
    Test, 9:150
Brazelton Neonatal Behavioral
    Assessment Scale, 8:108–109
BriefMAST, 8:207
CAGE questionnaire, 8:207, 272, 273–
    274
Career Assessment Inventory, 9:148
Career Value Scale, 9:149
Change Assessment Scale, 8:275–276
Child Behavior Checklist, 5:34–35, 53,
    7:11
Childhood Attention Problems (CAP)
    Scale, 5:54
Children of Alcoholics Screening Test
    (CAST), 8:42, 43
Children's Depression Inventory
    (CDI), 5:85
Children's Impact of Traumatic
    Events Scale-Revised, 5:35
Community Adjustment Rating Scale,
    5:205
Comprehensive Teacher's Rating
    Scale, 5:54
Conflict Tactics Scale, 6:8–9, 28
Constructive Thinking Inventory, 7:13
Consumer Employment Screening
    Form, 9:146
Cornell Medical Index, 7:54
Crawford Small Parts Dexterity Tests,
    9:150
Culture-Fair Intelligence Test, 9:217
Depression Scale of the Nurses'
    Observation Scale for
    Inpatient Evaluation, 3:169
Diagnostic Interview for Children
    and Adolescents (DICA),
    5:243, 7:12
Diagnostic Interview Schedule for
    Children (DISC), 5:243
Differential Aptitude Test, 9:150
Drug Abuse Screening Test (DAST),
    8:273
Drug Use Screening Inventory

(DUSI), 5:243
Drug Use Screening Inventory (DUSI-
    R), 7:5, 6, 8, 9, 19, 20, 21
Dyadic Adjustment Scale, 6:3–4, 27,
    226
Exchange Orientation Inventory, 6:7–
    8, 27
Family Adaptability and Cohesion
    Scales III (FACES III), 6:9–12,
    17, 28
Family Assessment Measure, 7:13
Family Environment Scale (FES),
    6:13–17, 28, 7:13
Geriatric Depression Scale (GDS),
    3:158, 6:180
Glasgow Coma Scale, 9:144, 155
Global Assessment Scale, 7:96
Gordon Occupational Checklist II, 9:148
Halstead-Reitan Neuropsychological
    Test Battery, 7:18, 9:147
Hamilton Depression Rating Scale,
    3:25, 26, 27, 42, 168, 169, 170,
    204, 209, 216, 217
Homeless Children Interview
    Schedule, 5:85
Homeless Children Interview
    Schedule-Mother Version,
    5:85
Instrumental Activities of Daily
    Living, 6:180
IPAT Anxiety Scale, 4:16
Kansas Marital Adjustment Scale, 6:3,
    27
Katz Index of Activities of Daily
    Living, 6:180
Kiddie Schedule for Affective
    Disorders and Schizophrenia,
    7:12
Kosberg's Cost of Care Index, 6:180
Learning Style Inventory, 9:215
Locke-Wallace Marital Adjustment
    Test, 6:3, 5, 27, 226
Luria-Nebraska Neuropsychological
    Test Battery, 7:18, 9:147
MacAndrew Alcoholism-Revised
    Scale (MAC-R), 8:71, 72
McCarron-Dial Work Evaluation
    System, 9:147, 149
Marital Attitude Survey, 6:226
Marital Interaction Coding System III
    (MICS III), 6:19, 32
Matching Families Figures Test, 5:55

Metabolic Screening Questionnaire,
    7:54
Michigan Alcoholism Screening Test
    (MAST), 8:42, 43, 57, 71, 200,
    207, 273
Millon Behavioral Health Inventory,
    7:12
Millon Clinical Multiaxial Inventory,
    9:148
Mini-Mental State Examination,
    3:154, 7:18
Minnesota Multiphasic Personality
    Inventory (MMPI), 3:183,
    6:14, 7:11, 9:148, 211, 217, 218,
    8:72
Multiaxial Problem-Oriented
    Diagnostic System for Sexual
    Dysfunctions, 6:192, 222
Multidimensional Personality
    Questionnaire, 7:11
Myers Briggs Type Indicator, 9:215
Parental Attribution Scale, 5:35
Parental Reaction to Incest Disclosure
    Scale, 5:35
Peabody Individual Achievement
    Test (PIAT), 9:149
Peabody Picture Vocabulary Test
    (PPVT), 9:216
Personal Assistance Satisfaction
    Index, 9:72
Personal Authority in the Family
    Systems Questionnaire
    (PAFS-Q), 6:17–18, 28
Personal Experience Inventory (PEI),
    5:243
Pittsburgh Initial Neuropsychological
    Testing System, 7:18
Rancho Scale, 9:144
Rand 36-Item Short-Form Health
    Survey, 3:205
Reading-Free Vocational Interest
    Inventory, 9:148
Relationship Communication Coding
    System (RCCS), 6:19, 32
Revised Children's Manifest Anxiety
    Scale (RCMAS), 5:7
Revised Consumer Employment
    Screening Form, 9:146
Reynolds Manifest Anxiety Scale,
    5:85
Rorschach Inkblot Test, 9:217
Schedule for Affective Disorders and

Schizophrenia (K-SADS),
    5:254
Schedule for Affective Disorders and
    Schizophrenia (SADS), 3:155,
    156, 166, 5:243
Scholastic Aptitude Test (SAT), 9:212
Short Portable Mental Status
    Questionnaire, 6:180
Sixteen Personality Factor
    Questionnaire, 9:148
Skill Checklist, 5:205
Social Adjustment Scale (SAS), 3:206,
    209
Sociomoral Reflections Measure,
    5:200
Spousal Inventory of Desired
    Changes and Relationship
    Barriers (SIDCARB), 6:6–7, 16,
    18, 27
State-Trait Anxiety Inventory for
    Children (STAIC), 5:7
Strong Vocational Interest Inventory,
    9:21, 148, 219
Substance Use Disorder Diagnostic
    Schedule (SUDDS), 5:244
Symbol Digit Modalities Test, 7:18,
    9:42
Taylor Manifest Anxiety Scale, 5:85
Teacher Rating Scales, 5:54
Teen Addiction Severity Index (TASI),
    5:244, 7:10
Trail Making Test, 7:18
Valpar Guide to Occupational
    Exploration, 9:148
Vocational Transit, 9:150
Ways of Coping Scale, 7:13
Wechsler Adult Intelligence Scale-
    Revised (WAIS-R), 9:42, 147,
    211, 216, 218
Wide Range Achievement Test
    (WRAT), 9:149
Worker Performance Assessment, 9:148
Zung Self-Rating Depression Scale,
    3:157
Scanning, 9:100
Scapegoat, 4:81
    co-dependent role, 4:77, 78
Scapegoating, 2:135, 5:186
    example of, 6:20
    in organizations, 4:36
Scenes from a Marriage (motion picture),
    6:271

Schedule for Affective Disorders and
    Schizophrenia (K-SADS),
    5:254
Schedule for Affective Disorders and
    Schizophrenia (SADS), 3:155,
    156, 166, 5:243
Schema, defined, 4:181
Schemata, 4:189
    maladaptive, 4:183
Schizo-obsessives, 1:31
Schizoaffective disorders, 3:142, 8:273
Schizophrenia, 1:37, 67, 197, 238, 239, 2:156,
    255, 261, 3:25, 107, 4:103, 117,
    5:162, 6:242, 251, 261, 7:38, 40,
    234, 8:247, 248, 251, 254, 257
    case study, 1:254–257
    double-bind theory of, 2:153
    in elderly, 2:200
    first person accounts, 1:252–254
    many DID patients once diagnosed
        with, 1:64
    motivation-based assessment and
        treatment of, 8:269–285
    obsessions and compulsions present
        in, 1:30
    PTSD in patients with, 1:16
    self-management approaches for,
        1:237–260
    statistics, 1:243, 247, 258, 8:273
    stress management techniques for,
        4:18–19
    vocational rehabilitation for patients
        with, 9:161–175
Schizophrenia Bulletin, 1:252
Schizophrenic disorder, 5:161
Schizotypal disorder, 5:13
Schneider v. Vine Street Clinic, 10:146
Scholastic Aptitude Test (SAT), 9:212
School
    dropout, 5:13, 160, 6:37
    intervention, for separation anxiety
        disorder, 5:10
    problems with in substance abusing
        youth, 5:231, 233, 239
    psychologists, 6:23
    records reviewed in cases of ADHD,
        5:54
    refusal, 5:8, 9
    suicide prevention strategies based
        in, 5:267–268
    suspension from, 5:49
    underachievement in, 6:36, 132

School Psychology Review, 1:193
Schools
    adjustment, 7:14–15
    children with ADHD and, 5:47
    in drug abuse intervention, 6:110
    as part of treatment collaboration,
        7:245
    problems in, 1:139
    require drug-free behavior, 6:112
    research dealing with ADHD and,
        5:59, 62–63
    trouble-filled, 1:138
Screening
    guidelines, 8:189–191
    instruments, 8:273–274
        See also Scales, Questionnaires,
            and Inventories
    multidimensional, 7:4
Scruples, former name of OCD, 1:30
Seasonal affective disorders, 3:245
Second fear, 1:100
Second-order change, 2:66
Secrecy
    and AIDS, 6:131, 133, 134
    seen in closed adoptions, 5:111–112
Security, parents represent, 6:46
Sedatives, 1:81, 8:58, 61, 65
Seduction theory, Freud's, 4:120
Seizure disorders, 1:82, 3:43, 7:41
Selective serotonin reuptake inhibitors
        (SSRIs), 1:21, 38, 44, 3:42, 59,
        61, 62, 108, 272, 273, 5:14, 57,
        6:262, 7:35, 80
Self
    actions of self toward, 2:90
    acts of, 2:89
    acts of others toward, 2:89
    anger at, 4:157–158, 165
    artificial, 5:114
    definition, 9:9, 14
    differentiation of, 2:156, 157
    false, 5:113
    institutional, 9:5
    interpersonal, 9:4
    knowledge, lack of, 9:193
    redefinitions of, 9:7
    true, 2:12, 5:114
Self-acceptance, 4:226–227
Self-actualization, 2:9, 12, 15, 9:200
Self-assertion, 4:122
Self-assertiveness, 4:228–229
Self-blame, 5:28, 29–31, 35

attributions, 5:30
Self-care, in counseling for relationship
    wounds, 4:186
Self-centeredness, seen in traumatic brain
    injury, 9:148
Self-Change Laboratory (Univ. of RI),
    phone number, 8:276
Self-concept, 2:7, 4:208, 8:165
Self-confidence, 4:56, 6:231, 9:164
    aerobic exercise helps build, 1:112
Self-control
    for children of divorce, 6:52
    therapy, for depression due to
        homelessness, 5:90
Self-criticism, and rehabilitation of
    criminals, 1:149
Self-destructive behavior, 6:259
Self-determination, 10:40
    defined, 10:21, 22
    rules based on respect for clients',
        10:29–32
Self-disclosure, 9:200
Self-discovery, 3:118
Self-efficacy, 3:83, 4:224, 7:230
    pillar of self-esteem, 4:219
Self-esteem, 1:17, 98, 2:260, 3:67, 192, 257,
        4:34, 35, 41, 44, 78, 80, 189,
        208, 209, 210, 211, 213, 215,
        5:43, 48, 6:271, 272, 8:140, 162,
        164, 216, 9:168, 192
    adoptees struggle with, 5:113
    attachments and formation of, 3:3
    case studies, 4:225, 226, 231
    challenged by stress, 1:23
    damaged, 6:260
    decreased, 8:9
    defined, 3:5, 4:219
    depends somewhat on past
        relationships, 4:181
    father's, 6:68
    if tied too closely to others' opinions,
        3:8
    impairment of in patients with
        history of incest, 4:122
    improving in jealous person, 6:256
    increased in mania, 1:213
    loss of in marriage, 4:207–208
    low, 1:39, 222, 5:24, 160, 7:11, 15, 8:123,
        9:191
        in COAs, 4:102
        in patients with anorexia nervosa,
            3:55

in depressed individuals, 3:184
lowered due to incest, 6:122
lowered when shame and guilt are
    present, 1:16
in maladaptive personality styles,
    3:7
need for, 4:219–222
questions to ask, 4:235–236
roots of, 4:223
sentence-completion program, 4:232–
    235
six pillars of, 4:223–232
    practice of integrity, 4:230–232
    practice of living consciously,
        4:224–226
    practice of living purposefully,
        4:229–230
    practice of self-acceptance, 4:226–
        227
    practice of self-assertiveness,
        4:228–229
    practice of self-responsibility,
        4:227–228
teen's, group therapist must not
    attack, 5:182
working with in psychotherapy,
    4:217–236
Self-evaluation, 4:220
    used in controlling anger, 5:218
Self-examination for Counselors
    Interested in Treating Older
    Adults (table), 3:75
Self-exploration, 9:11, 24
Self-gratification, countertransference
    reaction, 2:236–237
Self-help, 3:234
    in dealing with episodes of mania,
        1:211–230
    groups, 1:239, 5:178, 7:192, 202, 253,
        255, 8:74–76, 275
    directory listing, 8:156–157
    serenity concept in, 1:164
    literature, 1:112, 3:256, 4:84, 7:205
    as treatment of anxiety disorders,
        1:111–112, 114
    use of books in, 3:256
Self-identity, 9:199
Self-image, 3:67, 4:38, 211
    problems with, 4:103
"Self-in-relation" theory, 6:269
Self-management, 8:213–214
    approaches for seriously mentally ill

persons, 1:237–260
Self-medication, 7:225
    model of relapse, 7:219
Self-monitoring, 5:138, 142
    by counseling professionals, 10:38
    in cognitive therapy, 3:134–136
Self-observation, 2:256, 1:71
Self-presentation, of credentials, 10:82–83
Self-psychology theory, 6:268
Self-punishment, need for by gambler,
    1:157
Self-reflection, to ferret out recollections
    of sexual abuse, 4:143
Self-regulation, 4:2
    co-dependent person needs to move
        toward, 4:83
Self-regulatory disorder, 5:42
Self-reliance, 3:6, 4:212
    needs to be cultivated in therapy, 3:11
Self-Report Questionnaires (appendix),
    6:27–28
Self-report screening, 3:162
Self-respect, 4:224
    fertility as source of, 6:143
    pillar of self-esteem, 4:219
Self-responsibility, 4:227–228
    needed for relationship quality, 6:213
Self-reward, 5:145
Self-satisfaction, 6:177
Self-statement, coping, 5:144–145
Self-sufficiency, emphasis on, 6:201
Self-system, 2:7
Self-transcendence, 2:7, 12
Self-value, 4:226
Self-worth, 4:158, 159, 160, 161, 162, 165
    child's, 5:70
    gained from working within one's
        capability, 9:162
Selfishness, 4:82
Senile dementia
    See Dementia, senile
Senior Alcoholism Services (SAS), 8:211–
    212
Senior citizens
    See Elderly
Senior Companions, 6:183
Sentence completion, 4:232–235, 5:115
    exercise (appendix), 4:238–242
Sense of comfort, rational-emotive term,
    4:162
Sensitivity, extreme, 5:254
Sensitivity groups, 2:102

Separation, 1:120, 121, 3:12
   anxiety, normal, 5:9
   childhood, 1:123
   fear of, 5:2, 7
   from marital partner, 4:202
   from mothers, 3:188
   legal, defined, 6:41
   and loss, mastering, 3:3
   middle stage in divorce process,
      4:211
   reaction to, 3:3–5
   single fathers and, 6:58, 59
Separation anxiety, 3:9, 5:15
   felt by adoptee, 5:109
Separation anxiety disorder, 5:2, 5, 8–11,
   15
   statistics, 5:8–9
   symptoms, 5:9
Separation-individuation, 3:190, 5:185,
   229, 6:18, 273
Serax (oxazepam), 7:34
Serenity, concept of in self-help groups,
   1:164
Serotonin, 1:125, 3:25, 45, 99, 251, 5:6, 52,
   7:36, 67, 138, 142, 8:131, 250
   5-HIAA metabolite of, 1:42
   involved in pathophysiology of OCD,
      1:43
   low, associated with violent behavior,
      4:99
Sertraline (Zoloft), 3:272, 5:14, 57, 7:36,
   8:283
   and OCD, 1:21
Serum glutamic oxaloacetic transaminase
   (SGOT), 7:77
Serzone (nafazodone), 7:36
Sex
   as a basic intrinsic drive, 4:35
   group, as fantasy, 6:234
   safe, 6:125, 127, 143, 8:230, 236
   with therapists by patients with
      history of childhood incest,
      4:119
Sex education, 5:32
Sex therapists, 6:194
Sex therapy, 6:220
   historical perspectives, 6:193–195
Sex-role conflict, 7:11
Sexism, 2:232, 6:271
   defined, 6:268
   domination and subordination as
      manifestation of, 6:274–276

gender identification as source of,
   6:273–274
Sexual
   abuse, 1:23, 127, 3:255, 4:80, 114, 117,
      5:241, 242, 6:121, 122, 7:14,
      8:186
      case study, 4:137–139, 141, 5:25
      of children, 1:124, 125, 4:188, 189,
         192, 5:23–36, 8:95
      See also Childhood molestation;
         Incest
      assessment of is specialized
         skill, 4:144
      profound social problem,
         4:134
      treatment decisions, 4:144–
         148
      treatment models, 4:146
      ethical considerations in working
         with survivors of, 4:133–148
      intrafamilial
         See Incest
      prevention materials, 5:33, 36
      survivor of, 1:15
      survivors of, 4:134, 186
      suspicion of, 4:140–144
      syndrome, 4:127
      synonymous with incest, 4:115
      victims of, 1:13, 14
   aversion, 6:192
   aversion disorder, 6:235
   behavior
      ecstacy and, 7:143
      and exclusivity norms, 6:250
      frequency of, 6:222–224
      inappropriate, in incest victim,
         4:118
      LSD and, 7:139
   closeness, 6:271
   conduct
      improper, 2:219
      legal cases, 2:220–221
   desire
      hypoactive, cognitive-behavioral
         perspective, 6:219–235
      low, 6:191–213
   desire disorder, defined, 6:220–221
   deviance, 7:234
   disorders, 2:168
   dysfunction, 3:100, 6:260
   education, 6:229
   exploitation, of patient, 4:126

identity, 5:185
inhibitions, lessened with inhalants, 8:66
longings
    by therapist, 2:235
    for therapist, 2:233
molestation, 4:124
synonymous with incest, 4:115
orientation, 6:227
    questioning substance abuse
        client about, 8:228
relationships
    and mutuality, 6:277
    between supervisor and
        supervisee, 10:80
    with clients, 10:11–12, 119–120,
        195–206
        See also Clients, sexual
        boundary violations against
    ethical considerations, 10:51–
        53
    prohibiting, 10:46
    statistics, 10:196–197, 202
    time limits, 10:52
    as means of HIV transmission,
        10:212–213
response cycle, 6:192, 220, 224
trauma, 6:226, 229
Sexuality, 5:257
in developing teens, 5:185, 228
fear-driven, 4:218
inappropriate introduction to, 5:28–29
marital, case study, 6:197, 204, 205
problems with, 2:234
relational, 6:191–213
stepfamily and, 6:87
Sexualization, traumatic, 5:28, 32
Shame, 4:139, 142, 143, 158, 5:257, 6:226,
    229, 281
and AIDS, 6:118, 133
a core emotion, 4:191
Shaping, 5:138, 140
Shaw v. Glickman, 10:146
Sheltered employment, 9:165
Shock, as stage of divorce, 4:212
Short Portable Mental Status
    Questionnaire, 6:180
Short-term dynamic therapies
    See Psychodynamic therapies, short
        term.
Shyness, 4:218, 5:4, 43
Sibling
    bond, 6:150

coalitions, 6:10
Sibling position, influence of, 2:156, 159
Sibling rivalry, in organizations, 4:36
Siblings
of criminals, 1:140
drug use by, 6:105
of drug users, 6:121
of drug-abusing adolescents, 6:109
surviving, 6:150–151
unrelated, 4:97
whose parents have AIDS, 6:132
Side effects
expected, 7:30
extrapyramidal, 7:39
SIDS
    See Sudden Infant Death Syndrome
        (SIDS)
Signal functions, 3:3
Signs, behavioral, 2:4
Similarities Between Cognitive-
    Behavioral Play Therapy and
    Traditional Play Therapies
    (*table*), 5:136
Simple skill acquisition, 3:167, 168–169
Sinequan (doxepin), 3:272, 7:35
Sink-or-swim philosophy, by some
    employers, 4:39
*Sisson v. Seneca Mental Health/Mental
    Retardation Council*, 10:120,
    124
Situational analysis, 9:214–215
Six Pillars of Self-Esteem (*table*), 4:224
Sixteen Personality Factor Questionnaire,
    9:148
Skill acquisition, 5:197
Skill building, 9:89
Skill Checklist, 5:205
Skill deficiency, and aggressive youth,
    5:195
Skill level, employability and, 9:69
Skill transfer, 5:198
Skills, 9:88–89
communication, assessment of, 9:242
ethical reasoning, need for, 10:58–61
job, teaching, 9:91–93
job interviewing, assessment of,
    9:242
job-seeking, 9:93
lack of marketable in Native
    Americans, 9:187
social, 9:69, 163, 164–165
training, 1:244

durability of skills (*table*), 1:250
    evaluating, 1:252
    independent living, 1:247–251
    learning activities (*table*), 1:249
    symptom management (*table*),
        1:251
    transferability of, 9:89–90
    transferable, assessment of, 9:144–146
    work, 9:46, 87
        maintenance of, 9:122
Skinner's model, of operant conditioning,
    7:174–175
Sleep
    See also Insomnia
    changes in with drug abuse, 5:232
    deprivation of, 5:15
    difficulty, 7:34, 66, 76, 144, 161–162
    during divorce, 4:204
    disorders, 2:135, 5:7, 11
    disturbances in, 1:10, 81, 3:36, 38, 155,
        5:81, 156
        See also Insomnia
    REM, 4:13
Sleep-walking disorders, 8:252
Sleeper effect, 6:37
Sleeplessness
    See Insomnia
"Slips", 8:278, 281
Smart drinks, 7:132
Smoking, 3:101, 4:54, 59, 7:155, 164, 165,
    217–218
    See also Cigarettes; Nicotine; Tobacco
        abuse
    and decreased immune status, 3:28,
        29
    heavy, 8:274
    pregnancy and, 8:104–105
    withdrawal from, 8:111
    women and, 8:96
Sobriety, 4:84, 7:215, 8:202
    See also Alcoholism; Detoxification
    journal, 7:204
    marriage and, 7:124
    relationships and, 7:104–120
Sociability, 2:8
    stability, associated with successful
        treatment, 7:95
    support system, 7:206
Social
    age, 3:67
    drama, 6:104
        defined, 6:101

exchange process, 6:6
    functioning, post-stroke depression
        and, 3:41
    learning theory, 7:176–177
    life, as parenting task, 6:60
    phobia, 1:100–101, 3:266, 5:2, 3, 4, 5,
        13, 15
    rejection, 5:48
    skills, 5:198, 206, 208, 8:162, 163, 277,
        9:69, 163, 164–165
        competence in, 7:12–13.
        development of by children with
            ADHD, 5:66, 67, 68
        improvement in, 5:209
        not developed in aggressive
            adolescents, 5:195
        training, 3:232–233, 234, 6:22, 182
            for depression due to
                homelessness, 5:90
    stigma, and AIDS, 6:118
    support, benefit of, 4:188
    withdrawal, 5:159
    workers, 6:185
        credited with recognition of
            treating the family, 2:144
        needed for depressed homeless
            children, 5:91
Social Adjustment Scale (SAS), 3:206, 209
Social Security, subsidy, 9:154
Social Security Act (1982), 9:69
Socialization
    prior, and reasons for marriage,
        4:204–206
    sometimes contraincated for person
        with schizophrenia, 9:164
Society, pluralistic, 10:47
Society for Adolescent Medicine (SAM),
    8:188
Society for Psychotherapy Research, 2:251
Sociomoral Reflections Measure, 5:200
Socrates, moral philosophy and, 10:19
Socratic method, of teaching, 8:181
The Socratic Method (*table*), 8:182
Sodium benzoate, 7:52, 53, 54
Solipsism, danger of, 2:12
Solutions, attempted, 2:70
Somatic disorders, 4:6–12
Somatization disorder, 8:251
Some Definitions of Co-Dependence
    (*table*), 4:72–73
"Some Perspectives on the Legal Liability
    of Group Counseling in

Private Practice" (Paradise &
Kirby), 2:122–123
Sources for Information on Co-
Dependence (*table*), 4:86
Spanking, 1:205
Special education, 1:184
Specific phobia
See Phobia
Speech
See also Communication; Listening
of clients is frequently ambiguous,
2:17
freedom of, 4:163
problems with, 5:46
properties of clients', 2:18, 19
Speech and language pathologists, 9:150
Spelling, and children with ADHD, 5:47,
63
Spinal cord injury, 7:32, 41, 42, 8:56
drugs used in, 7:43
statistics, 8:80
study of patients with, 9:68
substance abuse and, 8:78, 80–81
Spiritedness, 2:40
Spirituality, client's, 10:241
Splitting, 2:114
Sports, as outlet for children of divorce,
6:50
Sports medicine, model of work
hardening, 9:132–133
Spousal Inventory of Desired Changes
and Relationship Barriers
(SIDCARB), 6:6–7, 16, 18, 27
Spousal Inventory of Desired Changes
and Relationship Barriers
(SIDCARB) for Mr. and Mrs.
Smith (*table*), 6:7
Spouse
abuse, 3:255
as caregiver of elderly relative, 6:170
of drug users, 6:130
new, commitment to, 6:92
SSRIs
See Selective serotonin reuptake
inhibitors (SSRIs)
Stabilization, 8:280
Staff
knowledge of supported
employment, 9:119–120
of work hardening program, 9:137
Stakeholders, in collaboration, 7:249, 251
Standard deviation

as a classification tool, 9:42, 43
to determine the severity of the
impairment, 9:45
Standard witness, contrasted with expert
witness, 10:98
Standardization, sample size for, 9:218–
219
Standardized tests, 9:38, 55, 114, 198, 198–
199
See also Scales, questionnaires, and
inventories
Americans with Disabilities Act
(ADA) rules governing
administration of, 9:55, 55–
56
imprecision of, 9:213, 215–218
quick method to collect objective
data, 9:243
Standards, professional, 2:123
"Standards for Employee Alcoholism
and/or Assistance
Programs", 8:40
Standards Manual for Organizations
Serving People with
Disabilities, 9:129
Standards of Practice (ACA), 10:46
Starvation, 3:52
See also Anorexia nervosa
self, 3:56
State-Trait Anxiety Inventory for Children
(STAIC), 5:7
Statement of Intent (*chart*), 1:232
Static ataxia, 4:100
Stealing, 5:106
Stepfamily, 6:75
incest in, 6:87
Stepmother, "wicked", 6:75, 93
Steps to Healthy Touching (MacFarlane &
Cunningham), 5:35
Stereotypes, job, African-American and,
9:181
Steroids, 3:22
anabolic, 5:240
physical fitness programs reduce use
of, 8:166
Stigma, 3:255
Stigmatization, 5:28
double in HIV positive drug abusers,
8:234, 242
of drug abusers, 8:94, 95
Stimulant abuse, 4:37
See also Addiction; Alcohol abuse;

Alcoholism; Chemical
 dependency; Drug abuse;
 Substance abuse; Tobacco
 abuse
Stimulants, 1:192, 5:12, 232, 7:130
 and ADD, 1:183
 for children with ADHD, 5:56, 57
 what they do, 8:251
Stimuli, 3:159
Stimulus fading, 5:138, 140–141
Stimulus variability, 5:217
Stock market, 1:159
 played by upper-class gamblers, 1:156
Stone Center for Developmental Services
 and Studies of Wellesley
 College, 6:269
Stories, fantasy, as means to help adopted
 child, 5:116
Storytelling, a distraction during group
 therapy, 5:186
Stout Vocational Rehabilitation Institute
 (*directory listing*), 9:61
Strategic Family Therapy, 2:146
Strategic planning, 9:100–102
Strategic therapy, 6:110
Strategies for Minimizing Caffeine Urges
 (*table*), 7:166
Stress, 3:266, 6:5, 9, 227, 229, 7:17
 acute, 3:255
 and changes in immune function, 1:21
 chronic, 3:255, 4:43
 and conflict, 6:138
 dampened with alcohol, 4:100
 defined, 8:202
 dimensions of traumatic events
  causing, 1:4
 disorders related to
  See Posttraumatic stress disorders
 of divorce, 4:202
 events, 6:135
 in explaining presence of disease, 4:54
 influence of disease on, 4:2
 interpersonal, 4:60
 life, 5:257
  assessment of, 1:8–12
 in older adults, 3:82
 overview, 4:42–46
 parental, 5:256
  affect child's sense of safety, 5:93
 in partners of drug abusers, 6:124
 psychological, can increase the

growth of tumors, 3:17
 related to physical illness, 3:16
 and trauma, 1:223–224
 traumatic, 1:8
  defined, 1:5
  factors affecting response to, 1:13–
   17
 unconscious processes and response
  to, 1:3
 work-related, 4:5, 43
 in the workplace, 4:33–49, 7:15
  case studies, 4:47–49
  diagnostic process, 4:46
  prevention, 4:49
  treatment process, 4:46–47
Stress management, 1:113, 115
 with anger and aggressive behavior,
  4:16
 with anxiety disorders, 4:14–16
 with behavioral and psychological
  disorders, 4:12–14
 clinical effects of, 4:19–20
 for depression, 4:16–17
 methods of relaxation, 4:2–5
 motivation and compliance, 4:5–6
 recent research findings on, 4:1–21
 for schizophrenia, 4:18–19
 for somatic disorders, 4:6–12
 for substance abuse, 4:17–18
Stress reduction techniques, 1:220, 221
Stress response, 5:89
Stress-related conditions, 2:261
Stressors, 5:255, 8:125, 284
 defined, 1:5, 7, 8
 life, 8:202
 protective factors against, 5:89–90
 psychosocial, 8:127
 types of and comorbidity, 1:13–15
Stroke, 3:100, 6:168
 defined, 3:34
 depression following, 3:33–45
 intellectual impairment and
  depression, 3:40–41
 location of lesions and depression,
  3:39, 40
 physical impairment and depression,
  3:39, 40
 rehabilitative treatment after, 3:41–
  44
 social functioning after, 3:41
 statistics, 3:35–36

Strong Vocational Interest Inventory, 9:21, 148, 219
Structural therapy, 2:146, 6:110
Structured Clinical Interview for the Diagnosis of DSM-IV Dissociative Disorder (SCID-D), 1:59–60, 61
Structured Clinical Interview for DSM-III-R (SCID), 1:8–9
Structured Learning Skill Curriculum, The (*table*), 5:212, 214
Structured Learning Training (SLT), 5:197, 202, 205, 210–211
Students
  college, 2:118
  in counselor training, dual relationships of, 10:191
Study skills, students with ADHD and, 5:62
Stuttering, 7:234
Subcommittee on Human Services of the Select Committee on Aging, 3:68
Subpoena
  duces tecum, 10:5
  psychological records and, 10:5
Substance abuse, 1:103, 2:103, 135, 3:236, 255, 267, 269, 4:80, 127, 5:13, 49, 106, 159, 163, 178, 256, 6:260
  See also Addiction; Alcohol abuse; Alcoholism; Drug abuse; Stimulant abuse; Tobacco abuse
  adolescent, 8:139–154
  diagnosing and treating, 8:188–192
  ethical issues in counseling, 8:175–193
  evaluation and treatment of, 5:227–245
  family therapy for, 6:99–113
  laboratory testing, 5:239–240
  physical fitness for, 8:159–170
  signs and symptoms, 5:232–234
  stages of, 5:234–235
  assessment of, 8:69–72
  causes wide range of psychoactive disorders, 8:94
  clinical signs, 8:70–71
  common substances, 8:61–66
  comorbidity in, 8:245–262

counseling certification in, 8:84–86
current trends in treatment, 8:76–78
defined, 8:59, 94
developmental problem, 8:160–162
disability and, 8:55–86
implications of, 8:8–12
job-based risk factors for, 8:38–39
motivation-based treatment, 8:269–285
parental, 1:22
and pathological gambling, 1:154, 155, 156, 162
persons at high risk for, 7:2
pregnancy and, 8:93–114
relationship to poor nutrition, 7:50
in patients with schizophrenia, motivation-based treatment, 8:269–285
scope of problem, 8:3–6
screening and assessment approaches for, 8:271–276
screening inventories and, 8:42–43
statistics, 7:132
stress management techniques for, 4:17–18
treatment, 8:72–76
  in veterans with PTSD, 1:15
  in the workplace, 8:1–44
Substance abuse counselor (SAC), 8:84
Substance abuse disorder, 5:156, 254
Substance Abuse and Mental Health Services Administration (SAMHSA), 4:70, 8:4
Substance abuser, 2:118
  effects of drugs on, 8:8
  motivation and, 8:270–271
Substance dependence
  criteria for, 8:251
  (*table*), 8:60–61
  defined, 8:59
Substance use
  defined, 8:59
  pattern of, 7:11
Substance use disorder, 1:33
Substance Use Disorder Diagnostic Schedule (SUDDS), 5:244
Substance-induced anxiety disorder, 1:102
Substance-induced disorders, 8:59
Substance-related disorders (SRDs), 8:58
  conceptual models of, 8:66–69
Substantial limitations, defined, 9:41
Sudden infant death syndrome (SIDS),

8:105, 106, 108
Suffer, some persons choose to, 4:251
Sugar, exacerbates depression, 3:249
Suggested Reading for Adoptive Parents
    and Adult Adoptees (table),
    5:119
Suggested Reading and Viewing for
    Adopted Children and
    Adolescents (table), 5:117
Suicidal ideations, 8:65, 123, 125, 128,
    131
Suicidality, 5:158–159
Suicide, 1:106, 2:135, 3:121, 195, 5:154, 240,
    8:149, 204, 255
    adolescent, 5:251–268
        high rates, 5:168
    of another family member, 5:256
    attempts, 6:37, 8:126
        and DID, 1:82
        phone calls to therapists may
            head off, 1:130
    attempts by substance abusers, 5:236,
        241
    cluster or grouped, 5:258
    considered half a murder, 3:124
    copycat dynamic of, 5:257
    dependency and, 3:185–186
    in dependent clients, 3:193–194
    depression linked to, 6:48
    and depressive gamblers, 1:166
    elderly, 8:205–206
    family history of, 5:159
    high risk of requires intervention,
        5:89
    in Huntington's disease, 3:105
    ideations, 8:125
    impulses, 3:128, 6:253
    liability for, 2:134
    media influence, 5:258
    and panic disorder, 1:105
    in patients with eating disorders, 3:62
    prevention, 3:260, 5:265, 267–268
        confidentiality and, 10:10
    rate in older white males, 3:72
    real danger in embarrassed manic
        clients, 1:228
    risk of, 3:120, 268
    statistics, 3:124, 5:252, 258
    surviving family members, 5:253
    thoughts of, 2:113, 3:36, 155, 4:79, 6:36,
        132, 7:96

warning signs, 3:258
Summary of Scores on Depression (table),
    5:87
Summary of Scores on Reynold's
    Manifest Anxiety (table), 5:88
Superego, 2:7, 80, 147, 3:193, 5:111, 229
Supervisees
    feedback provided by, 10:92
    rights of, 10:86–93
Supervision
    contrasted with therapy, 10:90
    defined, 10:77
    ethics in, 10:75–94
    parameters of, 10:89–90
    separating from therapy, 10:84–86
    videotaped, 10:91
Supervisors
    countertransference and, 10:191
    roles in dealing with troubled
        employees, 8:33–37
Supplementary Social Insurance, 6:183
Support
    agency-based, 9:152
    natural, 9:152
    as part of job, 9:109–124
    system, 3:256
    team, 3:246
Support groups, 6:179, 181
    for adoptees, 5:118
Supported exposure, 1:109
Supportive therapy, 3:115, 234
Surfak (docusate calcium), 7:43
Surrogacy, 10:59
Survival
    cancer, length of, 4:64
    elderly concerned with issues of,
        2:198
Survival of Treated and Untreated Cancer
    Patients (table), 4:65
Survivors
    of incest, 4:124
    of sexual abuse, 4:186
        ethical considerations in working
            with, 4:134–148
    of trauma, 1:3
        See also Posttraumatic stress
            disorders
Suspiciousness, 6:259
Symbol Digit Modalities Test, 7:18, 9:42
Symmetrel (amantadine), 7:39, 8:283
Symptom management module, 1:248,

254, 255
Symptomatic Jealousies, The (*table*),
    6:247
Symptomless autoimmune thyroiditis
    (SAT), 3:104
Symptoms
    cognitive, obsessions are, 1:30
    depression
        alleviating, 3:243–262
        recognizing, 3:244
    of OCD, 1:33–36
    psychiatric, may have medical causes,
        3:99
    of PTSD, 1:5
    recurrence of, 4:5
    removal of, 2:2
    substitute, 1:42
Synesthesia, 7:139
Syphilis, 3:106
System
    closed, 2:149
    cybernetic, 2:149
    healthy, 2:150
    open, 2:150
Systematic desensitization, 5:138–140
    as treatment for specific phobias, 5:14
Systemic Lupus Erythrematosus, 3:106
Systems theory, 2:149, 150, 151, 167, 6:195,
    209
Systems therapists, treatment of jealousy,
    6:257

T

T cells, 3:18, 19, 20, 22, 24, 26, 28
    collapse of, 8:226
    cytotoxic, 3:18
    growth factor, 3:20
    helper, 3:18, 20
    HIV and, 10:212
    inducer, 3:18, 20
    mitogens, 3:21, 25
    suppressor, 3:18
Taboos, sexual, 6:87
Tachycardia, 5:2, 232
Tagamet (cimetidine), 4:10, 7:155
Talk shows, presentations of COAs, 4:94
Talking About Touching (Beland), 5:36
Talking down, a bad trip, 7:146, 147
Tantrums, 5:236
Tarasoff v. Board of Regents of University of

California (1976), 2:133, 219,
    221, 222, 228, 5:281, 10:7, 139–
    146, 172–173, 213, 216, 233
    case described, 10:128–133
    critical response to, 10:133–134
    declining to follow, 10:138
    subsequent decisions, 10:134–138
Tardive dyskinesia, 7:39
Task, analysis, 9:117
Tavistock
    Clinic, 2:144
    group, 2:83
    Hospital, 2:102
Taylor Manifest Anxiety Scale, 5:85
TCAs
    See Tricyclic antidepressants
Teacher Rating Scales, 5:54
Teachers, 6:23
    adolescents and, 6:103
    adoptees acting out against, 5:115
    forming an alliance with, 5:8
    as inducers of anxiety, 5:2
    and students with ADHD, 5:43, 47, 48,
        59, 62–63
Teen Addiction Severity Index (TASI),
    5:244, 7:10
Teenagers
    See Adolescents
Teetotaling, 4:97
Tegretol (carbamazepine), 1:228, 5:166,
    7:41, 44
Telephone hot lines, 5:267
Television, excessive, 6:107
Temptation, contrasted with coercion,
    10:169
Tenormin (atenolol), 5:14
Tenth Institute on Rehabilitation Issues,
    9:39
Teratogen, alcohol most common, 8:102
Termination, of therapy, 5:148
Test anxiety, 9:243
Test bias, 9:215–218
Test taking, and students with ADHD,
    5:47, 62
Testimony, expert witness, ethical and
    legal issues of, 10:97–107
Testing
    See Family diagnostic testing
Testosterone, 6:221
Tests
    See also Scales, questionnaires, and

inventories; Standardized tests
for diagnosis of autism, 1:183
diagnostic tools for diagnosing DID, 1:59, 60–61
inventories for assessing PTSD, 1:8–12
medical
  for HIV, 10:212
  as part of legal trial preparation, 10:101
personality, to understand gambling disorder, 1:162, 163
to confirm diagnosis of ADHD, 1:197
Tests in Print (Murphy, Conoley, & Impara), 9:219
Tetrahydrocannabinol (THC), 3:102
Thallium, poisoning, 3:104
Thanatos, 2:7
Theobromine, 7:157
Theophylline, 5:162
Therapeutic alliance, 1:69, 240, 241, 2:166, 187–188, 3:60, 227, 229, 4:188, 6:160
in cognitive therapy, 3:133–134
crucial in counseling elderly, 2:199
impediments to, 4:124–125
Therapeutic community, 8:216
Therapeutic Goal in Managing Symptomatic Jealousy (*table*), 6:261
Therapeutic Goals in Managing Jealous Reactions (*table*), 6:255
Therapeutic privilege, 10:115
Therapeutic relationships
boundaries in, 10:84
erotic transference can tax, 10:206
initiated in cases of substance abuse, 5:237
power imbalances in, 2:215–223
private nature of, 2:217
warm, 5:132, 136
Therapist envy, case study, 2:239–240
Therapists
See also Counselors; Mental health professionals; Psychologists; Psychotherapists
and ADHD, 5:69–71
adoptees acting out against, 5:115
assessments in substance abuse cases, 5:237–239
beginner's anxiety of, 2:235
biases against providing therapy to

elderly, 2:197
cognitive-behavioral, 4:159
competence, 2:124, 4:136
  is necessary especially in sexual abuse cases, 4:145
conceptual orientation of
  Freudian, 3:114
  Jungian, 3:114
  Kleinian, 3:114
  Myerian, 3:114
considerations when counseling single father, 6:66–69
with countertransference issues, 2:112, 235–237
couples, 6:269
cynical, 2:53
dealing with grief, 6:43
denial by adoptive parents and, 5:119
gender differences, 4:125
gender of, 10:197–199
goals of decreasing parents' blame, 5:30
goals in therapy, 5:27
group
  inadequate training of, 2:123
  working with adolescents, 5:181–182
guide clients in cognitive therapy, 3:133
intervening
  with child's fear, 6:47
  with denial, 6:42
  with guilt, 6:44
  with anger, 6:45–46
might prefer to avoid treating clients with mania, 1:214
must develop awareness of self, 2:59
need professional commitment, 3:117
needed immediately in case of suicide risk, 5:258–259
often misunderstand clients, 2:53
play major role in suicide prevention, 5:268
as pro-child advocates, 6:38
questions to consider for EAP involvement, 8:31–32
rage and rejection felt by, 2:52
rational-emotive, 4:154
reactions to difficult clients, 2:52–54
reactions to DID clients, 1:72, 73, 74
as referees, 2:104
role in family therapy, 2:166, 169

role in treating dysthymia, 3:229
sex, 6:194
sexual exploitation by, 4:126
sexual involvement with, 4:119
sexually abusive
    profile of, 10:200–206
    impulsive, 10:204–205
    isolated, 10:204
    naïve, 10:203
    neurotic, 10:204
    psychotic, 10:205–206
    sociopathic, 10:205
sexually attracted to a patient, 2:112
strategies for counseling children of
    divorce, summary, 6:49–52
survey to decide on EAP
    involvement, 8:28–31
teaching self-help strategies to manic
    clients, 1:211–230
as threats to patient confidentiality,
    5:276–277
training, standards of, 2:125
as transference object, 2:104
viewed as authority or parent figures,
    2:52
vital functions in dealing with AIDS
    families, 6:126–127
working from feminist perspective,
    4:120, 122
working with a person who is
    experiencing mania, 1:224–
    226
Therapy
    See also Counseling; Psychotherapy;
        Specific types of therapy
    adaptive styles and, 3:11–12
    brief, with difficult clients, 2:63–77
    combined group and individual,
        2:109–113
    contrasted with supervision, 10:90
    defined, 2:64
    defusing failed prior, 2:68–69
    effective, 2:66
    failed encounter, 2:219
    family members may have conflicting
        goals for, 2:167
    group
        See Group therapy
    of incest victims, boundaries in,
        4:125–126
    individual, 4:62–63, 123
    outpatient, 3:167–168

study, 4:60–61
legal issues and, 2:217–222
postfusion, in DID, 1:82
separating from supervision, 10:84–
    86
sexualizing the end of the
    relationship in, 2:240
successful results in increased
    capacity to forgive, 4:255
termination of, 3:125, 5:148
verbal techniques, 2:73–74
withdrawal from, 2:131
Thinking
    abstract, capacity for in adolescence,
        5:156, 228
    child's, traits of, 5:131
    dialectical, 9:6
    negative, 6:225–226
        modifying, 6:232–233
Thioridazine (Mellaril), 10:114
Third-party reimbursement, for health
    care expenses, 3:82
"The Thirteenth Step", 8:152–153
30-week Sentence Completion Exercise
    for Self-Esteem Enhancement
    (*appendix*), 4:238–242
Thirty-Six Hour Day, The (Mace & Rabins),
    6:179
Thompson v. County of Alameda, 10:145
Thorazine (chlorpromazine), 7:40
Thoughts
    intrusive and repetitive in an
        obsession, 1:35
    recording, 5:138, 143–144
*Thoughts and Feelings: The Art of Cognitive
    Stress Intervention* (McKay,
    Davis, & Fanning), 3:253
Threat, perceived, theme of anger against
    others, 4:162–163
Threats, 6:246
3, 4-methylenedioxymethamphetamine
    (MDMA)
    See Ecstasy
Thrill-seeking, drug use as, 6:104
Thumbsucking, 6:46
Thyroid
    disease, 3:96
    disorders, 3:103–104
    dysfunction, 6:261
    hormone, 5:51, 52
Thyroid-stimulating hormone (TSH),
    3:104

Thytropin-releasing hormone (TRH), 3:104
Time line, family, 6:137
Time management, 6:61
Time-Limited Dynamic Psychotherapy, 2:88
Time-out, 5:59, 138, 142
    use of with ADHD children, 1:205–206
Title and Content of the Instructional Modules of the Ethical Practices in Rehabilitation Training Modules (table), 10:68–69
Title and Purpose of Each Instructional Unit of the Ethical Case Management Practices Training Program (table), 10:66–67
Title XX, 9:69
Tobacco, 8:62, 96
    See also Smoking
    abuse, 4:37
    sales, 7:64
Tofranil (imipramine), 1:44, 3:213, 274, 275, 276, 4:14, 5:56, 164, 7:35
Token economy systems, for behavior modification, 1:204
Tolerance
    defined, 8:251
    of pharmacologic regimen, 7:31–32
    substance use, 8:60
Torture victims, 1:2, 11, 13
Touching, 6:210–211
    in incest, 4:115, 116
Tough Love International (directory listing), 8:157
Tourette's syndrome, 1:38, 5:57, 8:252
    obsessions and compulsions present in, 1:30
    symptoms like, 1:44
Towards a Theory of Schizophrenia (Bateson et al.), 2:145
Toxicity
    relationship to health problems, 7:54, 56
    symptoms, 7:60
Toxicology tests, 8:272, 278, 282
Trail Making Test, 7:18
Trails, with moving objects, 7:140
Training
    on-the-job, 9:92, 93, 245

part of supported employment, 9:122
Traits, characteristics of individuals, 9:2
Trance logic, 1:57
Tranquilizers, 1:81, 82, 4:18, 5:241–242
    major
        See Antipsychotics
    minor, 8:129
        See also Anxiolytics
    minor abuse of, 8:124
Transactional analysis, 3:181, 193
Transactions, internal, 2:88
Transfer training, 5:211
    identical elements, 5:216, 217
    overlearning, 5:216–217
    positive transfer, 5:216, 217
Transference, 1:69, 129, 130, 2:49, 66, 80, 81, 82, 87, 92, 3:118, 186, 193, 4:122, 5:118, 6:201, 10:78–79, 86, 186, 187, 197
    defined, 2:81
    in divorce therapy, 4:213
    erotic, 2:233, 10:198, 199, 200, 206
        defined, 2:232–233
        interpretation of, 2:243
        therapeutic approaches to, 2:231–245
        therapists' need for consultation with colleague, 2:245
    multiple, 2:114
    negative, 1:120, 2:241, 5:187
    nurturing-symbiotic, 10:199
    psychosis, 2:117
    unhealthy, 10:117–118
Transference/parent link, 2:84, 85, 87, 91
Transformation, 9:9, 10–13
    career dilemma may trigger, 9:8
    personal
        moments of
            conscious conflict, 9:10, 13
            image, 9:11, 13
            interpretation, 9:11, 13
            pause, 9:10, 13
            repatterning, 9:11, 13
        promoting, 9:14
Transgression, against a rule as theme of anger against others, 4:163–164
Transition, 9:9, 18
    career dilemma may trigger, 9:8
    work programs, 9:128
Transportation, employability and, 9:69
Tranylcypromine (Parnate), 1:44, 7:36

Trauma, 3:255
  birth, 1:39
  childhood, 4:185
  defined, 1:5
  history of and BPD, 1:124
  metabolism of the, 1:70
  resolution of, 4:247
  severe childhood, 1:128
  and stress, 1:223–224
  victims of, objectives in treatment,
      1:19–20
Traumatic brain injury (TBI), 7:32, 41, 43–
      44, 8:56, 9:110, 112, 141–156
  case study, 9:155
  vocational evaluation of clients with,
      9:141–156
Trazodone (Desyrel), 3:42, 272, 7:36
Treatment
  abusive, 10:113
  acute phase, 3:270, 272–274
  addiction, 8:151–152
    role of, 8:140–141
  of addictive disorders, 8:256–259
  of alcoholism and substance abuse in
      adolescents, 8:188–192
  cognitive, duration of, 3:139
  in comorbidity, 8:249
    dual focus model, 8:249
    integrated model, 8:249
    parallel model, 8:249
    serial model, 8:249
  continuation phase, 3:274
  costs, 8:140
  of DID, 1:67–72
    should follow principles of
        posttraumatic therapies, 1:67
  of elderly alcoholics, 8:207–219
  failures, 3:94
  improper, 2:219–220
  maintenance phase, 3:275–276
  of mentally ill, 10:161–182
  motivation-based, 8:269–285
  of OCD, 1:40–44
  overview of techniques, 8:276–284
  pharmacologic, 8:260–261
  programs
    family programs, 8:76, 213
    halfway houses, 8:74
    inpatient, 8:73, 259
      See also Hospitalization
    outpatient, 8:73, 213, 233, 258
    self-help groups, 8:74–76

  therapeutic communities, 8:73–74
  of PTSD, 1:19–22
  recovery, 3:269
  recurrence, 3:269
  refusal, 10:176–177
  relapse, 3:269
  remission, 3:269
  resistance to in death of child cases,
      6:157–161
  response, 3:269
  of schizophrenia, community-based,
      1:243–244
  should not harm client, 10:27
  substance abuse, 8:72–76
  of substance use in pregnancy, 8:109–
      111
  termination of, 3:125
  unorthodox, 10:113–114
  women-sensitive, 8:109–110
Trends in Prevalence of Any Illicit Drug
    Use by Gender (*table*), 8:97
Trends in Prevalence of Cocaine Use by
    Gender (*table*), 8:98
Trexan, former name of naltrexone, 7:67, 69
Trial
  legal
    by nature adversarial, 10:104
    criminal, 10:106
    direct examination, 10:102–105
    preparing for, 10:101–102
Triangle of insight, 2:82, 84
  See also Insight
  (*table*), 2:82
Triangle of person, 2:82
  (*table*), 2:82
Triangling in, 2:156
Triangulation, 10:186
  example of, 6:10
  intergenerational, 6:17
  nuclear family, 6:17
Triazolom (Halcion), 4:13
Trichotillomania, 1:33
Tricyclic antidepressants (TCAs), 1:229,
      3:42, 53, 57, 59, 61, 62, 213,
      273, 7:35, 36, 8:129, 130
  See also Antidepressants
  for GAD, 5:12
  side effects, 5:165
  in treatment of separation anxiety
      disorder, 5:10–11
Triggers, 8:281
  of anger, 5:218

of anxiety, 5:27
Triglycerides, 7:60, 77
Trips
   See Hallucinations
Truancy, 5:9–10, 107
Trust, 2:65, 104, 109, 4:135, 181, 6:84, 231
   adoptees struggle with, 5:113
   after divorce, 6:77, 78
   interpersonal, difficulties with, 5:28
   needed for cognitive therapy, 5:132
   as part of intimacy, 6:199
   sacred, in counselors, 10:43
   in therapeutic relationship, 5:136
Tuberculosis, 5:162
Tuberous sclerosis, 1:179
Tumors, growth of, increased by stress,
      3:17
12-step Fellowship and Other Mutual Aid
      Groups (*appendix*), 8:156–157
12-step programs, 1:112, 2:100, 4:70, 71,
      82–83, 84, 85, 86, 87, 252,
      5:245, 7:64, 65, 79, 147, 201,
      202, 8:66, 77, 140, 141, 144,
      151–152, 232, 236, 240, 257,
      284
   closed meetings, 8:150
   counselors role in, 8:150–151
   open meetings, 8:150
   principles, 8:74–76
   treatment superior to others, 8:258
Twin studies, alcoholism and, 5:230
Twins, 1:38
   identical, concordant for OCD, 1:37
   study of COAs, 4:96–97
Tylenol (acetaminophen), 7:42
Tylox (oxycodone), 7:42
Type A, behavior, 3:74, 4:54, 59
Type A philosophy, 7:233
Type B, behavior, 4:54, 59
Type C, personality, 4:55
Types of Relationship Wounds and
      Associated Themes (*table*),
      4:182–183
Typification, warning against, 2:220

U

UCLA, study of schizophrenia, 8:272
UCLA Aftercare Clinic, 1:258
UCLA Clinical Research Center for
      Schizophrenia and

   Psychiatric Rehabilitation,
      1:258
UCLA Social and Independent Living
      Skills Program, 1:248
   multimedia modules
      medication management, 1:248
      symptom management, 1:248
Ulcers, peptic, 7:155
   See Peptic ulcer
Uncertainty, in counseling, principles for
      reducing, 10:32
Uncontested divorce, defined, 6:41
Understanding Co-Dependency
      (Wegscheider-Cruse &
      Cruse), 4:84
Unemployment, 4:45, 103, 6:175
   depression and, 3:217
   statistics, 9:80
Unification, 1:68, 83
Unintelligibility, 2:23
Universalization, 5:176
University of Chicago, 2:250
University of Michigan
   comorbidity study, 1:104
   survey on drug abuse, 7:130
University of Pennsylvania Medical
      Center, 2:251
University of Rhode Island, Self-Change
      Laboratory, phone number,
      8:276
Urinary tract, obstruction in, 3:43
U.S. Department of Health and Human
      Services (DHHS), goals for
      health, 8:160
U.S. Department of Labor
   selective worker certification, 9:145,
      154
   waiver, 9:153
Use of Alcohol and Drugs in the United
      States, 1985–1992 (*table*), 7:133
Utilitarianism, theories of, 10:214–216, 230

V

Validation, communication and, 9:244–
      247
Validity
   construct, 7:3
   incremental, 7:3
   predictive, 7:3
   psychometric, 7:3

Valium (diazepam), 2:220, 7:27, 34, 43, 147, 8:65, 80
Valpar Guide to Occupational Exploration, 9:148
Valproate (Depakote), 5:166
Valproic acid (Depakene, Depakote), 7:41
  and mania, 1:228–229
Values
  counselors', 10:18, 22–23
    case study, 10:23
    ethnic clients and, case study, 10:238–243
  cultural, 9:202
  family's, 6:16
  personal, 10:78, 81
Variables
  organismic, 3:159–160
  situational, 3:159
Venlafaxine (Effexor), 3:61
Verbal abuse, 1:123
  among clients, 2:127
Veteran's Administration, 8:213, 214
  behavioral model of alcoholism treatment, 8:210–211
  treatment of alcoholism, 7:93
Veterans' benefits, 9:69
VEWAA Glossary, 9:129
Victim, duty to warn, 10:131
Victimization, centrality of, 4:128
Victims
  of childhood abuse, difficulty in psychotherapy with, 1:129
  crime, 1:4
  crimeless, 4:247
  and forgiveness, 4:246
  of incest
    See Incest
  rape, 1:4
  of sexual abuse, 1:13
  of torture, 1:2, 13
  of trauma, objectives in treatment, 1:19–20
Video games, excessive, 6:107
Vietnam Experiences Questionnaire (VEQ), 1:11–12
Vietnam veterans, 1:15
  Mississippi Scale for Combat-Related PTSD, 1:9–10
Violence, 4:244, 6:242, 246, 249, 259, 10:2
  domestic, case study, 6:251
  duty to protect others from, 10:127–138

ethical dilemma in treatment agenda, 6:254
  part of our society, 5:192
  in relationships, 6:254
  risk of, 6:252
  in substance abusers, 5:240
  victims of, 2:103
  without forgiveness, 4:246
  witnessing, 3:255
Violent behavior
  associated with irrational demands about others, 4:158
  associated with low brain serotonin, 4:99
Violent Crime Index, 5:193
Virginia Commonwealth University Rehabilitation Research and Training (*directory listing*), 9:61
Visitation, 6:84
  rights, defined, 6:41
Visual impairments, 9:112, 221
Vita-lite, 3:252
Vitamin
  absorption, 8:205
  deficiencies, 3:106–107
Vitamin A, 3:29
Vitamin B^6, 1:183
Vitamin B^{12}, deficiency, 3:105, 106
Vitamin B-complex, 7:51, 60
Vitamin C, 7:51, 60
Vitamin E, 3:29, 7:51, 60
Vitamins, 7:53, 57, 60
Vivactil (Protriptyline), 7:35
Vocal tic disorder, 8:252
Vocational
  aptitude, 9:149–150
  assessment, 9:37–38, 134, 143, 234
    the Americans with Disabilities Act (ADA) and, 9:35–58
  evaluation, 9:38, 188
    of clients with traumatic brain injury, 9:141–156
    defined, 9:235
    effective use of, 9:233–247
    of Hispanic clients with disabilities, 9:209–224
  goals, 9:96
  interest inventories, 9:148
  preferences, 9:115
  rehabilitation
    for patients with schizophrenia,

9:161–175
programs, 9:87
specialist, 9:134
Vocational Evaluation and Work
      Adjustment Association
      (VEWAA), 9:129, 143, 234
Vocational rehabilitation, 3:236
Vocational Rehabilitation Act (1920), 9:128
Vocational Transit, 9:150
Voice quality, 2:23
Voices
    different seen in DID patients, 1:55
    hearing of as sign of DID, 1:58
Vomiting, due to acetaldehyde, 4:96
Voyeurism, 4:115
Vulnerability, 4:139, 6:231
    defined, 10:218
    principle of in ethics, 10:218–219
    to depression, 3:132–133

W

Wages, 9:112
    See also Income
War, 3:255, 8:191, 192
    Korean, veterans of, 8:211
    Vietnam, veterans of, 1:15
    World War II, veterans of, 8:211
"War on drugs", 6:108
Warfarin (Coumadin), 3:43
Washing, an OCD syndrome, 1:34
Watkins v. United States (1979), 2:226
Ways of Coping Scale, 7:13
Wechsler Adult Intelligence Scale-Revised
    (WAIS-R), 9:42, 147, 211, 216,
    218
Weight
    changes in, 5:154
    fluctuations in, 3:155
Welcome, Silence (North), 1:253
Wellbutrin (bupropion), 5:14, 7:37, 8:283
Wellness, working a major criterion of,
    9:173
West Virginia Research and Training
         Center (*directory listing*), 9:61
Western Interstate Commission for
         Higher Education, 7:254
Wey che, Chinese expression for crisis,
    4:42
White Americans, 9:178, 190, 191, 195
    more successful in obtaining

employment, 9:182
White v. United States, 10:146
"Who I Told" worksheet, 5:31
"Why List", 5:30
"Why Me?" story, 5:29
"Why Pie", 5:29
Wide Range Achievement Test (WRAT),
    9:149
Williams v. The Ohio State Medical Board,
    10:114, 124
Wilson's disease, 3:108
Withdrawal, 3:9, 6:268
    after death of close person, 3:6
    and aggressive youth, 5:195, 196
    alcohol, 7:66, 8:104, 122
    an adaptive response, 3:4
    benzodiazepine, 8:256
    death of child and, 6:149
    defined, 8:251
    in divorce, 4:203
    during pregnancy, 8:111–113
    from caffeine, 7:163–164
    from family interaction, 6:10
    opiate, 8:105–107
    opioid, 7:76
    protracted, 7:225
    sedative, 8:65
    social, 5:254
    substance use, 8:60
Withdrawal syndrome, 5:240, 241
    following cessation of gambling,
    1:155, 161
Witness
    See Expert witness; Standard witness
Women
    African-American, 8:247, 9:193
    capacity for connectedness in, 6:273
    as caregivers to elderly, 6:170
        greater stress in, 6:173
    depression and alcohol abuse in,
    8:124
    with disabilities, 9:80, 192
    poverty and, 9:191
    drug using, 8:95
    elderly, alcohol consumption in,
    8:199
    epidemiology of drug use among,
    8:95–99
    female self-identity and, 10:199
    Hispanic, 8:247, 9:193
    historically as subordinates, 6:274

lesbians, 8:231
low sexual desire and, 6:192
sex drive in, 6:222
Women's movement, 4:114, 6:58, 59
Woodstock, 7:136
Work
    conditioning, 9:128
    environment, effects on human
        functioning, 4:34
    hardening, 9:127–138
        defined, 9:128, 129
        models, 9:132–135
        process, 9:135–136
        program selection, 9:136–138
    monotony of, 9:162
    readiness, 9:89
    relationship between recovery and,
        9:163
    samples, 9:150
    site, location of, disabilities and, 9:70
    stress related to, 4:5, 33–49
    therapy, 9:128, 162, 168
        concepts underlying, 9:166–168
        expectations, 9:167–168
        mastery, 9:167
        rationale for, 9:165–166
    values, 9:149
Work capacity
    depression and, statistics, 3:200–202
    restoration of, 3:199–218
Work Item From the Beck Depression
    Inventory (*table*), 3:204
Work Item From the Hamilton
    Depression Rating Scale
    (*table*), 3:205
Work Items From the Rand 36-Item Short-
    Form Health Survey (*table*),
    3:205
Work Items From the Social Adjustment
    Scale (SAS) (*table*), 3:207,
    208
Work outcomes, 3:210, 211, 215
Work overload, 6:229
Work-based intervention programs, 8:3
Worker, identity of, 9:167
Worker Performance Assessment, 9:148
Workers
    injured, 9:130
    sequential phases of, 9:2
    supported, high rating by employers,
        9:87

Worker's compensation, 8:11, 57
Workers' compensation, spiraling costs
    of, 9:128
Workforce, demographic projections,
    9:178
Working
    equated with normalcy in our society,
        9:173
    major life activity of, 9:45–47
Workplace
    intervention programs in, rationale
        behind, 8:20–21
    medications in the, 7:26
    prevalence of substance abuse in,
        statistics, 8:4, 5, 6
    risk factors associated with, 8:38–39
    stress in the, 7:15, 16
    substance abuse in the, 8:1–44
Workshop on Self-Help and Public
    Health, 1:240
World Health Organization (WHO),
    guidelines on continuation
    treatment, 3:274
World views, of culturally diverse
    population, 9:179–187
World War I, work cure movement of,
    9:128
World War II veterans, 1:15
Wounds
    relationship
        assessment and treatment of,
            4:177–199
        case study, 4:192–197
        types, 4:182–183
Writing, journal, 1:220, 223

X

"X" culture, 7:132
Xanax, 8:65
    and PTSD patients, 1:21
Xanax (alprazolam), 5:14, 7:34, 147

Y

Yale University, study on alcohol-
    dependent patients, 7:70
Yes, You Can Say No (video), 5:33
YMCA, 7:253

Yom Kippur, 4:248
You Can Heal Your Life (Hay), 3:255
Your Personal Danger Signs Chart
    (*figure*), 3:250
Youth, myth of incompetence of, 6:107
Yugoslavia, study of stress and mortality,
    4:57

Z

Zinc, 3:29, 7:51, 60
    deficiency, 3:107
    poisoning, 3:104
Zipkin v. Freeman (1968), 2:220
Zoloft, and OCD, 1:21
Zoloft (sertraline), 3:272, 5:14, 57, 7:36,
    8:283
Zung Self-Rating Depression Scale (SDS),
    3:157